A HISTORY OF FRANCE

Richelieu

A HISTORY OF FRANCE

BY

LUCIEN ROMIER

TRANSLATED AND
COMPLETED BY

A. L. ROWSE

ST MARTIN'S PRESS · NEW YORK
1953

TO
THE ROCKEFELLER FOUNDATION
IN NEW YORK
AND THE HUNTINGTON LIBRARY
IN CALIFORNIA

PREFACE

THREE years ago in France I read this posthumous book of Lucien Romier's and was at once immensely struck by it. So many text-book histories are apt to be mere compilations of facts with not much conception of their significance ; whereas here was a work by one who, as both a trained historian and a writer closely in touch with public affairs, was able to make the history of France *intelligible* in a way I had not come across before. The book aroused my enthusiasm ; I found myself very much in sympathy with its point of view and with its whole approach. (Perhaps I may be forgiven for thinking it similar to my own approach in *The Spirit of English History*.) At any rate, I wished very much to introduce the book to the English-speaking public and to translate it myself. One certainly needs a more than ordinary feeling, I discover, to support the drudgery of translating ; but it did enable me to identify myself with the book, in some sense to make it my own.

The book as published in France, under the title *L'Ancienne France: des Origines à la Révolution*, stops short at 1789. But M. Romier had left a typescript of his history going up to 1885, and this Madame Romier very kindly made available to me. I am very much indebted to her for her kindness, and for her help and encouragement in every way ; and also to the distinguished medievalist, M. André Artonne, for many years President of the Association France-Grande-Bretagne, for his interest and his aid in forwarding the project. With their help over this single remaining typescript, it remained for me to add some three or four chapters. Now the English version is the only complete one of the book, the last and most mature work of its author, eminent both as historian and publicist.

M. Romier had had time neither to complete his book,
nor to revise what he had written. And that has added
immensely to the labour of giving his book a satisfactory
English form. Many passages in the original were written,
under the pressure of time, in a rapid, almost shorthand, manner:
whole sentences have needed disentangling, separating out and
re-presenting to turn them into English. At the same time,
I have tried to adhere as closely as tolerable to the original
text : only in a very few instances have I departed from it,
to correct evident mistakes of fact. A number of other corrections have been made, mainly of dates or — more important
— of figures. It is well known that medieval statistics — of
the numbers fighting in battles, for instance — have regularly
been over-estimated.

In making these and some other corrections I have been
greatly helped by the admirable medieval scholarship of Mr.
Lionel Butler, Fellow of All Souls College. I am indebted,
as ever, to my friend, Mrs. John Holdsworth (L. V. Hodgkin)
of beloved Bareppa, whose help has been invaluable, whose keen
eye has detected many blemishes and whose impeccable taste
has suggested many improvements. My greatest obligation is
to Mr. Norman Scarfe, of the University College of Leicester,
who has been through the whole translation with minute care :
his good scholarship, sense and literary discrimination have
been responsible for innumerable corrections and improvements of phrasing. He could himself have translated the book
better than I; without his most generous help I could not
have presented an adequate translation of it at all.

A visit to America now two years ago — made possible
by the generosity of the Rockefeller Foundation and of the
Huntington Library — provided me with an opportunity I
should not otherwise have had, in the interstices of other work,
of starting on the job of translation on board ship, on trains,
in hotels and elsewhere. From the point of view of my
American visit, concerned with English historical research, this
book is a by-product ; but I should like to offer it as a small

tribute of my appreciation for the generosity of those most public-spirited bodies, for without them it would not have come into being.

If my readers find the book in English half as interesting as I found it in French, I shall think the unexpected, unimagined labour of translation, in retrospect, more endurable.

A. L. ROWSE

Oxford
St. George's Day 1953

CONTENTS

	PAGE
PREFACE	vii

PART I
ORIGINS OF THE FRENCH PEOPLE

CHAP.
I.	NATIONAL CONTINUITY	3
II.	PEOPLES OF GAUL BEFORE CAESAR	10
III.	THE ROMAN CONQUEST AND ITS LEGACY	22
IV.	CONVERSION TO CHRISTIANITY	32
V.	BARBARIAN INVASIONS AND THE SETTLEMENT OF THE FRANKS	39
VI.	THE FRANKISH DOMINATION AND THE DEFEAT OF THE MEROVINGIANS	46
VII.	FRANKISH DOMINATION : CHARLEMAGNE	54
VIII.	BEGINNINGS OF THE KINGDOM OF FRANCE	67

PART II
THE SPIRIT OF MEDIEVAL FRANCE

I.	FEUDAL LORDSHIPS AND MONASTIC ACHIEVEMENT	79
II.	THE EXPANSION OF SOCIETY: THE CRUSADES	92
III.	THE WORK OF THE GREAT CAPETIANS	106
IV.	THE CIVILISATION OF THE 13TH CENTURY	123
V.	MISFORTUNES OF THE HUNDRED YEARS WAR	141

PART III
THE FORMATION OF MODERN FRANCE

I.	TOWARDS THE BOURGEOIS MONARCHY	163
II.	FRANCE AND ITALY	180

CONTENTS

CHAP.   PAGE

III. FRANCIS I AND CHARLES V   193

IV. THE REFORMATION AND THE WARS OF RELIGION   205

V. THE WORK OF HENRY IV AND RICHELIEU   220

PART IV

THE CLASSIC MONARCHY

I. FROM THE FRONDE TO LOUIS XIV   235

II. THE RISE OF LOUIS XIV   248

III. THE EXHAUSTION OF GLORY   260

IV. THE FRENCH MONARCHY AT THE CROSSROADS   272

V. THE RÉGIME BORNE DOWN BY SOCIETY   287

VI. ATTEMPTS AT RECOVERY   300

PART V

THE SIX REVOLUTIONS: FROM THE ANCIEN RÉGIME TO DEMOCRACY

I. THE CONSTITUTIONAL REVOLUTION   317

II. THE TERRORIST REVOLUTION   331

III. THE MILITARY REVOLUTION: BONAPARTE   345

IV. THE EPIC REVOLUTION: NAPOLEON   358

V. THE RESTORATION: A COMPROMISE THAT FAILED   373

VI. AN ATTEMPT AT MIDDLE-CLASS MONARCHY: LOUIS-
PHILIPPE   383

PART VI

UNIVERSAL SUFFRAGE

I. THE REPUBLIC OF 1848. NAPOLEON III   395

II. DIPLOMACY OF OPTIMISM. THE DISASTER OF
1870–71   410

III. BEGINNINGS OF THE THIRD REPUBLIC   423

CHAP.   PAGE
IV.   INTERNAL POLITICS : RADICALS IN POWER   436

V.   THE WAR OF 1914–18 AND RECOVERY   448

VI.   DEFEAT AND LIBERATION   463

INDEX   479

ILLUSTRATIONS

Richelieu	*Frontispiece*
Charles VII	*Facing page* 170
Francis I	194
Catherine de Medici	212
Louis XIV	270
Voltaire	290
Marie-Antoinette	334
Napoleon	358

MAPS

Gaul under the Franks	*Facing page* 46
France in 1328	142
France 1814–1914	448

PART I

ORIGINS OF THE FRENCH PEOPLE

CHAPTER I

National Continuity

❖

Ancient Names — Races and Peopling: Primitive Stocks — Local Types — Variety and Unity — Historic Consciousness

THE names of the greater part of our rivers come from times which have preceded history. They mark today, as they marked in the spirit of the men whose traces are almost entirely lost to us, the course and the aspect of the waters upon a particular territory which is ours. We repeat them with the same easy familiarity with which our ancestors repeated them, without having the least idea of him who first pronounced them. These names have gone all through our history, undergone — without being lost in it — movements of peoples, changes of customs, régimes, dialects. Like many names of very old places, they express what changes least in the frame of human society : the territory and natural sites.

But if they have been able to survive down to us, without being uprooted by the ebb and flow of events and losing nothing of their customary force, it is because the accidents of history have not prevented — beneath innumerable changes — a certain continuity through generations of inhabitants persisting in the same country. It would be absurd to pretend that from the origin of history the men of our territory have thought like us. But an obvious bond of words, images, customs, links us still, across thousands of years, with the ways of thinking and acting of those first inhabitants.

Races and Peopling: Primitive Stocks

Every people, once it has arrived at a certain degree of historic consciousness, turns back to its distant past to seek

there a continuity, true or false, that may fortify this consciousness and the rights it claims for itself. Nations, like
individuals, take pleasure in claiming noble ancestry for
themselves.

Most often they invoke race. The idea of race in a people
appeals both to the family instinct or sense of kinship, which
knits them together in mutual obligation, and to pride of
ancestry, the thing that an aristocracy values most.

Scholars deny any solid basis for the idea of race. Besides,
a race could only maintain itself pure by the rule of marriage
within the kin, which would bring about decline, and then
the disappearance of the enfeebled stock. Tribes that come
closest in the actual world to so-called racial purity are those
whom the conditions of their environment have impeded
from communicating easily with other men. They are also
the most arrested or degenerate. The civilising power of
Europe has, on the contrary, in great part come from the
incessant communication of its peoples among themselves and
outside, and from the extraordinary mixture of stocks which
has resulted thereby from the beginning of history down to
our time.

But if the title-deeds of a nation's continuity cannot be
sought in race, they appear clearly in the long continuance of
its peopling, such as it has been determined by the resources
of the territory, the attachment of the inhabitants to these
resources and the habits they produce. Rich lands, with easy
cultivation and varied productivity, are those that attract
men most; they are those also that retain men or make them
most determined not to be dispossessed. They constitute
zones of human stability as well as meeting grounds or
trek-ways. France is typical in this respect. Some leagues
from Paris, which has seen so many revolutions, and on
routes along which invasions have at all times passed,
one still finds numbers of peasant families whose presence
in the same district is attested for several centuries.
Doubtless they existed before there was any organised state.

Such ancient families are naturally more frequent in remote provinces.

France thus contains numerous elements of its primitive population. They have intermingled and undergone, in varying measure, mixture with the foreigner, but have kept their local character in mastering or absorbing occasional contributions from outside. In this way there is a French stock that is neither Latin, nor Celtic, nor Teutonic. Its temperament expresses the continuous influence of the land and the climate on families that have lived in our country from the most remote times.

Local Types

History suffers in some respects from an optical illusion. It is that record of events and changes which witnesses from the past have judged worthy of note. But for the common life of men it is not certain that the noteworthy events and changes that history records have more importance than the obscure joys and sufferings, which offer nothing singular to one's notice and are alike from one generation to another. Besides, history is above all the portrait of the ruling classes, which have occupied the attention of witnesses, inspired the documents, had their acts enrolled, left behind them works, institutions, monuments or something of renown. But the changes of fortune of the ruling classes are much more frequent and rapid than the modifications of the lot, way of life and habitat of the anonymous mass. For example, rural archives reveal that in our villages in the course of centuries the name of the lord of the soil has often changed, while the name of the occupier or cultivator of the same soil changed much more rarely.

One must admit then, as probable, the continuity from the beginning of obscure and tenacious elements in the French population, which owe their genius like their character not to the supposed virtues of blood, but to their communion time out of mind with the forces of the land.

Peoples of settled cultivators of the soil show an astonishing resistance to the action of invaders. Even when conquered or pillaged, they do not leave their fields, and, if they have been chased from them, they return when the time of trial is over. Witness the prodigious attachment of the Egyptian people to its soil for thousands of years. Witness the eagerness with which our peasants of the North and East returned to their devastated villages in 1918. Then, too, it is rare for invaders to care much for work : they collect tribute, take over public offices and titles to land, but they leave the real labours and joys of the land to the occupants who have already made it fruitful.

France has undergone innumerable invasions. The mixture of blood they could have brought about represents little enough in the character of our people, compared with the influences of the soil.

Variety and Unity

The land of France is one of the most varied, in relation to its extent, of any country in the world. This variety is reflected in the equally varied types of its population. A certain unity of manners exists among all Frenchmen, which makes them recognisable from the foreigner, as one distinguishes at first glance an Englishman from a Swiss, or a German from a Russian. But the unity of the French spirit is the result of political unity, as political unity in facilitating communication from province to province has permitted the birth of a certain type of Frenchman, who has recovered in course of time the diversity — greater perhaps than in any other European country — of its original local types.

These local types are still numerous and marked. They change sometimes from one canton to another. They have maintained up to a recent period a permanent conflict between the ancient principle of national unity and the obstinate survival of provincial feelings. The word 'province' with us retains a very living meaning. We can explain thereby the

effort towards internal conquest that the central power has
had to make during eight centuries — the Revolution included
— to ensure political unity.   And this unceasing effort at
internal conquest, pursued by force or through administration,
against resistance which had to be reduced gradually, is
doubtless one of the causes of the particular character of
centralisation which the French state finally took on.

The local types derive from a two-fold formation : that
resulting from kinship among families which are the distant
heirs either of primitive tribes or of immigrant groups ; or
the formation of physical and moral traits with a particular
colouring, under the influence of marriages and contacts
confined for many centuries to the inhabitants of the same
region, valley or estate.   On the frontiers and along the
coasts, the imprint of invasions or of immigrations is naturally
much more marked in the physiognomy of the local types
than in the interior of the land.

The variety of the territory of France — an aspect often
misunderstood but essential — has not prevented that territory
from developing in the spirit of its inhabitants, from very
early on, a vague aspiration towards unity.   France is the
oldest of unitary states and, in the political sense, the oldest
of the nationalities of Europe since the Christian era.   This
movement towards unity was to be counteracted not only by
the variety of soils and probably of population, but also by
the fact that our country opens on four different seas, each one
contributing its own particular influences and connections.

Doubtless France has natural frontiers which seem very
clear except on the North.   But natural frontiers are not enough
to make a nation.   The country whose natural frontiers are
most clearly marked on the map of Europe — Italy — achieved
unity only in the 19th century.   On the other hand, the
Netherlands, which have no natural frontiers, became a rival as
a nation with France and England from the 17th century on.

In truth, the most striking characteristic of our territory

and that which more than any other predisposed it to bear a great state is the facility it offers to internal communication, to mutual exchange, and in consequence to conquest and administration : a whole made up of small countries, of provinces or regions whose natural resources and trade were complementary to each other. Our unity represents the subordination of our varieties upon a territory in the interior of which differences of soil, altitude and climate are innumerable, but where the tracks of men never come up against a serious obstacle. All through history one observes that armies — armies of invasion, armies of defence, of civil war, armies of revolt or repression — run through France with astonishing rapidity. It was with the Arverni, who commanded one of the most important passages into Gaul, between the valleys of the Rhône and the Loire, that the first dream of our unity was born, as it was from the great crossroads of the Ile-de-France that the Capetians started to conquer their kingdom. Our great highways bring wonderfully to mind the peculiar mixture of resistance and facility that communications in general have always had for us.

Still, national unity in the geographical framework which corresponds to France today was not the work of a day nor of several years. The Gauls had glimpsed it. But it was not achieved until 1860 by the acquisition of Savoy and the county of Nice. Then Alsace and a part of Lorraine were not recovered, after a separation of more than half a century, till 1919.

Historic Consciousness

A nation does not develop like an animal or a plant by the drive of innate forces seeking simply an equilibrium of vital functions, subjected to the ineluctable cycle of youth, maturity and age. Every real nation defines itself, at first, in a consciousness of collective and willed effort. Its instinctive behaviour is developed not by chance encounters, but in relation to a soil, a tradition of morals and culture ; also to certain ideals which come from the past, are enriched every day with new experience and project their quality, constantly renewed, upon the future. This consciousness is the very complex product of all history, not only of the history that we know but of that which we cannot know. It is a consciousness that, once formed, does not die unless it deliberately renounces itself ; that can on the other hand renew itself unceasingly for different tasks or objectives.

Some nations have had only a single period of greatness. Others have had the privilege of producing or giving brilliance to successive and different civilisations. France is one of these. She owes such a privilege, doubtless, to her people's deep rooting in a land which always gives men, through all their trials or in spite of their weaknesses, sufficient means of livelihood and enough confidence in the future for them to begin once more to create.

CHAPTER II

Peoples of Gaul before Caesar

❖

*Prehistoric Remains — Primitive Forests — Ligurians and
Iberians — Celts — Marseilles — Independent Gaul*

MAN appeared on our soil in the quaternary age. We cannot
calculate the duration of the ages of French pre-history:
hundreds of centuries, a thousand — perhaps more. We
class them by the geological levels of excavation and the
remains of fauna or flora discovered. Changes or progress in
man's use of implements aid in describing these periods.

It was during an interglacial period, relatively warm, that
those men lived of whom we find the most ancient remains:
they have left tools of sharpened flint in the alluvial beds of
the Seine, Marne, Yonne, Oise and Somme. These implements
are called *chelléens*, from Chelles, near Paris.

From the following period, marked by a colder climate,
date objects — arms, implements, works of art even — in
considerable number. The authorities arrange these remains
in series under the names of places where the first discoveries
were made: such as the cave of Moustier in Périgord, the
village of Solutré in Maconnais, the cave of the Magdalen in
Périgord.

Already the hand of man is clever at reproducing the
image of living beings by engraving in line, by sculpture in
relief or in the round. It has left us small masterpieces, like the
reindeer of Bruniquel, the horses and wild bulls of Mas-d'Azil.

The traces of these men appear to us above all in the caves
or rock dwellings of certain cliffs or valleys, of which the
most characteristic is the valley of the Vézère. While caves
have served men of all periods, it seems that the men who

shaped stone did not always inhabit caves. It is simply that the human remains in caves have been better protected from destruction.

The following age — that of shaped stone — shows us new-comers on our soil : human beings much richer in resources, more industrious and more powerful. From that time there is an agriculture, bread, garments, an art of building and pot-making. It is the age of lake-dwellings, of huts on piles, of artificial caverns and numerous monuments of rough stone, upright or horizontal, which have left to certain of our villages names like 'Pierrefitte', 'Gros Caillou' and others of like meaning. To the same period belong the dolmens, menhirs, cromlechs and the alignments which remain above all in Brittany, of which Carnac is the most celebrated : religious or funerary monuments, which one finds from the British Isles to India, witness to the vast diffusion of certain ritual customs, as also to the existence of a social discipline.

Iron had been known, doubtless, for a long time already. But primitive man could not profit much from it, for lack of knowing how to give it resistance. On the other hand, the discovery of how to make bronze, by mixing copper with tin, transformed tool-making and increased men's means of action. Copper was widely distributed. But tin, necessary for making bronze, was rare: hence came the importance of the routes which led to the sources of tin. The most abundant source of this metal lay in Cornwall in the British Isles. To attain it by land, Mediterranean merchants had to pass through the whole length of our territory.

Primitive Forests

At the dawn of history our country bore large and dense forests. The warmer and wetter climate after the glacial period had made the trees grow at the expense of pasture. Grass-eating animals — reindeer, bison, horse — moved northwards to find open prairies. New fauna that went with trees

invaded the ancient hunting-grounds of man. Man, deprived
of the resources of big game which the herbivorous animals
formerly gave him, had to become more active and ingenious
to live. He took to agriculture, cattle-raising, above all
reclaiming land from forest. Our ancestors' first struggle was
against the forest. The profoundly man-made and variegated
character of our soil is the result of an effort of conquest
made upon the forest over thousands of years. Early modes
of reclamation and their development have left indelible traces
upon the face of France. The land that nourishes us has been
in large part created by the hand of man.

The first groups of settled cultivators formed in the clearings. The forest separated them. It was the chief barrier,
often more difficult or more dangerous to cross than the
discovered passes across the heights. Thus different regions
were defined, tribes rooted themselves and local customs were
born. Ancient frontiers were not lines but sterile areas or
those difficult to penetrate. Those parts of primitive forest
which took man longest to clear remained the real boundaries
of province from province. Even in our South, where the
drier climate aided man's struggle against the tree, the influence
of the forest is still visible on the defining of the regions. The
forest of Grésigne separates four countries, the Rouergue,
Albigeois, Quercy and Languedoc. The remains of the forest
of Belvès mark off the Agenais from Quercy and Périgord.
Between Lorraine and Alsace the great passage is a forest pass
— that of Saverne — which corresponds to the narrowest
stretch of the Vosges sandstone. The greater part of the
ancient strongholds or encampments in the North, East and
Centre — like Coucy, Pierrefonds, Chinon, Loches, Bourbon-
l'Archambault — are based on forest zones. To subdue the
recesses of our countryside to Christianity the monasteries had
to attack the forests effectually.

It is by the influence of the primitive forest on the nature
of the soil, the distribution of population and the formation
of local characteristics that France is chiefly distinguished

from the dry countries of the Mediterranean basin. One of the resources of Gaul which the Romans noticed at once — the number of pigs — came from the extent of the oak forests. From the forest tradition comes also the skill of our ancestors in building with wood. Gothic art, no doubt, would not have been born or would not have flourished to the same degree among a people with little skill for wood-work. The French Canadian, who came from our western provinces, is still today the best carpenter in America, as he was the most determined clearer of forest. It was the Gauls who taught the Romans the use of casks for wine.

There is a general relation between the character of the population or the look of a countryside and the ancient modes of reclamation. In regions where there are numerous springs, scattered reclamation by individual effort, slashing at the forest in a multitude of places, has caused it little by little to disappear. It has given us the regions of hamlets, of *mas*,[1] dairy-farms and isolated homesteads, where the habitation has retained through centuries the name of him who first broke it in. The tree has been driven back to the arid slopes, domesticated or replanted to form hedges and copses. On the other hand, collective clearance by communities has given us the countryside without hedges, the vast ploughlands of the North, East and part of the Centre of France, leaving forest areas to subsist on the margin of the rich lands.

Before the invention of heavy wagons, dating from the Middle Ages, the forest had as great an influence on the ancient ways of communication. To escape the obstacle of the forest, waterways, rivers and streams offered the most convenient passage. The system of watercourses in France, complex, organic, varied, was a factor in civilisation. Hence the importance, from the beginning, of internal navigation and riverside towns. On the other hand many migrations, contacts and diverse influences which passed through the great valleys reached only tardily or not at all the people of

---

[1] The large farms of southern France, particularly of Provence.

the clearings, of the little countrysides, of the hamlets and isolated farms. It is thus that our country from the first bore its double character of being easy for invaders or for commerce on one hand and of peasant stability on the other.

Ligurians and Iberians

The first inhabitants of France appear in history under the names of two groups of peoples : Iberians and Ligurians. Peoples more or less akin, doubtless, both of them connected with very extensive migrations and colonisations, covering a great deal of Western Europe, the Iberians more to the south, the Ligurians more to the north.

These peoplings, whose movements appear to us confused because they probably obeyed not so much an idea of methodical occupation of territory as needs, fears, ambitions which groped towards an objective — these peoples, at least in part, came to settle down. They have left a definite mark in a good number of the names of our rivers, mountains, localities. At certain periods they had a coherent social order and perhaps constituted primitive forms of empires. What we know of their temperament, ways of life and of working the soil reminds us of traits that are still frequent in the rural populations of the South and Centre of France. They belong to the dark type which seems to have peopled the Western Mediterranean basin and part of mid-Europe — very different from the dark type of Oriental origin. This was certainly the basis of the French type. It is still dominant in a great number of our families.

The memory of the Ligurians has been particularly alive, as well as their name, to the east of the Rhône and on the southern slopes of the Alps. The Iberians fixed themselves mainly west of the Rhône, in Aquitania and on both sides of the Pyrenees. It has been held that the Basques represent primitive Iberians ; but this identification remains doubtful. Auch is a name of Iberian origin ; Tarascon, of Ligurian.

Celts

About a thousand years before the Christian era a famous people enters into history : the Celts, fathers of the Gauls.

The migrations of the Celts, their exploits and conquests, their adventures and settlements, constitute one of the epic stories of the ancient world. They dominated, at one moment, almost the whole of Europe, except for the Mediterranean area. They burnt Rome and camped at the foot of the Capitol. They have left traces of their power and vestiges of their language from the Atlantic to the Dniester. Four centuries before Christ, they occupied France, the British Isles, half of Spain, central and southern Germany, northern Italy, the regions of the middle and lower Danube. This power sank gradually in the last centuries before the Christian era. Gaul, properly speaking, was a separate branch of it, the largest and the most alive.

The prodigious expansion of the Celts and their rapid conquests had for their principal cause, no doubt, the relative superiority of their weapons. Exponents of the technique of La Tène civilisation, they carried a sword of hard iron. Their most enterprising groups were formed in the regions where the influence of Greece and Italy penetrated, in that part of barbarian Europe where industry had been the most inventive. Thus they could easily subjugate the ancient peoples of our territory and found Gaulish civilisation.

But soon other influences and forces from the South made for the final conflict between the Celtic and Mediterranean worlds.

Marseilles

Towards the year 600 B.C., on the Ligurian shore of the Mediterranean which the Phoenicians and the Greeks had already visited, a group of emigrants from Phocea, a city of Ionia, founded Marseilles.

Marseilles, at first, was a weak colony. Its trade with the interior depended on the humour of the mistrustful tribes surrounding it. At sea its ships encountered bitter rivals, those of Carthage and the Etruscans. But from the beginning of the 5th century the power of Carthage weakened at the same time as the Etruscans drew back. Then Marseilles went ahead, extending its connections, installing stations from the Alps to Andalusia, founding maritime offshoots like Nice, Antibes, Hyères, Port-Vendres, establishing markets and fortified posts at the outlet of the routes from Gaul to the Mediterranean, organising the cosmopolitan crossroads of the lower Rhine, controlling the greater part of the commerce by sea and land between the reputedly barbarian West and the Hellenic world. Its luxury and its institutions make a striking contrast with the still primitive ways of the Celto-Ligurian tribes of the South of Gaul. It represents, at the very beginning of our history and before Rome became famous, a magnificent example on our soil of those Mediterranean cities of which the type survived till the death of Venice. These cities of free merchants, mistresses of a vast commercial network which they extend or defend — sometimes by means of diplomacy or ruse, sometimes by allying themselves to warlike peoples — are governed by an oligarchy of patrician wealth which has periodically to make concessions to the people and protect themselves against internal conspiracies and from the fierce covetousness of allies as of enemies. But their wealth, their spirit of competition, their very pride, encourage the arts and refinements of culture.

The influence of Marseilles is one of the most important facts in the history of our origins. Certainly Marseilles did not hellenise Gaul. But in establishing an Hellenic border all along our southern shore, she brought Gaul for the first time within the influence of the civilisations of the Eastern Mediterranean. This influence lasts far beyond the first impulse of Christianity, then of the Crusades, up to the Renaissance, up to the alliance of our kings with the Turks, up to our Romantic literature, to our Protectorate over the Christians of the Orient and to our mandate in Syria. For the rest, Marseilles contributes from the first by its trade, the diffusion of its currency and, above all, the effort of its merchants to open or re-open across Gaul the routes to the North, *i.e.* towards tin, copper and amber, to fix the axis of our nation.

Already Phoenician adventurers had crossed our country from the Rhône to the Channel, seeking Cornish tin. Marseilles extended this traffic by land, while its navigators, like Pytheas, reached the North Sea by the Atlantic. Similarly she attracted towards the Mediterranean merchandise brought from Northern Europe. She bought the metals of the Pyrenees, the Cévennes, the Alps. . . . A constant rhythm of our history will be the movement towards national unity through the success of relations between North and South, in spite of the insecurity of the East and the particularism of the West. This movement has its origin in the oldest channels of intercourse, linked to the first good fortune of Marseilles.

Lastly, Marseilles introduced the Romans into Gaul. She used them at first to resist the Etruscans and the Carthaginians, her competitors. Then she made herself the intermediary of the trade between Rome and Spain. After which she judged it convenient to call in Roman soldiers to curb the Gaulish tribes that pestered her. From that day her own independence and that of Gaul were condemned.

Independent Gaul

The word Gaul, from Gallia, Gallus, is the Latin adaptation of an old Celtic name, from which also comes Galatians.

The tradition handed down by Greek and Latin writers attributes to the Gaul tall stature, fair complexion and very light hair. This portrait perhaps corresponds to the image of the warrior Celt whose exploits terrified the ancient world, rather than to the common type of the populations living to the south of the Loire. The Mediterraneans, often small and very dark, were easily astonished by the height and whiteness of skin of the peoples of misty Europe.

There are good reasons for thinking that the basis of the population of Gaul was autochthonous. The descendants of the invading Celts — the Gauls properly so called — formed a layer superimposed on or mingled with the ancient stocks. They held the armed force, the property, the political power, the religion and the control of trade and communications. Their language was the common language. Their aristocracy held great estates, which pass later to the Gallo-Romans. But among the workers in the fields and in the lower strata of the towns, as with the population of poor or difficult regions, the autochthonous element remained, doubtless, the more numerous. Intermingling must also have weakened the original traits of the invaders.

Three types of Gauls corresponding to migrations, settlements and perhaps to different mixtures, were clearly defined upon our soil before the Roman conquest : in the South, and principally in Aquitania, a type which let itself be absorbed by the old Iberian or Ligurian population ; in the Centre, the type of Gaul brave, responsive to eloquence, ambitious and unstable, whom the narratives of Caesar have rendered familiar ; to the north of the Seine, a fiercer and harder type, difficult to subjugate amid the forests that protect him, the type of Belgic Gauls.

In the last centuries of its independence Gaul does not appear to be a savage country. Except for wars involving masses more or less numerous, its population is settled, divided into tribes, peoples and federations. The geographical organisation of the Gaulish population is retained by the Roman administration, then by the ecclesiastical system. Some of our provinces and the greater part of our regions owe their name or their early traditions to Gaulish tribes. Even the division of France into departments and districts has taken some account of this. The Soissonnais, Vermandois, Beauvaisis recall Gaulish tribes, like the Velay, Rouergue, Périgord, Saintonge and fifty other names of French regions.

Gaul had an already-developed agriculture. The quality

of its corn and of its light bread was renowned. Each region had its meadows or its pastures, as well as its cornfields. Farm stock and horses were raised ; plenty of pigs ; herds of sheep supplied wool for clothing. In the course of the eight years during which the Roman conquest was achieved, Caesar never had much trouble for long in revictualling his troops, which were often moved about without warning.

Gaul also had a trade, more or less prosperous according to periods of peace or trouble. Besides fortresses like Bibracte and Gergovia which were places of refuge, numerous towns or villages situated at the crossroads of valleys and uplands constituted centres of communication, of relays, posts for boats, places for fairs. Bourges, Orléans, Paris, Châlons, Rheims, Besançon marked meeting-points of this kind.

The Celts loved moving about. They understood communications and where to site a community. Outside of Gaul, they founded Milan, Brescia, Bologna, Belgrade. In Gaul itself tolls and customs were one of the principal sources of public revenue. Ordinarily the tribes did not think of disturbing the trade from which they profited. We know that in certain places penalties were laid down against those who harmed merchants. The Greeks considered their clients from the Celtic world as good payers.

Tracks and roads were already numerous in Gaul. Thanks to which Caesar could move his armies very fast over the whole territory. Later, the Romans straightened out and paved the principal highways to form the admirable network of routes from which came the general design of French communications.

The peoples of Gaul enjoyed the reputation of being hospitable, good-tempered, of an open mind and extreme bravery. They were reproached for intolerable boasting, the lack of follow-up in their designs, a leaning to indiscipline, to divisions of clans or parties, to the jealousies and hatreds of tribe for tribe.

Among the peoples, grouped in federations whose size

varied according to the ability of the chiefs or the power of some dominant group, there existed a certain unity of language, traditional customs and religion. They had a religion of nature, bound up with the spirits of the soil, forests and waters, upon which were superimposed cults of various origins, of which the chief was the cult of a sort of Mercury, patron of commerce and the useful arts. The memory of the Gaulish Mercury has survived in the names of places like Mercœur, Mercurey, Mercueil, Mirecourt.

A great religious corporation, that of the Druids, the organisation, influence and exact rôle of which are hard to grasp, cultivated theology and science, formed schools, provided a ritual, maintained practices, some of them inoffensive like the gathering of mistletoe, others cruel like their human holocausts. The Druids had the power of executing justice in fact or of right. Their chief place of meeting or pilgrimage was in the forest of Carnutes, near Chartres. It seems that Druidism represents a sect of northern origin which penetrated Gaul via the British Isles and won mainly the aristocracy.

The political and social system of the Gaulish tribes expressed the dual principle of the protection of the weak by the strong and of the material attachment of the weak to his protector. In the countryside it was the protection exercised by the great landowner over the tillers of the soil ; in the towns, the protection of the aristocrats over the common people or of the chiefs of clans over their followers. Still, as in primitive societies, the method of election was often used not only for civil magistrates, but for leaders in war. Hence frequent strife, even within the cities.

The tribes of Gaul could not experience the feeling of national unity such as we understand it. But they had a very clear notion of their kinship, their traditions, their common customs, of all that distinguished them from the German and from Mediterranean people, as they had of the ownership of their soil. In this sense they were patriots, and their patriotism was to be inflamed against the Roman invader.

Three peoples or federations of peoples emerged from the tribes as a whole before the arrival of Caesar. They were the Aedui who commanded the passages between Saône, Loire and Seine ; the Arverni, masters by possession or alliance not only of the central plateau but of the routes between the valleys of the Rhône, the Loire and the Allier; lastly, the Suessiones or Soissonnais, who held the crossroads of the Aisne and the Oise. Thus power and wealth tended to gather along the great commercial axis from the Mediterranean to the North Sea. The Aedui and the Arverni, who disputed the receipts of custom from neighbouring trade, were naturally rivals. As for the Suessiones, they had trouble in agreeing with the people of the Rheims region.

It was these rivalries that opened the way to Caesar.

CHAPTER III

The Roman Conquest and its Legacy

❖

First Roman Establishments — Campaigns of Julius Caesar
— Characteristics of Roman Gaul

THE Romans did not spread their civilisation gratuitously for the love of glory. They came to Gaul to seek lands they could obtain, resources to exploit and a defence base against invasions. Since the passage of Hannibal across the South of Gaul, they were anxious about the land-way between Spain and Italy.

It was the policy of Marseilles that brought them. The people of Marseilles had drawn too many advantages from their alliance with the military power of Rome against their Etruscan and Carthaginian competitors not to be inclined to abuse them. Like most trading nations, they thought that they could make use of the soldiers of others with impunity, for a convenient price. They first used Roman soldiers in 154 B.C. to drive back local tribes which threatened Antibes and Nice.

About a quarter of a century later, the Marseillese, vexed by new incursions of neighbouring tribes and probably disturbed by the control which the Arverni with their dependants, the Allobroges, exercised over the Rhône valley, called in Roman soldiers once more. But this time Rome needed lands for her poor and outlets for her traders. The legions came. They cleared the Rhône valley by two battles, one at the junction of the Rhône and the Sorgue, the other at that of the Sorgue and the Isère. The Gauls were crushed and the king of the Arverni, Bituit, taken by treachery. The Aedui, whose territory reached the junction of the Saône

22

with the Rhône at Fourvière, had favoured the invader against their rivals, the Arverni.

The Romans installed themselves first in the region to the east of the Rhône, then, crossing the river, extended their conquest to the frontier of Spain, from Toulouse to the Garonne and to the Albigeois. Henceforth they occupied the whole Mediterranean zone of Gaul, held definitively the routes from Italy into Spain, controlled the trade of Marseilles with the interior, barred the outlets of the Arverni towards the south, brought trade back on the axis of Rhône and Saône. The tribes which lived in the conquered countries were treated, according to merit and circumstance, as subjects, dependants or confederates. Colonisation began. Roman generals founded settlements like Narbonne, Aix-en-Provence and Toulouse. There were plenty of abuses or exactions on the part of the conqueror and several revolts on the part of the tribes before the vast province thus formed discovered the advantage of being Latin.

A quarter of a century after the first establishment of the Romans in the South, it becomes clear that independent Gaul, divided and probably weakened, can no longer defend itself against the menace of the barbarian peoples of Central Europe, each pushing the other on and whose hordes break out, with ever greater violence, under diverse names. The Romans themselves, after several expeditions the failure of which made them fear a new invasion of Italy, have to send Marius into Gaul to wipe out, near Aix-en-Provence, a horde of Teutons whom nothing till then was able to stop.

Frightened, the agrarian tribes took refuge in their mountain fortresses. The power of the Arverni was in retreat. Richer peoples, like the Aedui and their allies, who profited from the trade of the most frequented routes, sought effective aid.

It was then that Julius Caesar, who had entered into possession of the government of the Roman province of Gaul 1 January 58 B.C., saw his opportunity.

Campaigns of Julius Caesar

War-leaders are only reputed great according to the measure in which they succeed. Caesar succeeded in conquering Gaul after several years. He himself, both for his contemporaries and for posterity, set down the story of his campaigns in the sense which would best serve his glory. No evidence from his adversaries has come down to us. One can estimate his conduct, the means of his success and the superiority of his genius only on his own evidence.

He was a cool, hard man, master of his nerves if not of his ambition and his dislikes, prompt at judging a situation and deciding, a calculator practical and determined, quick to measure the forces before him and to make the most of his own; active, resourceful, brave. His foible seems to have been taking risks. His strategy, since it finally brought off victory, appeared marvellous. If the event had betrayed him, the historians perhaps would have condemned him as foolhardy.

A genius, without doubt ; but who owed his astonishing success largely to the tools and means of which he disposed. The Gaulish troops whose bravery he willingly praised to heighten his own, were insufficiently experienced in war, brought together on occasion and armed hurriedly. They went into battle or disbanded according to circumstances and local influences ; they showed themselves always uneasy at leaving their homes or their tribal domain and were open to all the causes of indiscipline. He opposed to them his legions, the best legions of Rome, formed of soldiers without equal : they were trained in the most meticulous discipline and broken in to every manœuvre, ruse or trial of war ; they were free of all cares other than fighting, imbued with professional spirit, indefatigable. They possessed superior arms both for the offensive as well as the defensive. The traditional processes and improvised expedients of the Gauls gave way to the skill of his engineers and to their experience : often, without their skill, he would have failed in the attempt or not even have made it. Lastly, although he refrained from mentioning it, we can read between the lines of the *Commentaries*, how easy it was for him to thwart or prevent the plans of the Gauls by spying and bribery, while his own designs remained secret.

The war of conquest which Caesar conducted from 58 to 51 B.C. presents two phases, distinguished not only by the character of the operations, but by the moral aspect of the conflict. In the first phase, Caesar gave the appearance of a liberator or rather of a protector of the quiet peoples of Gaul against the Barbarian invasions; his task, aided by those whom he helped or reassured, was relatively easy. In the second phase, Caesar appeared to the Gauls in his true character of conqueror who meant to enslave : now he aroused a general reaction of the spirit of independence, against which his good fortune almost broke.

Caesar entered into war at the request of the Aedui to throw back an invasion of the Helvetians. He defeated the Helvetians in the heart of Aeduan territory, near Bibracte. After which he made off towards the Jura to bar the path to another invasion, that of the Germans of Ariovistus. He drove back the army of Ariovistus towards the plains of upper Alsace, cut it in pieces and threw the remains of it across the other side of the Rhine.

Such successes won him many favours. The Gauls facilitated his passage, revictualled him and appealed to him. Drawn on by the tribes of the Langres and Rheims region, friends of the Aedui, he undertook to clear the passages of the Aisne and the Oise and pursued a campaign which drew him right up to the North Sea. This time he came up against the fierce peoples of northern Gaul, who defended their forests and to whom the Roman name was quite foreign. Owing to the crushing superiority of the engines and of the tactics of his legions, he subjected or intimidated the tribes from the Oise to the Scheldt. But not for long.

This move towards the North, inspired by a concern for security or by the desire to open up communications, began to arouse suspicions. The maritime tribes of the Cotentin and Brittany, whose fishing and trading boats went up as far as the Pas-de-Calais, began to stir. At once Caesar turned to the West. He attacked the Venetii, the most powerful of the maritime tribes, and destroyed their fleet in a sea-battle which his engineers had prepared with great skill. He sent his lieutenants to show the Roman eagle along the Channel and as far as Aquitania. He himself returned to the North to try and reach the mouths of the Rhine.

Perceiving a network of exchange, alliance or complicity among the northern Gauls, the Belgian, the Rhine peoples and the Celts of the British Isles, he wanted to break it. Twice he crossed the Rhine ; still more boldly, twice he crossed the Channel and, the second time, advanced with five legions on British soil beyond the Thames. Expeditions which testify to his audacity, but also to the passivity of the Gauls behind him.

After so many expeditions, exploits and victories, in which his legions and his engineers were as successful against natural obstacles as against resistance in mass and the dispersed ambushes of the Gauls, Caesar thought he had brought Gaul to submission. But Gaul suspected, now, that the Romans wanted to enslave her. Suddenly, in the year 54 B.C., the revolt for independence began.

The peoples of the North, under the lead of the chief of the Eburones, Ambiorix, set it in motion. A legion that was quartered on them was destroyed, other legions were surrounded and besieged. The uprising gathered strength from the Ardennes to the Loire. Caesar reformed his army, reinforced it and succeeded — thanks to the Aedui and the people about Rheims — in bargaining with the tribes that were hesitating ; then striking terror in the valley of the Seine and, advancing on the Belgae, he crushed them ruthlessly.

Gaul seemed to yield. But she was conspiring. The revolt

broke out in 52. The Roman merchants who profited by the passage of the Loire at Orléans had their throats cut. All the peoples, except the Aedui, the Remi and the Lingones, were more or less involved. The leadership of the revolt fell to the Arverni, led by their new chief, Vercingetorix.

It was the energy of this quite young man that brought the military fortune of Caesar to the edge of disaster. In comparing the forces, means and science of the old Roman campaigner with the astonishing improvisations of Vercingetorix, child of an inexperienced, undisciplined Gaul, the impartial historian does not know which to admire most : the calculating genius for conquest or the spontaneous genius for independence. But it is possible that Caesar exaggerated his opponent's valour in order to magnify his own achievement.

Vercingetorix grasped that it was necessary to divide the strength of the Romans, harass it unceasingly and wear it out ; to exhaust it and break it in detail ; to shun any direct collision and maintain communications among the revolted peoples. He had against him the incorrigible separatism of the tribes, the lack of cohesion among the contingents he succeeded in bringing together, conflicting demands, the palavers, mistrust and treachery of some of his associates, rivals and local adversaries, notably of the aristocracy ; and lastly, the equality in courage, the tactical superiority of the legions, their armament and equipment often impossible to resist.

To parry the blow Caesar tried first to break the communications between the tribes of the North and Centre, by occupying the routes between the Seine and the Loire. Then he laid siege to Bourges, a rich town, at the junction of the routes of the Centre, which succumbed after a terrible resistance. Next he struck against the Arverni, determined to take their chief stronghold, Gergovia. But there he suffered a defeat so heavy that even the Aedui and their followers deserted him. For months the Roman army had difficulty in defending itself and regrouping its forces ; in feeding itself and protecting its communications. At last, re-formed on the

Yonne, it seemed about to retreat to regain the Saône valley and return to Provence.

The Gauls, elated with hope, wished to hinder the retreat. They caught the Roman army as it was rounding the north of the Morvan. But they found it strengthened by a mass of German horsemen whom Caesar, fearing Vercingetorix's cavalry, had brought from the Rhine some time before. Pressed by the Aedui, who saw with terror the approach of the Romans they had betrayed, Vercingetorix gave battle. His cavalry was defeated by the Germans. Then luck turned. Vercingetorix let himself be pushed back and shut up in Alesia with the remains of his army, while waiting for the contingents levied over the whole of Gaul to come to the rescue: a tragic mistake, caused doubtless by the folly of the Aedui and perhaps foreseen by Caesar.

The Roman leader kept his adversary closely besieged. He himself remained free to negotiate or to bargain with the tribes. His engineers surrounded Alesia with works, notably with a double circumvallation, which greatly increased the means of manœuvre of the legions against sorties from within and attacks from without. At length the Gaulish army of rescue arrived. Ill-led and divided under rival chiefs, betrayed perhaps by some among them, it exhausted itself in a furious battle, then dissolved and disappeared. It left the besieged, suffering from fearful hunger and decimated by savage sorties, after forty days of vain efforts, at the mercy of the conqueror.

Vercingetorix, not wishing to be delivered up by his companions, yielded himself to Caesar. But Caesar did not pardon one who had humiliated him. Thrown into a Roman prison, the young Arvernian waited there six years until the conqueror of Gaul chained him to his triumphal chariot, then had his head cut off.

The Gauls' last armed attempt was the defence of Uxellodunum in Quercy.

Characteristics of Roman Gaul

For about five centuries Gaul depended on Rome.

It has been debated by historians whether, if she had remained independent, she would have produced a civilisation of her own. In truth, it was the Gauls themselves — like Marseilles — who, too weak to defend themselves against invasions, called the Roman forces to their aid. On the eve of Caesar's campaigns, Gaul was condemned to undergo either the irruption of waves of Barbarians or the domination of Rome. The Barbarians would not only have ravaged it but probably have submerged its population and changed its character. On the other hand, the Romans fixed the Gaulish people in marking it with their imprint. When the Barbarians came again later, in the decline of the Empire, Gaul found itself in a condition, if not to stop them, at least to convert them to its own civilisation, thanks to the memory of Roman prestige and to the influence of Christianity.

The Romans had the gift for formal definitions and logical construction. They created neither the personality nor the unity of Gaul, but in giving them a framework they gave them definition. After them, one knew where Gaul began and where it ended. They established a frontier there where nature had not marked one, to the North and East; and this frontier has survived, with the same significance, up to our time in spite of a hundred battles and numerous changes. The Roman frontier of Gaul became the most bloodstained line in Europe.

In the same way the Romans created neither the divisions nor the regional members of our country, but they did in a sense reconstruct them and give them precision. Out of the tribe they made the 'pagus' or 'pays' [1]; out of the people or 'nation', they made the city. Their conception of administrative hierarchy and of the rôle of regional capitals impelled them to found, rebuild, or enlarge numerous towns, all provided with public buildings of the same type.

Assuring the security of the whole territory by their army and police, they regularised traffic at the same time, increasing it and making it more active. To the Gaulish tracks they added a network of roads, solidly constructed, paved and straightened.

Of their conception of the general balance of Gaul, what has not survived is the preponderance they gave to lateral communications. They established the capital at Lyons and divided the land into four great provinces, Narbonensis west and east, Aquitania, Belgium, corresponding to the ancient relationships or acquired custom of the peoples. Based on Lyons, their organisation looked towards Italy. It was destroyed from the day when the movement towards French unity came from Paris.

Always, in the spirit of their own tradition, they multiplied magistracies, dignities and functions, more and more associating the local aristocracies with the honours, burdens and profits of the administration. They surrounded the Gaulish religion with an official guise, made its clergy servants of the imperial cult and of the state. They recruited soldiers, distributed ranks and privileges. They subjected social life to their law and their formularies. They imposed also what was less good, their fiscal system with its abuses.

With the Romans the urban element dominated the rural. Thus they gave a wholly new importance to the towns in Gaul. Our most Romanised provinces are those where there still survive the oldest towns, near each other. But Roman influence was not negligible on the richer parts of the country-side. In the same way as the Romans fixed the administrative and provincial framework of our country, they laid down the lines of rural property. They gave a precise form, legal and social, to the great estates. From these great estates were born many of our villages, which still bear the name of a Roman or Gallo-Roman master : Sabinius — Savignac, Savigneux, Sévigné, Savigny ; Florus — Florac, Fleurieu, Fleuré, Fleury, etc. The great estates of which each one constitutes an agrarian unity called 'fundus', 'villa' or 'cortis', inscribed on the official survey in the name of a family, later became in times of trouble refuges for the people of the fields. They foreshadow the feudal system long in advance.

In spite of the clearness of the imprint they have left on our country and on our mind, the Romans latinised only a small proportion of the peoples of Gaul. Outside the Mediterranean South, the furrow of Rhône and Saône, the great lateral routes their merchants followed to the Atlantic and the areas where the legions were stationed, Latin immigration did not penetrate very deep. The remains of their buildings, some of them magnificent like the Pont du Gard, are only really numerous and considerable in the South. Outside the towns the Latin language, even, spread very slowly. Six enturies after the Conquest, bishops were still complaining of not being able to make themselves understood by the peasants. Many things in which we think we recognise the trace of the Romans themselves, recall simply the effort of the Gallo-Romans to copy or imitate their masters.

What is sure is that Gaul, by the charm of its life, its resources, its natural balance and the candour of its spirit, appealed to the Romans, as the Roman name flattered the vanity of the Gaulish upper class. Several emperors were pleased to live in Gaul, and Julian, the cultivated emperor who embellished the town of Lutetia, expressed his particular affection for our country.

But one may doubt whether the Roman imprint would have indelibly marked our nation, if this imprint had not been maintained by Christianity, revived by the jurists of the Middle Ages, then by the scholars of the Renaissance, glorified by our classical literature, and finally engraved by education in all our habits of mind.

CHAPTER IV

Conversion to Christianity

❖

*First Christians in Gaul — Bishops and Cities — Pagan
Opposition — Rural Resistance: St. Martin*

THE Christian religion came to Gaul not from Rome but
from the East, through the Greeks or Syrians whose ships
visited the coast of Provence. The Mediterranean merchants
had formed colonies in the chief towns of southern Gaul and
at the great crossroads of internal trade. Some of them, in
the 1st or 2nd century of our era, must have brought the echo
of the preaching of St. Paul and the seeds of the apostolic
mission. Long after, the Greek language still served for the
epitaphs of the faithful.

It is at the centre of communications and the capital of
Roman Gaul, at Lyons, that the Christians appear for the first
time in our country, grouped in a solid community, active and
resolute even to martyrdom. This community comprises
Orientals such as Bishop Pothinus, an Asiatic by birth, the
physician Alexander, a Phrygian, and one Attalus, from
Pergamos. It includes also Gauls or Gallo-Romans, nobles
even, poor, young men or young women like the praise-
worthy servant-girl Blandina who suffered, with numerous
martyrs, under Marcus Aurelius in 177, in the fearful sacrifices
of the amphitheatre of Fourvière.

Bishop Pothinus having been put to death, another
Oriental, the priest Irenaeus, a native of Smyrna, famous
for his learning and his charity, succeeded him. Fairly soon,
communities swarmed not only in southern but in central
Gaul — where a young noble of Autun, Symphorian, allowed
himself to be martyred — and up to the Rhine region. Soon,

the Bishop of Lyons, Irenaeus, extended his range of action very considerably.

Having brought in the Christian faith, the Greeks and Syrians also introduced heresies. Thus one sees the first apostles of the Gauls burdened with the triple care of spreading the Gospel, bearing up against persecutions and preserving the orthodoxy of their disciples. This struggle for orthodoxy later exercised a decisive influence on the coming of the Frankish monarchy.

Bishops and Cities

The Christian religion won the towns a good deal before penetrating the countryside. The rural population, inhabitants of the *pagi* or *pays* — *pagani* — the peasants or pagans, hardly understood Latin, and Greek not at all. Their conversion came only slowly, through the effort of missions, of monasteries and through the foundation of parishes on the great estates. Christianity found a far more favourable environment in the cities than in the countryside.

Roman civilisation had brought, in Gaul as in the rest of the Empire, a rapid growth of towns. This civilisation, however — of which we admire at a distance the material achievements, its power of political diffusion, the laws, the formal culture — lacked social foresight and, still more, warmth of spirit. Attracting the masses, it never knew how to raise their level or guarantee them a stable way of life. The old problem of the plebs, common to all the Mediterranean republics, became transformed gradually as the towns grew larger, into a problem of pauperism. The 'bread and circuses' of periods of prosperity was not a solution for periods of misery.

For another thing, Roman religion under the Empire became a sort of deification of political power and of public pomp which offered no help of a spiritual kind to the common man, most often never even touched him, and left without nourishment the aspiration of sensitive souls towards a

non-material ideal.   In the eyes of discerning men, the prestige
of the Roman tradition did not succeed in disguising a dryness
of heart within it and a vulgar immorality.   The first Christian
apostles from Asia Minor brought — in addition to their
ardent faith and the charm of the Orient — the spirit of
Hellenic culture, more humane, more athletic and seductive
than the pompous rule-making spirit of Latin functionaries.
They brought a wonder-working virtue — charity — which
bound the faithful together as brothers by mutual help and the
hope of a return after death, with no distinctions of rank or
fortune, to the family of one and the same eternal Father.

Founded on the dictates of an inner faith and taking its
sanctions from a domain beyond the reach of all political
power, the Christian ideal denied the very definition of the
Roman state, offended the external and theatrical cult of it by
the Latins.   That is why the first Christians were persecuted
with such revolting cruelty.   They sapped the moral basis of
the whole Roman edifice.   In addition, by their connections
or their kinship with the Orient, as well as by their withdrawal
from life, they brought down upon themselves the xenophobia
and hateful suspicions of the populace.

At the end of the 3rd or beginning of the 4th century, a
score of bishoprics already existed in Gaul.   After 313, when
the Emperor Constantine by the edict of Milan had proclaimed
liberty of conscience, and had accorded Christians the right to
exist, to celebrate their rites and possess goods, the number of
conversions increased rapidly.   Bishoprics became numerous.
The bishops gained a moral authority and a power in fact
which, in the decline of Gallo-Roman administration, made
them the real protectors of the cities, sometimes even the
arbiters of social life.   So too the ecclesiastical organisation
fixed itself in the local or regional framework which the
Romans had superimposed on the divisions of ancient Gaul :
the cities became the sees of bishops, and the ecclesiastical
province, governed by a 'metropolitan' prelate, corresponded
to the administrative province.

The bishop was elected by the faithful. When the see was vacant in a town, the bishops of the province assembled there, presented a candidate to the people who elected or rejected him. As the authority of the episcopal function increased over social life, the elections gave place to more disputes, sometimes even to disturbances in which the secular powers and agents intervened.

A century after the edict of Milan the bishops appear as the principal personages of the cities, already administering considerable property arising from the gifts of the faithful, and not only as religious judges but, in a measure, civil judges. Their theological activity is also worthy of attention. The Gaulish episcopate asserts its spirit and character strongly in the Councils. One of its members, Hilary of Poitiers, a great opponent of the Arian heresy, did not hesitate to reprimand the Emperor Constantius himself in the name of the churches of Gaul. From the beginning of Gaulish Christianity, Irenaeus, the Bishop of Lyons, had recognised the pre-eminence of the Bishop of Rome. It needed, however, a great number of discussions or decisions and even the intervention of emperors to subordinate the Gaulish bishops definitively to the authority of the Pope. The Pope was represented in Gaul by the bishop of Arles, the town where the Roman prefect resided.

Pagan Opposition

On the eve of the dismemberment of the Empire, Gaul, with the Greek cities and Italy, was the principal base of Christianity in Europe. But the Christian conquest still met with strong resistance in some towns and made little advance in the countryside. Under Constantine the bishopric of Tours remained vacant 'on account of the opposition of the pagans'. Aristocratic Gallo-Roman families, whom their official fortune or their education had attached more than the emperors themselves to the ancient religion of Rome, regarded with displeasure the favours which Christian propaganda enjoyed.

When Julian dared to react against the Christian impetus in Gaul, he expressed the resentment of what we should call 'the conservative world'. The Christians did not rest till the moment when in fairly large numbers they could get possession of administrative offices and functions.

From this moment, too, they were free to build public edifices to shelter their cult. They had assembled at first in cemeteries and catacombs, because Roman law protected colleges or funerary associations. This protection having been abolished specially to prevent the first Christians from meeting in cemeteries, they took refuge in private houses. After the edict of Constantine they openly possessed buildings for the practice of their religion and began to build shelters, preferably in suburbs where lived the faithful poor.

The oldest vestige of a church in France is an inscription, discovered at Minerve (Aude) and now in the Narbonne Museum, recording the construction of a basilica by Bishop Rusticus before the middle of the 5th century. The oldest of our churches, properly speaking, is the baptistery of St. John at Poitiers which appears to go back to the 6th century. The crypt of St. Laurence at Grenoble and the crypt of Jouarre date from the next century.

Rural Resistance: St. Martin

In spite of the marked preponderance the Romans had given to the towns, Gaul remained rural and agricultural. In the countryside, however, the Christian religion had great difficulty in penetrating and establishing itself. Two or three hundred years after the arrival of the first apostles large villages possessed not a single Christian.

It is probable that the peasants of some regions for a long time kept the use of their indigenous dialects, a mixture of Celtic vocabulary with older words. Even after these linguistic survivals had partially yielded to popular Latin, the speech of the countryside remained under local influences : dialects modified, without being confused with, each other.

In these circumstances the townsman and still more the stranger had difficulty in making themselves understood. For the simple needs of daily life the inconvenience was not very great. But to propagate from village to village a doctrine and a faith completely foreign to the habits of the peasants was a singularly arduous task. In order to spread itself the Christian religion was forced at the same time to propagate spoken Latin among populations up to that time ignorant of the language.

On the other hand the peasants were much more devoted than the townspeople to beliefs and cults which they attached to the spirits of the place, the sites of the neighbourhood, the customs of their ancestors, the good or evil influences of nature and the seasons. Christian missions, running up against this religion of nature which they condemned, did not hesitate to exorcise it or in other words to empty it of its barbarous content and adopt, and even bless, harmless traditions or poetic forms. So the Christian imagination comes to take the place of the pagan imagination. In the spots to which the pagan had brought his offerings, he would find henceforth a holy image before which to pray with less fear and more hope. . . . But in the country as in the towns the decisive power exercised by early Christianity was in its charity.

Christian missions in rural Gaul developed from the end of the 4th century. This evangelising work had for its guide and hero an ascetic who had been a soldier, then an officer, in the Imperial army — St. Martin. His charity was proverbial : at Amiens in the depth of winter he had cut his officer's-cloak in half with one stroke of his sword to give the other half to a poor man. Entering the religious life his virtues made him so popular that he was acclaimed, against his will, bishop of Tours. Near this town he founded the monastery of Marmoutier, where missionaries and bishops were trained. He himself journeyed through the countryside incessantly, exemplifying the only way of life that could convert the peasants : an ascetic frugality, manners as simple as their own, a sleepless spirit of charity, a systematic effort to substitute the concrete symbols of the Christian faith for pagan monuments and images, and, lastly, a courageous assiduity in denouncing the abuses of public power, even to reprimanding emperors themselves. He died in 397. . . . France was not to forget this rough warrior. On our soil there are hundreds of churches dedicated to St. Martin ; his name still designates scores of our towns, villages or hamlets.

The disciples of St. Martin continued his work. But several centuries of new efforts were necessary to conquer the pagan soul of the countryside. It was necessary to multiply oratories and chapels, to clothe with a Christian meaning the aura of mountains, the beneficence of springs, the mystery of forests, to raise a statue or a calvary in place of each idol overturned. It was necessary above all to found monasteries in great number to bind together the Christian example with life itself, with the work and the security of the labourers of the fields.

Monasticism was born in Egypt. It was introduced into Gaul at the moment when St. Martin began his labours. From the 5th century, under the influence of a theologian of the South, Cassian, who had visited the famous convents of the East, the desire for monastic life spread rapidly in select Christian circles. The strict rule of Oriental ascetics was in any case modified with us to take account of the function of monasteries in rural society.

CHAPTER V

Barbarian Invasions and the Settlement of the Franks

❖

Peaceful Incursion, Invasion by Force — Barbarian Settlements and Kingdoms — Frankish Conquests : Clovis

FOR roughly a thousand years, that is to say from the birth of Marseilles, southern immigrations and Mediterranean relations dominated or determined the progress of Gaulish society. Greece and Asia Minor sent merchants. Then Rome conquered Gaul and left on it a strong imprint. Lastly Christianity came to change its religion. Gaul seemed to have to obey, in its destiny and its civilisation, influences from the South.

But, in the 5th century, the Barbarian invasions and the Germanic penetration modified this tendency. Henceforth, Gaul would be governed and organised, no longer from the South to the North, but from the North to the South. She would become France, from the name of the Franks who came from the North to conquer her.

Peaceful Incursion, Invasion by Force

Gradually, through all the ways open to them, the Barbarians, known under the name of Germans, penetrated into the Roman Empire. They were more boorish and primitive than the Latinised Celts. But they allowed themselves to be recruited easily. Children of inhospitable mountains or of unreclaimed plains from the Rhine to the Vistula and from the Danube to the Baltic, they came down towards the lands of the South, in numerous bands, to seek work, vacant ground, some occupation that permitted them to live better and get near to civilisation. They were hired as workmen or colonists in agrarian regions. The Empire made auxiliaries of them for its army and cheap cannon-fodder.

This invasion, up till then peaceable and military, suddenly— towards the year 400—took on a tumultuous character, violent and large-scale. The Empire was overrun by whole peoples no longer satisfied with a modest place, advancing aggressively, breaking down resistance and destroying at random, pushing one another along like pieces in an avalanche.

The cause of the avalanche was the brutish irruption of a new mass from the depths of Asia, Tartars and Huns, yellow nomads of frightening aspect, upon the already vast body of Germans, overcome with panic. For more than a century the barbarian peoples, tribes, armies ravaged the civilised world, as if a hurricane had succeeded the avalanche and had raised up whirlwinds of peoples. The Huns, crossing Europe after Asia, led by Attila — a little man, thick set, with a big head, dark complexion, slanting eyes, flat nose — arrived before Paris, where St. Geneviève prayed ; they then laid siege to Orléans where the Bishop St. Aignan distinguished himself, to cross the Loire ; finally, coming up against the army of the Roman general Aetius, they were repulsed at the Catalaunian Fields, near Troyes, and beaten in 451.

Thirty years later, the German invaders having settled here and there, the ancient territory of the Empire appeared to be covered with a crop of Barbarian kingdoms.

Three Germanic kingdoms divided Roman Gaul.

The western Goths or Visigoths dominated the land from the Loire to the Pyrenees, the Mediterranean and the Ocean. Beyond the Pyrenees they had conquered Spain. Their capital was Toulouse. Their king, Eurich, proudest of the barbarian princes, proclaimed himself a sovereign independent of the Imperial supremacy. His successor, Alaric, had a summary digest of laws drawn up, the *Breviary of Alaric*. The Visigothic power surpassed the others in prestige.

The kingdom of the Burgundians, whence came the name

of Burgundy, covered almost the whole basin of the Rhône
and the Saône. It was bounded on the South by the Durance
which separated it from Visigothic lands. The Burgundians
were tall men, good workers, carpenters or masons, considered
easy-going. Their king, Gondebaud, showed a marked
deference for the Roman tradition.

Lastly, the Salian Franks from the Scheldt and the Meuse
defeated a lingering Gallo-Roman troop at Soissons in 486 and
later put to flight the Alemanni who tried to open out from
Alsace. These Franks dominated all the northern half of our
country, from the Rhine to the Loire and from the Morvan
to the North Sea. Their king, Clovis, was to be the founder
of our first dynasty.

Barbarian Settlements and Kingdoms

One must picture the Barbarians entering Roman Gaul not
as an army with any ideal they wish to realise or any desire
to impose laws, institutions, customs, but as bands of adventurers, loud, gluttonous, malodorous, ruthlessly led by chiefs
who reward themselves and their men out of pillage. Far from
contemning or despising comfort, riches and all the delights
of the world into which they irrupt, they aspire only to
participate in them without restraint. When they arrive in
a villa it is the kitchen that interests them first. Then they
demand that lands be given them, but do not dispossess the
first occupant entirely. Their domination springs from their
brutality and from their warlike practices against a population
which has lost the habit of arms during the long Roman
peace. War is for them the means of taking things, not
changing them. Their chiefs even deck themselves out
ostentatiously with cast-off Roman things, as a negro king
puts on European uniform.

So the Barbarians do not expel the old population. At
most they molest it to get what they want. They treat it
not like a conquered population, still less like an inferior
one, but like a population which should share with them

what it possesses. Then, too, they mingle little with it. For a long time they retain their laws and customs, leaving the Gallo-Romans to go their own way. Formerly, the Empire in making use of them in its armies termed them guests, which meant soldiers quartered on the inhabitants. They continue to behave as guests, but guests who cannot be shown the door and whom it is the interest of the inhabitants to placate by doing what they can for them.

The Germanic penetration into Gaul exercised a lasting influence on the political life, social condition and even the temperament of our people.

Doubtless the first troops of invaders did not comprise very numerous effectives. Except in the North and East, where the Franks pushed back some of the occupants of the soil, the coming of the Barbarians, following the easiest routes and seeking to reach towns to pillage rather than spread over the countryside, modified the basis of the population along relatively restricted lines. But the incursions by force were followed by a continuous immigration. For four centuries at least, up to the decline of the Carolingian dynasty, Gaul and Germany — South-West Germany from the time of Clovis's sons, the whole of Germany from Charlemagne's — lived under practically a common rule, obeyed leaders sprung from the same stock and governments of the same nature : open one to the other as they had never been. The peopling and the customs of Gaul, its political make-up, felt the effect of this long association with Germany.

Alongside the Gaulish people, light and gifted, softened in the Roman peace, is juxtaposed the Frankish people, hard, enterprising, little civilised, hungering for land and war, bent on work and conquest. Where the Romans made Gaulish civilisation develop in the direction of urbanisation by giving the social, political and administrative predominance to the towns, Frankish rule brought this civilisation back to the military and rural type, which ultimately ended in feudalism. Lastly, the force of domination and conquest being thenceforth

located in the North, French unity was created under the
influence and pressure of the North. Paris dethroned Lyons
as capital. The knot of valleys of the Seine, Oise and Aisne
formed the great crossroads of France and its real dynamic
centre, while the importance of the Rhône valley diminished.
The regions slowest to come into French unity, paradoxically,
were those where the Roman conquest encountered least
resistance : the South, South-West and West.

From the names of places, remains of Barbarian cemeteries
and distribution of dialects spoken at the beginning of the
Middle Ages, we derive a fair idea of the extent and density
of the Germanic colonisation on our territory. These colonies
were compact between the Rhine, Seine and the Pas-de-Calais,
numerous to the east of the Saône, thinly sown between
Seine, Loire and Saône, a little more dense in the old domain
of the Goths, the basin of the Garonne. One finds hardly
any trace in the South around the Rhône, in the mountain
country of the Centre and its tributary valleys, or in the
West properly speaking. On the Norman coast some colonies
of Saxons had come by sea and settled. In Armorica, a region
partly waste and wild — first oppressed, then neglected, by
Roman officials — bands of Britons, driven from Britain
before the Anglo-Saxons, found a refuge. They retained the
use of the Celtic language as they spoke it on the other side
of the Channel.

Frankish Conquests: Clovis

In 481, at the death of his father Childeric, who claimed
to be descended from Merovius, Clovis, quite a young man,
became king of one of the most active tribes of the Franks,
which occupied the region of Tournai in Belgium. It seems
that the Franks were the best disciplined and trained for
battle among the Barbarians. They formed themselves into
warrior-groups and farming communities.

In 486, when hardly twenty, Clovis defeated at Soissons
a troop of Gallo-Romans led by one Syragius, and by this

victory made himself master of all the country from the Scheldt to the Loire. The Franks thus appeared as conquerors in the heart of Gaul. Henceforward their superiority could be presumed over the other Barbarians who were settled and quiet, caring more for good living than fighting.

The bishops, who were in fact the guardians of the people in the cities, lived in continual anxiety. There was no more help to expect, in material things, from the Roman power from now on. Nothing would prevent the Barbarians from remaining masters. But the two Barbarian peoples who had already established their domination over a large part of Gaul, the Visigoths and Burgundians, professed the Arian heresy, which might be imposed by force or spread of itself among the mass of the Gallo-Roman faithful. The one hope was Clovis. Clovis had power on his side and therefore could ensure order. He was young : therefore responsive to pressure or advice. He was a pagan : therefore stripped of theological prejudice and ready for conversion to the true faith. On his side, Clovis, whose whole career attests that he had a calculating, crafty mind, understood very well that if he obtained the favour of the Catholic clergy and of the Gallo-Roman people his advance would be easy.

From the time of his first campaign against Syragius the young king was on good terms with the bishops, as the anecdote of the vase of Soissons shows. This precious vase, pillaged from a church, was claimed from Clovis by the bishop of the place. A soldier broke it rather than hand it to Clovis for the bishop. Shortly after, the king dashed out the brains of the culprit in front of his troops.

The decisive victory of the bishops was to marry Clovis to a princess ardently devoted to the Catholic faith — Clotilde, niece of Gondebaud, King of the Burgundians. In three years, by her influence and with the zealous aid of St. Remi, Bishop of Rheims, she brought the fierce pagan to declare himself a Catholic. Clovis received baptism at Rheims in 496, along with three thousand of his warriors.

Then the real miracle was accomplished. With an army much less numerous than Julius Caesar's, Clovis took hardly more time to establish his ascendancy over Gaul. Already, before being baptized, he had managed to throw the Alemanni back across the Rhine. In 500 he defeated the Burgundian king near Dijon and forced him to pay tribute. In 507 he crushed the Visigoths and killed their king with his own hand, at Vouillé, near Poitiers. Then turning against the chiefs of the Frankish tribes of Thérouanne, Amiens, Cambrai, Le Mans and Cologne, he had them assassinated and took over command of their warriors. He thus built up a vast Gallo-Germanic kingdom, covering almost the whole of Gaul and a part of Germany, from the Pyrenees to the Weser.

In spite of his odious ways and his proved crimes, the bishops did not cease to support him, as he did not cease to lean on them. He received the dignity of Consul and Imperial legate. He died at Paris in 511 and was buried in the church which he and Clotilde had had built and which later became the church of St. Geneviève.

The career of Clovis reveals, besides the exceptional gifts of this Barbarian chief, the lamentable disorder into which Gallo-Roman society had fallen and the predominant influence which, in this state of affairs, the episcopate had acquired as protector of the terrified peoples.

The Frankish Domination and the Defeat of the Merovingians

❖

Sharing and Warring among Frankish Chiefs — Decline of
Civilisation : Prestige of the Church and of Monasteries
— Degradation of the Merovingian Monarchy : Mayors
of the Palace

THE descendants of Clovis, who are usually called Merovingians, reigned over our country nearly two hundred and forty years. But their effective government hardly lasted more than a century and a half, before real power passed to the 'Mayors of the Palace' who were to produce the Carolingian dynasty.

This Merovingian or Frankish epoch of our history presents on the surface an appearance of frightful barbarism. The example of barbarism is that set by the Franks themselves and their kings. But the alliance of Clovis and the bishops preserved the future in three ways : it canalised the waves of invasion in making Frankish power a rampart against other Barbarians ; it prevented the Gallo-Roman population from being irremediably pushed out or uprooted ; it enabled the Church, under cover of its privileges, to save a part of Latin culture and to consolidate the first achievements of Christian civilisation. Thus, at a deeper level, continuity was assured of those elements which would one day triumph over barbarism itself.

Sharing and Warring among Frankish Chiefs

Following Frankish custom, the four sons of Clovis shared out his goods and his kingship like so much booty. The capitals of the four kingdoms, Rheims or Metz, Soissons,

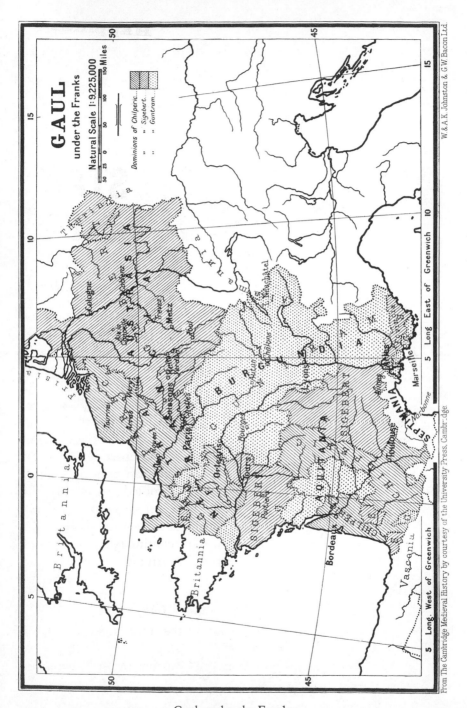

Gaul under the Franks

Paris, Orléans, were chosen, not far from each other, in territories of Frankish colonisation. They shared territories of conquest or military occupation in the same way. The system was then extended to the new acquisitions of the dynasty. This system entailed the creation of numerous enclaves, and encouraged trickery, mistrust, vendettas : it was the prime cause of the almost incessant dissensions of the Merovingian princes, of their wars and family crimes.

In spite of their settlement and the conversion of some of them, the Franks did not lose the taste for adventure. After the death of Clovis, their impetus continued to carry them forward. They waged war as far as Thuringia, Italy, Spain. In Gaul itself they accomplished the conquest of the Burgundian kingdom and occupied Provence. Only the region of Narbonne or Septimania remained attached for another century and a half to the Visigothic kingdom of Spain.

Fifty years after the death of Clovis, the last survivor of his sons, Clothair I, reunited under his sceptre the whole of Gaul, except Septimania. But on his death his sons made a new partition, taking the same capitals as the sons of Clovis had chosen. This second division was more ephemeral and gave place to as many dissensions as the first. In 613 the unity of Frankish territory was re-established under Clothair II. At last, in 634, Dagobert divided these territories into two kingdoms, Austrasia in the East, Neustria in the West, giving each in principle equal territory and population.

At bottom, the political history of Gaul under the Merovingians reflects three antagonisms : between the eastern region, Austrasia, which was under Germanic influence, and the West or Neustria which retained something of Celtic and Roman traditions ; antagonism between Frankish territory as a whole, Austrasia and Neustria, and the strongly Latinised territories under the military occupation of the Franks, Aquitania and Burgundy ; finally, opposition between Burgundy and Aquitania themselves.

Austrasia or the eastern kingdom was the country of

Frankish colonisation *par excellence*, a country of vast estates, where the towns — Trèves, Metz, Rheims — are scarce, with a rude and war-like population.

Neustria or north-west Gaul, from the Scheldt to the Loire, contained big towns : Paris, Rouen, Soissons, Tours. The Franks were numerous here, but without contact with Germany and mingled with Gallo-Romans whose superior civilisation had its influence on them. Their temperament was quieter.

In Aquitania and in Burgundy, the contrast with the Franks comes both from the definitely Romanised spirit of the old aristocracy and the grudge of the first Barbarian conquerors, Visigoths and Burgundians, henceforth in subjection.

It is clear that when Clovis died, the Merovingian dynasty failed in political sense. For, in contrast with what the Romans had done, it favoured a division of Gaul which could become irreparable, conforming with natural compartments. Austrasia meant the Rhine and Meuse valleys ; Neustria the watershed of the Channel and the Seine basin ; Aquitania, the Atlantic watershed and the basin of the Garonne ; Burgundy, the basin of Rhône and Saône. Thus may be defined the centrifugal forces, which remained strong till modern times. Still, the memory of Clovis, aided by the tradition of the Gaulish episcopate, remained strong enough to save the principle of a certain unity.

Decline of Civilisation: Prestige of the Church

The quick triumph of the Franks, the passive attitude of the Gallo-Romans in relation to them, and the very duration of the Merovingian dynasty — in spite of terrible dissensions — would be incomprehensible if we did not know that the Frankish domination had, on the whole, a remarkable capacity for handling the possessions, customs and habits of the earlier occupants. The parts of Gaul, in the North and East, where they established their most numerous colonies, had already been given over to them by the Roman Empire when it was making use of them as soldiers and pioneers clearing the land. These parts had long experience of invasions and were the least peopled with indigenous inhabitants. Besides, the Franks, who owed their rapid conquests either to the complicity of the bishops or to the easy tolerance of the population, settled down without much violence.

Merovingian Gaul presents us with three juxtaposed societies, each with its traditions, customs or laws, its habits and systems : old Gallo-Roman society, without any political support and much disorganised, but retaining certain propensities of culture and some of its possessions ; Christian society, which comprised almost all the townspeople and already many of the upper class, having the episcopate as its effective expression, political support and in a way patron of the dynasty ; lastly, Frankish society proper with its laws, customs and institutions of Germanic origin.

The Merovingian kings are not kings of Gaul, they are kings of the Franks. They are careful to preserve the marks of their origin. They wear long hair. They obey the Salic law, which excludes daughters from owning land and commands equal partition among sons. They prefer to live in the country on great estates, in villas where they keep their treasure. They usually confuse their ministers with their domestic servants, among whom the major-domo or mayor of the Palace achieves dominance. They send into the provinces lieutenants, called 'dukes' and 'counts', whom they provide with lands and who, gathering all power into their hands, sometimes become real tyrants. They reform laws and do justice in patriarchal manner, assisted by counsellors. They have a vast personal following, distinguished from their subjects by duties and rights. They strike money by counterfeiting Imperial coins. They raise armies, through the medium of dukes, counts and other officials, among the populations concerned, and attract soldiers by offering them part of the booty.

Of these kings the best was Dagobert who, following the

advice of his treasurer, the goldsmith St. Eloi, tried to represent a type of paternal monarchy, legal and just for all, reconciling the Frankish with the Roman tradition. He richly endowed the abbey of St.-Denis, which afterwards became the burial-place of the kings of France.

But, too frequently, the Merovingians spent their time in family conflicts. The most terrible of these struggles raged for nearly half a century between Queen Brünhilde, an educated princess of Visigothic origin, wife of Sigebert, and a Frankish woman, formerly a servant, Fredegonde, wife of Chilperic. Brünhilde had a tragic end : betrayed by the great landowners of Austrasia and delivered up to the son of her enemy, she was dragged to her death by the hair, an arm and a foot at the tail of an untamed horse.

To escape from all this violence, Gallo-Roman and Christian society moved towards the system of feudal commendation, that is to say, of reciprocal engagement of the weak to the strong. Owing to the influence of the Church, slavery was mitigated.

Then, too, the Church was growing increasingly in stature : not only did it dominate religious and moral life, but it represented what there was of intellectual life. The best writer and chronicler of the Merovingian epoch, Gregory of Tours, author of the *History of the Franks*, was a bishop, like the poet Avit. By the fear of Hell that the Church inspired in the powerful, by the jurisdictions it held, by its right of sanctuary that men recognised, by the very extent of its possessions which permitted it to welcome or protect a multitude of people, it checked, dispelled and sometimes eradicated the brutalities of the time. Still more, if Gaul retained a certain sentiment of its unity, it was because the Frankish Church constantly affirmed its own unity, in spite of territorial divisions and intestine wars. Already, kings and magnates were exerting pressure on the episcopate, attempting to falsify elections and claiming to supervise councils. A Syrian merchant, Eusebius, by means of presents, purchased the bishopric of Paris. Officials or domestics of the Palace, simple laymen, became bishops, to the detriment of clerics.

Monastic life was in full flower. Already the monasteries, ruled by abbots, seeking to emancipate themselves from episcopal power, increased their estates and resources from the gifts of rich persons who wished to ransom their faults or their crimes. Already, too, the monastic rule was relaxing. At the end of the 6th century, an Irish monk, St. Columbanus, brought to Gaul both a monastic reform and a penitential system for the faithful. The saintly figure of St. Radegund makes its appearance. Far removed from the grossness of the age, a Thuringian captive of royal blood, she was the wife of King Clothair, and foundress of the monastery of Sainte-Croix at Poitiers, a woman of ardent spirit and cultivated mind.

The towns no longer have the grandiose aspect of Roman times. The public monuments, half destroyed or decayed, are overrun by hovels and serve as shelters or improvised fortresses. The urban population is diminished. Industry and trade, however, exist. Gold- and silver-smiths, of whom St. Eloi provides an illustrious example, are making brilliant arms, embossed shields, enamelled ornaments for belts and brooches, gold and silver plate. Oriental merchants still come in, either by Marseilles, Arles or Narbonne, or by the Danube route. The celebrated fair of St.-Denis is held for four weeks every year at the gates of Paris.

In the country, life is distributed between the great estates, the villas, of which each bears the name of its owner (Gerbeviller, Ramberviller, etc.) and the small towns of free men, the *vici* (Vy, Vic, Neuvic, Longwy, Vivonne, etc.). The villas cover the greater part of the soil : they already comprise, in the dependants on the great landowner, the whole personnel and organs of a future village ; each has its tillers of the fields and artisans, its chief dwelling and church, its jurisdiction. The great landowners, from the Merovingian epoch, begin to consider themselves as lords on their lands. The kings, too, in granting charters of immunity to their followers, despoil themselves of a part of their sovereign rights.

Degradation of the Merovingian Monarchy: Mayors of the Palace

After the death of Dagobert, the Merovingian dynasty declines to such a point that tradition calls its last kings the *rois fainéants* and represents them as having no real authority, passing their useless lives at the mercy of their domestics, carted wretchedly to their assemblies on an ox-wagon. In fact, most of these kings die when hardly adolescent, children of an enfeebled stock, or still young, worn out by precocious debauchery. Others, unable to bear the brutality of the times, take refuge in the religious life. Incapable of keeping the effective government in their nerveless hands, they abandon it more and more to the mayors of the Palace.

The function of the mayor of the Palace, like all functions of the Frankish state, is very ill-defined. It broadens or narrows according to the talents of the person in question. As the dynasty weakens or gives way, the mayor of the Palace becomes more than a minister, a sort of substitute for the king, who levies taxes and regulates expenses, exacts military service and directs external relations or enterprises, decides peace and war. Representative of the king in relation to his subjects, he is at the same time spokesman of the magnates at the side of the king. That is to say, that he disposes of very varied means of action. From the middle of the 7th century, a mayor of the palace in Austrasia tried to take the title of king.

This function exists in the 7th century in Neustria, Austrasia and in Burgundy. It is naturally much coveted and disputed within each kingdom and each possessor exercises it in his fashion amid a growing anarchy. Conflict develops too between the ambitions of the mayors of the Palace of different kingdoms. At last, after a long rivalry between Austrasia and Neustria, the battle of Tertry, near St.-Quentin, in 687 assured a definitive predominance to the mayor of Austrasia, Pepin, of Héristal, near Liège. This personage, founder of the fortune of the Carolingians, himself represents a sort of hereditary dynasty of mayors of Austrasia — the origin of whose power was the alliance of the family of Pepin with that of Arnoul, Bishop of Metz.

The descendants of Clovis yield place not as the result of a revolution, but because they do not in any way fulfil the rôle for which the Frankish monarchy was instituted, recognised and consecrated in the West. Far from assuring order, their weakness, dissensions and vices encourage anarchy. Far from bearing themselves like conquerors charged with spreading Christianity and civilisation, they get themselves defeated by the pagan Barbarians, who destroy the first churches of Germany and push the missionaries back over the Rhine. Far from educating themselves, they corrupt the Church. However, new dangers, singularly urgent, menace the Christian West. For its defence the Church chooses among the Franks a family of leaders altogether stronger and more gifted.

CHAPTER VII

Frankish Domination: Charlemagne

❖

*Saracen Invasion — Charles-Martel — Accession of Pepin
the Short — Charlemagne and the Western Empire —
Characteristics of the Carolingian Empire — Carolingian
Civilisation*

AT the beginning of the 8th century, dangers for the Christian
West come at once from North, East and South. But it is in
the South that the peril grows most formidable, by the startling
advance of the Arab conquest.

Less than sixty years after Mahomet's death, the Arabs,
having already conquered Syria, Egypt and Persia, completed
their crossing of North Africa and reached the Atlantic.
The Byzantine Empire, shaken by their exploits, could neither
stop them nor still less protect the Christians of the West from
the scourge of Islam. Only the Berbers had retarded the
invasion without succeeding in preventing Byzantine Africa
from breaking up. The Oriental merchants who frequented
Italy spread alarming news there.

In 711 the army of Islam crossed the Straits of Gibraltar.
A few years sufficed to conquer the greater part of Spain. Then
it advanced into Septimania and occupied Roussillon, Lower
Languedoc and Narbonne. Overrunning itself, it was held up
on the route from Carcassonne to Toulouse by Eudes, Duke
of Aquitania. But soon the Mussulman cavalry went ahead
again, pushed up the Rhône and Saône valleys and penetrated
deep into Burgundy, pillaging, razing and overturning what
it came up against and sacking the town of Autun. Some time
after, another mass of cavalry debouched from the Pyrenees
by the pass of Ronceval and followed the highway from
Dax to Bordeaux; there it forced the crossing of the Garonne

and thrust forward to reach Poitiers and Tours. Thus the Saracens, having already taken Autun, the town of St. Léger, the popular saint of Burgundy, threatened Tours, the sanctuary of St. Martin.

Germany was beginning to stir. The Frisians and Saxons were in revolt against Frankish penetration. The Alemanni sought their revenge. Bavaria was insecure. The pagan and savage peoples were lifting their heads again.

In Italy other Germans, apparently Christianised — Lombards or Longobards, men of the Long Lance — who had come in the wake of the Goths, having pushed back the Byzantine Empire and parcelled out the territory, were now threatening to take possession of Rome and the Pope.

Charles-Martel

Who was to defend the West? Frankish Gaul seemed demoralised. In the South, leading families, officials and counts, were in treaty with the Saracens. The *rois fainéants* thought only of reviving the conflict between Neustria and Austrasia. Pepin of Héristal died, leaving young grandchildren. At the very moment when the Saracens were crossing the Pyrenees, Aquitania sought to detach itself from the North.

And then the man who was needed came forward : a Frank, in whom the warlike gifts of his race were incarnate, the handsome and valorous Charles-Martel. Natural son of Pepin and a concubine, he was imprisoned on his father's death. He escaped and drew round him the most valiant of the Franks of Austrasia. In three years he established his authority over Austrasia, Neustria and Burgundy and put the Aquitanians to flight. Then he turned against Germany, inflicting a severe lesson on the Frisians, deposing the duke of the Alemanni, and defeating the Saxons. At last, in 732, at the entreaty of the Aquitanians themselves, he marched to encounter the Emir Abd-al-Rahman, who, after burning the churches of Bordeaux, was besieging Poitiers. Franks and Saracens confronted each

other at the junction of the Vienne and the Clain. 'The men
of the North', says a Spanish chronicler of the time, 'were like
an immovable wall, frozen by the cold.' Against this wall the
Saracen cavalry was broken. The Emir was killed ; his army
fled. For a long time yet the Arabs occupied the South of
Gaul, trying to push up the Rhône Valley, penetrating into
Italy, finding people ready to combine with them for pillage.
But Charles-Martel and his Franks pushed them back gradually. Gaul was saved from Islam.

The Church regarded such a warrior with favour. Besides,
was it not under the protection of Charles-Martel that the
Christian missions with St. Boniface tried to save the wildest
peoples of Germany from paganism ? In 739 Pope Gregory,
shut up in Rome by the Lombards, cut off from all communication with the Eastern Empire, sent a mission to the Frankish
chief to put the 'keys of the confession of St. Peter' in his
hands and asked for his help. But the conqueror of the
Saracens hesitated to attack the Lombards who had helped
him to retake Provence. Though an admirable soldier, he
remained timid and inexperienced in politics. He died in 741
at Quierzy-sur-Oise, leaving to his son, Pepin the Short, the
chance to be crowned king.

After Vercingetorix and Clovis, anticipating many others,
Charles-Martel provides the third example of this faculty for
recovery which characterises the history of true nations and
particularly of ours.

Accession of Pepin the Short

Of the two legitimate sons of Charles-Martel, who shared
the succession, Carloman, the elder, was soon in orders ; he
founded a monastery on Mount Soracte, near Rome, then
retired to the convent of Monte Cassino. The family of the
mayors of Austrasia had a reputation for piety. Pepin the
Short, now sole master of the Frankish state, was to make
himself the ally, protector, benefactor of the Church, from
which he drew remarkable profit politically.

Brought up at the monastery of St.-Denis, he was a man of rare culture among the warriors of his time. He was sufficiently versed in religious matters to collaborate effectively with the great Anglo-Saxon monk, St. Boniface, Apostle of Germany, in the reform of the Church. He was interested in Greek books, in geometry and even in Aristotle. Arrived at power at the age of maturity, Pepin was also a subtle politician, determined, prudent, calculating.

He did not wish to usurp kingship, he wished it to be conferred on him. The abbot of St.-Denis in Neustria, St. Boniface and his disciples in Austrasia, prepared the ground for him. An assembly of the Frankish people at Soissons in November 751 deposed the last Merovingians, who were tonsured and shut up in a monastery, and elected Pepin king. He rewarded the clergy with rich donations, then led an expedition against the Saxons whom he forced to receive Christian missionaries.

Pope Stephen II did not know how to free himself from the Lombards, who started their attacks against Rome and Ravenna anew. He asked Pepin for an interview and begged him to supply a bodyguard for his visit. The meeting took place at the royal villa of Ponthion in Champagne. The new king swore that he would free the Pontiff from the Lombards. Stephen II passed some months at St.-Denis. During his stay the monks sang their pupil's praises to him. On 28 July 754 at St.-Denis the Pope solemnly blessed Pepin, his wife and children, and forbade the Franks on pain of excommunication to choose a king outside this family henceforth. Thus for the elective kingship of the Franks was substituted kingship by divine right, for Germanic custom Roman principle, in place of the brotherhood of warriors the alliance of throne and altar — the work of the monastery of St.-Denis, cradle of the real monarchy and tomb of the kings.

The same year Pepin paid his debt. Out of scruple or to avoid offending the susceptibilities of the Frankish ruling class, now become suspicious, he tried at first to negotiate with the Lombards. Then, having crossed the Alps, he

defeated them at Susa and took their capital, Pavia. After
which he prudently hurried to treat with them, imposing on
them the restitution of Ravenna and eleven other towns.
Encroaching on the rights of the Byzantine Empire, Pepin
gave these towns to the Holy See. Suddenly with one stroke,
he created the Papal state, which lasted up to 1870. . . . He
had to return to Italy once again to constrain the king of the
Lombards to keep to his engagements. It was the occasion for
him solemnly to confirm the donation made to the Holy See.

Afterwards, Pepin was occupied in imposing his authority
in his own kingdom and in reconquering the parts lost; after
a new expedition into Germany against the Saxons, he drove
the Arabs out of Languedoc. But the most difficult task was
to subdue Aquitania, from the south of the Loire to the
Pyrenees; it claimed to be independent and its fortresses formed an offensive line right into the middle of
Gaul. A barbarous war broke out — the first of the wars of
the North against the South — in which we already recognise
the passion that later inspired Simon de Montfort. Pepin and
his Franks ravaged Berry, Limousin and Auvergne, taking
Bourges, Thouars and Clermont and destroying the castles of
Bourbon-l'Archambault and Chantelle; they advanced as far
as Quercy and defeated the Aquitanians in pitched battle.
Held up for a while by threats from Germany, the Franks of
the North soon decided to finish the war. Pepin established
his base at Bourges, whence his troops attacked Languedoc
and occupied Toulouse, Albi, Rodez and the Gévaudan. The
young Duke of Aquitania, Waifer, attacked on all sides, was
killed and his family captured: Aquitania was subdued.
Pepin sent reliable officials there; he reopened abandoned
churches, reassured and flattered, the clergy. He made a
triumphal entry at Saintes, where his wife, Queen Bertrade,
was awaiting him.

On his return from this campaign, he went to his beloved
abbey of St.-Denis to die, 24 September 768, aged fifty-four
years.

Pepin the Short has benefited in the eyes of posterity, as with his contemporaries, from the renown which churchmen gave him — a renown which extended as far as Persia. That did not prevent him from being a consummate master of manœuvre, a war-leader as fortunate as he was wise, a king sure of his rôle and of his designs. By his alliance with the Church, he opened up to the Franks the road to an unforeseen greatness along which Charlemagne continued to march. He achieved this for them almost in spite of themselves — for they resisted — in ceasing to be their elected head and becoming a consecrated king.

Charlemagne and the Western Empire

The two sons of Pepin did not agree. The division of the succession would no doubt have turned out ill if the younger, Carloman, had not died unexpectedly after a reign of two years. Charles, the elder, whom legend and history call Charlemagne or Charles the Great, found himself sovereign of a territory which the successes of his father and grandfather had extended from the Mediterranean to Frisia, from the Atlantic to the Danube and almost to the Elbe : all ancient Roman Gaul and almost all Germany, without counting a sort of protectorate over Italy. He got this immense state in most favourable conditions, when the insurgent peoples and the invaders had just been beaten, with the Frankish armies well trained and well armed, and with the unreserved support of the Church and the prestige of a sort of Roman heritage. Charlemagne was assuredly a magnificent figure. But Charles-Martel and Pepin the Short had prepared exceptional opportunities for him. He had, too, the further good fortune of reigning, an absolute master, for nearly half a century.

Little resembling his legendary portrait, Charlemagne was a man of sanguine humour, vigorous rather than majestic, big and heavy, with thick neck, round head, prominent nose, eyes wide-open and lively, with long hair, a moustache in the Frankish fashion without any beard, his voice too small for his body. He was married four times. Of simple manners, he showed himself habitually sober, but did not dislike banquets and good wine. He liked swimming and hunting, had a taste for witticisms, oratory, the animation of feasts, the scene, movement, life. He was a ready speaker, knew some Latin, studied astronomy, rhetoric, dialectics and, like his father, interested himself particularly in religious matters. For the rest, generous and good-natured, without haughtiness or false dignity, welcoming to all, familiar with his guests.

He had numerous residences or villas in Gaul and in Germany. He went from one to the other, travelling indefatigably. But the dwelling he preferred was at Aix-la-Chapelle, where he built baths, a palace, a church, and where he dreamed of making a 'new Rome', in the heart of the old country of the Franks, on the line where Gaul and Germany were soldered together.

Charlemagne's armed expeditions were very numerous, but were, in general, police-expeditions, repressing troubles in the interior and on the frontiers rather than wars of conquest properly speaking. All in all, he did not much enlarge the framework of territorial possessions and protectorates that Pepin the Short had left him. He gave a civilising character to Frankish expansion.

As faithful ally of the Holy See, he began by breaking for good the power of the Lombards who terrorised Italy. He took Pavia, their capital, imprisoned their king and, placing the iron crown on his own brows, proclaimed himself their sovereign. Practically speaking, Italy passed under his authority.

Next, he determined to put a term to the Arab penetration which menaced the South of Gaul. This was a long, hard struggle. He had to undertake seven expeditions in twenty years. He experienced some reverses, of which the most famous was the massacre of his rear-guard at Ronceval by the Basque mountaineers, sworn enemies of the Franks — the disaster in which Roland perished, Duke of the Marches of Brittany, hero of the *Chanson de Roland.* In the end, he succeeded in establishing and consolidating a zone of defence on both sides of the Pyrenees, the March of Spain, with Toulouse as its capital. But he could not subdue the Basques.

In Germany, in spite of numerous expeditions and short-lived truces, the Franks had never curbed the Saxons. These wild heathens — worshippers of Irminsul, a colossal wooden idol, and refractory to the activity of Christian missionaries — inhabited a region of forests and marshes, between the Low Countries and Denmark, where their swarming tribes hid themselves in huts that the stranger had difficulty in recognising. Charlemagne waged a war against them, relentless, carefully thought out and without pity. He employed in it all the military science that his father had handed on to him. After the first expeditions, the chief, Widukind, was in vain converted and came solemnly to receive baptism at Attigny-sur-Aisne — the war against the Saxons all the same lasted thirty-two years. Charlemagne vainly tried to shorten it by terrible reprisals, mass executions and the deportation of entire tribes; he triumphed only after the exhaustion of the Saxon forces. At least this fearful tragedy had decisive results for the future of Germany and Europe. Roads were constructed, towns founded round Frankish fortresses like Bremen, Magdeburg, Halle; civilisation penetrated into savage haunts. What the Romans had not dared or been able to attempt, Charlemagne succeeded in : in his brutal way, he shaped Germany.

This Germanic construction, in order to last, had to be protected by a girdle of defences. Charlemagne threw back the Danes, the Slavs and pursued the Avars, descendants of the Huns, into Hungary — their fortified camp or ring, filled with treasure pillaged from a score of nations, fell into the possession of a Frankish army. The eastern frontier of the Carolingian state was organised into military territories or marches from which were born later Brandenburg — kernel of Prussia — and Austria.

The sequence of wars and conquests of Charlemagne has left a romantic and legendary memory from which sprang the principal themes of the *chansons de geste*. In fact, these wars seem to have been waged in pursuit of a design as calculated and determined as it was grandiose : to gather Catholic Europe into a single empire, as extensive as possible and with frontiers strong enough to stop the barbarians, whose destructive impetus had not ceased during four centuries. A design evidently inspired, like all the work of the first Carolingians, by the Church, the bishops, the abbots of the great monasteries and the missionaries. A design the amplitude of which can only be measured in taking account of the enormous distances which then separated the Spanish March from the March of Brandenburg — perhaps two months' journey. A design that the Franks accomplished under Charlemagne, but which was to miscarry afterwards because of its very size, leaving ancient Gaul and ancient Germany marked with a common imprint, more divided than ever : design or clerical dream, the temporary realisation of which the Church hastened to bless.

Christianity was born and had begun to grow in the environment of the Roman, the Imperial, peace. The very memory of the persecutions that the pagan Emperors had inflicted on it made it all the more attached to the prestige of the Imperial idea from the moment they abjured paganism to become Christian.

But, in the 8th century, what was the Empire ? It was a far-away power seated at Byzantium, vaguely tinged with heresy, quite incapable of protecting the widespread, but fragile, Christianity of the West against the double menace of barbarians from the North and Saracens pushing up from the South. The Western Church was awaiting the opportunity to give life and force again to the function as well as to the title of Emperor.

Charlemagne was manifestly the person designed by destiny for such a resurrection. If he had chosen to proclaim himself Emperor, no-one would have been able effectively to oppose it. It is supposed that he had the idea without daring to express it as long as there lived a megalomaniac Pope Hadrian who dreamed of uniting pontificate and Empire himself. But on Hadrian's death, his successor Leo III, a former small official, who was pursued by the hatred of the Roman nobles and had just escaped their blows, hastened to give himself the protector whom Christianity required for itself. On Christmas Night 800, Charlemagne, passing through Rome, was praying in the basilica of St. Peter when Pope Leo, almost by surprise, placed the Imperial crown on his head.

The Byzantines naturally made prolonged objections. They took half a century before deciding to recognise officially the accomplished fact of the Western Empire.

Characteristics of the Carolingian Empire

The Empire of Charlemagne was founded on two forces : one material — military supremacy ; the other moral — religion. It lacked a real political and administrative framework. Military supremacy could not last indefinitely. As for religion, it could bind together beliefs, but it could not bind territories. The Carolingian structure was the more fragile because it remained subjected to the Frankish custom of dividing the inheritance.

Alone, the character of royal power, formerly elective, henceforth theocratic, appeared changed. Did this change give to the Carolingian princes the right to make or modify at will the laws, the famous 'Capitulations'? The Capitulations, collections of legislative acts or customs, were the common work of people and king.

The political and administrative frame of the Carolingian epoch does not appear very different from the Merovingian. The ministers are still of the household or private servants of the king. There is no fixed capital. Government moves about incessantly with the king and his friends. From time to time a general assembly is called together, where the people and the magnates speak of all that concerns them in the presence of the king.

The administrative division into counties continues. Under Charlemagne, naturally, the counts obey. Later, the counts, marquises and their lieutenants keep for themselves both the excessive powers which they have been given and the territory they administer. This constitutes the origin of great lordships. Charlemagne had their administration inspected periodically by men in his confidence, laymen or clerics, the *missi dominici*.

Military service is exacted henceforth only from men possessing some fortune, an estate of at least three *manses* (= farms) : that amount by reason of the increase of cavalry since the invasion of the Saracens, each horseman being held to furnish his horse and to provide for it. Military duty, become very onerous, is soon rewarded with privileges.

The administration of justice was strengthened by the tribunal of appeal of the *missi dominici* and by a new personnel of professional judges, the *scabini*, who replace the ancient juries. As under the Merovingians, the king possesses immense domains from which he draws his immediate resources. For the rest, the state draws direct and indirect taxes. The central power has a good deal of trouble in hindering local officials from multiplying them to their own profit. Under Charlemagne the coinage is a royal monopoly, but his successors allow great lords to strike their own moneys.

The evolution of great rural estates progressively confuses land-holding and political authority. The landowner and the official become less and less distinguishable : the fusion of both will be found in the lord. Immunity — that is to say, administrative, fiscal and judicial autonomy—remains still rare for lay lands; it becomes the normal rule for Church property.

Carolingian Civilisation

It is not in vain that an authority with such an aura assures security and peace over a territory as vast as the empire of Charlemagne. Agriculture works better, trade and traffic increase, resources fructify and multiply, the arts and civilisation progress.

Northern Gaul, at length given shelter from invasions and civil wars, is cleared and broken up with quite new vigour. In time it becomes one of the richest agricultural regions of Europe. Great abbeys, like St.-Waast of Arras, St.-Bertin of St.-Omer, St.-Riquier near Abbeville, encourage the development of agriculture in Artois and Picardy. Following Charlemagne's own example, the abbeys establish model farms around which colonists and workers cluster more and more. By the fact of this inflow of people coming to seek security of work and life, as by the fact of pious gifts which increase the Church's fortune unceasingly, the monastic estates constitute enormous areas of agricultural exploitation. The abbey of St.-Germain-des-Prés possesses about 90,000 acres, employs on its lands nearly 3,000 families and more than 10,000 persons. The abbey of St.-Remi of Rheims exploits 693 manses or farms, that of St.-Wandrille in Normandy 1,727 manses. The abbey of Luxeuil comes to have even more. In the dependencies of St.-Martin of Tours live some thousands of workers. And already, as at St.-Riquier, the artisan township grows alongside the abbey; the artisans install themselves near the agricultural estate.

Trade is very active on the Seine, the Scheldt and the Meuse, the Rhine and the upper Danube. The valleys of the Rhône and the Saône become again the great artery of traffic between the North and the Mediterranean : Lyons and Vienne recover wealth. Arles is the principal entrepôt for products of the Levant. Nîmes, with a partly Greek population, develops its industries. Narbonne, a cosmopolitan port where Frankish officials jostle with Spanish merchants and Jews, rivals Marseilles. Charlemagne protects the Jews, values their knowledge, and uses them in the Orient and with the Arabs. Bordeaux, Nantes, Etaples, Boulogne, Ghent are increasingly frequented by ships. Entrepôts are established at the crossroads of the

Frankish Empire, at Tournai, Maestricht, Worms, Mainz —
meeting-points of Gaulish and German trade. Trading settlements grow up along the new frontiers. Thus appears a double
system of fruitful exchange between the different regions of
the Empire on one side, between the Empire, the Orient, the
Mediterranean and the barbarian peoples on the other. For
the first time Europe becomes aware of its economic opportunities.

Charlemagne strove, along with the monasteries, to
challenge the ignorance into which Gaul fell under the
Merovingians. He encouraged the teaching of reckoning,
grammar and then of fine writing or calligraphy, without
which manuscripts remained unreadable even to most clerks.
The writing of Carolingian manuscripts, sometimes decorated
with miniatures, letters of silver or gold, is one of the clearest
and closest to the printed book that we know. The Emperor
drew round him, too, scholars or learned men from all
countries, without distinction of race : such as the historian
Paul the Deacon, Italian by origin ; the poet Theodulph, a
Goth ; the writer and chronicler Einhard, born in Franconia ;
and above all the celebrated teacher Alcuin, an Anglo-Saxon.

The simple comparison of Merovingian with Carolingian
coins shows the progress of art. But of the edifices of Charlemagne's time, most of them made of wood and so exposed
to frequent fires, little enough remains to us. The chapel of
the palace of Aix-la-Chapelle, the chief monument remaining
from that time, seems to have been imitated from the Byzantine
architecture of Ravenna. We recognise the same influence
of Byzantine architecture in the little church of Germigny-les-
Prés, not far from Orléans. The rebirth of the arts in Gaul,
after long relapse into barbarism, is made, then, as always in
such cases, by bringing in models from outside.

CHAPTER VIII

Beginnings of the Kingdom of France

❖

*Weaknesses of the Frankish Empire — Treaty of Verdun
— Invasion of the Normans — Powerlessness of the Last
Carolingians — The Dukes of France: Hugh Capet, King*

THE Empire of the Franks, the Gallo-Germanic Empire as
it was built up by Pepin the Short, then consolidated, increased and made famous by Charlemagne, lasted hardly a
century. Its principle was recognised for nearly three centuries. Napoleon's Empire, less vast considering the relative
ease of communication and government, was to last only a
few years. Even the Roman Empire, much more solidly
constructed and administered, had not preserved its real unity
for more than three centuries.

We must not misunderstand either the greatness or the
significance of the work of the Franks. The Roman Empire
had been above all Mediterranean. The Frankish Empire was
exclusively European : from the memory it left came the
notion of Europe as one, as from its divisions were born
several historic states which are living still. It fixed the
character and ethnic constitution of the West, in raising
barriers which have never since been permanently overstepped,
against Moslem invasion, the Slav advance, the irruption of
Asian nomads. It lacked the brilliance of science, letters and
the arts to make it famous. But without the protection that
its power, put to the service of the Christian idea, gave to
the clergy and particularly to the monasteries, guardians of
ancient culture, the creative impulse of the Middle Ages would
not have been possible.

The Frankish Empire did not fall by accident. It carried
in it the causes of its dislocation. It was far too much extended

for the means of control of the time, both military and administrative. The custom of dividing the inheritance condemned it to be parcelled up, in spite of dynastic ties. The need for each territory, region or province to watch over its own immediate security against dangers equally urgent elsewhere was to break the unity of military organisation and disperse resources : each prince, duke, marquis or count had his men to organise, his lands to defend, his treasure to provide, followers to maintain. The onerous nature of military service prevented the Aquitanian from going to fight in Saxony, and conversely. Charlemagne had only to defeat adversaries on the Continent. He had little cause for anxiety on the sea-coasts. The influx of the pirates from the North, the Normans, at the mouth of all the rivers from the Scheldt to the Adour, completely changed the conditions of the problem : the Empire was attacked on all sides : every region, distracted, wanted defenders for itself alone. Even in the interior of the Empire, the custom of paying officials in lands, in grants on the taxes, in benefices more or less hereditary — joined with the accumulation of powers in the same hand — opened up all the opportunities for disorganisation, for the day when the dissensions of the royal family, the old clan rivalries, the quarrelsome temperament of the Frankish people and chance incident would give a pretext for indiscipline. Finally, the notion of the state in men's minds was destroyed by the multiplication of personal ties, of which even Charlemagne's Capitulations had encouraged the habit.

Treaty of Verdun

Charlemagne died in 814. The unity of the Empire subsisted after a fashion under his heir, Louis the Pious or the Debonair, a weak and blundering character. Dissensions and wars for the division of territories under the Franks began in the lifetime of the Debonair and continued under his sons. After the battle of Fontenoy, in Auxerre, a treaty of partition was signed in August 843 at Verdun.

The Treaty of Verdun founded the kingdom of France, as it was to subsist up to the end of the Middle Ages. This treaty ensured the absolute independence of the kingdoms bespoken for each of the three sons of Louis the Pious. Charles the Bald obtained the western part of the Empire, from the Scheldt to Spain; Louis the German took Germany proper, from the Baltic to the Alps and the Save; between the two, Lothar received, besides Italy, a large band of territory of ancient Gaul, from the mouths of the Rhine to those of the Rhône. This creation of an independent Lotharingia (origin of the name of Lorraine), taking away from our country the great routes from the Mediterranean to the North Sea and the Rhine, has weighed heavily on the history of France. In the intermediate zone thus established two new kingdoms soon formed, vassals of the future Germanic Empire: the kingdom of Lorraine and that of Burgundy, later of Provence. During long centuries French policy has exerted itself to get back these regions, essential parts of the national patrimony, inhabited almost entirely by people of Romance tongue.

The unity of the Carolingian Empire was reconstituted for a moment, at the end of the 9th century, first by Charles the Bald, then by one of the sons of Louis the German, Charles the Fat. Both received the Imperial crown from the Pope, anxious to restore unity. After which the Empire broke up again into five kingdoms: France; Germany with Lorraine added; Burgundy; Provence with the Lyonnais; Italy, itself divided up.

At Strasbourg in 842 two of Charlemagne's grandchildren, Louis the German and Charles the Bald, in league against their brother Lothar, had sworn an oath of alliance before their troops. Louis the German, in order to be understood by his brother's troops, pronounced his oath in the Romance tongue derived from popular Latin; Charles, to be understood by the Germans, swore in Teutonic speech. The oath of Strasbourg is the first document in the vulgar tongue in both German and French history. It proves that already the Franks of France had adopted the language out of which French came and that they knew no other.

The name of *Francia*, France, had appeared from the Roman epoch to designate the right bank of the lower Rhine, the country of the Franks. This designation still survives today in the name of Franconia. Then *Francia* extended itself to the left bank of the Rhine, to the Low Countries and, after the victories of Clovis, down to the Loire, without comprising Aquitania or Burgundy, in spite of their submission. Under Charlemagne, the name of *Francia* covered the whole Empire of the Franks, except Italy. For a long time Germany was called *Francia Orientalis*, eastern France. But the name of France ended by attaching itself to the Seine country, which had been since Clovis the centre from which Frankish conquests radiated. At the end of the Middle Ages the Ile-de-France meant the country between Seine, Oise and Marne to the south of the Valois and the west of the Brie.

Invasion of the Normans

In the course of the century that followed Charlemagne's death, western France lived in terror under the frequent and destructive attacks, growing ever bolder, of the pirates of the North, the Normans.

Norwegians, Swedes, Danes — it was chiefly the Danes who invaded France — setting forth from Scandinavia where life was difficult with too hard a climate and too poor a soil, came down towards the South in search of booty and fertile lands. The advance of Charlemagne's armies, driving back the Saxons towards the North, had doubtless barred the route to Scandinavian immigration into Germany. Whence the necessity for Nordic tribes to seek adventures by sea more than ever.

Harsh and merciless as they were, the Normans did not lack the qualities that make conquering peoples. They had strong discipline and a knowledge of the methods of war shared by few. Their fleets, planned for long cruises, enabled them to operate by surprise. Their tactics on land revealed an astonishing promptitude of calculation and action.

From the beginning of the 9th century, they were to be seen at the mouth of almost all the rivers and streams, in the North Sea, the Channel and the Atlantic. They attacked the Empire of the Franks on the side least well defended and most difficult to defend, the whole effort of the Frankish armies being directed towards Central Europe and Spain. They went up the rivers, fell by surprise on the inhabitants, carried off harvests, pillaged treasures, burned townships and monasteries.

They advanced very far, by repeated cruises the frequency of which demoralised the local populations. Not only did they devastate the future Normandy, but they pushed on to Beauvais, Noyon, Chartres, Paris, Soissons, Melun and Meaux. They pillaged Anjou, Vendée, Poitou, advanced beyond Orléans, penetrated to Poitiers, Limoges, Angoulême and even to Clermont-Ferrand. Passing through the Straits of Gibraltar, they arrived at the Rhône valley. They appeared at Arles, Nîmes, Valence. The people, lay and clerical, fled. The monks carried their relics and their sacred objects from one refuge to another across terrorised France. A moment came when the Normans roamed in Burgundy, in Champagne, in Lorraine.

Evidently the Carolingian princes, occupied with their disputes and their partitions, were surprised and overwhelmed by the Norman invasion. Most often they did not know how to make the invaders withdraw, except by purchasing their departure for gold. This procedure found its solemn — and, for the rest, efficacious — sanction when in 911 Charles the Simple concluded a treaty at St.-Clair-sur-Epte ceding to the Scandinavian chief Rollo the territories near the lower Seine, which the Normans, coming in greater and greater numbers, already occupied in force.

Although mingled little by little with the indigenous

population of ancient Neustria, the Normans or Danes of the lower Seine and of Calvados remained in contact for two or three centuries with their kin of the Baltic.

Powerlessness and Divisions of the Last Carolingians

The danger of the Norman invasion prepared the accession of the future Capetians, as the incursion of the Barbarians had made the opportunity of Clovis and the onrush of the Saracens the prestige of Charles-Martel. For the third time the terror of the people and of the clergy engendered a royal house.

Towards the middle of the 9th century, the great-grand-father of Hugh Capet, a Frankish lord named Robert the Strong, commanded for Charles the Bald a region comprising Anjou, Touraine, Maine and the upper valley of the Orne. Soon, from being Count he became Duke—in other words, chief of the military forces of the country between Loire and Seine, the area most threatened. He succeeded in defeating the Bretons in revolt, then in surprising and massacring bands of Normans. His command was enlarged as far as Auxerre and Nevers. His exploits were already becoming legendary and bringing hope to the people, when he fell, pierced by a Norman arrow, at Brissarthe in 866.

His son, Odo, was Count of Paris. The Normans had sacked and burned Paris twice. They came back in 885 with a cloud of sailing ships covering the Seine for two or three leagues. But this time — thanks to Count Odo, the Bishop and the Abbot of St.-Germain-des-Prés — the town, withdrawn within the rebuilt and fortified city, withstood the siege. The Normans of the Seine, swollen by bands from the Loire, in vain constructed their siege engines, built a camp, pressed their assaults : Paris resisted them for nine months and was not taken. In the end, Odo escaped to Germany to solicit the help of the Emperor Charles the Fat. The latter, having arrived at the foot of the heights of Montmartre with an immense army, found nothing better to do than to buy

the retreat of the Normans for money and to offer them the
pillage of Burgundy.

The people placed all their confidence in Odo. Soon,
Charles the Fat was deposed and Odo elected king. Thenceforth Odo had to fight both the Normans and the partisans
of the Carolingian dynasty whom the Franks of the East
supported. He endured reverses. Finally, before his death
(as he had no child), he recognised the right to the crown of
Charles the Simple, who was to treat with the Normans.

Odo left his brother Robert master of Paris, Blois, Tours
and Angers. The discontented lords of western France
pushed Robert into revolt and elected him king. A battle
followed at Soissons between Charles' army, composed of
Lorrainers, and the troops of the king-elect, in which the latter
was killed.

The Dukes of France: Hugh Capet, King

Robert's son, Hugh the Great, showed himself a subtle
politician. Instead of declaring his candidature for the title of
King, he saw to it that his protection or his services to the
Carolingian princes were highly paid and applied himself to
enlarging his possessions, his effective power and his following, clerical as well as lay. Recognised as Duke of the Franks
or of France, exercising in the end the functions of Regent of
the realm, he increased and consolidated the dominant position
of his family. Sure of the future, he died in 956.

His son, Hugh Capet — the man with the little cape —
came up against the same hostility from the Franks of the
East, faithful to the Carolingians, against the Western Franks.
He waited more than thirty years. At last, thanks to the
support of a great prelate, Lorrainer by birth and brother of
the Count of Verdun, Adalbéron, Archbishop of Rheims
(inspired by his secretary, the scholarly Gerbert), the long-
contemplated manœuvre came to a head. In 987 the young
king, Louis, was going to denounce the conspiracy against
his throne, when he had a mortal fall out hunting. Two

assemblies of the magnates followed. The first, at Compiègne, was stormy but dominated by the skill of Adalbéron. The second, at Senlis, elected as king Hugh Capet, who was crowned and anointed at Noyon, 3 July 987. The new king then got rid of the last Carolingian and his family by treachery, shutting them up in the tower of Orléans.

Hugh had henceforth a great title and impressive rights, but little means and few resources. To arrive at the throne, pay the upkeep of the western lords and buy the adhesion of the people of the East, he had to consent to many concessions, recognise numerous usurpations, close his eyes to encroachments of every kind. He had had even to beg the support of the Normans and the Germans. Here was a monarchy very frail in its beginnings, which imposed itself not all at once, as the Carolingian monarchy had done by shining deeds, but gradually, by realistic calculation, good sense and political ruse, while awaiting the opportunity of genius or luck. A true peasant kingship, eager to take or defend land, clever at lawsuits against neighbours, very pious with the priest and adroitly demagogic elsewhere.

Hugh Capet is King of France and of Aquitaine. The clerks of his entourage call him the 'glorious' and 'august' as they called Charlemagne. The lords who elected him recognise his dignity. He represents both the Frankish idea of the chief chosen by his peers and the Roman idea of the sacred monarch. But all that is very theoretical. The first Capetian figures simply — amid the old officers, counts, marquises, dukes, lay or ecclesiastical lords who appropriated to themselves the lands and the authority they had received from Charlemagne and his descendants — as the repository of a double principle of suzerainty and unity. This principle has hardly a real application any more, except to confirm, by means of the homage rendered to it, the usurpations committed by the great.

Actually, the king can command only on his own lands, in his domain. This domain, much diminished, comprises in all a band of territory from the Oise to the Loire, with Senlis, Étampes, Dreux, Orléans. Even Paris is still subject to a count of its own. Of his ancestors' dominion in the West, there remains to the king only the title of Abbot of St.-Martin of Tours, the right of direct supervision over the counties of Blois, Anjou and Maine, an indirect control over the Breton counties of Rennes and Nantes. He also possesses Montreuil-sur-Mer. The monasteries of St.-Denis, St.-Germain-des-Prés, St.-Maur-des-Fossés, St.-Aignan-d'Orléans, St.-Riquier, and many others recognise him as patron.

All the rest of the realm is divided into lordships, of varying size, more or less independent of the royal authority and of which the chief correspond to the old military commands of the Carolingian epoch: the county of Flanders, the duchy of Normandy, the duchy of Burgundy, the duchy of Aquitaine or of Guyenne, the duchy of Gascony, the county of Toulouse, the marquisate of Narbonne, the county of Barcelona. All Lotharingia, *i.e.* Lorraine, Franche-Comté, Lyonnais, Savoy, Dauphiné and Provence, are outside the kingdom, under the suzerainty of the German Holy Roman Empire. The title of Emperor was restored by Pope John XII in 962 in favour of Otto the Great, second king of Germany of the Saxon dynasty, conqueror of the Lombards like Charlemagne before him.

PART II

THE SPIRIT OF MEDIEVAL FRANCE

CHAPTER I

Feudal Lordships and Monastic Achievement

❖

Meaning of the Feudal System — The Great Fiefs —
Weakness of the Early Capetians — Widespread Power of
the Church — Prestige of the Monasteries — Influence of
Cluny: Genius of St. Bernard — Awakening of the
Communes

THE seigneurial or feudal system, which became between
A.D. 900 and 1000 the rule not only of French society but of
almost the whole of Europe for several centuries — it was to
last in some regions up to the 20th century — is difficult to
understand from the point of view of modern principles and
habits.   It is difficult, besides, to judge it fairly against
traditions that are wholly hostile to it.   It has united
against it, later, the monarchy and the Church, the lawyers and
the clerics, the partisans of authority by divine right and those
of democracy, the absolutists and the parliamentarians. Above
all, it has not been pardoned for having retarded, at least in
appearance, the unification and centralisation of the state.

In fact, the feudal system, however numerous and detestable its abuses may appear, was not a phenomenon of
barbarism.   On the contrary, it probably prevented society
from becoming barbarous again after the break-up of the
Frankish Empire.   In the almost complete collapse of the
political framework, it saved enough fragments of the past
for the emergence in less than two centuries of the high
civilisation of the Middle Ages, far superior to that of
Charlemagne.

The system of feudal lordship was born of insecurity

and was a reaction against it. In the absence of a general system for maintaining public order, officials, landowners and lords defended themselves and their goods, as did their dependants or their serfs, by means usurped in theory, which could only be local. They were linked together by ties of mutual aid and of personal dependence. In default of legal protection and guarantees of public order, the mass of poor people put their fate into the hands of those who possessed the land that fed them and also the arms to fight. Thus the whole society was built up on the exchange of personal services. Naturally the strong were masters of interpreting the personal contract rather as they chose. The only safeguard was in the conscience of the powerful and in their fear of moral sanctions or of Hell. The system permitted many exactions and brutalities, but gradually it became more regular. In truth, it only lasted so long because the personal bond corresponded to the state men were in, insecure, anxious, weak. As for territorial divisions, people in the Middle Ages did not see the same inconveniences as we do. A confined frame satisfied their particularism. They preferred being commanded by men of their own countryside to being administered from afar by an unapproachable authority. Then, too, considering the difficulties of communication at that time, the great fiefs like Aquitaine or Normandy represented an area comparable to that of a modern state.

It is usual to consider the formation of the unity of France as an entirely political achievement. But the political achievement was only effective in so far as it suppressed barriers and shortened distances in creating more rapid means of communication. The apparent unity of Gaul under the Romans had depended on the unity of the road system. Under the Merovingians roads were hardly kept up any more. Charlemagne bothered himself only with the military roads of Germany, and we know that in his time trade flowed mainly along river routes. After six or seven centuries of neglect in regard to communications, feudal particularism reflected in part the splitting up of any wider area of exchange.

The Great Fiefs

In the France of the early Capetians, the North and the South, separated by the valley of the Loire, still form two territories and two very distinct peoples. The king himself is called 'King of the Franks and the Aquitanians'. The North, formerly favoured in all respects by the Frankish ascendancy, is rich and — thanks to the absence of natural obstacles — more open than the South to general movement. On the other hand the Frankish Empire has given a new impulse to trade between northern Gaul, Germany and Central Europe. Oriental merchants arrive henceforth in the West via the Carpathians and the Danube. Northern France, the France of the Franks, more and more affirms its economic, political and religious predominance — the North is very Catholic — over the South.

The richest fief of the North is the county of Flanders, which includes the country of Ghent, Bruges and Ypres, speaking a Teutonic dialect, and the country of Lille, Douai, Arras and St.-Omer, where Romanised inhabitants speak a French dialect, Walloon. To the county of Flanders are attached, as vassals, the counties of Boulogne, Guines and St.-Pol. It is ruled by a dynasty whose chiefs call themselves from father to son Arnoul, Baldwin or Robert. This dynasty seeks to enlarge its possessions on all sides, towards Zeeland, towards Hainault and towards the Vermandois. It establishes its capital at Lille, which it embellishes and increases in size. An enterprising dynasty, warlike, prompt to make itself obeyed.

The duchy of Normandy, the frontier of which cuts the Seine below Mantes, belongs to the family of the old Scandinavian chief Rollo. Mingling with the indigenous population, the Normans gradually adopt Christianity. Order is restored and wealth returns. Rouen, Dieppe, Caen, Alençon attract trade. The clergy re-establish themselves at Rouen, seat of an archbishop, and in the five episcopal towns Évreux, Bayeux, Séez, Lisieux, Coutances. The abbeys of Jumièges, St.-Wandrille and Fécamp lift up their heads again. The ducal dynasty is vigorous, adroit, sometimes brutal or cynical, given to ambition and a certain magnificence. At first allied to the kings of France, it does not hesitate to threaten them by its power.

The counties of Blois and Champagne envelop the royal domain to south and east. The county of Blois includes, with that town, Tours, Châteaudun and Chartres ; the county of Champagne, Meaux, Provins, Troyes and Vitry. The families that possess them are related and practise partition of inheritance in the Frankish manner. Hence sometimes the reunion, sometimes the division of the two counties. Most of the counts are men of mediocre character, blundering, adventurous, without any capacity for consistent drive.

On the other hand, the county of Anjou, which gradually enlarges itself to cover Maine, Touraine, a part of Poitou and Brittany, is ruled by active spirits, strong of temperament, wary and combative. One of them, Fulk Nerra, renowned for his boldness, his crimes and his political vigour, becomes a legendary figure. In less than three hundred years, the Angevin dynasty comes to dominate half France and all England. It represents the great danger for the future of the Capetians.

The counts of Nantes and Rennes dispute the title of Duke of Brittany. Brittany, except for Nantes which serves as maritime outlet for the Angevins and Poitevins, is a closed country, speaking a Celtic tongue, primitive in manners, split up into small fiefs : it appears to the French chroniclers of the time as 'a real land of savages'. However, there is besides that a French Brittany, bristling with military lordships, Rais, Clisson, Ancenis, Vitré, Fougères, Combourg.

Finally, the duchy of Burgundy, with the valleys of the upper Seine and the Saône — the Saône from the middle of the 10th century forms the frontier between the kingdom of France and the Germanic Empire — completes the series of great fiefs of the North. The first Burgundian dynasty springs from a branch of the Capetians. But the dukes have to deal with strong opponents over this territory which has suffered less than others from the ills of the Carolingian epoch and where the triple tradition of Aedui, Romans and Burgundians has produced a spirit difficult to master. The local lordships, Nevers, Auxerre, Sens, Semur, Chalon, Mâcon, Beaujeu, are intractable. A vast clerical and monastic power holds the duke in check. There are the bishoprics of Mâcon, Chalon, Auxerre, Autun and Langres. There are above all the great abbeys : Cluny, Vézelay, Flavigny, Tournus, St.-Pierre-de-Bèze, Pothières, St.-Bénigne-de-Dijon, which claim to owe obedience only to God and deference only to the Pope.

To the south of the Loire, we enter the duchy of Aquitaine, a vast group of territories — a veritable state, in practice quite independent. It unites, to begin with, Berry, Poitou, Saintonge, Angoulême, Limousin, Auvergne and Périgord. Soon it annexes the duchy of Gascony. Thenceforward, it covers almost a third of the France of today. The Duke of Aquitaine or of Guyenne appears, in the eyes even of certain popes, to be the real king. The dukes have themselves crowned at Limoges in the manner of sovereigns. They are of Poitevin origin. They make a great figure in the world by their magnificence, their taste for display and for letters, their external relations, their ability and their conquests. They several times refuse to render homage to the Capetians. The heads of the ducal family almost all bear the name of William. Their heiress is ultimately Eleanor, for a time Queen of France, then repudiated ; whose second marriage, bringing Aquitaine to the Count of Anjou, future King of England, marks one of the gravest checks to the fortunes of the Capetians.

However powerful it is, the Poitevin dynasty which rules Aquitaine does not succeed in subjecting all the South. Without speaking of Pyrenean lordships, almost inaccessible in their valleys, the county of Toulouse, stretching from Provence to Rouergue, remains irreducible, ruled by the family of St.-Gilles. The Counts of Toulouse are in turn threatened by the Counts of Barcelona, who aim at creating a Franco-Spanish monarchy uniting Languedoc and Roussillon to Catalonia.

Weakness of the Early Capetians

On their own domain, which is in fact the smallest of the great lordships of their kingdom, the first Capetians — Hugh Capet, Robert the Pious, Henry I, Philip I — do not have an existence sensibly different, domestic, political or military, from that of heads of dynasties regarded as vassals of the Crown. It is the same way of life, the same manner of ruling, the same piety or brutalities, the same ambitions of a mainly local significance. The particular mark of the Capetians is seen less in manifestations of authority or of magnificence than in a watchful prudence and good sense that keeps them from adventures. Their domain, if it seems small, is nevertheless the best placed, at the crossing of the principal routes not only of France, but of the West. Dynasty and domain can wait on fortune.

Occupied primarily in keeping order at home, the first Capetians do not seek to conquer France. They have not the means. If by chance they succeeded, it would be a precarious achievement. France is not ripe for political unity. Under the Romans, the unity of Gaul represented only the common submission of the Gaulish peoples to a foreign power. Under Merovingians and Carolingians, unity was made at certain moments between the Franks, but not between the territories they dominated. In the 10th and 11th centuries, there is no longer a common ascendancy, either Roman or Frank, to impose upon the different parts of France a unity at least in appearance. Henceforth it would be necessary for unity to come from the nation itself, according as this unity seems beneficent ; and it is accomplished from within, the work of the kings being consolidated and sometimes preceded by the adhesion of the peoples.

It is a false view of history that considers the Middle Ages as a period of retreat, from the point of view of the unification of the country. There is no retreat, there is change in the nature of the forces which should finally bring about unity. An external or superior ascendancy cannot in itself make the unity of divided or distinct peoples. The Romans themselves did not make the unity of the peoples their empire brought together. In the modern epoch, the Habsburgs did not make the unity of their subjects. For populations to unite lastingly, in the double consciousness of their common interest and ideals, to the authority that claims to unite them, their desire to be united must correspond. French unity makes progress according as the kings offer the people better order, a better government and administration.

But in the 10th and 11th centuries, unity hardly exists any more within the great fiefs than in the realm itself. The dukes and counts, in strengthening their individual power, create zones of local order and unity which are later absorbed by monarchical order and national unity.

Widespread Power of the Church

It is clear, in any case, that the power which curbs the excesses of seigneurial rule, inspiring it with sentiments or ideas other than the love of fighting and the search for gain, does not reside in the monarchy. This power is that of the Church and, most of all, of the monasteries.

The Church, though it does not dispose of armed forces and possesses less land than the great lords, dominates the evolution of society. Its influence imposes itself ultimately because it represents a power both general and constant, while the authority of each lord remains local, disputed, more or less ephemeral. At this period of intense piety, of concrete faith, in which men believe in constant miracles and the Devil intervenes in the familiar life of everyone, a lord can certainly kill, rob, burn, lead a scandalous life, throw scorn or insults in the face of the clergy: he will not go further because all

Christian society, that of his own fief and outside, from the humblest to the greatest — serfs, king or pope — deny him, condemn him, league together against him. He risks excommunication, a formidable kind of outlawry, both material and spiritual. Robert the Pious, King of France, is excommunicated for marrying a relation, condemned to seven years' penitence and denounced to the Christian world because the manners of his court do not please the monks of Cluny.

The Church also dominates society because it almost alone is instructed, reads and writes, distributes knowledge to the rich as well as the poor, keeps up continuous relations between one country and another, preaches constantly to the masses, guides public opinion, fixes the current version of events and makes history.

It represents at once a moral safeguard, a political support, the focus of civilisation and a mass of inexhaustible riches towards which everybody looks. Through the bishoprics, it holds many of the towns, the centres of activity and of social life : for, since the later Roman Empire, the power of the bishops has not ceased to be chiefly urban. Around the towns and in the country, another power, another form of wealth grows up, more independent and also more ambitious, that of the abbeys or monasteries. From Charlemagne's time, the Emperor had his model farms as the monasteries had theirs. Under the first Capetians, the monasteries were much to the fore in agriculture, directing clearing and breaking in the land, to create wealth and improve the conditions of life.

Prestige of the Monasteries

The truth is that feudal abuses and the vices of the lords corrupted the episcopate in so far as it submitted to the pressure of the lay powers. This pressure continues to grow throughout the 11th century. The attraction of church property is too evident : the lords cannot refrain from seizing a part of this wealth in procuring episcopal elections or in directly nominating members of their family or household to bishoprics.

Simoniac or prevaricating bishops are to be seen, fighting and robbing bishops, bishops with wives and children. There are even dynasties of bishops. And these bishops, naturally, are more and more jealous of their independence, less and less careful of the discipline of the Church.

But against them — to subdue them, dispossess them, or overthrow them — is raised the whole power of monasticism, entirely devoted to the principle of religious unity, faithful to the Pope and provided with efficient weapons.

The first of these is the prestige of monastic life, of monks and monasteries in the eyes of all Christian society. The more brutal the lords are, the more the people and the best among the great turn towards the Church. But the Church towards which they turn is less and less the episcopal Church, half corrupt, locally enslaved and preoccupied with temporal interests ; it is the monastic Church that represents a higher ideal of the Christian life. So, gradually, the abbeys or monasteries attract the respect of the masses, the land and money of benefactors, the elect among the clergy. Kings or princes — laymen themselves — according to the degree of their piety, bow before the monastic ideal and pay over to the abbeys in favours and gifts ransom for the crimes they have committed.

A conflict rages not only in France but in all Christian Europe between the bishops, representing an authority that becomes local at the same time as it is feudal or temporal, and the abbeys, which claim to depend only on God. Out of this struggle the feudal episcopate emerges vanquished and subjected to Rome, while the French monarchy — bringing the episcopate over to its side away from the lords — raises the Gallican standard against Rome and the monks.

Influence of Cluny: Genius of St. Bernard

The chief agents of the monastic supremacy were the monks of Cluny. The name of Cluny in the Middle Ages did not designate only an abbey : it was the symbol of a sort of religious empire that transcended political frontiers.

From its foundation in 910, the abbey of Cluny enjoyed complete independence, in right and in fact, of lay powers. Situated in Burgundy, in a neutral zone between France and the German Empire, it has been compared to an autonomous island in the midst of an ocean of jurisdictions and feudal servitudes. Its founder, Duke William of Aquitaine, had proclaimed it freed from all temporal overlordship. For two or three centuries, this independence was not contested by any sovereign, any more than was the liberty for the monks to elect their abbot without subjection to anybody's influence. The Bishop of Mâcon, in whose diocese the abbey was situated, had no more control over its affairs than the Duke of Burgundy. The sole authority it recognised was the Holy See. In fact, it often inspired the policy of the papacy rather than obeyed it.

The first abbots of Cluny were superior men in their character, the loftiness of their conceptions, their gifts of administration and their piety. Two of them, Odilon and Hugh I, without abandoning the humility of the monastic calling, appeared at certain moments as the arbiters of Christian Europe, capable of subduing kings and resisting the most authoritarian of Popes. A Duke of Burgundy entered the cloister of Cluny as monk, and the King of France, Philip I, nearly entered it too.

Cluny's empire, its moral and temporal empire, was more important for a century or two than any secular state. Its possessions formed seven provinces in France : in Provence alone Cluny possessed forty-four monasteries and eighty-one priories. Spain, Italy, England, Germany, Poland were filled too with Cluniac priories. No other influence equalled Cluny's on the formation of the Christian spirit in the Middle Ages. Without Cluny, Europe would perhaps have undergone an irremediable retreat of its civilisation.

Cluny's strength was derived from its government, its discipline and its charity. Its government was absolute in the hands of the abbot. All the dependent houses formed with the mother-house a single congregation which obeyed the abbot through the medium of priors or superiors. This government was not a fiction, it was effective and actual. The abbot of Cluny visited the priories of the different provinces of its empire, regulated affairs and decided how men should be employed. Some abbots were travellers of a disconcerting activity and hardihood.

The rule of Cluny, a more supple version of the rule of St. Benedict, placed in the first rank with prayer, the work of the spirit, teaching, hospitality and charity. These last two virtues assured Cluny the affection of an immense following. Thanks to the many-sided support of the Congregation of Cluny, the popes of the 11th century could proceed to the reform of the episcopate, against the savage resistance of lay lords and part of the higher clergy and could deny to lay powers all right of conferring 'investiture' of ecclesiastical dignities. So the Church escaped the hold of feudalism on it ; in escaping it, it became its judge.

The faith of the time was never satisfied. At the beginning of the 12th century ardent souls undertook to reform the reformers. The reform of the monastic world was to complete that of the episcopate.

There was first the foundation of the abbey of Prémontré, near St.-Gobain, where regular canons submitted themselves to a rule after St. Augustine, severer than that of the Benedictines. Then, in the South, began the order of Grammont, called the 'Bonhommes', practising an almost inhuman austerity. About the same time, the Carthusians of St.-Bruno set the example of contemplative isolation. Lastly, the wandering preacher, Robert d'Arbrissel, drawing with him an army of penitents from Anjou to Languedoc, instituted the abbey of Fontévrault, whose rule condemned women to the punishment of absolute silence.

But it was Burgundy again, the province where Cluny reigned, that gave to France and Europe of the Middle Ages its greatest religious reformer, one of the astonishing figures of our history : St. Bernard.

Bernard was born of a rich family at Fontaines-les-Dijon. From his childhood he was possessed with a passion for preaching and for the life of the cloister. He entered the Benedictine abbey of Cîteaux, drawing his brothers with him. Then he founded a new monastery in the waste and wild valley of Clairvaux. His monastic cell there was a sort of prison. The man who dominated Christian Europe lived there, under a roof that constrained him to bend his head in order to sit or stand up, with a bed of wood and straw — for thirty years.

He was a person of an astonishing vitality, a mixture of storm and sweetness, a terrifying will-power that went with a kind of tenderness for children and the unhappy, for the oppressed and for animals; a man of humility and a conqueror, a peasant skilful at handling the scythe of the harvester and a philosopher, a great orator and a subtle writer, with a gift for irony and poetry; by nature physically splendid, rendered infirm by privations, but of indomitable strength: all the contrasts incarnate in the service of a faith.

He reformed the monastic world. He reformed the episcopate. He reformed the papacy in spite of itself. He made the Cistercian rule and the Cistercian monk the models of Christian asceticism. He stood up against Cluny even though loving it. He made emperors and kings bend the knee. He carried across Europe the two-fold torch of his reason and his burning sincerity. His external work was precarious, but his mark on men's minds decisive.

Awakening of the Communes

On the margin of the feudal lordships and sometimes under the protection of the clergy, sometimes against it, a third force begins to appear : that of the burghers, merchants, artisans of the towns.

This force is born of the necessity, for people who live by trade, to protect their movements and their transactions, to assure the orderliness of markets, to resist spoliations of every kind, to acquire — for money or otherwise — guarantees that are called privileges. The insecurity of trade forces merchants and artisans to cluster together. As they pay taxes, people come to take care of them, flatter them, attract them into 'new towns'; and as wealth procures them means of action, people bargain with them even while fearing them.

In the 10th and at the beginning of the 11th century, the existence of towns was unsure, in jeopardy. It is the period of the break-up of public authority, of great domains sufficient to themselves, of seigneurial anarchy, of exactions and brutalities. Trade cannot develop when contracts depend on personal good will.

But at the end of the 11th century, the intervention of the Church, which is itself becoming liberated from the seigneurial yoke, and the influence of the monastic empire exerting itself beyond frontiers, re-establish free currents of trade in a time of relative security. Men hasten, as if coming out of prison, to breathe the open air. They begin to travel in all directions. Along the roads the monks in the ascendant pass by, the pilgrims in masses, companies of knights on expeditions or in search of shining adventures, artisans offering their skill from one halt to another, merchants ever more numerous. Then, there is a swift and widespread economic expansion. The small wars had hampered commerce. The Crusades and the big wars encourage a sort of speculation and the re-establishment of trade with the East.

So, newly enriched and repeopled, their minds opened by contacts with outside, the towns and townships deal with their lords, extract concessions from them by agreement or by force — their 'charters'.

The communal movement — or, as some historians exaggerate it, the communal revolution — takes on a particularly active character in Northern France, in the towns of the valleys of the Oise, Aisne, Somme, Lys and Scheldt, there where industry and commerce had developed most since the time of the Carolingians.

CHAPTER II

The Expansion of Society: the Crusades

❖

Castles — The Countryside — The Towns — Vitality and
the Need for Expansion — William the Conqueror —
Migration of the Crusaders — Two Tongues: Oïl and
Oc — Architecture and Sculpture

THE concrete sign of feudal power is the castle, raised most
often on a natural height, sometimes on an artificial motte,
at the mouth of the valley, at the junction of rivers, at the
crossing of routes, at all the points that must be taken advantage
of or defended, and in frontier zones. It is at once the abode of
the lord or of the castellan who represents him, the seat of his
command, a barracks for his soldiers and, in case of danger, a
refuge for the inhabitants of the countryside.

The castle as such is a creation of the Middle Ages. It
was invented by the Franks. What brought it into existence
from the beginning of the 9th century is the same cause that
brought to birth the feudal system: fear, the urgent need of
immediate protection and of a local refuge against invaders,
killers or simple robbers, in particular against the Normans.
At the end of the Roman Empire, the population lived mostly
in towns. After the Germanic invasions and the colonising
of the Carolingian age, people spread into the countryside:
insecurity reappearing, it was necessary to fortify the countryside by building numerous castles.

The elements of the castle are practically the same everywhere. The lord's dwelling, the keep — as strong as possible
and several stories high, with its own defences, dwelling-
rooms, store-rooms, recesses, its cistern or its well — dominates the place. Square or rectangular at first, later on the

keep takes various forms, most frequently round. The approach to the keep and its annexes is defended by one or several containing-walls protected by ditches or moats. In wooded country to the north of the Loire, castles were for long built almost wholly of wood and surrounded with thick palisades. Progress in the art of shooting, so to say, necessitated the gradual abandonment of wood for stone in the building of castles, as in that of churches, from the middle of the 11th century. A hundred years later, castles, like churches, witness to the new science of architects and have a style of their own.

The castles sheltered men as rough and enterprising as they were vigorous. The energy of these men — heirs of fertile families in which from generation to generation only the healthiest children survived — is disconcerting to our way of estimating human activity. To understand the early Middle Ages, before Christian refinement, scholarship and culture, regular administration and social politeness had penetrated manners, one must concede to persons of the time a vitality much more powerful, more spontaneous and simple than that of people in the modern age. Their feelings, their passions, their exploits and crimes, their repentances and even their faith were in proportion to this vitality. The same vitality partly explains the importance of the personal tie between individuals.

Later, the monarchy was to destroy the importance of the personal tie, mainspring of feudal society, in substituting for it the prestige of the king and the law. In the 11th century the Church alone, face to face with the lords, could only try to transform this tie of warlike or barbarian origin into a sort of religious and moral discipline. Thus knighthood was created, or rather nursed up, consecrated and propagated, like a lay congregation of warriors established in the interior of the feudal hierarchy, which was watched over from outside by the monastic congregation.

Knighthood represented the body of duties and obligations assumed by the young man destined for the military profession on the day when, arrived at the age to fight, he received the investiture of arms. The old obligations were exclusively of a military nature : bravery, loyalty, fidelity to his leader. The Church introduced a more extended morality into it : the defence of religious institutions, protection of the weak, of widows, orphans, merchants, pilgrims, respect for women, and temperance. The knighthood was recruited by co-optation : one found in it not only lords' sons, but promoted commoners and even people of servile origin. It did not change the temperament of individuals. It did not make brutalities disappear. But it established in society a sort of idealised type which served as reference and a rule by which to measure the conduct of everyone.

Addressing itself to the conscience of the adolescent and the self-respect of the man, under the seal of a rite of dedication which struck men's imaginations, knighthood succeeded in softening manners. It was much more effective in this respect than the oaths and ephemeral agreements, known as 'truces' or 'the peace of God', by which the clergy tried to stop feudal wars and depredations.

The Countryside

Under the domination of the castle, sometimes protective, sometimes oppressive, lived those of the peasants who did not depend on an abbey.

Local wars, pillaging and devastation, resulting in the weakening of order and security, had rendered the people in the country very unsettled. This instability of the rural population threatened to deprive the feudal domains of the large labour-force that the processes of a rudimentary agriculture demand. Hence the constant effort, often brutal, sometimes odious, of the lords to tie the peasant to the soil, preventing him from moving away, from marrying outside the domain or from disposing of his children as he liked. This is what is meant by serfdom. A revolting state of affairs from the point of view of our law, but in fact much less cruel than ancient slavery and less inhuman than certain forms of forced labour which have continued in some countries up to our day. Bound to the soil, the serf at least had the soil and a part of its fruits.

Troops of tillers of the soil and wandering workmen were numerous, employed mostly in clearing and breaking up land, making 'essarts' as they are termed. There were also free or half-free peasants, who defended as they might their relative independence by yielding dues, fines, forced labour. Nor were all these men borne down like beasts of burden without mind or dignity. Some serfs attained to important functions on the estate to which they were attached. Some entered the order of knighthood. The earliest peasant risings, if they reveal the excesses or stupidity of the lords, show also the promptness of the people of the fields to lift up their heads. One must not imagine the humblest of our ancestors as passive beasts. The French peasant knew how to defend himself long before mastering the legal formulae of his freedom.

From the end of the 11th century, under the impetus of the peasants themselves and under the influence of the Church, chiefly of the monasteries, the lords, understanding their interest better, treat with the peasants, seek to attract them rather than to force them, fix and limit their dues, grant them charters and franchises. Soon, associations of peasants grow up, then real rural federations, communities of all kinds, linking families or villages — all revealing rapid progress in the enfranchisement of the countryside. Groups of villages, as in the Soissonnais, become rich or strong enough to constitute themselves into communes and buy their full liberty.

The Towns

The inhabitants of the towns are grouped by the very fact of agglomeration. The town of the Middle Ages comprises a community much closer than our modern towns. It has a wall and ramparts within which families or individuals are constrained to crowd together, with less and less space at their disposal as population grows. Hence the narrow streets, the overhanging house-fronts, the intensity of life and the frequency of epidemics. When an abbey exists in a suburb, it protects itself by a wall of its own surrounding its precincts. Artisans of the same trade and merchants of the same kind habitually occupy the same street : a very old usage, which makes contact easy, simplifies trade, mutual regulation, order and the collecting of tolls. Already there are corporations more or less organised, which soon possess heads and rules. Commerce from one town to another is made by caravans guarded at the common expense. The town has its notables, recognised by the name of 'prud'hommes' (aldermen), 'échevins' (provosts), 'juges' (councillors), who deal with the lord or the bishop and who have certain powers of administration.

From the time when manners became more tolerable and the general security was bettered, at the end of the 11th century, the towns increased in number, then grew very quickly. The countless monastic establishments, which provided areas of relative quiet, enabled people to hive in clusters. As the people of the fields became settled and tillage increased by clearing the waste, new markets had to be established, the 'new townships'. Churches, monasteries, sanctuaries of all kinds attracted a multitude of pilgrims who increased local trade. In many parts lay lords began even before clerical lords to create 'new towns', 'free towns', 'bastides' or refuges, to grant charters for peopling towns and selling liberties to the townsmen.

But the towns were to benefit above all by the new currents of trade that resulted from the French expansion abroad, especially from the conquest of England and from the Crusades.

Vitality and the Need for Expansion

The people of the Middle Ages, by their very vitality, were prolific and mobile. As peace was re-established and violence and misery got fewer victims, as the rights acquired along with the means of keeping order restricted opportunities

for local adventure and families became more stable, this vigorous world felt itself too much confined on lands or in towns the
resources of which remained insufficient.   The influx of men
into monastic life and the clerical state revealed already an
excess of population over subsistence.   This excess was felt
in seigneurial families all the more because fiefs could not be
indefinitely divided and means of usurpation diminished.   It
was necessary to find an outlet for surplus energies.   The
Normans, who had not forgotten their ancient migrations, set
things in motion.

From the beginning of the 11th century people set out for
war against the Saracens of Spain who threatened the Christian
principalities beyond the Pyrenees and prevented pilgrims
from reaching the shrine of St. James of Compostella.   A first
expedition was led by a Norman knight, Roger of Conches.
Then bands of knights from Aquitaine and Champagne,
attracted by hope of booty or obeying the injunctions of the
Church, crossed the Pyrenees in their turn.   At length, the
Burgundians, under the influence of Cluny, which had priories
in Castile and Navarre, could not content themselves with
warring against the Saracens : they founded settlements and
dynasties in the peninsula.   The Dukes of Burgundy allied
themselves to the reigning house of Castile, and the county of
Portugal was constituted in favour of a Burgundian prince
named Henry.

In the same age, the Normans conquered southern Italy
and Sicily.   The Norman sanctuary of Mont-St.-Michel had
been for long connected by a chain of pilgrimages to the shrine
of San Michele of Monte Gargano on the Adriatic.   Already
Norman pilgrims, of warlike temper, had taken the opportunity to try out the ground.   They did not take long to see
that there was a place to occupy in this southern Italy where
Greeks, Italians, Saracens and Lombards milled about.   Soon
they arrived in numerous bands under the lead of the sons of
Tancred of Hauteville.   Led successively by William Iron-arm,
Humphrey, Roger and Robert Guiscard, they took less than

thirty years to possess themselves, by bravery, trickery or intimidation, of Campania, Apulia, Calabria and Sicily. Palermo fell into their power in 1072. They founded the Norman kingdom of the two Sicilies, one of the most astonishing political works of the Middle Ages, from which emerged a curious civilisation, a sort of synthesis of three civilisations, French, Byzantine and Arab. The Normans did not stop there. They invaded Greece and dreamed for a moment of taking Constantinople.

William the Conqueror

The Normans of France won their greatest renown by the conquest of England.

The operation was planned and carried out with a masterhand by the Duke of Normandy himself — William the Bastard, later called the Conqueror, natural son of Robert the Devil and a daughter of the people called Arlette. William was a powerfully built man, bald, fat, with a hard face, an irritable temper, and a resounding voice. He was at heart lonely, thoughtful, determined and possessed by the idea of power. Numerous bonds of trade or kinship existed already between Normandy and England. On the death of the English king, Edward the Confessor, without a direct heir, the chief of the Saxon nobility, Harold, placed himself on the throne, as Hugh Capet had done in France. But at once William the Bastard, asserting his kinship with the dead king and having won the support of the Holy See, claimed the succession to Edward the Confessor. He assembled at the mouth of the Dive an army of about 1,500 horse and 4,000 foot, composed not only of Normans, but of contingents from all the countries of the West. A large fleet of boats was built and assembled at St.-Valéry-sur-Somme. On 28 September 1066 they set sail to land in England the next morning.

A fortnight later, 13 October, at Hastings, Saxons and Frenchmen of the West confronted each other in a terrible battle. Harold was killed, the Saxon army annihilated.

William subdued England so rapidly that he was able to return to Normandy some months after without fear of losing his new possessions.

The union of England to Western France was to entail consequences of a lasting importance, not only for the political evolution of the two countries, but also for their economic and social development, as in the realm of the intellect and of the arts. Through their alliances and their struggles, the French and the English, by their contacts of every kind, were going to form the spirit of the West.

Migration of the Crusaders

Thirty years after the conquest of England, it is not only bands of knights or troops of adventurers, nor even an army properly speaking, it is the peoples of Western Europe who set themselves in motion to deliver the Holy Land from Moslem oppression. Under the sign of the cross — whence the name 'crusade' — the masses of the people, like their lords, join the march against the power of Islam. The centre of disturbance in this vast migration is France.

The crusade results from a number of causes of diverse but concordant nature. There is the discipline of ideas and designs established among Christian peoples of the West under the influence of Cluny and its monastic empire : a discipline that gives extraordinary power to religion. There is the pressure of population, of needs, forces and aspirations of every kind brought about by the suppression of local wars or of disorder in general in a social environment of limited resources. There is the recent arrival in Asia Minor of the most fanatical and aggressive tribes of Islam, who break the two-fold current of traffic between West and East, that of trade and pilgrimages. The maritime republics of Italy push forward an operation from which in any case they hope to derive benefit. Lastly, the ambition of the Normans of Sicily and the appeal of the Byzantine Emperors attract enterprises towards Constantinople.

Pope Urban II, having passed through Cluny and arrived in Auvergne, launched the project of the crusade in November 1095 before the Council of Clermont, which assembled a crowd of prelates, priests and knights of the Centre and South. In the North arose a monk of Picardy, Peter the Hermit, who drew a multitude around him; barefoot, a serge frock over his thin body, eyes burning and of moving voice he passed through France and Lorraine in midwinter, giving the poor the money he received and preaching the deliverance of the Holy Places.

The enthusiasm spread at once among the masses of the people as well as among the knight-hood; the people were the first to catch fire. A mass of 40,000 or 50,000 persons — men, women and children — set out under the lead of Peter the Hermit and of a poor knight, Gauthier Have-Nothing, crossed the Rhine, drew the German pilgrims along with it and, after traversing Europe — not without committing immense damage on its way — arrived at Constantinople. The Byzantine Emperor, Alexis Comnenus, hastened to get rid of them. He had this multitude transported into Asia where the Turks were waiting to dispose of it.

The main mass of the crusade set out on 15 August 1096. It comprised four armies which followed separate routes to meet at Constantinople. The army of the North, led by Godfrey of Bouillon and Baldwin of Flanders, took the Danube route. The army of the South, commanded by Raymond of Toulouse, crossed northern Italy and the Balkans. The army of the Ile-de-France and the Loire, under the orders of a royal prince, Hugh of Vermandois, and the Count of Blois, went to embark at Brindisi with the army of the Normans.

To pass through, the crusaders had to obtain leave of the Emperor at Constantinople. After much bargaining, they touched Asian territory in May 1097. From this moment they had to defend themselves against the perfidy of the Greeks, the attacks of the Turks, the perils of heat and thirst. Crossing the plateau of Asia Minor and the chain of the Taurus, they arrived in front of Antioch, which they besieged for eight months. Having captured the place, they were themselves besieged by the Turks and endured a fearful famine there. At last, they defeated them and resumed their painful march. Three years after leaving France, on 6 June 1099, they at last saw the ramparts of Jerusalem. The city was defended by a numerous garrison ; the crusaders were now probably no more than four thousand, exhausted and consumed by thirst. The rest of them, many thousands of human beings, had perished or disappeared. At Antioch alone, immense numbers had succumbed. In a sort of frenzy, against all apparent hope, the crusaders made the assault on 15 July, and by a miracle Jerusalem fell to them.

Thus was founded the Latin kingdom of Jerusalem ; the most popular leader of the crusade, Godfrey of Bouillon, took the government with the title of defender of the Holy Sepulchre. To this kingdom was attached the principality of Edessa, conquered by Baldwin of Flanders ; the principality of Antioch, occupied by Bohemond of Sicily ; and the principality of Tripoli, which fell to Raymond of Toulouse. The conquerors introduced the feudal system and Western customs into the territories they occupied. They did not fail to enjoy the pleasures of Oriental life.

The first crusade is, without doubt, the greatest witness of the religious faith of the French Middle Ages. The extreme endurance, the determination and bravery of the crusaders, like their ultimate success, are only explicable by moral causes. The enterprise, however, exemplifies other qualities besides faith. It is evident that the knights already possessed military knowledge, tactical skill, equipment and methods of organisation without which their faith would have remained powerless against all the adverse circumstances. The crusade reveals an inventive and creative spirit which begins now to flower in France itself.

Two Tongues: Oïl and Oc

The expansion of French society in the 11th century, the knightly expeditions and conquests, the monastic connections, pilgrimages and migrations of people had not only material consequences. Along with the increase of wealth due to more widespread trade, there came a new activity of men's minds. This was to show itself in literary or philosophical works and in the admirable works of art known as *romans*.

While the clergy continue to write and speak Latin, lords and people use a vulgar tongue quite distinct from the low Latin from which it derives: the Romance tongue, first form of the French language. Underneath numerous dialects, corresponding to the political fragmentation of the territory, to the traditions received or influences felt by each group of people, we recognise in the realm two Romance tongues: that of *Oïl* and that of *Oc*. *Oïl* and *Oc* mean the same thing as *Oui* later. The language of *Oïl*, French properly speaking, which triumphs with the political supremacy of the people of the North, is muffled and contracted: it is spoken from Hainaut and Lorraine to Saintonge, Berry and Burgundy. The language of *Oc*, which is sometimes called Provençal, more clearly enunciated, is spoken from Lyons and Bordeaux to Catalonia. The oldest relic of literature in the language of *Oïl* is a poem in assonance, from the middle of the 11th century: the legend of 'Saint Alexis'. The language of *Oc* yields a poem from the 10th century on 'Boëce'.

At the end of the 11th century the literature in both languages bursts into flower. The first of them produces the epic of war, the masterpiece of which appears in the *Chanson de Roland*. The second of these languages gives birth to the poetry of the troubadours. There is a striking contrast between the inspirations and themes of the two literatures. The poetry of the language of *Oïl* witnesses to the persistence in northern France of heroic legends celebrating the glory of Charlemagne and the Franks, as well as the

CH. II THE CRUSADES

battles for the Christian faith. The poetry of the language of
Oc sings the courtier's life and love, exalts the pleasures of
the world and turns its oddities to ridicule. The one, that
of the North, is collective in its inspiration; the other, the
Southern, individual.

These two literatures are spread abroad by minstrels,
bards and wandering story-tellers, the 'trouvères' of the
North, the 'troubadours' of the South, who go from one
castle to another, from monastery to monastery, from one
band to another along the roads, to provide distraction for
knights, pilgrims and merchants.

Outside the cycle of purely literary works, the beginning
of the 11th century is marked by a welling-up of intellectual
activity. The lofty spirit of St. Bernard dominates all this
epoch. Schools are multiplied. The teacher Abélard, whose
adventure with one of his pupils, the young Héloïse, creates
a scandal, brings about a revolution in the philosophical
methods and scientific ideas of the scholastic world. His
dialectic, in which Christian theology is strangely mingled with
profane literature, brings him a clamorous popularity among
the students which intoxicates him. St. Bernard, disturbed
by the agitation and dissension that this too advanced teaching
produces, has it condemned by a Council. Abélard, not
relishing the risks, takes refuge devoutly among the monks of
Cluny to escape the thunders of the terrible Abbot of Clairvaux.

Architecture and Sculpture

The men of the 11th and 12th centuries have left us
of their civilisation a witness before which we must bow:
Romanesque art. Romanesque architecture and sculpture produced simple and great works, the remains of which move
us still.

After the ravages of Saracen or Norman invasions, churches
had been rebuilt of wood. Almost all these buildings were
destroyed by fire. Local wars, disturbances and poverty prevented their rebuilding. So, towards the year 1000, it was

mostly ruins that were to be seen. When the feudal system brought back some security, people began to build once more. 'The world', says the chronicler Raoul Glaber, 'covered itself with a white robe of churches.' These new edifices of stone and wood did not resist long : most of them were reduced to ashes. Fire seemed to be one of the worst scourges men had to fight. Hence the abandonment of wooden building for stone. On the other hand, the churches became the centre of collective life, the meeting-places of large crowds. They had to be built on a bigger scale. The economic improvement at the end of the 11th century gave resources with which to pay for new buildings. A magnificent effort was to raise Romanesque works of art, pure and of great nobility, on our soil.

The chief characteristic of Romanesque architecture is the introduction of vaults in the churches. Three kinds of vaults borrowed from the Romans replace the old structure of timber : the cradle or semi-circular vault, which wonderfully suits the long bodies of the new churches ; the arris vault, formed by the intersection of two cradle vaults, which stands on four separate supports, permitting the thickness of the walls to be reduced and the nave or aisles to be divided into rectangular compartments ; the cupola, a vault in the form of a hemispherical dome, employed most often for round or polygonal churches. Inside the building the vault is supported on pillars or columns, and on the outside on plain buttresses. An inventive and very living sculpture covers the capitals of the columns, the entrances, the façades. Often two or three steeples are raised on the same church.

Later, St. Bernard and the Cistercian monks, reacting against the luxurious decoration of the Benedictine abbeys, impose on the churches of the Cistercian order a style of a monumental simplicity, excluding sculptures, paintings and objects of gold.

During the 11th and 12th centuries, the impetus towards these constructions was provided mainly by the monks, and chiefly by those of the Cluniac order. The abbots rivalled each other in zeal to give their monasteries vaster and more sumptuous churches.

They were not the only ones.   Many bishops and clerics of every kind had acquired enough knowledge to make plans for works and inspire craftsmen — architects, masons, sculptors. Princes and lords, too, were equally keen on buildings which bore witness both to their power and their faith.

This extraordinary expansion of the religious art of the Romanesque epoch would not have been possible without the generous adhesion of the mass of the faithful multiplying their gifts or without the skill of numerous lay craftsmen. We meet the names of laymen among the builders of illustrious monastic edifices, like the abbey church of St.-Benoît-sur-Loire.

Thus Romanesque art, at the same time as it is a sudden outburst of the creative genius of our country as a whole, expresses the variety and originality of local inspiration.   This art only takes on its full significance beneath the characteristics of each region.   We recognise a Norman architecture, the masterpiece of which is St.-Etienne at Caen ; a Provençal architecture, typified by St.-Trophime at Arles; a Burgundian architecture, direct child of Cluny ; an architecture of Auvergne, of which the purest type is the church of Orcival ; a Toulousan architecture, which built St.-Sernin ; a style of Poitou, represented by Notre-Dame-la-Grande at Poitiers with its exuberant sculptures. . . . Deep in the lost corners of our countryside, the Romanesque age has left, in local stone or brick, the impressive evidences of its simple, but creative, energy.

CHAPTER III

The Work of the Great Capetians

❖

*The Founders of French Unity: Philip Augustus, St. Louis,
Philip the Fair — Conquest of the West, North and South
— Army, Administration, Justice — Influence of the
Lawyers — Conflict with the Papacy — Financial Methods*

UP to the end of the 12th century, the lords bend only before
the Church and above all before the monastic power which
dominates all classes of society. The king enjoys a nominal
suzerainty over what is called the kingdom. He administers
his narrow domain as best he may, tries to obtain respect and
homage, seizes some lands here and there ; but, outside his
kinsmen and neighbours, the magnates have little regard
for his authority. The first crusade, which draws scores of
thousands of Frenchmen, is made without him, as the conquest
of England was achieved without him.

The first Capetians would appear very mediocre if, amid
their weaknesses, one did not see them at least secure the
permanence of their dynasty and the cohesion of their domain.
Putting aside gradually the two-fold Frankish custom of
electing the chief and dividing the succession among male
children, they succeed in making the monarchy unitary and
hereditary : that alone guarantees to their family opportunities that neither Merovingians nor Carolingians had. On
the other side, they spare themselves the risk of great adventures or foolhardy ambitions : by calculation or perhaps
for lack of means, they keep to their domain and only expand
slowly. They take a century and a half to free this domain
from the exactions or brigandage of local lords, then in
extending it to Sens, the Gâtinais, the Vexin, to Bourges and
Issoudun. Lastly, they present themselves very skilfully to

both people and clergy as defenders of justice and order. One of them, Louis VI the Fat, makes a great reputation for himself in turfing out troublesome neighbours and in pursuing bandits. He and his son Louis VII the Young, counselled by Suger, the wise Abbot of St.-Denis, procure the support of the Church and the small people, assert their suzerainty all they can, and gain prestige.

But Louis VII had not got the practical sense of his father. He set out on a second crusade, preached by St. Bernard, which ended in disaster and from which he returned almost alone. After which, he had his marriage with Eleanor of Aquitaine annulled (1152) and thus lost at one stroke the vast possessions this marriage promised the dynasty : Auvergne, the Limousin, Poitou, Périgord and Gascony.

On the death of Louis VII, in 1180, the royal domain was reduced once more to a band of territory from Senlis to Bourges, which hardly went beyond Mantes on the Seine and Sens on the Yonne. This domain seemed wretched besides the properties which the powers growing up against the Capetian monarchy could dispose of.

One marriage brought together Normandy, Anjou, Maine and Touraine for the benefit of the Angevin family of the Plantagenets. Another marriage, that of Eleanor of Aquitaine, repudiated wife of Louis VII, with Henry Plantagenet, had given the Angevin house the Centre and the South-West. This same Henry Plantagenet became King of England. There then is a vassal, master of England, who possesses in the realm of France a territory ten times larger than the royal domain : about thirty-five of our departments.

To the east, the German Empire dominates the Rhône valley, a part of the Cévennes, the Saône, the Meuse and extends to the Scheldt. Flanders, Champagne, Burgundy and the county of Toulouse escape the effective authority of the king.

The first six Capetians have not in 200 years succeeded in equalling any of their great vassals in the extent of their possessions. But kings of an altogether different calibre now succeed them, to whom a century suffices to subdue almost the whole of France.

Philip Augustus, St. Louis, Philip the Fair

Three sovereigns eminent for their conquests, as for their government, created the power of the monarchy and determined the orientation of French unity : Philip Augustus, Louis IX — known as St. Louis — and Philip the Fair. Without their activity with its lasting effects, the shape of our history would have been entirely different.

Philip Augustus (1180–1223), son of Louis the Young, deserves perhaps the first place among the founders of royal greatness. He was tall and burly, with a high complexion, little hair, and a friendly face. He liked wine, food and all pleasures, but subordinated his tastes to his aims. Matured very early in the experience of men and things, knowing how to make religion, ruse and force play their part, he succeeded in diplomacy as well as in his wars. During more than forty years' rule, he asserted a remarkable mastery.

His son, Louis VIII, reigned only three years. Then the crown fell to the young Louis IX, the future St. Louis, watched over by his mother, Blanche of Castile, a woman of ability and great energy.

St. Louis (1226–70) was a large youth, thin but wiry, fair, prematurely bald, of clear complexion, his eyes lit up with life and goodness, gracious in manner, with an expression in turn determined, thoughtful and smiling : a personality of great charm. He had an open and cultivated mind, quick to brush away sophisms, a character resolute and brave, good-humoured, sometimes joking, often gay, a delightfully human spirit, which did not exclude either prudence or determination.

St. Louis' son, Philip III the Bold, did nothing remarkable. But after him another great king mounted the throne : Philip IV, called the Fair. As his sobriquet indicates, Philip the Fair (1285–1314) attracted attention by his handsome face and bearing. He had the fair hair and blue eyes of his grandfather

St. Louis. He showed the same graciousness as his ancestors, the same determination, the same taste for learning and, in a measure, the same piety. But he was far less scrupulous than St. Louis.

These three sovereigns — Philip Augustus, St. Louis, Philip the Fair — freed the royal power from feudal constraint and ecclesiastical tutelage to put it at the service of a properly French civilisation.

Conquest of the West, North and South

First, it was necessary to break the power of the Plantagenets, demolish the Angevin empire, which covered both England and almost all the west of France.

In this direction, the policy of Philip Augustus was undeviating. He devoted himself to dividing the family of the Plantagenets, setting its members one against another and weakening the head of the family by supporting the revolt of his heir.

First, he upheld against Henry II his son, Richard Cœur de Lion. Then when Richard succeeded his father, Philip set out with him for the third crusade, left him over a quarrel at St. John of Acre, returned to France, allied himself with Richard's younger brother John Lackland, and recognised him as King of England, in return for the cession of part of Normandy and Touraine. But Richard in turn, after two years of captivity, defeated Philip, got his lands back and, to bar the way to the Capetian, built the fortress of Château Gaillard.

On Richard's death, Philip employed the same tactics against the new King of England, John. Philip upheld John's nephew Arthur of Brittany against him, and on the pretext that John had violated feudal custom, condemned him to lose all the lands he possessed in France. A war followed. Arthur disappeared mysteriously. But Philip took Château Gaillard after a siege of six months, invaded Normandy, Anjou, Touraine, Poitou and even Brittany. John Lackland had to resign himself to keeping only southern Poitou and Guyenne.

The Plantagenet dominance on the Seine and the Loire was broken.

It was essential to prevent any recovery. In 1223 Louis VIII consolidated his father's conquests and took La Rochelle by an energetic expedition against the English. Later, the lords of Poitou having revolted with the connivance of the King of England, St. Louis defeated the English anew at Taillebourg and at Saintes (1242). Finally, by the Treaty of Paris (1259), Henry III of England renounced Normandy, Anjou, Touraine and Poitou absolutely. He recognised himself liegeman of the King of France for the possessions which the generosity of St. Louis left him on the Continent : Guyenne and a number of fiefs in the dioceses of Limoges, Cahors and Périgueux.

At the end of the 13th century, Philip the Fair, on a poor pretext, claimed to confiscate Guyenne and sent his troops to invade it. But he had to restore it some years later.

In the North, the authority of the Capetians came up against the power of the Count of Flanders, ally sometimes of the English, sometimes of the Germans.

The wife of Philip Augustus, Isabella of Hainault, had brought him the province of Artois as dowry. The Count of Flanders formed a coalition of great lords to try and get the province back. Philip succeeded in breaking the coalition, then forced the Count to cede him the country round Amiens and the Vermandois (1183).

Thirty years later Ferrand, Count of Flanders, entered into a new coalition with John, King of England, the Emperor Otto, the Count of Boulogne, the lords of Holland and Lorraine. The allies disposed of greatly superior forces. The Emperor commanded a large army : the German and Flemish troops together were some 15,000. The King of France had only 10,000 men. But Philip was an experienced tactician, aided by a remarkable adviser, 'Brother' Guérin. In a terrible battle at Bouvines, 27 July 1214, where he was nearly killed, he defeated his adversaries. This victory resulted in the German

Emperor Otto losing his throne, King John being discredited in the eyes of his subjects, and brought the Capetian domination up to the gates of Lille.

St. Louis confined himself to trying to extend French influence peaceably over Hainault and Flanders. But Philip the Fair brought less gentleness to it. To punish the Count of Flanders, who had allied himself once more with England, he invaded Flanders. The Flemish communes had revolted and their militias massacred the French cavalry at Courtrai ; Philip marched against them and after a fierce battle defeated them at Mons-en-Pevèle (1304). He kept Lille, Douai and Béthune, which were united to the royal domain.

On the east, the Capetians had to guard against the Count of Champagne, the Duke of Burgundy and the Emperor of Germany.

Philip Augustus in the first years of his reign forced the submission of the Count of Champagne and the Duke of Burgundy. Later, as we have seen, he defeated the Emperor Otto at Bouvines. St. Louis' mother, Blanche of Castile, obliged Count Thibaut of Champagne to cede to the king the counties of Blois and Chartres. Then the wife of Philip the Fair brought him the county of Champagne itself as dowry. Elsewhere Philip the Fair never ceased to sap the positions of the German Empire. He succeeded in detaching the Barrois, the Vivarais and the Lyonnais. Lyons became a royal town in 1310.

There remained the South. From 1212 Philip Augustus occupied Auvergne. Soon after, the crusade preached by the Pope against the Albigenses prepared the way for the annexation of Languedoc to the royal domain.

The Albigenses, thus called from the town of Albi, principal centre of their propaganda, called themselves Cathares or the 'Pure'. Their religious doctrine spread very rapidly in Languedoc, which had never been properly evangelised — which oriental, Semitic and Saracen influences had long penetrated and where the Catholic clergy, very dissolute, lacked prestige. By its essential purity, this doctrine seduced refined spirits ; by its almost complete lack of formal demands, it pleased others. The Count of Foix and the Viscount of Béziers adopted it. The Count of Toulouse himself, the greatest prince of the South, showed himself sympathetic.

In 1207 Pope Innocent III, ceasing to oppose the progress of the Albigensian heresy by persuasion, invited Philip Augustus and the northern lords to extirpate it by force. The king held back. But, the following year, the Papal legate — Pierre de Castelnau — having been assassinated in Languedoc, northern and even German lords rose in great number to follow the new legate, Arnault Amalric, Abbot of Cîteaux. The men of the North had always detested the South, which in return despised their rudeness. The crusade against the Albigenses, led by a squire from the Ile-de-France, Simon de Montfort, ambitious and implacable, led to frightful devastation. It provided a pretext for killing. In some places it covered up summary and brutal acts of dispossession.

Violence lasted for more than a decade. Descending by the Rhône valley, the crusaders conquered first the country of Béziers and Carcassonne. The capture of Béziers was followed by the massacre of thousands of people, and by the sacking and burning of the town. The country round Toulouse resisted longer. The King of Aragon having sent an army to the aid of Raymond VI, Simon de Montfort defeated it at Muret. But he did not enter Toulouse until 1215. The town revolted three years later ; he had to besiege it again and perished, his head crushed by a stone ball.

His son, Amaury de Montfort, gave up and ceded all his rights and domains to the King of France. The son of Philip Augustus, Louis VIII, took definitive possession of Languedoc by force of arms in 1226. Some years later Pope Gregory created the Inquisition to extirpate the remains of the Albigensian heresy.

The South was never to forget this story of bloodshed.

In truth, the weakness of the southern lords, softened by comfort, gave free rein to bands of unscrupulous and greedy adventurers whom the pretext of a crusade had brought together.

Army, Administration, Justice

The rapid and lasting successes of Capetian power from the accession of Philip Augustus to the death of Philip the Fair were not the fruit of chance. One must seek the causes, on one side, in the reform of the royal army and, on the other, in the attraction felt by the population for the ordered government of the great Capetians.

In place of the fleeting contingents, ill-trained and un-disciplined, with which lords formerly furnished their suzerain to form the host or feudal army, Philip Augustus constituted a regular army, hardened to war, ready and available for use. It included one or more corps of paid knights, aided by squires on foot and mounted, and was reinforced by bands of professional mercenaries.

On the other side, Philip Augustus prided himself on his skill as an engineer and his gifts of organisation. He cease-lessly improved the armament and engines of war of his troops, and transformed the art of constructing, attacking and defending fortresses. Thanks to which he was able to capture Château-Gaillard. He himself had numerous castles built, the great tower of the Louvre and a wall surrounding Paris. Remains of his constructions, much better designed than those of the period just before, still exist at Dourdan, Issoudun, Gisors. He fortified not only towns, but even simple town-ships that were threatened.

During the whole of the 13th century, the tradition of Philip Augustus inspired the royal army and its engineers. Philip the Fair went further, in practice, to a form of conscription.

But it was not enough to conquer territories : it was necessary to win over the people.

Philip Augustus instituted the regular administration of districts which depended on the crown, by officials strictly subordinate to the king : bailiffs and seneschals. The bailiwicks were, on the whole, in the North and East; the seneschals' districts in the South and West — except for Touraine and the mountains of Auvergne which were bailiwicks. To the bailiff or seneschal the sovereign delegated very extensive powers: in administration, finance and justice; regulative, economic, military. These agents tracked down feudal abuses, protected the people and assured order in all respects.

Upon the institution of bailiffs and seneschals was imposed that of royal inspectors, the real controllers of the administration. The inspectors accomplished a most useful work from the time of St. Louis onwards. Their reports, which have survived, give us a living picture of the manners of the time. Under Philip the Fair, an inspector stayed four years in one single district of the West to reorganise public security and correct the misdeeds of the local officials.

Supreme head of justice in principle, the king had much ado, in practice, to get the judiciary function back into his hands. In fact, since the Carolingians, justice had been gradually split up among numerous, more or less independent, jurisdictions : there was seigneurial justice, lay justice, that of the Church and of the communes. However, without justice, administration could not be rendered seriously effective. The great Capetians put up a stubborn struggle always to reconquer their sovereign right of justice.

They began by turning feudal custom against feudalism itself. They authorised the subjects of the lords to appeal directly to the king, to be admitted as burghers of the king and consequently to escape seigneurial justice. Then they extended this procedure, not only to persons, but to churches, towns, districts, which were thus placed under royal safeguard. On the other side, they reserved a certain number of judicial cases, those affecting the rights of the king (*lèse-majesté*, carrying arms, coining false money, exploiting the public interest), the list of which they gradually lengthened. At last, they struck the decisive blow against private jurisdictions by extending the right to appeal from feudal courts to the king's courts.

In proportion as he recovered his rôle as universal judge, the king saw cases flow into him. The Sire de Joinville, councillor and historian of St. Louis, shows his master thus rendering justice beneath the Oak of Vincennes. In practice, the Capetians delegated the judicial function to judges named by them : in the first degree, provosts, castellans, wardens ; in the second, bailiffs and seneschals ; in the third, the Parliament.

Parliament, the judicial division of the King's Council, emerged regularly constituted under St. Louis. It held several sessions a year at Paris in the Palace of the Cité. Composed at the beginning of prelates, lords, officials and lawyers, it soon fell under the effective influence of these last, who performed a permanent function. St. Louis' son, Philip III, then his grandson Philip the Fair, divided up the judicial work of Parliament among specialised courts.

Thanks to this supreme court of justice, the law was interpreted and applied uniformly for the whole realm, in spite of local customs. In addition, Parliament aided the king to draw up and state the law. It thus became one of the principal organs of national unity, the promoter of the formula : one king, one law.

Not content with making their army an effective instrument of domination or repression and with offering the peoples of the realm administrative and judicial advantages, the great Capetians sapped feudal independence by all the means law placed at their disposal.

Outside their own domain, it was on the lands of the Church that their authority encountered least resistance, since the clergy had need of royal protection. And the possessions of the Church, episcopal or monastic, covered an area and

represented a wealth growing constantly in proportion to the
generosity of the faithful. The numerous estates of bishoprics
and monasteries constituted gradually a second royal domain,
according as the king's protection was extended over them.
This protection presented such advantages that the sovereign
could soon exchange it against a partial cession of seigneurial
rights. The Capetians got themselves recognised, by contracts called those of '*pariage*', as associates or partners in lay
or ecclesiastical lordships situated outside their domain.

Lastly, taking their feudal rights literally, they played rigorously on the right of suzerainty and the sanctions it carried
with it. With the aid of their lawyers, they excelled in
reclaiming vacant fiefs, and in pronouncing judicial confiscation of the property of vassals reputed felons — to the profit
of the crown. This procedure of feudal confiscation permitted
notably Philip Augustus to invade the possessions of John
Lackland and, later, Philip the Fair to seize Guyenne.

Influence of the Lawyers

The Merovingians, Carolingians and the first Capetians had
not distinguished the offices of central government from the
functions of their household. Hence the titles, in origin
domestic, that the great dignitaries bore : the seneschal,
charged in principle with the royal table ; the constable,
placed in charge of the stables ; the chamberlain or roomsman,
the butler, the equerry, the grand almoner. . . . From the
time of Philip Augustus the offices of government began to
be distinguished from domestic functions. Beginning with
St. Louis, the king's household, grouping all the domestic
functions, was clearly separated from the offices of the
Chancery and the king's secretaries, who were occupied with
administrative or political business.

In the offices were installed the literate officials — jurists,
clerks of the courts, scribes and secretaries ; studying Roman
law, they gradually formulated the doctrine of monarchical
unity and pushed it through to victory. Already under Philip

Augustus lawyers, real 'knights in law', worked for this unity. A century later, under Philip the Fair, they were the inspirers and the boldest agents of royal policy. From the central government, their activity overflowed into the provinces.

Among them some figures stand out. Such as Philippe de Remi, lord of Beaumanoir, who after St. Louis' death formulated the maxims of the new kingship. Or the Norman advocate, Pierre Dubois, who wanted to confiscate the property of the Church and dreamed of a kind of French Imperialism. Or the Auvergnat, Pierre Flote, who from being a plain serjeant became ambassador and chancellor of France, a great orator and a passionate partisan of monarchical authority. It was he who treated Pope Boniface VIII as 'Satan, half blind in body and wholly in spirit'. Such was the Toulousan, Guillaume de Nogaret, former teacher of law, judge of the district of Beaucaire, then Chancellor of France, who managed the kidnapping of Pope Boniface VIII at Anagni. Such too was the man of Dauphiné, Guillaume de Plaisans : also a jurist and an implacable enemy of the Templars. Such was, lastly, the smooth and calculating Enguerrand de Marigny, principal councillor of Philip the Fair, who became so rich that in the end he was accused of peculation and hanged on the gibbet of Montfaucon.

Conflict with the Papacy

The lawyers — who had usually come from the middle or lower classes — detested the feudal magnates. In addition, they represented almost the only educated class outside the Church, in competition with, and sometimes in opposition to, the spirit of the Church : hence the definitely anti-clerical character which they gave, from time to time, to the policy of the pious Capetians, and even of St. Louis.

The clergy of the parishes and the monasteries had a vast amount of property at their disposal. Of whom was this property held, the Pope or the king ? In the age of feudal particularism and of the pullulation of local powers, the Church had been the sole common authority, in fact ; the only organised monarchy. This ecclesiastical monarchy reached its full extension in the 13th century under the illustrious Pope Innocent III, veritable arbiter of kingdoms. It was inevitable that there should be a clash between the pretensions of this ecclesiastical monarchy and the rights which the Capetians, with a new vigour, insisted on in their kingdom. In particular, the King of France, whatever deference he showed to the Church, considered it an encroachment for the Pope to receive taxes and subsidies or to award benefices at his will on French territory. St. Louis himself affirmed : 'the temporalities of churches are held of the king alone'.

Under Philip the Fair, the conflict suddenly broke out with extreme violence. The two lawyers who were then advising the king, Guillaume de Nogaret and Pierre Flote, were southerners not much embarrassed by scruples. Pope Boniface VIII had the defects of a proud and sensitive man.

In 1301 the king had a protégé of the Pope, Bernard de Saisset, Bishop of Pamiers, arrested for high treason. On which the Pope addressed Philip a bull that was a stern warning. To get public opinion on his side, Philip called an assembly to which Pierre Flote communicated a shortened version of the pontifical bull, falsified and offensive. The representatives of the clergy themselves were roused by the Pope's tactlessness. But Boniface, far from quietening down, learning of the massacre of the king's cavalry at Courtrai and of Pierre Flote's death, threatened to depose the king 'as a wicked boy'. Then, before a council of French bishops at Rome, he proclaimed the absolute supremacy of the spiritual power over the temporal.

Philip the Fair, anxious, had begun to weaken when Guillaume de Nogaret got him to accept the plan of a sudden *coup* against the Pope. An act of accusation, charging Boniface with the most odious crimes, was read at a crowded assembly in front of the royal palace. Warned of it at once, the Pope placed the whole realm of France under an interdict and loosed Frenchmen from their allegiance to the king. But Nogaret had set out secretly for Italy. He got in touch with the powerful family of Colonna, enemies of Boniface. On 7 September 1303, Nogaret and Sciarra Colonna with a band of 1,600 adventurers surprised the villa at Anagni where the Pope was residing. The populace joined with the attackers to pillage houses. On a throne in pontifical vestments, tiara on his head, the keys of St. Peter and the cross in his hands, Boniface awaited death with dignity. Nogaret confined himself to reminding him of the accusations that lay against him and to making him prisoner. But two days later, the people of Anagni changed sides, forced Nogaret to flee and freed the Pope. Broken by this shock, Boniface came back to Rome to die a month later.

In 1305 Philip the Fair had one of his followers, Bertrand de Got, Archbishop of Bordeaux, elected Pope, who took the name of Clement V. The new Pope did not hesitate to absolve Nogaret. He was the first Pontiff to instal himself at Avignon (1309), where the Popes were to stay for seventy years.

Thus, more fortunate or less scrupulous than the Emperors Frederick Barbarossa or Frederick II, who had fallen before the authority of the Holy See, Philip the Fair — grandson of St. Louis, heir of a family pious above all — frustrated the hopes of the Papacy.

Financial Methods

The Capetians, from Philip Augustus to Philip the Fair, accomplished great things. But it was expensive. They had to find new resources to supplement the revenues from their domains. At the end of the 13th century, under Philip the Fair, the state of the royal finances became critical. The lawyers who surrounded the king, ready for anything rather than arrest the impetus of the monarchy, employed various means to reinforce the treasury. They did not hesitate to use rough and even criminal methods.

Not content with contracting loans and receiving the tenth of the revenues of the clergy, Philip the Fair created taxes on commerce known as '*maltôtes*'.   Then, he forced all his subjects, after subjecting them to the principle of obligatory military service, to ransom themselves by paying him a royal impost under the form of a subsidy.   Besides the Parliament of justice, a chamber of accounts was organised to examine financial affairs.

Soon, means of taxation no longer sufficed.   Breaking with the honest tradition of St. Louis, who had made the royal coinage the safest and most widespread of currencies, Philip the Fair debased the gold and silver pieces made in his mints.   He imposed on the pieces in circulation an arbitrary value, variable according to requirements.   Impoverishment, conflict, complaints and even outbreaks among the people resulted.   He deserved the name : 'false coiner'.

Afterwards he went for the financiers and institutions possessing capital.   Operations of exchange, banking or loan constituted an important commercial activity already, exercised chiefly by Jews, Italian bankers who were referred to as 'Lombards', and by some religious orders which — thanks to their establishments or connections in different countries — received considerable sums, sometimes to hold, sometimes to transfer.

Jewish communities were then numerous in the realm, principally in Champagne, the Loire valley and Languedoc. Formerly, Charlemagne had treated them well.   In the 12th century, St. Bernard had defended them.   In the 13th century, their wealth provoked envy, complaint and suspicion. Their influence, not only economic, but intellectual and religious, was constantly spreading in the South.   Christians adopted Judaism.   St. Louis, always careful to avoid violence, strove to convert the Jews.   But Philip the Fair had other concerns.   His least scrupulous councillor, Nogaret, who had been a teacher at Montpellier, knew well the wealth of the powerful Jewish communities of Languedoc.

A beginning was made by hitting these communities with such heavy impositions that some Jews emigrated. Then their credits were examined and denounced as usurious. Finally, 21 June 1306, order was given to the royal officials to arrest all Jews, to seize their goods and account books. Embezzlements, misappropriations, irregularities were common. Confiscation did not yield the profits expected. The middle class of the towns seem to have regretted the Jews. They were allowed to take up their activity again some years later. Some came back, but ruined and demoralised. Many of the Jews of Languedoc had sought refuge in Spain.

The Italian bankers or 'Lombards', who then exploited the kingdom — money-changers, collectors of taxes, coiners — had for long deposited large subsidies or credits with the treasury. St. Louis, who did not like the financiers, had already pounced on them once. In 1311 Philip the Fair had them expelled and substituted himself for the recovering of their debits. But the 'Lombards' were too good supports of the treasury to remain banished for long.

The most scandalous operation of Philip's reign was the trial of the Templars.

The military order of the Temple, founded after the first crusade for the defence of the Holy Places, constituted a sort of independent power alongside states and lordships. Its military rôle in the East had gradually lost its value. But its following and wealth had steadily grown in Europe, where it possessed numerous houses. Excellent administrators, installed in fortified houses, protected by their double character, religious and military, the Templars had figured early on as useful guardians of valuables or capital. Popes and kings used them to handle their funds. The Temple, as the solidest of credit establishments, had on several occasions held the treasure of the Capetians. It had lent them a great deal of money, in particular to Philip the Fair who was much embarrassed by his debts.

Such power and riches were vulnerable. People told tales

of the avidity or the morals of the Templars which were doubtless inaccurate, but which fortified the malevolence of public opinion towards them. Other religious orders were jealous of them. In truth, the Temple had almost forgotten its original mission and so lost its *raison d'être* in the eyes of the faithful. It appeared no more than a vast concern for landed and financial exploitation and so offered itself a prey to the aggressive cupidity of Philip the Fair and his councillors.

The king and his confidant Nogaret prepared their bold stroke by a campaign of ignoble calumny against the Order. On 13 October 1307 the Templars were arrested *en masse* throughout France, and denounced to the Inquisition. A trial of such perfidy and cruelty was arranged against them that it ended by turning a section of public opinion in favour of the accused. Fifty-four Templars were burned alive in Paris in 1310. The Grand Master of the Order himself, Jacques de Molai, suffered at the stake. To get possession of the property of the Temple, Philip the Fair by harsh threats obtained from Pope Clement V and a Council at Vienne the abolition of the Order in 1312.

The accused had protested their innocence before dying courageously. No impartial witness believed in the crimes of the Templars. The affair reveals the atrocious rapacity of the grandson of St. Louis.

The political deterioration that is evident in Philip the Fair's methods of government reveals the decline of the monarchy's moral standing and marks the end of one of the most splendid phases of French civilisation: the 13th century.

CHAPTER IV

The Civilisation of the 13th Century

❖

Elevation of the Human Spirit — Apogee and Limits of Ecclesiastical Power — The Mendicant Orders — The Art of the Great Cathedrals — Vitality of Economic Life — Appearance of the Towns — Prestige of the French Language: Influence of the University of Paris

THE 13th century shines not only in its political achievements — it was a century of expansion in every respect of spiritual, as well as of material, civilisation.

Man in this age was elevated, cultivated, purified in spirit. His character appears to us with the definite traits we recognise in persons of great epochs : a mixture of vitality and restraint, of creative initiative and calculation, exuberance and taste, energy and understanding, of ardent faith in principles and pity for weakness. The horrors perpetrated in this age, like the massacre of the Albigenses, the crimes of the Inquisition and later the trial of the Templars, move us in so far as they disturbed contemporaries who felt they ought to explain them, if not justify them : a scruple quite foreign to men of earlier centuries.

This refinement is manifested in the most Christian society in history. But one recognises it as well, in the same epoch, among non-Christians like the Jews and the Moslems of Spain or Egypt.

St. Louis, who incarnates the ideal of government as the public opinion of his time conceived it, is not a person of puerile or simple traits. On the contrary, he represents a complex type, whose virtues and thoughts, like the elements of a cathedral in this splendid age, are balanced in a harmony as subtle as it is vigorous. Addressing himself to his son, in the *Precepts*, he says : 'If a poor man quarrels with a rich one, support the poor man more than the rich, until the truth is discovered'. It is more than charity or pity, it is a thoughtful care for the balance of the conditions in which justice ought to be pronounced. He says later on : 'Be rigid and loyal in keeping to justice towards your subjects, without turning to the right or the left hand'. It is a precept that is opposed not only to violence or faction, but to weakness and to the compromises of political interest : a precept of virtue, perhaps, but still the virtue of balance. One day, the same St. Louis declares to his brother Charles of Anjou, who had committed an abuse of power : 'There ought to be only one king in France, and do not think, because you are my brother, that I shall spare you against right and justice'. This is not the bluster of a barbarous king or the frown of a majesty which delights in itself : it is the affirmation of a general duty, superior to private sentiments. It is still the notion of balance, of royal power considered not as personal property but as the keystone of society.

Equally complex is the religious and moral personality of St. Louis. His exceptional religious devotion came less from the heart than from the mind : he sought not consolation, but the truth. He preferred the reading of sacred texts and theological discussions to ritual practices. He loved to talk of problems of the faith, even at table. He ignored nothing of the difficulty of believing. He did not dislike the company of people whose good sense and honesty were allied to the confession of very human weaknesses : such as that seneschal of Champagne, the chronicler Joinville, who drank his wine neat and 'always the best first', sought money and the joys of life, exposed himself to dangers only in moderation and recognised that 'he would rather have committed thirty mortal sins than be a leper'.

This king with his prodigious charity, scattering alms without reckoning, himself caring for the poor and the sick, sending back the receipts of the treasury to provinces suffering from famine, founding hospitals for all sorts of ills and visiting the contagious in spite of the 'corruption of the air' and the odour of infection which upset his men-at-arms: this king, of whom a contemporary said that his generosity 'went beyond the limit', was not blind to the things of the world, nor easy to dupe. He had a wilful temperament, a lashing repartee, an unsparing humour. To a lady of ripe age who wished to attract his attention by a showy *toilette*, he said: 'Madame, formerly you were beautiful, but what is past is past. Put then all your care into acquiring beauty of soul.' He treated the pretensions of certain bishops with contemptuous roughness. He listened to his counsellors, but decided brusquely by himself. Faithful to his wife, Marguerite of Provence, he stopped her from intriguing and held her in check with a rigour that did not give way.

Two of the brothers of St. Louis were men of worth. One, Alphonse of Poitiers, poor in health and retiring, governed the South of the realm from afar. He reveals himself to us through his correspondence as a model administrator, just, exact and jealous of his rights. The other, Charles, Count of Anjou and Provence, foreshadows Philip the Fair by his energy, hardness and audacity: he was an astonishing adventurer, became senator of Rome, king of the Two Sicilies, pretender to the throne of Jerusalem and to the Latin Empire of Constantinople, roused half Europe and got himself praised or cursed in every language.

The court of St. Louis presented still a patriarchal appearance. It moved ceaselessly from monastery to monastery, from one royal house to another, around Paris. His principal residences were the castle of Vincennes, St.-Germain-en-Laye, Fontainebleau, Lorris, Montargis, Poissy, Vernon. St. Louis had neither first minister nor favourite. He recruited his counsellors and the leading personnel of the monarchy almost exclusively in the old provinces of his domain, between Somme and Loire. Later, particularly under Philip the Fair, people from the new provinces, southerners and Normans, flooded into the Capetian court and changed its spirit : to the *prud'hommes* of the North, balanced and just, there succeeded the lawyers of Languedoc and the Norman advocates, much more ingenious, but less sensible and, above all, less Christian.

One of the most characteristic aspects of the 13th century is the mixture of reflective wisdom and adventurous imagination. Something of the overwhelming vitality of preceding centuries still animates people. Hundreds of knights, the best of French chivalry, departed to conquer southern Italy with Charles of Anjou, brother of St. Louis, and thousands of Frenchmen of every condition set out in their wake to colonise the kingdom of the Two Sicilies.

St. Louis himself, peaceable, economical, prudent on every other occasion, was as excited as an adolescent brought up on romance as soon as it was a question of war against the Saracens. To conquer the infidel was his constant dream. For a great price he bought the relics of the Passion from the Emperor at Constantinople : the Holy Crown of Thorns, the True Cross, the Holy Lance and Sponge. In spite of his mother and his counsellors, he spent four years preparing a crusade : he embarked at Aigues-Mortes, 28 August 1248, and passed the winter in Cyprus ; after taking Damietta he suffered a total defeat at Mansourah in February 1250. Held prisoner by the emirs of Egypt, he was ransomed, but remained several more years in Syria, whence he seemed unable to tear himself away. Ill, enfeebled, blamed by all people of good sense, nothing deflected him from his dream : he patiently organised a new expedition, more absurd than the first and, setting out from Aigues-Mortes, 1 July 1270, died of plague near Tunis some weeks after.

His son, Philip III, had a still more marked leaning to chivalrous adventures ; he wasted the money and resources of the Capetian house in profitless enterprises. By their intrigues against the Angevins of Sicily the Aragonese had become involved in the revolt known as the 'Sicilian Vespers' ; Philip III took the cross to declare war on Aragon and was

defeated. These adventures prepared the way for the exactions of the reign of Philip the Fair. They foreshadowed the
futility and knightly disorder of the Hundred Years War.

Apogee and Limits of Ecclesiastical Power

The civilisation of the time of St. Louis, in the kingdom of
France, had a character clearly French. Yet this flowering of
French culture did not come only from the action of the
Capetian kings. It reflected the general progress of the West.
This progress was in large part the result of the efforts of the
Church and especially of the monastic orders during two
centuries to instruct, and give order and morality to feudal
society.

The Church was naturally the first to draw advantage
from the order that was established. But it did not take long
to perceive that this very order brought with it a limitation
of the material authority and political influence it claimed to
exercise. So the 13th century marks both the supreme height
attained by the Church and its first recoil. The double
attitude of St. Louis, his very sanctity and ardent devotion
to religion, on one side — his mistrustful vigilance in regard
to the Holy See and the bishops, on the other — betray
already a latent conflict, which breaks out under Philip the
Fair. The Church appears then as a monarchy that surpasses
other monarchies — centralised, omnipresent, with its energy
and its demands, with its legates ordinary and extraordinary,
its justice and its tribunals, its court or Curia and its numerous
bureaucracy, its system of taxation fed by very various imposts,
dues and revenues. The Pope commands the clergy of different countries, not as the first of pastors, but as an absolute
master. The bishops are no longer elected by their peers or
by the canons, they are most often chosen by the Pope ; they
call themselves 'bishops by the grace of God and of the
Holy See'.

The Holy See has not only its own domain in Italy.
Several realms — England, the Two Sicilies, Aragon, Portugal

— recognise themselves its vassals and as such pay it dues of a political character. It gets taxes even from Bohemia and Scandinavia. After a century of efforts and trials, is not the Papacy triumphant in the famous struggle of the Church against the German Empire?

This struggle comes to its end in Italy, in the lifetime of St. Louis, actually in the kingdom of the Two Sicilies which a troop of Norman lords founded in the 11th century and which has become one of the most civilised states of Europe. At the end of the 12th century, by the marriage of the eldest son of the Emperor Frederick Barbarossa to the heiress of the Norman kingdom of the Two Sicilies, the German dynasty of Hohenstaufen extended its dominion over southern Italy. In the time of St. Louis, the crown of the Hohenstaufen is borne by the Emperor Frederick II, grandson of Barbarossa. Frederick II, born of a Sicilian mother, represents a quite Oriental culture, half-Greek, half-Arab. Small and puny, short-sighted, bald, he was an intellectual, speaking four or five languages, interested in all the arts and sciences, given to the life and habits of the califs rather than those of knights, in touch with the researches of the Arab scholars of Egypt and Spain, allied with the Sultan of Egypt, of a sceptical mind and as little Christian as possible ; finally, a cunning enemy of the Holy See. Struck by Pope Innocent IV with a sentence of major excommunication and deposition, he provoked fierce struggles in Italy between his partisans, the Ghibellines, and his adversaries the Guelfs. He died of a bout of fever in 1250. His sons—Conrad and after him, Manfred—continued the struggle. The Pope called in against them St. Louis' brother, Charles of Anjou, who received the crown of the Two Sicilies. At length, in 1268, the last of the Hohenstaufen, Conradin, son of Conrad, was captured and executed. It was a brilliant triumph for the Holy See. Germany and Italy, henceforth split up by anarchic rivalries, paid the price of it over centuries.

The Mendicant Orders

The centralisation of ecclesiastical power and the disappearance of social insecurity entailed the weakening or discredit of the monastic orders. The monks had been the precursors of the new civilisation. The monastic empire had prepared the way for the Papal monarchy. For more than two centuries, the great abbots of Cluny, then of Cîteaux and Clairvaux, had by their material power and spiritual authority defended Christian society against outbreaks of brute force. But, in the 13th century, with order re-established and sanctions effectively exercised against wrong-doers — either by the king's agents or by delegates of the Pope — there was no longer any reason for devout Christians to live in monasteries and to constitute them in some sort Christian fortresses or strongholds apart from the secular world. It was in the world and in society that the Christian spirit had need to guard souls against perils of another nature : the growth of prosperity and the spread of heterodox ideas. From these new needs, to which the monastic orders did not respond, were born the great orders known as 'mendicant', the Franciscans and the Dominicans.

The founder of the Franciscan Order, Francis of Assisi, son of a rich merchant of Umbria and himself a worldly knight, at twenty-five became the wandering apostle of the renunciation of goods, of gentleness towards all creatures and of smiling charity. He formed the confraternity of the Friars Minor, which the Pope approved in 1210. The Franciscans mixed with the people, going barefoot in wooden sandals, clothed in a thick robe of brown wool, with a cowl, a cord around the body — which caused them to be called, later, Capuchins or Cordeliers. The Order of the Friars Preachers or Dominicans was founded at the same time (1215) in the South of France, by a Spanish noble, Dominic, who had resolved to fight the heresy of the Albigenses by preaching and by leading the life of the humble.

The two orders resembled each other by the following traits which distinguished them from the monastic orders : their members mingled in the crowd, lived only by their work or from alms, allied an extreme simplicity to intellectual speculation and were obedient and zealous agents of the Pope. St. Louis himself was affiliated to the lay tertiary Order of St. Francis. The Franciscans, by the works of St. Bonaventura and Roger Bacon, and the Dominicans, through the genius of their great doctor St. Thomas Aquinas, exercised a profound influence on Catholic thought. Their numbers grew very rapidly, witness to their popularity. At the end of the 13th century the Franciscans were many thousands in number. The Dominican missions extended as far as Greenland.

The rise of the Mendicant Orders coincided, too, with the exaltation of popular piety, which henceforth surpassed that of the upper classes of society. In 1212 a little shepherd of twelve years preached a children's crusade : thousands of children embarked at Marseilles and were caught by traders who sold them as slaves to the Moslems of Egypt. This popular piety explains the diffusion of the cult for, and trade in, relics ; the growing importance and enrichment of centres of pilgrimage — Jerusalem, Rome, Compostella, Tours, Vézelay ; the social efficacy of ecclesiastical sanctions and penitences, of excommunication and interdict. It also explains why, in spite of the resistance of some members of the Church, public opinion tolerated the abominable methods of the Inquisition.

The Art of the Great Cathedrals

Lastly, popular piety, by means of its material gifts and an outburst of collective creativeness, rendered possible the art of the great cathedrals. In few words, Suger, Abbot of St.-Denis, paints this enthusiasm of a people for building their church : 'every time', he relates, 'that great blocks of stone were drawn by cables from the quarry, the people of the country and even from neighbouring districts, gentry or peasants, had the cords attached to their arms, chests or shoulders and drew the loads along like beasts of burden'.

Romanesque art had been especially the work of the monks. Most of the Romanesque churches recall the power of an abbey or a lord. On the other hand the immense cathedrals of the end of the 12th and of the 13th century, bringing into the world a style as fertile as that of the Greeks, the ogival or French style — absurdly called 'Gothic' by the Italian pedants of the Renaissance — was the work of towns-people, craftsmen and workmen, packed inside the walls of vivacious communes, industrious and free.

Ogival or pointed architecture is the result of the conscious effort of medieval builders to reconcile the use of the stone vault, replacing the timber-work of the old basilicas, with the necessity to build churches ever longer, more majestic and soaring. To counteract the pushing out of the walls under the weight of the vault, the Romanesque builders had narrowed the nave, thickened the walls and strengthened the buttresses. The builders of the ogival period, much bolder, invented the pointed vault : beneath a vaulted bay, two diagonal arches intersect each other and support the weight. Hence, the weight being directed on the strong points of the arch, the architect distributes it as he likes : he can distend or contract his arches, bend them back or open them, give to each compartment of the edifice the form he needs. Between the bases of the arches, the wall becomes redundant : the buttresses are now only external arches shoring up the crossings of arches — they make flying buttresses : vast windows, filled with painted glass, replace the heavy Romanesque masonry.

It was in the Ile-de-France towards the middle of the 12th century that the pointed style was invented. It grew out of a transformation of the Romanesque style that took place in the royal domain. From that time the architectural superiority of the new style was so evident that everywhere it entered into competition with the Romanesque styles of the different provinces. In the 13th century the pointed style

finally triumphed over the survivals of the Romanesque. Each
province in adopting it gave it a particular character. The
same provincial inflections marked the extraordinary development of sculpture and decoration. Thus the pointed style
expressed both the sovereign unity and the manifold local
genius of the realm of France. It had, also, enormous influence
abroad : from the 13th century on, it was imitated in Germany,
Italy, Spain, Sweden and as far as Cyprus.

Of the architects, artists and workmen who made the age
of St. Louis an epoch comparable to the greatest age of Athens,
we know almost nothing, save the ingenuity and audacity, the
precision and fertilising flow of their discoveries. In spite of
the mystery which surrounds these builders, each of their
works presents a personal accent. They worked within a
collective impulse, but with individual manners. Nothing
would be more false than to consider the great monuments of
the Middle Ages as the product of a society crushing the
individual : they bear witness, on the contrary, to the flowering
of a multitude of personal fantasies and virtuosities collaborating in the same design. What we know — at least from
certain documents like the sketch-book of Villard de Honne-
court, contemporary of St. Louis — is that the master builders
of the time possessed a very wide range of knowledge and
capacity, at once architects, sculptors, decorators, geometers
and engineers.

King, lords and towns employed a 'master-workman' or
accredited architect who traced the plans and drew up the
specifications ; he chose the materials, discussed the prices
with the contractors and surveyed the works. He received a
regular salary, with allowances and gratuities. Artisans and
workmen were paid sometimes by the day, sometimes for the
job, by piece-work or by contract. The accounts of expenses
reveal to us families of artisans who worked for more than
a century at the same building — sculptors, image-makers,
stone-cutters, painters, carpenters, joiners — transmitting the
traditions of their craft from father to son.

St. Louis' masters of the works were Pierre and Eudes de Montreuil.

Like architecture and sculpture, the art of stained glass at the beginning of the 13th century is largely a French and Flemish art. It attains its high point of perfection in the workshops of St.-Denis, Chartres and Paris, where most of the industries were concentrated.

The great cathedrals express a precise moment of the faith and of French genius. This period was brief enough — less than a century. The cathedrals that could not be finished under St. Louis had their building afterwards interrupted or slowed up. For enthusiasm, forced labour had gradually to be substituted. The effort and the generosity which such enterprises demanded—raising up mountains of stone, without which architects and artists would have had to occupy themselves with something other than realising their ideal — presupposed an exceptional energy in society. From the end of the 13th century onwards, zeal relaxed and means diminished.

Vitality of Economic Life

For the rest, faith could not suffice for everything : wealth was necessary. The century of the great Capetians was a century of economic progress and improvement of standards.

The cultivators of the soil feel secure and settle down. Everywhere clearings gain upon the forest. The soil is cultivated with more care. Low-lying lands are drained in Picardy, the Cotentin, Poitou and Languedoc. The Flemings raise dikes and establish the first polders. A beginning is made of controlling streams and rivers, notably the Rhône. Corn and wine show the most extensive cultivation, along with flax and hemp. Food-giving plants are imported from the East, from Sicily and Spain : rice, maize, buckwheat, spinach, aubergine, artichoke, shallot, tarragon ; and fruit-trees like the apricot. Farmyard animals, pigs and sheep multiply. Bees yield the honey that serves for sugar, and the wax with which tapers are made. Every peasant, like every district, tries to be

self-sufficient.   The vine is found as far north as Normandy
and even in Flanders.

The country people become gayer too.   The *fabliaux* or
popular tales show us peasants full of banter, bold and sly,
with whom impertinence in argument goes with the habit of
slandering the master as well as heaven itself.

However, the mass of the peasants remain still deeply
ignorant, given up to superstitions and irrational impulses.
In 1251, on the news of St. Louis' misfortunes in Egypt, bands
of men, women and children — the 'Pastoureaux' — gathered
in the northern provinces, under the leadership of an old
fanatic, to go and deliver the king and conquer Jerusalem.
These unfortunates denounced traitors everywhere ; they beat
up the clergy and demanded the suppression of monks and
nobles and the massacre of Jews.   It was not easy to disperse
them.

In the towns, the progress of society was striking and
continuous.   Under the influence of security regained, of
easier communications and of increased trade with the freeing
of the towns, industrial and commercial activity ended not only
in generating wealth but in creating a powerful and articulated
organisation of labour.

All the towns had their craft gilds or corporations.   In
Paris alone, under Philip the Fair, there were one hundred and
fifty.   The gild grouped together workmen and masters ; no-
one could enter a trade without joining the corporation.   A
young man began as an apprentice to become, later, a journey-
man ; then, if he succeeded in passing the test of the 'masterpiece', he was admitted as a master.   An elected council of
aldermen or masters administered the gild and defended its
interests against other trades ; it tested the quality of the
products and repressed frauds ; it saw that statutes or regulations, which were very rigorous, were respected.   Under
St. Louis, the provost Etienne Boileau gathered together a
large number of gild regulations in a collection called the
Livre des métiers (Book of Crafts).

In view of the slowness and cost of transport, every town
or province had to be self-sufficient in essentials.   Thus
industry remained chiefly local.   But already there were areas
of large industrial production or of specialised products.
Such as the northern region : St.-Omer, Lille, Valenciennes,
Ypres, Ghent manufactured from English wools cloths famous
for their fineness and colour, and exported even to the Orient.
Consequently the Flemish towns prospered rapidly and built
their halls, belfries and palaces.

While in regions where industry kept its local character
union seems to have prevailed between masters and workmen,
who worked together and ate at the same table, social conflicts
broke out in areas of big production, like Flanders and
Tuscany, another centre of the cloth industry in the Middle
Ages.

But wealth comes especially from commerce.   In the
13th century international traffic takes on new scope with
the developments of long-distance trade between the West,
Northern Europe, the Mediterranean and the East.   Great
associations or trading companies are constituted under the
name of 'hansas' or 'gilds', which exploit chiefly transport
and allied activities : such as the powerful gild at Paris of the
Merchants by Water, enjoying a virtual monopoly over the
trade of the Seine — and giving its arms to our capital ; [1] such
as the gild of the Seventeen Towns, which includes the merchants of the cities of Picardy, Champagne, Flanders and
Hainaut.   Such, too, abroad are the 'Hansa' of London and
the famous Hanseatic League controlling affairs and navigation
from the North Sea to the Baltic.   Across the Mediterranean,
since the Crusades and the foundation of the Christian principalities in the Levant, trade has become very considerable.
The merchants of southern France have agents at Alexandria,
in Cyprus, at Beyrouth and Byzantium, besides in Italy, Sicily,

---

[1] These show a ship afloat on the water with the famous motto beneath, *Fluctuat
nec mergitur* (it floats and does not sink) — not less to the point, nor less moving, now
than at any other time in the history of the city.—A. L. R.

Spain and Moslem Africa. It is the moment when the fortunes of Venice and Genoa reach their apogee. Marco Polo traversed Central Asia and sojourned seventeen years in China, in the time of Philip the Bold.

Roads were improved and bridges constructed — such as the famous bridge at Avignon — hostelries were established and refuges or hospices for travellers. Navigation at sea became easier, thanks to the new use of the mariner's needle, the employment of the first marine-charts and the installation of lighthouses.

The sudden intermixing of trades of different countries encouraged exchange-operations, in which Jews and Italians excelled, with the Catalans and bankers of the South of France.

Never were the great fairs more animated or more coloured. The fairs of Champagne, at Provins in spring, at Troyes in summer, out-vied all others : the merchants met there from Northern and Central Europe, the Mediterranean and the West ; there were sold Flanders cloth and Morocco leather, furs from Scandinavia and spices from Asia. Paris had its famous fair of 'Lendit', which resembled a popular feast, in the plain of St.-Denis in the month of June. But nothing equalled in picturesqueness the fairs of the South, especially that of Beaucaire to which the traffickers and brokers of the Mediterranean ports came. At Montpellier, recounts a witness, one saw 'Arabs from Morocco, merchants from Lombardy, Rome, all parts of Egypt, from Palestine, Greece, Spain, England, from Genoa and Pisa, speaking all tongues'. In the West, Rouen, La Rochelle and Bordeaux profited from the growing trade of England with the Continent. On the Flemish coast, Bruges was the common entrepôt for the countries of the North.

It is impossible to understand the expansion of French civilisation in the 13th century if one does not realise that the realm of France was then the principal highway between the old Mediterranean Europe, which the Crusades had just liberated, and the new Central and Northern Europe pulsating with activity and enterprise. From Augsburg and Nuremberg into Spain, from Sicily and Tuscany into England, the main trade routes passed through our country.

Appearance of the Towns

Within their fortified walls, the towns look over-populated. The houses even press on to the bridges. At Paris, the Pont-au-Change is covered with the booths of the money-changers. Along the winding streets encroached on by shops, the fronts are so huddled together as to lean on one another. Each house has its sign : the Tin-Pot, the Golden Mortar, the Fishing Cat, the Smoking Dog, the Spinning Sow. The shopkeepers hail the passers-by, the innkeepers vaunt their hot bread, their herrings, their fresh tun of Auxerre wine. The cries of the street merchants date from this period. There is a regular population and one of interlopers, that of vagrants, swindlers, beggars, tricksters. After nightfall well-to-do people do not expose themselves to the risks of the street. The constable or the night-watchman perambulates ; but it is a poor safeguard.

The towns run several risks in addition. Fire is frequent because most of the houses are of wood ; curfew is rung for people to put out their lights ; night-work is forbidden. In one year alone, under Philip Augustus, Rheims, Beauvais, Troyes, Provins, Arras, Poitiers were all burnt. In twenty-five years, Rouen was burnt six times. And then there were epidemics caused by the lack of ventilation and the heaping up of filth. King Philip Augustus, opening a window of his palace, felt ill on breathing the smells of the street.

These stifling towns attract more and more inhabitants, because they represent all the joys of communal life for people who for centuries have been condemned to miserable isolation. Life in common means movement and contacts, the gaieties of the street. It means too the spectacle of costume, which becomes rich and decorated, access to the pleasures of the table which are greatly increased by imported products and more complex or more comfortable furnishing. It means above all feasts and games, a whole gamut of enjoyment, from processions to tournaments or mock-battles and dramatic representations, which were revived to accompany religious ceremonies.

Prestige of the French Language : Influence of the University of Paris

While Latin still remains the language of clerks and teachers, common speech — the Romance tongue of France, or French — has become not only a spoken tongue but a literary language. The *chansons de geste*, and the works of minstrels, ballad-makers and troubadours, no longer constitute the whole of literature. Romances like *Tristan and Iseult* begin to appear, tales and *fabliaux*, in which are expressed sentiments much more complex and refined than hitherto. The 13th century produced two historians in popular prose, Geoffrey de Villehardouin, chronicler of the fourth Crusade, and especially the Sire de Joinville, whose *History of St. Louis* is a work exquisite in tone and in sense of life. At this period, too, the French language, impure as yet, but supple and savoury, enjoys a diffusion it does not find again till the 18th century. It is the international tongue of Europe, or at least of cultivated people in Europe. The Italian Brunetto Latini writes in French, 'because', he says, 'the speech of France is most delightful and commonest to all peoples'. The Venetian Marco Polo dictates the accounts of his travels in French. Soon, other spoken tongues reduce the field of expansion for French. Dante writes the *Divine Comedy* in Tuscan dialect ; in Germany the epic poem of the *Nibelungen* triumphs.

The diffusion of the French language in the 13th century is due to several causes : to its native qualities, to the prestige conferred on it by the recent greatness of the Capetian kings — and in particular the fame of St. Louis — to the commercial importance of the French fairs, and to the expansion due to the conquests and settlements of French chivalry from England to Asia Minor. But among the most decisive causes is the influence of the university of Paris. At the end of the 12th century the teachers and students of Paris formed an association, following the example of the artisans and merchants. This association, called the 'University of the masters and scholars of Paris', rapidly became the most powerful and illustrious of its kind in Europe. Philip Augustus granted it privileges which freed it from the tutelage of the king. With the support of the Pope, it liberated itself, later, from the control of the Bishop of Paris. It constituted thus, on the left bank of the Seine, along the slopes of Mont-Ste.-Geneviève, in the domain called later the Latin Quarter, a sort of autonomous republic counting thousands of students of all countries, secure in its relations with the whole of Europe and capable of intimidating authorities which tried to embarrass it. To interfere with it was an international scandal. Speaking of it, Pope Honorius described it as 'this river of knowledge that waters and fertilises the land of the Church Universal'.

Under St. Louis it had four faculties or teaching orders : Theology, Canon Law, Medicine and the Liberal Arts. The students, like the teachers, following the countries of their birth, were grouped in 'nations': France, Normandy, Picardy, England. . . . Each faculty was presided over by a dean. The dean of the Faculty of Arts, controlling much the most numerous body, soon became Rector or head of the whole university. He had the appearance of a sort of sovereign in the Latin Quarter. In ceremonies he took precedence of cardinals. He governed, not only teachers and students, but all the common people and tradesmen who lived by the university, from paper-sellers to innkeepers. This government did not proceed without difficulties, on account of the always turbulent and often violent habits of the students. Some students were so poor that hospices and colleges had to be founded to receive, and enable to work, those who could not live on their resources. Thus, in 1257, Robert de Sorbon, almoner of St. Louis, founded the famous college which gave its name to the Sorbonne. The colleges, subjected to a rigorous discipline, raised the moral level of university life.

Other universities were constituted at Toulouse and Montpellier in the 13th century, at Orléans at the beginning of the 14th : the study of law flourished henceforth at Toulouse and Orléans, that of medicine at Montpellier.

French students also frequented foreign universities, notably those of Italy.

CHAPTER V

Misfortunes of the Hundred Years War

❖

The Valois and the Knighthood — Causes of Franco-English Conflict — Defeat of Philip VI — Anarchy under John the Good — Wisdom of Charles V — Madness of Charles VI : Civil War : The English in Paris

THE work of the great Capetians and the progress of moral as well as material civilisation in the West since the Crusades made France, at the beginning of the 14th century, not only the richest country in Europe, but one whose inhabitants had already some sense of their national destiny. The French population attained a figure it hardly exceeded till much later ; nor perhaps greatly exceeded until the rise of industry in the 19th century. The framework of the monarchy was made, the bases of social life and of intellectual development fixed, the currents of general activity directed, initiative and advance stimulated in all domains. France seemed in the way to extending her influence over Europe.

But this strength acquired was incapable of employing itself in construction or conquest. It served only to sustain French continuity through a long series of invasions, devastations and misfortunes of every kind that is known as the Hundred Years War. Without the material resources and moral traditions that the age of St. Louis left to France, it would have been impossible to hope either for the resistance our country put up to its miseries, or for the rebound of liberating energy that Joan of Arc was to incarnate in her person.

The misfortunes came, first, from the sudden decline in the personalities of the kings. The Capetian stock had produced three great kings, and chance given them three long reigns, in a century. Philip Augustus, St. Louis, Philip the Fair had been great men, robust, sane, exceptionally gifted. Later, the sons of Philip the Fair — Louis X, Philip V and Charles IV — succeeded each other on the throne at intervals of a few years, leaving only daughters. Women having been excluded from the succession to the throne, the crown fell to a nephew of Philip the Fair, Philip of Valois, in 1328. Before Louis XI, the new Valois dynasty was to give France two brainless kings, Philip VI and John the Good ; one mad, Charles VI ; and two infirm, the only ones who showed themselves capable of much thought, Charles V and Charles VII.

To make matters worse, during the same period, the opponents of the reigning king were men of ability. John the Good, a real fool, had to struggle against the 'diabolical' intelligence of the king of Navarre, Charles the Bad. The brother of the mad King Charles VI, Louis, Duke of Orléans, had much more brains than his elder brother. The same Charles VI and his son Charles VII found themselves in conflict with the Dukes of Burgundy — Philip the Bold, John the Fearless and Philip the Good — three strong characters.

On the other hand, the three first Valois made war and governed under the banner of chivalry — if you like, in the spirit of the nobility. It was the worst spirit with which the monarchy could be inspired, completely counter to the great traditions of the Capetians, who had worked precisely to break the feudal world by relying on the clergy, the middle class and the people. Chivalry, instituted to purify and discipline a half-barbarous feudality, had lost its purpose in proportion as royal power asserted itself and imposed its order, justice and administration. Lords and nobles, dispossessed of their local power but not of their property, constituted henceforth a caste, vain, lazy, given to all sorts of sports and romantic adventures, in quest of pleasure, luxury and glamorous deeds, united in an exhibitionist pride of caste, but devoid of real discipline.

Repressed for a century, this nobility rose up again

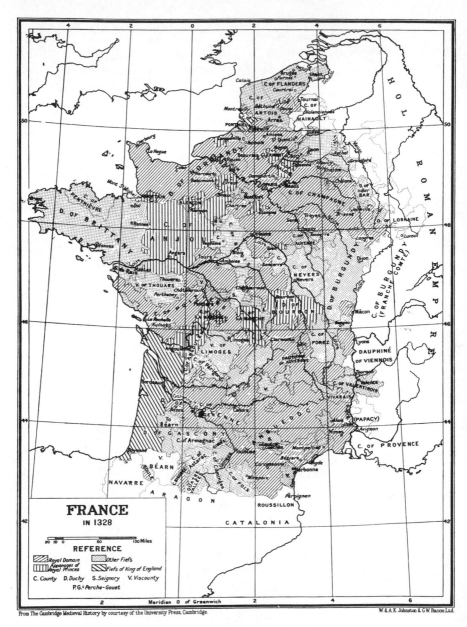

France in 1328

immediately after the death of Philip the Fair, under his feeble sons. It drew strength from the unpopularity of the lawyers or advocates, the old king's counsellors, who had engaged in too many scandalous lawsuits, debased the coinage and increased taxes. It was an assembly of great lords and nobles who, excluding women or their heirs from the succession to the throne, gave the crown to Philip of Valois in 1328. The new dynasty was, then, from its accession, prisoner of, or at least one with, the nobles.

The nobles, accustomed to jousts and feats of individual prowess but not to military discipline, transformed the royal army into a presumptuous mob, in which the horseman, alone considered as a man of arms, made a show of his plumed helmet, his armour, the trappings of his horse, his spurs, absurd footgear, and his disproportionate lance — all the paraphernalia of tournaments — bullied the infantry (termed foot-sloggers), obeyed as he pleased and despised peasant arms even when they were decisive.

This kind of chivalry, of a mad bravery and puerile silliness, was to come up against English troops, less numerous but better disciplined, organised and armed. Formed of excellent recruits, the English infantry was national, very well trained, made up of bill-men and archers manœuvring according to a new system of tactics, issued with powerful long-bows. The English cavalry, composed of nobles and small gentry, ignoring caste-spirit, obeyed and fought in their ranks.

Causes of Franco-English Conflict

Considered narrowly, the Hundred Years War between the realm of England and the realm of France arose from the claim of Edward III, King of England, grandson of Philip the Fair through his mother, to the throne of France, which the decision of an assembly of magnates had just given to Philip of Valois, nephew of Philip the Fair.

In reality, the Franco-English conflict had begun from the establishment of the Normans in England, and it was to last well beyond the time of the first Valois, up to the modern period. This, the longest and bitterest conflict in the history of the West, was fed by all sorts of dynastic rivalries, incidents and pretexts. But it had one cause, profound and constant, which alone explains its duration : the impossibility for the English nation to develop, become rich or even to live comfortably in too confined an island, if it did not have an external outlet. Before the discovery of the New World and the British expansion overseas, there was no outlet for the English nation save on the European continent. However, for the English, the European continent means, in the first place, Western France and Flanders. In addition, there was the significance of Gascony and its all-important wine-trade with England as a factor in Anglo-French rivalry. Capetian designs on Gascony were resented both by Edward III and his subjects.

Edward III did not declare his claim to the French throne until the moment when Philip VI of Valois had beaten the army of the Flemish communes at Cassel and threatened to deprive England of the vital outlet that the great cloth industry of Flanders provided for her woollen merchants. It was then that a draper of Ghent, Jacques van Artevelde, linked the cause of Flemish industry to that of English commerce, preaching to the Flemings that 'without the King of England they could not live, for all Flanders is founded on cloth-making, and without wool one could not make cloth'. Upon which the Flemings recognised Edward III King of France, and the English destroyed Philip VI's fleet in the harbour of Sluys (1339–40).

Defeat of Philip VI

Philip VI had inherited from the Capetians resources and a prestige such that he could keep the advantage as long as he did not engage in an all-out struggle with the English. In 1344 he succeeded in adding further to the crown's possessions by the acquisition of Dauphiné, which was to be reserved henceforth as an appanage for the king's eldest son, with the title of Dauphin.

The English troops invaded Normandy, then pressed forward almost to the approaches of Paris. Philip VI pushed them back towards the north and forced them to give battle at Crécy, near Abbeville. Edward III's army was about 12,000 strong; that of the King of France perhaps twice as strong. Philip's lack of self-control and the disordered tactics of the French knights gave every opportunity to the discipline of the English. A disaster ensued. Philip himself with a handful of men escaped at night to seek shelter at a neighbouring castle. The old blind King of Bohemia, John of Luxembourg, sacrificed himself at the head of the knights. This was in August 1346.

The English lost no time. They laid siege to Calais, the capture of which was to assure them a complete mastery of the passage from England into France. The governor, Jean de Vienne, was the rough chief of an heroic population. The town yielded only to famine, after six months. Edward III, angered by this long resistance, thought of putting the inhabitants to the sword. He consented to spare them, on condition that six burghers 'of the most notable', barefoot, in their shirts and cords around their necks, should bring him the keys of the city and be put to death. The richest townsman, Eustache de St.-Pierre, and five others volunteered at once. The Queen of England, by her moving appeal, saved them from death, had them 'clothed and fed, and conducted into safety'. But the population had to leave the town: only twenty-two burghers remained. The empty houses were given to the English. Calais was to be an English town, in the full sense of the word, for more than two centuries. Philip VI had made a feeble attempt to relieve the besieged. The English were henceforth sure of being able to disembark in France at will (1347).

The realm, demoralised and exhausted, suffering from famine and ruined by the monetary expedients and tax-demands of the government — which reduced it to borrowing no matter how or from whom — was suddenly afflicted by a more horrible scourge than all other ills : the Black Death. Brought from the Orient through Italy, the plague reached France and spread till it destroyed a quarter of the population. In the course of 1348 and the beginning of 1349, the West was occupied almost wholly in burying the dead and enlarging cemeteries. The people, in terror, left their work. Men's minds were distracted ; they denounced poisoners everywhere. Jews were persecuted. Production and commerce were disorganised. Strange sects appeared, like that of the Flagellants. Then, the epidemic over, relaxed morale and the thirst for pleasure caused new disorders. Land remained in part uncultivated ; dearth and want grew fast.

Philip VI died in 1350, leaving the crown to his son John, who was mentally deranged.

Anarchy under John the Good

John II, surnamed the Good on account perhaps of his bravery, was thirty-one. But his mind was not adult. Violent, credulous and spiteful, a crazy romantic, he belonged to the type of men who bring disaster down upon themselves. His very qualities, his courage and his liking for chivalrous gestures, were to aggravate the consequences of his defeats. He chose his counsellors badly and changed suddenly from confidence to hatred towards his familiars. When he had but just been crowned, he had the Constable Raoul de Brienne executed without trial for some unknown reason.

The most attractive figure of the royal family at that time was a young man, Charles of Navarre, grandson of Philip the Fair through his mother, affable, adroit, a good talker, witty and acute. He possessed, besides the kingdom of Navarre, enormous estates in Normandy, in the Caux country, the Eure and Seine valleys and up to the gates of Paris. He believed in his rights to the crown and allowed adventurers to draw him into conspiring against John the Good. The latter at first showed great weakness in regard to Charles and left him plenty of time to strengthen his side. Then suddenly, in 1356, he

decided to arrest him with his own hands, in the course of a
banquet at Rouen.   Charles's supporters, the Navarrese, led
by the Norman family of Harcourt, thereupon delivered
lower Normandy to the English.

War had broken out again, first in Brittany — where the
French captain Beaumanoir and his companions distinguished
themselves against a band of English in a curious combat
called the 'combat of the Thirty' — and then again in the
north and centre of the realm.   The Prince of Wales — who
has become subsequently known to history as the Black Prince
— had just ravaged Languedoc and was returning towards the
Loire.   Learning that the King of France was marching to
meet him with 15,000 or 20,000 men, he beat a retreat to a
place just south of Poitiers; there, strongly entrenched on a
plateau cut up by hedges and vines, he waited to deny his
adversary the road to Guyenne.

On 19 September 1356 John the Good, mounted on a white
charger, gave the order to attack, in spite of the contrary
advice of the marshal Clermont.   It ended in a worse disaster
than Crécy.   All 'the flower of the chivalry of France' perished
in the battle: twenty-two bannerets, 2,426 men-at-arms.
John fought, battle-axe in hand, at the head of his knights;
he was taken prisoner with the youngest of his sons, Philip,
fourteen years old.   The Black Prince treated him magnifi-
cently and took him to Bordeaux, then to London; no prisoner
ever received such deference.   The realm, however, was given
over to the foreigner, to misery and civil war.

The people lamented the misfortune of its king, then cried
out against the nobility, which was denounced and derided in
ballads and libels as responsible for the disasters.   Traitors,
corrupt and cowardly play-actors, the knights were made
to appear as having 'dishonoured France'.   A breath of
revolution blew through town and countryside.

The indignation of the towns expressed itself in the States
General.   Since Philip the Fair, the kings had taken to the
habit of calling together representatives of the 'orders' or

'estates' to demand subsidies whenever the government was in need of money. On the morrow of the disaster of Poitiers, the young Dauphin Charles could not dispense with convoking them. Many nobles having disappeared — many dead, others prisoners, and the survivors having lost their arrogance — it was the middle-class townsmen who played the leading rôle at the States General. They found a revolutionary leader in the person of Étienne Marcel, provost of the merchants of Paris.

Two parties joined in the agitation against the incompetent government. One, represented chiefly by the middle class, did not put the claims of the dynasty in question, but violently attacked its counsellors. The other, denouncing the Valois as both usurpers and incapable, having got the throne by fraud and done nothing but ill, upheld the claims of either Charles of Navarre or the King of England to the crown. So long as these two parties acted together, the monarchy appeared in danger. But, as soon as they were divided, it easily kept the upper hand.

The Dauphin Charles adroitly let his adversaries compromise themselves, and then profited actively from the reaction of opinion in his favour. The leader of the middle class, Étienne Marcel, lost hold through not knowing how to choose in time between a useful reform of government and a conspiracy against the dynasty. The anti-dynastic party and the Navarrese, whose spokesman was Robert Lecoq, Bishop of Laon, came up against the sentiments of the people, that of loyalty towards an anointed king and of revolt against the accomplices of England. The prestige of the king anointed at Rheims and hatred of the invader were the levers which Joan of Arc was to use, eighty years later, to save French unity.

The States General — supported by the forces at the disposal of Étienne Marcel, who put Paris into a state of siege — exacted from the Dauphin the arrest of the principal counsellors of the crown and the promulgation of something like a

Parliamentary control, as expressed in England by Magna Carta. On this basis, in spite of the flexible but tenacious resistance of the Dauphin, the middle class would perhaps have won, if Étienne Marcel had not used violence, placed the dynasty in question and provoked civil war. He welcomed the pretender Charles of Navarre to Paris, himself invaded the Dauphin's palace with an armed band and killed two of his counsellors, the marshals of Champagne and Normandy. The Dauphin feigned submission, then succeeded in escaping and appealed to the loyalty of the provinces, which responded. Henceforth, the game was lost for Étienne Marcel. He demanded help from the Navarrese and the English. The Parisians themselves cried out against treason. On 31 July 1358 Étienne was attacked unexpectedly and killed by a band of townsmen. The Dauphin re-entered Paris and was greeted with acclamation.

The revolutionary attempt of the States General and of Étienne Marcel had expressed the discontent of the towns. The anger of the countryside manifested itself by a real rising of the peasants, called the 'Jacquerie', from the nickname 'Jacques' or 'Jacques Bonhomme' given to the labourer in the fields. The movement started from Picardy and quickly gained Champagne. It was above all an explosion of hatred against the nobles. Not only did the famous 'chivalry' appear responsible for defeat, invasion and the general misery, but many gentlemen, instead of protecting the country people, had joined troops of disbanded soldiers to organise brigandage. The families of those who had been taken prisoner claimed that they were robbing the peasants of their cattle, food and equipment to pay the ransoms exacted by the English.

Long in preparing, the fury of the peasants exploded with terrible violence. Numerous bands were formed to burn castles, cut the throats of the nobles, ravish women and girls, to pillage and destroy. The Jacques found leaders among the relatively instructed people of the small towns and villages, merchants, craftsmen, the lower middle class. Officials and

even priests mingled with them. They provided a leader or
captain, who understood soldiering : Guillaume Karle, of
Mello, a good-looking fellow, 'intelligent and well-spoken'.
From the Beauvaisis as far as St.-Dizier for a couple of weeks
the hunt was up against the nobles and their manors were
laid waste. The principle of loyalty to the king was, however,
not questioned.

But the nobles, who had at first fled in fear, soon recovered
themselves, and they all forgot party to repress the revolt.
Charles of Navarre captured Guillaume Karle by treachery.
Caught off their guard, the Jacques allowed themselves to be
attacked and massacred. The nobility was pitiless in its
vengeance : in a few days, they killed some thousands of
peasants, guilty or innocent, tracked down like mad dogs, 'the
halt as well as the lunatic' say the chronicles.

The Jacquerie marked a decisive breach of trust between the
peasantry and the nobility. The people knew henceforth that
they had no safeguard or justice other than the authority of
the king. For centuries the people were often more royalist
than the king, until the day when the king became the instrument of the nobility.

In fact, from the disaster of Poitiers to the death of John
the Good, the people of France had no other defender than
themselves against the English, the Navarrese and brigands
of every kind. It is then that one sees symbolic figures of the
resistance on the land grow up, like that of the 'Grand Ferré',
that peasant of Herculean mould who, with his village companions, went out 'to kill the English'.

In the secrecy of peasant huts a national consciousness was
gradually forming which would one day find expression in
Joan of Arc.

For the present, the mistakes committed received their
reward. While the countryside held out against misfortune as
best it could and the towns, big and small, shut themselves up
within hastily built ramparts, the King of France — by a
treaty signed at Brétigny, near Chartres, in 1360 — ceded to

the King of England a quarter of the kingdom outright : Calais, Montreuil, Ponthieu, Saintonge, Périgord and all Guyenne.   Besides which John the Good undertook to pay a huge ransom.

The people handed over to the English protested.   In the rest of France the treaty did not even procure a respite ; once peace was signed brigandage returned in earnest.   Countless soldiers of all countries who were now out of employment and bands of vagabonds or adventurers formed themselves into 'great companies' to ravage the realm.   In these 'great companies', organised and disciplined with as much rigour as regular armies — in fact, collective enterprises for military pillage — were found English, Germans, Spaniards, Gascons, Bretons, Flemings, mercenaries of every origin, nobles, ruined bourgeois, peasants and unscrupulous clerics such as the archpriest Arnaud de Cervole.

Almost all the provinces experienced this scourge.   The 'companies' went right up to the walls of Avignon to threaten the Pope, and he had to buy their retreat very dear.   John the Good, at liberty again, sent a royal army against them : it allowed itself to be surprised and crushed at Brignais, near Lyons.

At last, the unfortunate John died in 1364, leaving the crown to a more solid head.   The old adversary of Étienne Marcel, the Dauphin Charles, was anointed Charles V.

Wisdom of Charles V

Charles had suffered in his youth from a 'very serious and protracted illness'.   He remained frail, pallid, thin, subject to 'fevers' and 'colics', his right hand swollen, his body affected by latent tuberculosis.   But his delicate health had kept him from the brutal attractions and puerile habits of chivalry.   His mind had matured by the study of what one could learn in written works and the watchful, reasoned observation of men and events.   He saw through things, knew how to decide and act with effect and loved above all the two least practised virtues of his time : moderation and order. He took St. Louis as his model and he resembled him in certain traits of character, notably the mixture of religious devotion and shrewd good sense. The trials he had been through and his tough struggle against Étienne Marcel, had added a touch of cunning to his wisdom.

He was fortunate in war, intelligent in his reforms, beneficent and splendid — one of those whose memory honours the history of the monarchy most — in any case, the sovereign best equipped in the things of the mind that France has known. Unhappily he reigned only sixteen years : he had neither the time to realise all that his rare intelligence promised nor, in particular, to consolidate his work of recovery for France.

From the depths of his castle of the Louvre or from the *hôtel* of St.-Pol, where he took pleasure in living amidst jewels and books, conversing with artists and scholars, this king — always careful to conceal his illness under a fine bearing — conducted government in masterly fashion.

He realised at once that he needed an army remodelled and solid, disciplined and well-armed, provided with the new artillery, and substituting determined and thought-out tactics for the absurd improvisations called 'chivalrous'. To command this army, he knew how to choose a real leader, not remarkable for his birth, nor for beauty of looks nor grace of manners, but who incarnated all the virtues of war : a Breton, poor, 'flat-nosed, dark, sullen', brave and resourceful : Bertrand Duguesclin, eldest of a family of six children, of poverty-stricken stock of small squireens.

Duguesclin had won his title of Chevalier of Brittany in the struggle between the house of Blois, who defended the French side, and the house of Montfort, whom the English supported. Then he made his reputation as a great soldier in various places, notably in Normandy. On the accession of Charles V he was forty-four, had arrived at a good position and was in command in two bailiwicks. The new king discerned the merits of this rough fighter, loyal and loved by his troops : he chose him for his man.

Duguesclin defeated the Navarrese at Cocherel, near Évreux, in 1364, and this forced Charles of Navarre to treat. In the following years, twice made prisoner — first in Brittany, then in Spain — and twice liberated, the rough Breton succeeded at least in driving most of the partisan companies outside the realm. Then, as Constable of France, he waged war so successfully that, when he died in front of the fortress of Châteauneuf-de-Randon where he was besieging brigands (1380), the English had lost almost all their conquests and occupied only the ports — Calais, Cherbourg, Brest and Bordeaux. His master had him buried beside the kings, at St.-Denis.

For government and administration, Charles V chose his counsellors as he had chosen Duguesclin for war, among men of solid worth. He gathered round him not only officials, diplomats and jurists as devoted as they were well-informed — the brothers de Dormans, the chancellor Pierre d'Orgemont, the advocate Hugh Aubriot, the chamberlain Bureau de la Rivière — but also real political thinkers, a Raoul de Presles, a Philip of Mézières, a Nicholas Oresme, all persons of refinement of culture and elevation of mind.

While engaged in freeing his territory, Charles V busied himself in re-establishing a sound currency, improving the administration of the Treasury and assuring regular resources to the monarchy. He created over the whole realm tax-districts — the 'elections' with agents, the 'elected', named by the States General to sit and levy taxes promptly. He instituted a financial administration presided over by the 'Court of Aids'. The 'aids' were taxes on trade destined, with the imposts on houses, to furnish extraordinary receipts to complement the ordinary receipts from the royal domain, now become insufficient. He did not succeed, however, in avoiding the necessity of raising heavy loans.

He survived his great servant and friend Duguesclin only

two months. On 14 September 1380, he died in the peace of
his country house of Beauté on the banks of the Marne, having
asked pardon of all those — nobles, bourgeois or villeins —
who might have cause to complain of him and having affirmed
his contempt for the things of this world.

Charles VI's Madness: Civil War: The English in Paris

The heir to the throne, Charles VI, was not twelve years
old. He was good and generous and his father had taken
great care with his education. But the child lacked spirit.
His four uncles, the brothers and brother-in-law of the dead
king — the Dukes of Anjou, Berry, Burgundy and Bourbon —
after quarrelling, then took to sharing power to exploit the
realm.

The gravest error of the Capetians, from the beginning of
the 13th century, had been to give vast domains, entire provinces, as appanages to the younger sons of their house. Thus
were formed once more, to the detriment of monarchical
authority, seigneurial powers at once parasitical and
indisciplined. The first Valois, with their usual irresponsibility, constituted half the realm into appanages. This error
was to subject French unity to a terrible trial. Of the four
possessors of these great domains, who bore down on the
weakness of Charles VI, one — the Duke of Bourbon — was
descended from the sixth son of St. Louis. The three others
were sons of John the Good. The last, Philip the Bold, already
Duke of Burgundy and soon to be Count of Flanders, had a
strong personality at the service of great ambitions.

The people were not long in finding that the king's uncles
made their government cost them too dear. Risings in Flanders
and in England were the news just then and in 1381 risings
broke out at Béziers, Rouen, Amiens, St.-Quentin, Rheims,
Paris and several other towns. The 'Maillotins' — the nickname given to the Paris insurgents who armed themselves
with lead mallets — killed collectors of taxes, broke open
prisons and sacked shops. They were suppressed with

ferocity. Philip of Burgundy carried the little king into Flanders, crushed the rebels of Ghent at the battle of Roosebeke and had their throats cut 'like dogs'. Returning to Paris, which he entered as a conqueror, Charles VI presided over the execution of a great number of notables executed by way of example. All the rebellious towns were punished and ransomed in the same manner.

After some years, the young king tried to rid himself of his uncles and to recall his father's old counsellors, bourgeois or men of the small gentry, whom the great lords called derisively the 'Marmousets'. But, too frail, highly strung and impressionable, worn out early by pleasure and too much exertion, he fell ill. When hardly recovered, he decided to set out for the country to revenge Olivier de Clisson, who had been attacked by Pierre de Craon, cousin of the Duke of Brittany. On 5 August 1392, as he was riding out of the forest of Mans under a burning sun, the shock of a lance against a steel helmet made him suddenly tremble : he rushed forward, sword in hand, striking his escort. They held him with great difficulty : he was raging mad. Thenceforward he remained mentally unstable, suffering from attacks of dementia which became more and more frequent.

His uncle the Duke of Burgundy had made him marry a pretty German, Isabel of Bavaria, 'short and a brunette', attractive and given up to pleasure. When he became mad, she was twenty-two. She had not the character to bear the burden of politics : she asked only that fêtes might continue to go on. The fêtes did go on to the point of frenzy, in a riot of luxury and extravagant fashions. In the course of one of these fêtes called the 'ball of the savages', the king, disguised in cloth smeared with pitch and covered with linen tow, was nearly burnt alive.

The leader of the dance at court was the king's brother — Louis, Duke of Orléans, a sensitive youth, charming and cultivated, a good talker, but extravagant and with a passion for elegance. Philip, Duke of Burgundy, died and his son,

John the Fearless, succeeded him.   The two cousins, Louis of Orléans and John the Fearless, detested each other.   The new Duke of Burgundy, rough in manner, negligent in his appearance, a bad speaker, but determined, violent and vindictive, had no scruples.   He had the Duke of Orléans assassinated as he left the Queen's apartments, one night in November 1407.

Civil war was thus let loose between the Burgundians and the Armagnacs.   These last represented the family of Orléans, whose heir was married to a daughter of the Count of Armagnac.   The Burgundian party — green hood and red cross — supported by the lords of the North and East, the Dukes of Brabant and Lorraine, had the populace of Paris with it, affronted by the arrogance of the house of Orléans. The Armagnac party — red scarf and white cross — drew on the Gascon nobility, the lords of the Centre and the West, the Dukes of Berry, Bourbon and Brittany.   The kingdom fell back into the disorder and miseries that had marked the reign of John the Good.   Popular discontent developed into a rising. It broke out in 1413 at the instigation of the Duke of Burgundy, among the butchers and skinners of Paris, led by one named Caboche, who gave his name to the movement 'Cabochien'. As in the time of Étienne Marcel, the rioters invaded the royal palace and had the most hated courtiers given up ;   they extracted from the poor king and his son a charter of reforms inspired by the middle class, and established a reign of terror in the capital.   After some weeks, the peaceable people had had enough of it ;   they threw out John the Fearless and got the Armagnacs to return.   The Cabochien leaders were executed.

Upon this, the new King of England, Henry V, concluded a secret alliance with John the Fearless and landed in Normandy.   He could not advance far, and turned back towards the north.   The French army, after Duguesclin's death, had again become the absurd mob of chivalry of the time of Philip VI and John the Good.   At Agincourt in Picardy, some 20,000 strong, it joined battle with the English army, only one-half its size, but disciplined and solid. It underwent a disaster worse than Crécy and Poitiers. Henry V, afraid of being overwhelmed by the number of his prisoners, had them massacred in cold blood (1415).

In the following years the English installed themselves in Normandy. Rouen, then the second city of the kingdom, had to surrender to Henry, after a fearful siege of seven months, in the course of which thousands of useless mouths were sacrificed — old men, women and children.

The Burgundians, having regained Paris by treachery, gave the signal for new massacres. John the Fearless was master of the person of the unfortunate Charles VI and dominated Queen Isabel. Alone, the little Dauphin Charles, sixteen years old, had succeeded in flying to Bourges. John the Fearless tried to entice him back : an interview took place, 10 September 1419, on the bridge of Montereau, where, quite unexpectedly, the Dauphin's men threw themselves on the Duke and killed him.

The son of John the Fearless (out of revenge), Queen Isabel (out of villainy) and the Parisians (out of hatred of the Armagnacs) delivered France to England. In 1420 Charles VI had to sign the Treaty of Troyes which recognised the King of England as heir to the throne, confided the government of the realm to him and gave him in marriage Catherine, sister of the 'so-called' Dauphin. Henry V with his troops made a solemn entry into Paris. He died two years later, the same year as Charles VI himself, in 1422.

This date marks the lowest point in the history of the French monarchy and, practically speaking, the end of the monarchy based on chivalry.

The period of the first Valois, which the death of Charles VI closes — that is to say, the 14th century and the beginning of the 15th — presents to our judgment astonishing contrasts and incoherences, in some ways mysterious.

One sees the foundering of the principal forces which

supported, and then disciplined, the impulse of the Middle Ages. The Church is weakened by the great schism of the West, which raises two Popes hostile to each other, the Pope of Avignon and the Pope of Rome. Heresies begin their attack on it from several sides, notably those of Wyclif in England and of John Huss in Bohemia. The authority of the Sovereign Pontiff bends before Councils. The old monastic support disappears or gives way. The French kingship, apart from the temporary recovery brought about by Charles V, seems to have lost almost all its traditional virtues : prudence, the capacity for any consistent drive or taste for order, any sense of opportunity or love of the people. It allows itself to be crushed in three disastrous battles — Crécy, Poitiers, Agincourt — by its vassal, the King of England, whose forces and resources are quite small. At home it is menaced by movements of a new character, social risings and Jacqueries, attempts at political revolution. Finally, both the knighthood and the nobility discredit themselves lamentably.

Yet in this century appear great Christian teachers, like Gerson, Chancellor of the University of Paris, and personalities ardently devoted to the Church, like St. Catherine of Siena. Never, on the other hand, have monarchs and princes, magnates and simple lords so much loved *décor*, the refinements of luxury, art and even of culture. And it is at the hour when the kings by their shortcomings provoke foreign invasion, risings and brigandage, and bring all sorts of ills on France, that national feeling takes life in the humblest dwellings, by a rebound of loyalty towards the unhappy dynasty.

Against the English, against the companies of mercenaries and innumerable brigands, walls are hastily built round towns, new castles rise in the villages and fortified granges in the hamlets. But, at the same time, palaces, *hôtels*, country seats to provide repose and pleasure, are erected. Military and religious architecture invent nothing : they refine upon the inventions of the preceding age. Civil architecture, in contrast, bursts out in sudden brilliance. At the same time the

arts of ornamentation are growing : tapestry, miniatures,
painting and especially sculpture, as illustrated by the admirable
works of Claus Sluter, master of the Burgundian school.

It is an age in which foolery and finesse neighbour together
strangely ; massacres and subtle debates, insecurity and fêtes,
misery and luxury, cynicism and candour ; popular outbreaks
of violence, bourgeois intrigues and lordly presumption ;
weakness and vitality.

An age of superficial decadence : the collapse of the
framework of the Middle Ages allows deep currents to appear,
of an intellectual and moral character as well as material, which
give promise of a decisive transformation to come.

The great chronicler of the 14th century, Froissart, has a
backward-looking mind, but a marvellous gift of portraiture
and writing that is already modern.

PART III

THE FORMATION OF MODERN FRANCE

CHAPTER I

Towards the Bourgeois Monarchy

❖

General Disorder — Joan of Arc, Heroine of the Liberation
— Expulsion of the English — Economic Revival —
Ambitions of the House of Burgundy — Louis XI and
Charles the Bold — Aggrandisement and Unification of the
Realm — Regency of the Beaujeu

THE land of France deserved great pity under the blows of so many misfortunes. In parts depopulated, given over to brambles and thorns, one can say — as a chronicler observed — 'rather desert land than land of France'. When invasion and civil war finished, there remained but few inhabitants at Limoges; Rouen, Rheims, Toulouse had lost half their population; in Paris there were hundreds of empty houses.

There were two kings. One was the frail Charles VII, aged nineteen, who seemed to unite all the physical and moral blemishes of his family. 'Son of a madman and a loose woman', he had short legs, knock-knees, a head too large and ill-made, thick speech and poor sight; feeble in character, mistrustful and fearful, hypochondriac, he let himself be dominated by his entourage; lastly, in spite of his wretchedness, this Valois liked pleasure and extravagance. He reigned precariously over the country of the Loire and the Centre, Languedoc and Dauphiné. His government was seated at Bourges and at Poitiers.

The other king, Henry VI of England, was a very young child. His uncle, the Duke of Bedford, an energetic and able regent, governed English France : Paris, Normandy, Picardy, Champagne, the Barrois, the south of the Seine to Le Mans and the gates of Orléans, Guyenne. The powerful ally of the English, Philip the Good, was master of all Burgundy,

Nivernais, Artois and Flanders. The English troops were making progress. Soon they were attempting to take Orléans and cross the Loire.

The Christian world remained deeply troubled. For half a century, the Western Schism kept pious souls in agony, no-one knowing of the two Popes who excommunicated each other which was the right one : men saw the rivalry of Rome and Avignon produce two bishops for the same diocese, two abbots for the same abbey, two curés for the same parish. At Constance a great council was assembled to reform the Church : a multitude of clerks and laymen from all Europe came there to voice its anxiety and its complaints. At length, the schism came to an end. But immediately a terrible religious war began, the Hussite war, which shook Bohemia and Germany.

Farther away, on the Danube and in the Balkans, the Turks were advancing, throwing back the knights and enslaving Christian peoples. . . .

Amid this confusion in both temporal and spiritual spheres, the French people brought forth their great heroine.

Joan of Arc, Heroine of the Liberation

About 1412 Joan of Arc was born at Domrémy, an obscure village on poorish soil, between a slope covered with copses and the meadows where the river Meuse glided by, separating Champagne from Lorraine, some leagues from Burgundy. A corner of the country curiously preserved from the ravages of invasion and of civil war, but not from anxiety due to threats quite near at hand. The English and Burgundians had not yet reached this village that depended on the castle-ward of Vaucouleurs, faithful to Charles VII. The peasants were good French, pious and charitable. Joan, a child of honest labourers, had the temperament of a healthy peasantry. She grew tall, robust and strong, with brown hair, a pleasant countenance and lively expression ; with the spirit of repartee, great good sense and shrewdness ; of incredible determination and a compassionate heart. She needed this solid balance and these natural gifts to avoid being treated as a madwoman.

The documents do not permit us to doubt that Joan obeyed, in her illustrious adventure, a kind of genius that gave her not only courage, but clairvoyance.

At thirteen she heard voices which she attributed to the patron saints of her country, St. Michael, St. Margaret and St. Catherine, already exhorting her to a great mission of deliverance. It was not at all by chance that the girl's imagination was awakened and her faith exalted : a band of Burgundians had just carried off the flocks of Domrémy, the English were invading the Barrois, and had burned Revigny. At sixteen, she experienced the direct impact of war : the English attacked the surrounding places and the terrified villagers of Domrémy took refuge at Neufchâteau. Her voices urged her on and she resisted no longer, but departed, in the modest dress of a peasant girl, for Vaucouleurs. The Armagnac captain of the place, a man called Baudricourt, who knew her father, laughed at her and wished to send her back to her parents. She insisted with a disconcerting firmness on the mission she must accomplish. She was watched, was exorcised by the parish priest ; the people listened to her and respected her. This modest and sane girl, who spoke clearly and said firmly what she wished to do and whose piety influenced all around her — it was impossible to take her for a witch or for feeble-minded. The inhabitants of Vaucouleurs bought her a horse and equipment. Baudricourt ended by giving way : he gave Joan a sword, letters of recommendation and six men-at-arms to accompany her to Chinon in Touraine, where Charles VII was residing. For greater safety, she was dressed in man's clothing. She set out in the depth of winter, 13 February 1429.

The first wonder was that she escaped the dangers of such a journey. After ten days on the way she reached Chinon. Would she be received ? The king's entourage subjected her for two days to surveyance and various interrogations. But she emerged unscathed from suspicion and was introduced into the royal presence. Without hesitating, she recognised Charles VII, went straight to him and, as he mistrusted himself, murmured to him some words which left him deeply moved. Franciscans were sent to make an enquiry at Domrémy. After new interrogations and new hesitations, Joan was sent to Poitiers to undergo a double examination — that of the theologians of the Armagnac party who examined her religion, and that of the matrons who affirmed her virginity. She astonished everybody by her robust uprightness, her discreet but brisk speech. A Limousin monk asked her in his dialect what language St. Catherine and St. Margaret spoke — 'Better than yours', she replied. The doctors were conquered by the virtue of this extraordinary maid.

But Joan disliked these delays ; she became impatient. The English were besieging Orléans ; it was high time to act. The old soldiers of the royal army — La Hire, Xaintrailles, Bueil, Ambroise de Loré, the Sire de Rais — offered to follow her lead. The young Duke of Alençon was enthusiastic. Some thousands of soldiers gathered at Blois. The Maid was given armour and a white banner with the badge of the Franciscans : 'Jesus-Mary'.

The great work of Joan, whether with the aid of the Armagnac officials or no, was to have discerned at once, in the task to be accomplished, the importance of the preconditions to it. It was essential to restore the morale of the people by stopping the English and breaking their military prestige. It was essential to quash doubt about the birth of Charles VII, who was regarded as a bastard, and on the legitimacy of his rights ; hence the decisive value of the anointing at Rheims, after which the faithful people would rally to their king. Lastly, it was essential to appease the resentment of the Duke of Burgundy. All the rest would come afterwards. Joan had a doctrine and would never vary from it, notably as to the importance of the anointing and, in consequence, of legitimacy — principle of national adhesion. Her solid reasoning in this respect was the reasoning of the people, the argument of village evenings, an answer to the uncertainty of common folk as to where right lay.

The least defeat to begin with, and it would be the end of the miraculous adventure . . . Joan did not hesitate. The English were besieging Orléans : she would go and defeat them. On 29 April she penetrated into the town on her white horse. From 4-7 May the relieving army captured the English forts. On Sunday 8 May the English retreated, abandoning artillery and provisions. Both sides were astounded. Then enthusiasm burst forth throughout loyal France and crowds of people rushed to place themselves under the orders of the Maid. At Patay, 18 June, the best English captains, Talbot and Fastolf, again let themselves be routed by Joan's army ; Talbot was captured. Joan had her idea : to defeat the English gave confidence back to people. But to keep the popular impetus firm, the most urgent thing henceforth was to crown and anoint the king. Charles VII and his favourites showed no great desire to take the road for Rheims, exposed as it was to enemy ambushes. The Maid insisted and at last Charles set out. As by enchantment towns, big and small — Châlons, Troyes — surrendered and opened their gates to him. On 16 July he entered Rheims and the very next day was anointed in the cathedral. The Maid of Domrémy, erect with her standard in her hand near the altar throughout the ceremony, prostrated herself in tears before her 'gentle king' as soon as he was anointed.

The enthusiasm of the people gained northern France and even Normandy. But Charles's counsellors left the English time to recover themselves ; two months and a half went by before the royal army attacked Paris. On 8 September, before the St.-Honoré gate, Joan had her leg pierced by an arrow. She had to be carried away by main force. With her away, the king gave up and returned to his indolent life in the castles of the Loire.

In the spring of 1430, Joan, impatient, got away with

some companions and went to aid Compiègne, which was besieged by the Burgundians. On 23 May, in a sortie, she was surrounded, thrown under her horse and taken by a leader of a Burgundian band, Jean de Luxembourg. He kept her for six months, expecting a ransom, and then sold her to the English for ten thousand gold pounds. Doubtless Charles VII could have bought her back in time, but his favourites did not like the Maid who had scorned them.

As for the English, to do away with this heroine of eighteen would not serve them at all, if they did not first try to dishonour her and so undermine the faith of the people and, by the same token, the prestige of the king anointed at Rheims. The idea was to show that the pretended Charles VII was only a fool in the hands of a witch.

On Bedford's orders, about fifty theologians and canons of Paris and Rouen, where almost everybody had taken the English or Burgundian side, assembled at Rouen to try the poor girl from Domrémy. Pierre Cauchon, an old Cabochien rioter, now Bishop of Beauvais, presided over this tragic trial. The sentence being prearranged, the girl might have been spared additional suffering and humiliation. But it was necessary to sully her, to extract confessions from her, force her to deny her mission. For four months, tormented and questioned, subjected to all sorts of traps, she defended herself with superhuman spirit against the grossness of her gaolers, the perfidy of her judges and the physical and moral temptations of her own weakness. Better than anything else the evidence of the trial at Rouen bears witness to the transcendent character of Joan of Arc.

Finally, 28 May 1431, she was declared a 'lapsed' heretic. On the morrow, when she was told that she would be burnt alive, the girl cried out in terror and despair. But on 30 May, when she arrived on the old market square at Rouen she recovered her courage to mount the stake. Seeing the flames burn up around her poor body, she raised herself up in a last surge of faith. Cauchon himself wept.

Expulsion of the English

In a year Joan had brought about a great change in the history of France. She had rendered the realisation of a Franco-British state impossible. The idea of it may seem chimerical today, but the weakness and discredit of the first Valois, except for Charles V, made it appear at that time less absurd than it seems to us.[1] Cauchon and his troop of judges from Paris and Rouen, calculating men, would not have committed the terrible crime of burning a maid, pure and loyal above all, if they had not believed in the lasting character of the Anglo-Burgundian régime they served.

Joan, on the other side, had put French unity and its symbol, the legitimate king, under the protection of the people. It is the first time in our history that the feeling of the people for safeguarding the work of the monarchy outweighs the foresight and decision of the monarch himself. Joan of Arc's initiative marks the authentic awakening of our national consciousness in the modern sense.

Lastly, the Maid, in raising the people to the rank of guardian of French unity and of the king who represents it, corrected the disastrous error of the first Valois kings who, forgetful of the Capetian tradition, delivered themselves over to the nobility.

By the Treaty of Arras in 1435 the two hostile Frances, the Armagnac and the Burgundian, were reconciled. In the following year, Paris opened its gates with joy to Charles VII. The king, ripened by experience and drawn away from his worst favourites, profited by the opportunities given him by the Duke of Bedford's death and the disorder into which English politics fell. From 1449 to 1453 his army reconquered Normandy and then Guyenne. The English kept only Calais.

Economic Revival

A strange personality, this Charles VII! At the same time as he seemed to regard Joan of Arc's adventure as a passive

[1] Thus Romier writing in 1939.—A. L. R.

and almost indifferent spectator, anxious, for the rest, not to run any risks himself, he presided over the reconquest of his realm and the expulsion of the English almost without taking part. He figured in hardly any expeditions. He disliked danger and seemed to shrink from action. He lived almost heedlessly, hidden and inaccessible in his castles along the Loire. Belatedly, at forty-five, he fell for women. He brought to Court from Nancy a beautiful woman of loose morals, Agnes Sorel, whom he displayed to all and sundry as his mistress, heaped with presents, revenues and lands — a fact without precedent in the history of the kings — and by whom he had four daughters. After her death, he took another mistress, Antoinette de Maignelais. Finally, old, morose, infirm, he took his pleasures in the gutter, dragging in his train a troop of unsavoury women, in which figured Marion the plough-girl, and Alison the washerwoman.

But this man who seemed self-effacing, weak, incapable of generous feelings, knew admirably how to profit from opportunities and make use of others, while he was punctual and meticulous in his work with his counsellors. Thus his person repels sympathy, but his reign was a triumph.

Under Charles VII not only are the English driven from France, but the monarchy is reorganised and the state strengthened : the King's Council becomes an effective and energetic institution in which influence is exerted by middle-class men of practical mind, assiduous at business, able and informed — like Jacques Cœur, the brothers Bureau, Guillaume Jouvenel des Ursins, Étienne Chevalier, Guillaume Cousinet. The finances are reorganised, the Treasury revenues secured by indirect imposts — the aids and the salt-tax (*gabelle*) — and a direct poll-tax (*taille*), which remain the monarchy's chief resources for three centuries. Justice is reformed and the Parliament of Paris takes up its old functions once more; provincial Parliaments are created at Toulouse and Grenoble. The army is remodelled and enlarged, and rendered regular and permanent by the formation of companies of orderlies or 'gendarmes';

Charles VII

a solid infantry of 8,000 or 10,000 bow-men is trained; the artillery is strengthened with hand-cannon, the first guns, with culverins, throwing-engines — bronze-pieces throwing iron balls.

Still more, this king who owed the recovery of his fortune to the 'voices' of Joan of Arc, to St. Michael, St. Margaret and St. Catherine took up again the tradition of Philip the Fair against the Holy See. By the Pragmatic Sanction of Bourges, a kind of ordinance or law concerning the morals and discipline of the clergy (1438), he deprived the Pope of the temporal resources he found in France and restricted as much as possible the intervention of the Court of Rome in the choice of bishops.

Charles VII's government had luck with it. As soon as peace was re-established, it benefited from an economic revival from which it drew the best advantage. The cloth industry had a great expansion, notably at Rouen, at Montivilliers in the Caux country, at Bourges and Paris. The exploitation of mines — coal, iron, silver, copper, lead — made headway. Trade revived everywhere, thanks to the establishment of a sound currency and the security of the roads. Under royal patronage, Lyons created its famous fairs which took a part of international traffic away from Geneva. Aigues-Mortes on the Mediterranean and La Rochelle on the Atlantic acquired a monopoly of the import of spices. The king sent trade-missions as far afield as Morocco. He concluded trading treaties with German principalities and Denmark, with Castile and Aragon.

Then, when the nobles, who would not work, remained impoverished by the losses of war and, in order to live, put themselves more and more at the service — that is to say, in the pay — of the sovereign, the middle classes grew rapidly richer. At the same time as Charles VII's reign marked the powerful awakening of national consciousness among the mass of the people, it coincided with the first expansion of bourgeois ambitions. The bourgeois — drapers, grocers, mercers, butchers, big shopkeepers — bought castles, manors

and lands from ruined gentry, acquired official posts in the
law courts and in finance, and were ennobled to form the first
noblesse de robe.

Jacques Cœur, son of a merchant-furrier of Bourges,
represents best this ascent of the middle class. He knew how
to profit from war in all kinds of speculations. His firm,
situated first at Montpellier, then at Marseilles, traded with
the Mediterranean ports, with the Levant and Egypt. It both
imported and exported, made armaments and took commissions on every kind of product, arms, cloths, carpets, silks,
spices, perfumes. Its fleet carried precious merchandise as well
as slaves. From a trader Jacques Cœur became an industrialist : he possessed a factory at Florence, a dye-works at
Montpellier, mines in Lyonnais, paper-mills. He gained a
fortune such that he could buy thirty manors. He became the
king's financial agent and counsellor, and the Treasury banker.
But he had too many enemies and too few scruples. In 1451
he was imprisoned and his goods were confiscated. He escaped
and fled to Rome ; he died eventually in the service of the
Pope, at Chios.

Ambitions of the House of Burgundy

At the end of Charles VII's reign the English no longer
had any possessions on the Continent, except Calais. The
Burgundian power remained, more or less reconciled to the
King of France, but still ambitious, a menace.

No region in Europe at that time equalled the Low
Countries in wealth. The court of Philip the Good was the
most brilliant in the Christian world, the centre of the life of
luxury and aristocratic extravagance. The family of Burgundy,
whose head was entitled Duke of Burgundy, Brabant and
Limburg, Count of Flanders, Artois and Boulogne, Palatine
of Hainault, Holland, Zeeland and Namur, Marquis of the
Holy Roman Empire, lord of Frisia, Salins and Malines,
realised greatness after the ideal of the first Valois, his ancestors.
The Dukes were indeed Valois, ambitious, thirsting after

adventures and luxury, a bit touched, but with a vigour of temperament that the elder branch had not had for a long time.

Philip the Good, who founded the chivalrous order of the Golden Fleece in 1429, dominated the figures about him, tall of stature, pleasure-loving and violent, of an extreme pride, liking fêtes, the arts and women, liable to accesses of temper that made him severe. His monarchical government, strong and disciplined, concerned itself chiefly with the rich towns of Flanders and Brabant which gave it its opulence. His tax-demands provoked discontent and sometimes raised revolts. His external relations were involved and precarious. He aimed at the title of king for his possessions within the Empire. He was called the 'great Duke of the West', but this greatness was not enough : he wished to be the equal of his cousin, Charles VII.

Louis XI and Charles the Bold

Joan of Arc's 'gentle king' finished miserably, suffering from abscesses in his limbs, a swelling in the mouth and a softening of the brain. He died 22 July 1461. His son, Louis XI, who was not inconvenienced by family feelings, forgot to be present at his funeral.

The new king was — like his father, grandfather and great-grandfather — a nervous type, impulsive and suspicious, tricky, cynical, superstitious ; a man in perpetual agitation, an incorrigible chatterer, who spoke ill of everything and everybody, thick of speech, rolling his tongue, incapable of pronouncing the letter *r*. He ruled only by intrigue and fear. He wheedled and bribed people, excelled in withdrawing from a false step, then revenged himself diabolically. His contemporaries compared him to a spider. He covered himself with sacred medals, murmured paternosters and claimed he could seduce or buy all the saints in Paradise ; but, if it had been possible, he would have put God in prison. A born traitor, a bad son, a bad husband and a poor father,

he exposed himself to his adversaries' laughter by his unfortunate body, his hunched-up shoulders and his too thick neck,
his common appearance and his 'every-day' hat or bonnet, his
buffoon-like look.   His greatest defect as ruler was a febrile
quality that made him commit hasty and imprudent deeds.

Fate served him strangely well, as it had served Charles VII.
But he had also exceptional gifts : capacity for work, vivacity
of intelligence and a promptness of judgment that we find in
no other prince of his time.   For the rest — an incomparable
advantage for a Valois — he detested the nobility and despised
the follies of chivalry : there lived in him the secret passion
of a leveller—which was precisely what the monarchy needed.

He was going to come up against his cousin, the young
heir of the house of Burgundy and son of Philip the Good —
Charles the Bold, an unbalanced type also, but of another sort.
One cannot imagine greater dissimilarity between two men.
Charles's mother was a Portuguese, arrogant and headstrong.
The marriage of Philip the Good's exuberant temperament
and the sombre humour of Isabel of Portugal had produced
a child of high bearing, but rigid, inordinately pretentious,
taciturn, inclined to nurse obsessions.   A youth of rare distinction of appearance and, for the rest, a hard worker, educated, chaste, sober to the point of foregoing the use of wine
without water, which much amused Louis XI.   His handsome
face, with clear blue eyes that contrasted with his brown
complexion and thick black hair, had the imprint of a sort of
fixed melancholy.   Erect and robust, inured to the hardest
exercise, he believed himself, however, destined to an early
death.   Pride in him came near to madness.   He was incapable
of listening to advice, of keeping any self-control, of moderat-
ing his anger or, if the case arose, his cruelty.   He lacked, above
all, what his adversary possessed in excess : trickery.

Louis XI had had the less commendable youth.   From the
age of sixteen he had declared himself his father's enemy and
had a hand in a revolt of some nobles, the 'Praguerie'.   Forced
to submit, he had taken part for a time in war against the

English and in Switzerland. Then he had been established in
Dauphiné as an independent ruler. Recalled by Charles VII,
he took care not to obey and passed over to the Duke of
Burgundy, where he lodged and lived at the latter's charges.
Married at thirteen, a widower at twenty-two, he remarried
at twenty-eight without consulting his father : 'Am I not old
enough', he said, 'to choose a woman for my own convenience ?'

He was barely crowned before he made himself hated ; he
disgraced Charles VII's counsellors and recalled those who had
been condemned, surrounded himself with mischievous and
unworthy people, upset the clergy, exasperated the nobility
great and small and oppressed the people, so that revolts
broke out at Rouen, Alençon, Rheims, Aurillac. The 'League
of the Public Good' was formed in 1465 to bring him to
reason. After a short war, he yielded everything demanded
of him — provinces, towns, villages — to his brother, to the
Duke of Brittany, the Duke of Burgundy. But in three
months he succeeded in dividing and embroiling his opponents,
and took back what he had promised.

In 1468 there came a new rising against his bad faith.
Charles the Bold, who had just succeeded Philip the Good,
prepared to join in. Louis XI asked for a safe-conduct and
went to Péronne to negotiate with Charles, while sending
emissaries of his own to raise the town of Liège against the
Duke. Unfortunately, Liège revolted too soon, while the
king was still at Péronne and proofs of his treachery arrived.
Louis, caught in a very bad posture, was obliged to give
fifteen thousand gold crowns to some of Charles's counsellors.
On their advice, Charles confined himself to imposing on his
treacherous cousin the Treaty of Péronne, which assured free
passage through Champagne between Burgundy and Flanders.
Louis XI accompanied the Duke to punish the people of
Liège, crying — 'Long live Burgundy!'

Two years after this misadventure, in 1470, an assembly
of notables at Tours annulled the Treaty of Péronne. From

then on, luck turned.   A French army took the towns of the
Somme from Charles.   The latter, in exasperation, invaded the
kingdom, but his fury broke against the ramparts of Beauvais
and he had to accept a truce.   His accomplice, Charles of
France, brother of Louis XI, who aimed at the throne, died in
1472.   From this moment, almost without fighting, the King
of France by the varied resources of his diplomacy pushed
the Duke of Burgundy relentlessly to destruction.   Like his
father, only still more ardently, Charles dreamed of being
King of Lotharingia and — who knows ? — claimant to the
Imperial throne.   Already he had had his crown made.
Louis XI did not fail to excite the suspicions of the Emperor
of Germany, Frederick III, on this subject.   There was one
who would never favour the ambitions of Burgundy.

Charles hoped to make an ally of Edward IV, King of
England, and draw him into France.   Louis offered the
Englishman a pension, which was accepted : by the Treaty of
Picquigny (1475).

At length, in order to realise his Lotharingian dream,
Charles sought to take Alsace and Lorraine, so as to assure
the link between his Burgundian domains and Flanders.
Louis XI exhorted the Duke of Lorraine to defend his independence and the Swiss cantons that of the towns of Alsace.
Charles was defeated by the Swiss at Granson and at Morat in
1476.   He was killed before Nancy in January 1477.

Aggrandisement and Unification of the Realm

Louis XI had only to gather the harvest, but with his
nervous feverishness, he tried to harvest too quickly.   Charles's
heir was a daughter, Mary.   God-child of the King of France,
she solicited his protection.   With a little persuasion, he could
have married her to the Dauphin, the future Charles VIII.
But not content with seizing Burgundy — a male appanage
which naturally reverted to the crown — he annexed the
county of Artois and even Franche-Comté, an Imperial fief.
Mary, thus dispossessed, found a refuge with the Flemings,

and in revenge, she married Maximilian of Austria, a marriage which engendered two centuries of war between France and the House of Austria.

The regulating of the Anjou succession was better managed. The chief of the Angevin house, 'King' René, died in 1480. At once Louis XI gathered in the duchies of Bar and Anjou, with all the rights of the deceased in the kingdoms of Naples and Jerusalem. René's nephew, Charles of Maine, soon disappeared : Maine and Provence, too, came back into the royal domain.

Louis XI has been much praised for having almost achieved French unity. Doubtless he was expert in profiting from opportunities and, sometimes, in creating them. He had a genius for diplomatic intrigue and he knew how to profit extraordinarily from the means left him by Charles VII. He knew how to choose his agents and how to make himself obeyed by inspiring the fear of his vengeance. Nothing was repugnant to him ; nothing moved him. He terrified the nobles, he checkmated the towns. He had two of the greatest lords executed — the Count of St.-Pol and the Duke of Nemours ; he incarcerated a Cardinal, his old favourite, Jean La Balue ; he had many people executed or put into the iron cage without sentence. When Arras hesitated to take his side, he put the aristocrats to the sword and expelled the inhabitants. Lastly, he knew how to flatter the class which was growing, the class of merchants and ambitious bourgeois whom the war and then the peace had enriched. He stimulated commerce and encouraged the establishment of new workshops and industries ; he installed silk-weaving at Lyons, then at Tours, and conferred important privileges on the fairs at Lyons. He attracted traders and foreign craftsmen in every way he could and concluded commercial treaties with Portugal, England and the German Hansa. He even knew how to make use of what was disordered in the spirit and the society of his time : shady types, spies, unscrupulous lawyers and adventurers of every sort.

He had sleepless cunning, a cynical sense of realities, practical judgment, a greedy eye and a hand prompt to seize. But, taking all his capacities into account, one cannot compare him with the great Capetians of the 13th century, either for his grasp of the whole picture or for love of the people, or for his idea of the royal office. He was, in spite of all, a Valois — infirm, highly excitable, cruel ; he dealt harshly with the people. Unexpected luck made half his fortune, and death, which struck down successively those he feared or whose inheritance he awaited, was his best accomplice. One cannot overlook his fatal lack of foresight in allowing the house of Austria to seat itself in the West.

Important in its practical results, Louis XI's reign is equally so in the realm of the mind. It marks the coming of modern politics, of politics which seeks an end in itself, outside all preoccupation with religion, justice or morality : in short, politics for politics' sake, such as was already practised by the Italian princes and republics, and such as it is later described by Machiavelli. It is the bourgeois idea of politics.

Regency of the Beaujeu

Louis XI passed the last period of his life barricaded in his castle of Plessis-lès-Tours, in terror at the approach of death. He tried up to the last to bargain with sickness by loading his doctor, Jacques Coitier, with presents, and with Heaven by giving money to the churches or begging the intervention of holy men, such as the hermit, François de Paule. Even when moribund, he did not cease his chatter. He died 30 August 1483.

His son, Charles VIII, was thirteen : puny and ill-made, red-headed, with a fixed look and nervous temperament, hasty and headstrong, but of an affable character : sprig of a race that seemed to reserve its degenerates for the throne.

Louis XI's daughter, Anne, nine years older, was a solider character. She had married Pierre de Beaujeu. With her husband she assumed the tutelage of her little brother.

The Beaujeu saved the work of Louis XI against the

demands of the States General of 1484 and against an aristocratic rising, the 'Mad War', of 1485. The king's brilliant
cousin, Louis, Duke of Orléans, leader of the malcontents,
succeeded only in getting himself defeated and taken at
St.-Aubin-du-Cormier in 1488. A large French army forced
the young heiress of the duchy of Brittany, Anne, to marry
Charles VIII.

The monarchy, for a time, was free from all menace. It
needed only to be on guard against its own spirit of adventure.

CHAPTER II

France and Italy

❖

*Complexity of the 15th Century — Italian Renaissance —
Activity of Flanders and of Germany. First Printers —
French Luxury and Refinement — Displacement of Com-
munications from the Mediterranean towards the Atlantic —
Italian Influence on France — Expeditions of Charles VIII
and Louis XII*

THE 15th century — the age of Joan of Arc and Louis XI —
marks one of the most complex and fertilising periods in the
development of civilisation. In it the medieval spirit attains
forms of refinement very near to corruption, while it is
surprised by discoveries of every kind, already expanding its
horizons. This century presents, in certain of its works, a
mixture of extreme maturity and youth, a subtle equilibrium
that does not recur again.

This complexity — easy to recognise in intellectual life,
in manners and, especially, the arts — results at bottom from
a like complexity in human commerce and the currents of
wealth.

Italian Renaissance

From ancient times, commercial life was concentrated in
the Mediterranean basin, along the course of traffic between
East and West. Each time that this traffic was interrupted by
whatever event, wealth contracted in the West. So the Arab
invasion, followed by the Norman incursions, appears to be
one of the chief causes of the sudden set-back to civilisation in
the West in the 9th century. On the other hand, each time
that traffic between Asia and Europe was freed, there followed

a new impulse of civilisation in the West. Such was the case after the first Crusades, which were followed by the expansion of the age of St. Louis.

In the 14th century, while the realm of France was undergoing the ravages of the English invasion, the Italian merchants — taking the place of the declining Byzantines — conquered or occupied all the commercial routes of the East. The Genoese — early established at Pera — and the Venetians installed factories, colonies or ports not only in the Mediterranean basin, but around the Black Sea and up to the coast of the Sea of Azov. From then on, wealth flowed into Italy ; luxury, the arts and all forms of culture flourished there.

At the beginning of the 15th century, as a result of technical progress in ship building and navigation, the maritime expansion of the Italian republics takes on an imperial character. Venice, notably, becomes the queen of commerce : she has more than three thousand ships, employs 36,000 sailors, plants her flag — the lion of St. Mark — on the coasts of the Adriatic and as far as the mouth of the Don. Her head or doge every year goes on board a gilded galley, the *Bucentaur*, and throws a gold ring into the sea as a sign of espousal. All the Italian towns in varying degrees share in this expansion and, to protect their wealth, build walls, maintain troops, pay *condottieri* who later become their dukes or princes. Florence, especially — where the Medici, thanks to their gold and their sly demagogic politics, are transforming themselves from merchants into tyrants — is the great centre of banking and industry.

In spite of her divisions, and in the same measure that wealth feeds the rivalries or emulation of its states, Italy produces a magnificent flowering of works of every kind. She becomes once more the chief focus of Western civilisation. This is the 'Italian Renaissance', the creative impulse of which lasts for two centuries, from Petrarch to Michelangelo.

The intellectual character of this movement is that of individualism, breaking with the collective disciplines of the 'Christendom' of the Middle Ages. The individual gradually

gains on the group ; liberty breaks the bonds of social dependence. In politics, individualism, abolishing the intermediary
orders between the citizen and public power, produces tyranny
or absolute monarchy ; and this in turn, by accustoming
citizens to the undisputed supremacy of the state, prepares the
way for the fusion of state and nation, otherwise called national
sovereignty.

Activity of Flanders and of Germany.   First Printers

While Italy thus finds fortune and glittering prestige,
another focus of wealth, culture and art develops in the North
of Europe — in Flanders and Germany.   Certain factors that
operate to Italy's profit also do to Northern Europe's.   The
dispersion of political power secures a quasi-independence to
trading towns and a sort of pre-eminence to international
trade.   Technical progress in navigation facilitates traffic in
the North Sea and the Baltic.   The organisation of regular
stages on the land routes between Flanders, Germany, the
Danube, the Carpathian passes and the Black Sea, is another
factor. . . . Yet other causes favour the civilisation of the
North.   Most important is the rise of industry and the trading
companies.

For several centuries Europe bought from Asia and Africa
products the demand for which grew with improved standards
of living and particularly with the development of towns.
These products were spices of every kind, silk, gum and
lacquer, perfumes, gold and precious stones.   Their prices
varied with the number of middlemen, the transhipments
necessary, the customs paid and distances covered.   Spices
were sold three times dearer at Alexandria than at Calicut,
incense five times dearer than at Mecca.   The aims in commerce
were then, first, to seek the shortest routes to the East ;
second, to economise the West's diminishing reserves of gold
and silver, by offering manufactured objects in exchange for
exotic products.

The Italians were shippers, importers and bankers, but

— except at Florence — they had few industries. Flanders possessed a powerful cloth-industry which had been exporting its products for a long time. As for Germany, it was the country, above all, of the technical arts. Nürnberg and Augsburg were the leading centres of the artisan crafts of Europe. The great commercial association known as the Hanseatic League comprised eighty towns, among the most prosperous being Lübeck, Hamburg, Bremen, Danzig, Cologne. Like the Templars formerly, it had its fortified trading-posts in the whole of Northern Europe and right in the heart of Russia. Its four chief stations were at Novgorod in Russia, Bergen in Norway, Bruges in Flanders and London. It maintained armed forces and possessed ships of war as well as merchant fleets. Lastly, the fairs of Antwerp had become the meeting-place of the merchants of the West, and an international Exchange was founded there in 1460.

This economic activity supported in the Northern countries, notably in Flanders, a series of great painters like Hubert and Jan van Eyck — who painted the famous retable at Ghent, the 'Adoration of the Lamb' — and in Germany, dynasties of armourers and goldsmiths, sculptors, painters and engravers from whom sprang such men of genius as Dürer and the Holbeins, elder and younger.

In the Low Countries, at Haarlem, one Laurent Coster — at the beginning of the 15th century, it seems — first thought of the principle of printing by 'characters' or movable letters. The invention was carried into effect, between 1440 and 1450, at Mainz, and was put into practice by two citizens, Johann Gutenberg, who worked first at Strasburg, and his associate Peter Schoeffer.

Printing, in permitting the rapid and unrestricted diffusion, at a low price, of news and writings, of thought and the sciences, transformed the conditions of human progress. A first printing-press was set up in Paris in 1470 by the Rector of the University, Guillaume Fichet.

French Luxury and Refinement

These two great movements, economic, intellectual and artistic — the Italian on one side, the Flemish and German on the other — were in constant contact with each other. They were in communication through France, which was thus subject to varied influences under which she reacted according to her condition at the moment.

The regions of France that benefited most from the meeting of these two influences were those traversed by the route from Italy to Flanders — those precisely that the King of France only recovered at the end of the 15th century : Burgundy and Provence. Hence the leading place occupied in French civilisation and art of the 15th century by the Burgundy of the Dukes and the Provence of Count René, better known as King René because of his rights to the crown of Naples. On the banks of the Rhône, too, since the 14th century, the Popes at Avignon, builders of palaces and patrons of the arts, established a centre of artistic activity which attracted Northern and Italian artists.

Up to the reign of Louis XI, the main current of traffic and the arts passed outside the realm of France. Under Charles VII, a first effort was made by Jacques Cœur to attract part of the contacts of the West with the Mediterranean basin towards Aigues-Mortes, Montpellier, Lyons and Bourges. Jacques Cœur, however, had to transfer some of his affairs to Marseilles and to Italy. In the North, it was the towns under the economic influence of the Flemish-Burgundian group, like Arras, St.-Quentin, Compiègne, that built sumptuous houses — evidences of their wealth.

It was a masterly move on the part of Louis XI to grant exceptional privileges to the fairs of Lyons and so to intercept the traffic between Italy and the Northern countries to the profit of the realm. The success of this move made Lyons in a quarter of a century one of the most flourishing places in the world, the chief centre of Western communications and

the intellectual focus of the French Renaissance : a success
that contributed to draw the policy of the kings into the
Italian wars.

If, up to Louis XI, the Flemish-Burgundian state remained
the chief beneficiary of the economic revival, of the love for
luxury and fêtes, of refined or exotic fashions, the same taste
for the arts spread through the whole of France. At the court
of the kings, in the great appanages — with the Duke of
Berry, the Duke of Bourbon and even the Duke of Brittany —
there was a singular mixture of financial embarrassment and
extravagance, of poverty and patronage. Out of which came
works of art like those of the school exemplified by the Master
of Moulins, like the treasury of miniatures of the *Très riches
Heures du duc de Berry*, or the admirable portraits of the
Touraine painter, Jean Foucquet.

French castles at this period became palaces with towers
or ramparts half defensive, half decorative : such as Pierrefonds,
Mehun-sur-Yèvre in Berry, or Bonaguil in Guyenne. The
churches were covered with 'flamboyant' motifs. Sculpture
pushed realism sometimes into the extremes of tragic expres-
sionism. The artistic patronage of the middle class already
competed to a fair extent with that of the princes, while the
nobility of chivalry went to ruin. Down in the poorest
classes in the towns this contrast appeared between misery
and gay life, refinement and depravity, expressed with so much
vivacity in the poems of Villon.

Few epochs have produced types at once so contrasting
as that of Joan of Arc, who was the incarnation of the people's
purity of heart, that of the decadent 'Bohemian' represented
by Villon, the type of the business entrepreneur as we see it
in Jacques Cœur, and the cold politician as Philippe de
Commines, the historian of Louis XI, depicts that monarch.

From the Mediterranean to the Atlantic

From the middle of the 15th century the line of communication between East and West, which so enriched the

Italian republics, was threatened. On 29 May 1453 the Turks, under Mahomet II, took Constantinople. Some years after, they conquered the Morea and then Bosnia. Soon they dominated territories from the Adriatic to the Sea of Azov, from the Carpathians to the Euphrates. The trading-posts of Genoa and Venice in the Orient were ruined, the Mediterranean trade-routes with Asia cut. Traffic did not recover till much later and with difficulty, in the 16th century, by the alliance of Francis I, King of France, and the Sultan Soliman.

This disaster to Mediterranean commerce hit the Italian republics first. Its repercussions affected the whole West: they were both economic and also, more strictly, monetary. The excess in imports of luxury goods, without counterpart in exports, brought about a dearth of means of payment. Gold and silver, disappearing gradually, doubled their value in a century: money became scarce, the price of goods fell. The European in quest of new sources of precious metals and unexplored riches turned towards the ocean routes which the progress in navigation at sea — the perfected compass, portulans or marine charts, star-maps or astronomical tables — enabled him now to attempt.

Portugal was first to seek her fortune in this direction. Freed early from the Moslem dominion which she drove back into Africa, Portugal, from the mid-14th century onwards, discovered the Canaries, Madeira, the Azores. In 1433 her sailors reached Cape Bojador — already visited by a Norman, Jean de Béthencourt — and in 1445 Cape Verde. In 1486 Bartholomew Diaz reached the Cape of Good Hope and rounded Africa. In 1498 Vasco da Gama crossed the Indian Ocean, touched India at Calicut and prepared the way for Portuguese settlement on the coast of Malabar.

However, men were searching for another route to India by the west. Italian geographers, Genoese bankers, the entourage of the Kings of Portugal and Castile were speculating on the earth's being round and on the idea that the eastern coasts of Asia were not so far from the western coast of

Europe. From 1492 to 1502, Christopher Columbus, setting out from Spain, crossed the Atlantic four times; he first landed in the West Indies, later he reached the mouth of the Orinoco and finally Honduras, believing that he had touched Asia. A Bull promulgated by Pope Alexander VI, 3 May 1493, partitioned the world to be discovered between the two Kings of Castile and Portugal. A crowd of explorers — Portuguese, Spaniards, English, French, Dutch — leapt forward to the search for new lands. The main currents of wealth shifted from the Mediterranean to the Atlantic. The economic, political and social equilibrium of Europe was profoundly changed by it, the intellectual and moral horizon prodigiously expanded.

From the political point of view, the great discoveries had the result — after displaying in Portugal a dazzling flame of wealth, magnificence and art — of furnishing Spain with the means to exercise the imperial function which Charles V imposed on her : a function of which England possessed herself later, at least as to the empire of the seas.

From the economic aspect, the influx of gold and silver from the new lands lowered the value of money and greatly increased the nominal prices of goods, encouraged trade, speculation and all exchange operations — in other words, money-changers, brokers, transporters and other middle men.

On the other hand — here is the social aspect of it — the class that lived by fixed dues and rents, the nobility of feudal origin soon found itself so poor that it either had to beg favours or gifts from the king, or sell its lands to the new rich of trade and commerce. The king himself, whose finances were affected by the debasing of the currency and the growing dearness of things, in order to meet expenses, ended by selling offices and public places to the sons of grocers, drapers and bankers, who gradually formed the ruling class in the state under the name *noblesse de robe*.

So modern Europe, capitalist and bureaucratic, was born.

Italian Influence on France

Faced with this great change, France hesitated and badly bungled her maritime opportunities, which were equal to those of Portugal, Spain or England. She experienced a sort of retarded impulse of the chivalrous spirit and lent herself — instead of turning her forces towards the Atlantic or the North — to wasting them in a vain attempt to conquer Italy.

Here appears one of the traits that are characteristic of our nation in the modern epoch : the dispersion of efforts and enterprises outside, the lack of plan or cohesion, of consistency in the policy of expansion. After Louis XI, the unity of France was practically achieved. The English having been defeated, and Burgundy and Provence reunited to the domain of the crown, the realm acquired that ease and activity which the balance of her resources naturally produced. It remained to direct her surplus energies wisely. France is an agricultural and continental country, open to four seas, predisposed to centralisation, but divided among divergent needs of expansion, towards the Ocean, Flanders, the Rhine and Italy, towards the Orient even and Africa. She never succeeded in choosing definitely between her external ambitions, either on land or sea.

At the end of the 15th century, at the very moment when the Italian republics were declining and the princes, less sure of their resources, were beginning to look for protection or loans from abroad, France got a fixation on Italy. It would seem that the newly annexed provinces, Burgundy and Provence, induced the realm to incline towards the South-East. For so long the rich trade on the road from Italy to Flanders had by-passed France : now it was a question not only of exploiting it, but of moving into Italy to take possession of all the riches and arts which had been debarred. While the Portuguese, Spaniards and Genoese launched their navigators on the ocean to discover unknown deposits of gold and silver, French chivalry — impoverished by the Hundred Years War and thirsting for wealth — expected to find fortune and treasure in Italy. After all, the inheritance of the house of Anjou, fallen to the house of France by King René's death, carried with it rights to or claims on the kingdom of Naples, which were withheld by the King of Aragon.

Then, too, since the end of Louis XI's reign, the Italians had taken to coming to France to seek benefices and employments. The French dreamed of remunerative adventures in Italy. The Italians knew that France was exploitable and willing to pay for any political services and lessons in education, culture or art that she received. For more than half a century the French tried to conquer Italy, while the Italians colonised France : our kings granted them innumerable favours, gifts of money, employments and lands. The French victories in Italy were ephemeral ; but many Italian families acquired a permanent footing with us. The 'French Renaissance' was good business for the Italians.

Expeditions of Charles VIII and Louis XII

When barely come of age, Charles VIII thought only of Italy. He disengaged himself from other affairs, abandoned Artois and Franche-Comté to Maximilian of Austria, Mary of Burgundy's husband, and restored Roussillon to Ferdinand of Aragon. What interested him was the alliance offered him by the intriguer Ludovico Sforza, Duke of Milan, to make war against the King of Naples. In September 1494 he crossed the Alps and five months later made a triumphant entry into Naples, which welcomed him. No sooner was he installed there than all Italy turned against him and he had to beat a retreat. His enemies in coalition formed an army which barred the way at Fornovo. But the furious charges — *furia francese* — of the king's cavalry forced a way out (5 July 1495).

An accident suddenly put an end in 1498 to the puerile career of Charles VIII. Dying childless, he left the crown to his cousin, Louis of Orléans — Louis XII — descendant of Charles VI's brother and Valentina Visconti, daughter of the first Duke of Milan. The new king then had claims not only

on Naples, like his predecessor, but also on Milan. He set
out at once for the Milanese and captured it. He then contested the kingdom of Naples with the Spaniards in a war in
which Bayard achieved fame — the knight *sans peur et sans
reproche* — and finally had to cede that territory to the Spanish
general Gonsalvo de Cordova, by a truce signed in 1504. A
few years later the French renewed the war in Italy in the
service of a 'Holy League' formed by the bellicose Pope
Julius II against the Venetians. Louis XII's army defeated the
Venetians at Agnadello in 1509. Soon after the Pope changed
sides, betrayed the King of France and ranged against him
England, Spain, Venice and the Swiss. A young hero with
a great talent for war, the prince Gaston de Foix defended the
Milanese brilliantly against the Spaniards, but was killed at
Ravenna on the day of his greatest victory, 11 April 1512 ;
after which, the Milanese was lost. France was invaded by
the English, the Germans and the Swiss. Louis XII tried to
buy them off with money. In 1515 he died.

The crown passed to his son-in-law and cousin the young
Count of Angoulême, who became Francis I. This handsome
young man of twenty, drawn on by the lure of chivalry,
hastened in his turn to win glory in Italy. He secured
the alliance of the Venetians against the Duke of Milan and
the Swiss. In the month of August 1515, his army crossed the
Alps by the pass of Argentière — where 3,000 sappers drove a
way in a few days — and made a sudden descent on Lombardy.
The Swiss fell back to Marignano, near Milan. There they gave
battle, 13-14 September, and, in spite of their solid defence, had
finally to give ground before the French infantry. 'For two
thousand years', wrote Francis I to his mother, 'there has not
been so grand or so hard a battle.' It was a hand-to-hand
engagement without any manœuvring, decided by the reinforcements from Venice.

Some months later, the Swiss signed a treaty of perpetual
peace with the King of France, by which they undertook never
to fight against him and to permit him to recruit from them

as many mercenaries as he pleased, in return for the payment
of an annual sum. In the same year, 1516, Pope Leo X conceded
the king the concordat of Bologna. Lastly, by the Treaty of
Noyon, Francis I acquired the Milanese, while the new King
of Spain, Charles, kept the kingdom of Naples.

When the war was renewed five years later, in Italy and
elsewhere, it was for France a question of something quite
different from chivalrous adventures and exploits : a question
of holding at bay the new and formidable power that the great-
grandson of Charles the Bold — Charles V — now raised
against the kingdom.

The expeditions of Charles VIII and Francis I into Italy,
with the contacts and relations of every kind that resulted from
them, brought about the expansion of the artistic and intellectual movement which historians call the French Renaissance.
In reality, it was not a rebirth, properly speaking, but a
quickening of, and a divergence from, certain traits of the
French genius which lent themselves to Italian modes.

The Renaissance — in part a negation of the creative effort
of the French Middle Ages — is nothing other than a return to
antique forms under the inspiration of Italy. French artists
at first copy the Italian works, then gradually make use of them
to attain a new creative phase, that of 'classic art'.

Italy brings no instruction to French builders and architects, except for the decoration of buildings. The Gothic
style long persists, especially in church architecture. On the
other hand, quite early there appear on civic buildings and even
on the churches, figures clothed in Roman fashion, sculptured
medallions, pseudo-antiques and bas-reliefs. One sees busts
of Caesars and effigies of pagan gods decorating chapels as well
as castles and private houses. The French architects, heirs of
the skill of the old Gothic masters, often succeed in giving to
these artificial and borrowed ornaments a living expression
that the Italian models sometimes lack. From the beginning
of the 16th century on, copies of the antique in France display

an ease and verve in which one recognises the work of hands made supple by a tradition of their own, that of the virtuosos of the flamboyant style and of realistic sculpture.

In the intellectual field, the Renaissance was more fertile than in the arts. For a couple of centuries, the exclusive admiration of ancient literature and history became a dogma with a class of Italian scholars — the Humanists. From the day when the printing-press permitted the diffusion of classical texts, learning spread and, with it, the taste for criticism — literary, philosophical, scientific.

The extent of the change the Renaissance brought about in mind and morals, as in the arts, is illustrated by the fact that, less than a century after the martyrdom of Joan of Arc, the stalls of a cathedral — like that of Auch — were decorated with figures of Venus and Cupid, Hercules and Ganymede. With the images of the saints and angels to whom the Maid had prayed are mingled fauns and bacchantes.

CHAPTER III

Francis I and Charles V

❖

Character of Francis I — Charles V's Position in Europe —
Rivalry of Francis I and Charles V — Henry II and the End
of the Italian Wars — Spirit of the Renaissance

In the Middle Ages, from the 11th to the 15th century, conflict — armed or political — hardly ever ceased between the
French and the English. The Capetian kingdom was made
in the struggle against the English, or, more exactly, against
the ambition of the Kings of England — heirs of the feudal
houses of Anjou, Normandy and Guyenne, then claimants to
the inheritance of Philip the Fair — to constitute a Franco-
English state. It was against the English that France gained
consciousness, so to say, of her nationality. It was the idea
of the Franco-English state that was finally defeated by the
popular mission of Joan of Arc. In the modern period, maritime discoveries having changed the whole conditions of
expansion for the English, the Franco-English conflict was no
longer continental, but naval and colonial.

Starting with the 16th century, the continental conflict
was between France and the house of Austria. This conflict
lasted in the reflexes of diplomacy up to our time. The bias
it created affected the treaties of 1919.

In the same way as the Franco-English conflict, earlier,
had for its occasion the divorce of Louis VII and Eleanor of
Aquitaine, the source of the conflict between France and the
house of Austria may be traced to the error of Louis XI in
pushing — by his tactlessness — Mary of Burgundy, Charles
the Bold's daughter, into marrying Maximilian of Austria.

In times when kingdoms and lordships were considered

the property of a family or 'house', a simple marriage could change the map of Europe. The young man who mounted the Spanish throne in 1516, Charles V, was the heir of four houses — Burgundy, Austria, Aragon and Castile. He accumulated thus the Low Countries, Flanders, Artois, Franche-Comté, the arch-duchy of Austria and its dependencies, Aragon, Sardinia, Sicily and the kingdom of Naples, Castile and the Spanish colonies of America. In spite of Francis I, three years later, in 1519, Charles succeeded, by hard bargaining, in getting himself elected Emperor of Germany. He was only nineteen.

Character of Francis I

The conflict between the exigencies of French and those of Imperial policy would have broken out under no matter what princes. But the two men who began it, Francis I and Charles V, presented a contrast in personalities which one would have said was made by design for the gallery.

Francis I was a strong and healthy Valois, splendidly endowed for life — a rare case in that family which, since John the Good, had only produced infirm or sickly kings. The witness of contemporaries is unanimous : 'as handsome a prince as the world has seen'. His good looks lay doubtless in his bearing and expression rather than in the king's features, which lent themselves to caricature. Always dressed richly and with care, he was in deportment, dignity and easy grace, the ideal of nobility. He loved violent exercise, tournaments and duels, and even war as a sort of game of bravery. He talked a great deal, with a facility of learning and intelligence that gave his charm all the more effect. He was cultivated and wrote verses ; he loved literature and the arts, fêtes and women. He has been reproached with displaying a mixture of sudden whims and indecision, irresponsibility and bungling, egoism and senseless extravagance. . . . In truth, he had the most brilliant, if not the safest, qualities that a prince can display to the world, with almost all the defects of a spoilt

Francis I

child. He carried on the Valois tradition of chivalry with
splendour and he made superb use of it in some respects —
especially in the art of patronage. His intentions were good.
He had set-backs, but also strokes of good fortune for him
and his realm. He is one of the most fascinating figures in the
history of our kings.

Francis I benefited at the beginning of his reign from the
prosperity that had developed in France during the last years
of Louis XI. For forty years the realm — notably increased
in size and open now to international traffic — had not
experienced serious war on its territory. Charles VIII's and
Louis XII's Italian expeditions had had no effect on the
internal peace. New generations replaced the fearful gaps
made earlier in all classes by the Hundred Years War, by
epidemics and famines. This increase of population extended
clearings and cultivation and gave trade opportunities all the
greater, since a single authority and system of order henceforward protected all the main routes of communication with
abroad. An historian of the time, Claude de Seyssel, noticed
this fact : 'for one merchant that one found in the time of
Louis XI, one finds more than fifty. And there is nowadays
less difficulty in going to Rome, Naples, London and overseas
than there used to be formerly in going to Lyons or Geneva.'
At the Lyons fairs the money that changed hands amounted to
more than two million gold crowns. France, too, began to
be interested in distant discoveries and to draw profit from
them. The ports of Dieppe, St.-Malo, La Rochelle, Bordeaux
went ahead. Le Havre was founded in 1517. A Dieppe
shipowner sent ships to America, to the Indies and as far as
Sumatra. On behalf of Francis I, the Florentine Verazzano,
and later Jacques Cartier of St.-Malo, explored the North
American coast. The estuary of the St. Lawrence and Canada
were discovered by Cartier in 1534.

So the court of Francis I from the beginning provided a
spectacle of external wealth and magnificence that had not
hitherto been equalled. The needy nobles put themselves in

the pay of the sovereign and competed with each other in zeal or intrigue to obtain employments, favours and gifts from him. The middle class and the people were too content with the internal tranquillity to criticise the means. Royal power became personal and despotic, with favourites of both sorts, counsellors and agents promoted or disgraced according to the day's humour. Government was directed by a council or dominated successively by personal favourites : Chancellor Duprat, the Constable de Montmorency, Cardinal de Tournon, Admiral d'Annebaut, joining with the favourites, among whom the Duchesse d'Etampes was the most famous.

But soon the expenses of the court, the gifts distributed in profusion and the cost of new wars exhausted the Treasury. It was found necessary to tighten up and centralise the administration of the finances, constantly increase taxes, to borrow and thus start — what had been unknown hitherto — a public debt with state interest, and to ask capital advances from foreign bankers. Lastly — a very serious innovation — public employments and offices were sold, and since that made them practically hereditary it increased the monarchy's need for money. From then on everybody aimed at buying an office : bureaucracy became one of the characteristics of French society, and the multiplying of offices led to a growing centralisation of the state.

The great feudal houses had disappeared, except that of Bourbon. Its head, the Constable Charles de Bourbon, married to a daughter of Anne of Beaujeu, was very wealthy, possessing the Bourbonnais, Auvergne, the March and Beaujolais. After his wife's death in 1521 he quarrelled with Francis I's mother, Louise of Savoy, a grasping woman who disputed part of his inheritance. In exasperation he committed treason and fled to the service of Charles V ; his estates were confiscated. The Bourbons continued in disfavour till the time of Henry IV.

Charles V's Position in Europe

Francis I's kingdom constituted a block of territory, a homogeneous nation, a state already centralised. But it was three parts surrounded by the Empire of Charles V. It could not expand or, perhaps, breathe without conflicting at some point with this empire which stifled all chances of French expansion and, moreover, was a direct threat to the country.

Charles V's possessions were three or four times larger than Francis I's. But the Emperor was not satisfied : he aimed at European ascendancy and claimed, in particular, the whole heritage of the house of Burgundy.

His personality was a mixture of true grandeur and oddness, as complex as his empire, the offspring of marriages between four families of contrary temperaments. He had the pride of his Burgundian ancestors and the solemn megalomania of Charles the Bold, the calculation of the Germans, the cunning and tenacity of the Aragonese, the mystical and imperialist piety of Castile. His countenance, which betrayed a determination to dominate, with its projecting chin and under-jaw, expressed too a noble self-sufficiency, and a set expression, vaguely inhuman.

His possessions bordered France without a break, by Flanders, Artois, the German Empire and Franche-Comté, from the North Sea to the junction of the Seille with the Saône. The Duke of Savoy who, by his possession of Bresse, reached to the gates of Lyons, soon became his ally. In Italy, Charles possessed Naples and Sicily and had dependants everywhere. He captured the Milanese and held Genoa and Florence at his convenience. From Naples to Sardinia, and from Sardinia to Spain, he was able to cut the Western Mediterranean. If he allied himself with England, he closed all the outlets from France. Finally, to the north and east, one victory was enough to put Paris in danger.

But his position had a certain weakness in general as well as defects in particular. The great weakness was that his possessions were dispersed, badly linked together, strangers to one another : if some parts gave way, the dislocation of the rest might follow. He had to live with this fear and, as the danger came clearly from French expansion, his determined plan was to beat France down or, at least, to hold her in check. The particular defects of his position were in certain areas of instability or weakness, like Lorraine and the Three Bishoprics (Metz, Toul, Verdun), or like Savoy and Italy itself with its kaleidoscopic republics and its princes up for sale.

Such are the conditions of the struggle between Charles V and France. France strikes at the points of particular weakness, in Savoy, in Italy, then in Lorraine ; she knits together alliances in Germany and, far beyond Italy, with the Turks. Charles V, for his part, ceaselessly tightens his pressure on the realm, in the North, from Italy, even by the invasion of Provence. Both sides try to neutralise England or to win her.

Rivalry of Francis I and Charles V

The first war turned into disaster for the French. At the interview of the Field of the Cloth of Gold, the king failed to win Henry VIII of England, who thereupon gave his support to Charles V. The Imperialists invaded northern France and laid siege to Mézières. In Italy, the Milanese was lost. The Constable de Bourbon went over to the enemy and led the Imperialists to ravage Provence and attack Marseilles. Francis I reacted quickly, took the offensive and reconquered the Milanese. Then, at Pavia, he met with a complete defeat and was himself taken prisoner, at the mercy of his enemy (24 February 1525). He bought back his liberty by the Treaty of Madrid (14 January 1526), which gave the whole of Burgundy to Charles V and handed over the king's sons as hostages.

But once he was free, Francis refused to give up Burgundy. French diplomacy was very effective : it produced a more favourable attitude on the part of England, concluded an alliance with the Protestant princes of Germany and negotiated a close alliance with the Sultan Solyman the Magnificent, whose victorious armies in Hungary were now drawing near to Vienna and threatening Charles V's possessions in the rear. In 1536 the famous Capitulations were signed by which France received the privilege of trading on all the coasts of the Turkish Empire, with the protectorate of the Holy Places and of the Catholics in the Orient : the foundation of French pre-eminence in the Levant. The fleet of the Pasha Barbarossa joined with the French fleet against Spanish ships in the Mediterranean.

This diplomatic campaign, bold and in some ways revolutionary — since the Infidel and the heretics allied themselves with the Most Christian King to conquer Most Catholic Spain — reversed the fortunes of war. After a new check in Italy, Francis returned to the attack and conquered Bresse, Bugey, Savoy and Piedmont. Charles V invaded Provence again, but was repulsed with heavy losses.

Some years later, the King of England, Henry VIII, went over to Charles V's side once more ; the Spaniards invaded Champagne and got as far as Meaux, some leagues from Paris. But the Duc d'Enghien's army in Italy brought off the victory of Cerisola (1544).

Francis I died in 1547. The net benefit of his reign was twofold : the affirmation of French unity and power, which brilliantly came through a most critical period ; the formation of a diplomacy, the principles and methods of which remained effective for more than a century.

Henry II and the End of the Italian Wars

As vigorous in body, with more application but much less charm and liveliness than Francis, Henry II, who succeeded him, might have achieved more renown than he did if he had not died unexpectedly, in an accident, after reigning only twelve years, and if his policy had not been abruptly deflected by alarm at the progress of the Protestant Reformation. He showed an absurd weakness for his mistress, who was much older than himself — Diane de Poitiers. But he had a counsellor of great good sense in the Constable Anne de Montmorency, an able general in the Duc de Guise, and valorous captains and clever diplomats whom he well knew how to employ, in spite of the intrigues of the court.

The first part of his reign was fortunate and even glorious. He had the newly acquired provinces — Bresse, Savoy, Piedmont — wisely administered. He occupied the Three Bishoprics — Metz, Toul, Verdun — which had remained outside the realm since the Carolingian partitions. This advance threatened Charles V's empire at its most vulnerable point. With an army of 60,000 the Emperor tried to recapture Metz. The Duc de Guise, who defended the town, inflicted on him a heavy defeat. In Italy the French established themselves at Siena, in the Tuscan Maremma, and gained a foothold in Corsica, re-establishing thus the maritime link between the kingdom and the peninsula.

Ill and discouraged, Charles V abdicated in 1555, leaving Spain, Naples, Franche-Comté and the Low Countries to his son Philip II; Austria, the hereditary possessions of the Habsburgs and the Imperial Crown to his brother Ferdinand, already King of Bohemia and Hungary. The old Emperor retired to die in the monastery of San Yuste. France seemed to have won the game.

But in 1557, led on by Pope Paul IV — a Neapolitan Caraffa, who dreamed of liberating his country from the Spaniards — and by the ambition of the Guise family, Henry committed the mistake of reopening hostilities. The Duc de Guise failed to conquer Naples. The Spaniards invaded France from the North and crushed the Constable de Montmorency's army at St.-Quentin (August 1557). On returning from Italy, Guise fortunately captured Calais from the English, allies of the Spaniards (January 1558).

France and Spain no longer had the resources to continue the war. Henry II was preoccupied with defending religious orthodoxy, in his own realm and even at court, against the progress of the Protestant Reformation. Philip II had the same cares on his mind. The two kings hastened to sign the Treaty of Cateau-Cambrésis in April 1559. France kept the Three Bishoprics and Calais. She lost Bresse, Bugey, Savoy and Piedmont, which were restored to the Duke of Savoy, Emmanuel Philibert. She abandoned Corsica and the Tuscan coast.

Spain remained powerful, but deprived of the Imperial prestige. France had at the last moment forfeited half her gains; but she had totally ruined Charles V's designs and fortified her unity in the struggle to such a point that twenty-five years of civil wars were not to diminish her territory by an inch.

Henry II perished in July 1559, three months after the conclusion of peace, having been wounded in the eye by a lance-thrust in the tournament given for the marriage of his daughter Elizabeth with Philip II, widower of Mary Tudor.

Spirit of the Renaissance

The period that covers the conflict of Francis I and Henry II with Charles V, marks the highest achievement of the artistic, intellectual and social forms of the Renaissance in the West. The power of these opponents, the resources at their disposal — the King of France by the wealth of his kingdom, the Emperor by that of the Low Countries and the influx of precious metals into Spain; the sums they pour out in support of their cause, notably in Italy; lastly, their similar love of luxury, refinement, pomp — provoke on both sides a magnificent flowering of achievement of every kind.

In Italy, famous painters like Leonardo da Vinci, Raphael, Michelangelo, then Titian, Tintoretto, Veronese, dominate the arts. In 16th-century France, as in the Middle Ages, it is above all the architects and sculptors who show genius. Pierre Lescot, of Paris, designs and begins the building of the new palace of the Louvre. Philibert Delorme, son of a Lyons architect, builds the castle of Anet, near Dreux, for Diane de Poitiers, before constructing the palace of the Tuileries for Catherine de Medici. Jean Bullant, architect to the Constable de Montmorency, builds the castle of Ecouen, near Paris. Thenceforward the Classical style, Graeco-Roman in inspiration, is established — a complete break with Gothic tradition. Before, during the first years of the century, the castles built — notably in the Loire valley, in Touraine and Anjou — still recalled in their decorative effects the forms of the older castles : such as the châteaux of Amboise, Blois, Chambord, Chenonceaux, Azay-le-Rideau, le Lude. And right up to that time Gothic of the Flamboyant style continued to produce masterpieces, like the law courts at Rouen.

Among French sculptors, two schools can be recognised equally : one that continues and refines upon the realism of the preceding century, the other adopting the Classical style. The great artists of the first are : Michel Colombe, the Breton, maker of the Duke of Brittany's tomb at Nantes ; the Lorrainer, Ligier-Richier, who sculpts the 'Entombment' of the church of St.-Mihiel ; Pierre Bontemps, whose chief work is the tomb of Francis I at St.-Denis. The most celebrated sculptor of the new school is Jean Goujon, maker of the trophies of arms on the façade of the Louvre, of the 'Diana' at Anet and of the 'Nymphs' of the fountain of the Innocents at Paris.

Leonardo da Vinci, a sort of demi-god of the Renaissance, died in France, at the manor of Clos-Lucé, near Amboise, as Francis I's guest. Francis also invites Benvenuto Cellini, master sculptor, to his court and gives him employment. Bernard Palissy of Périgord, scholar and artist, recovers the secret of enamel applied to terracotta. The Pénicauds and the Limousins, both families from Limoges, excel in the painting of enamel on copper.

The first half of the 16th century is the time when humanism spreads and triumphs in Western Europe. In leaving Italy, it becomes less artificial and draws nearer to life. The erudition, the criticism of texts, the feeling for form which it took with the Italians are enriched, outside Italy, with the gift of observation, the deep sensibility and thoughtfulness of the Western peoples who made medieval civilisation. This mixture brings about a sudden and expansive movement in the realm of the mind. In its Italian aspect, humanism is in danger of leading to a dry academicism. Transplanted abroad into a milieu more complex, richer and more realist, it produces the modern mind.

The Italian literature of this period shines above all in historical discourse, scholarship, poetry and the mock-heroic genre : it reflects the cult of antiquity, the intrigues, fêtes, the insatiable taste for *décor*, for the rhetorical and romantic, and for tragic or pleasing complication such as the small courts of the peninsula loved. Machiavelli, a Florentine official, writes the *Prince*, a sort of picture of political manners, then the *Discourses of Livy* and a *History of Florence*. Guicciardini, teacher and man of action, redacts in his cold style, the *History of Italy*. A poet full of the comic spirit, Ariosto, publishes *Orlando Furioso*, a mock epic. Later, Tasso produces a serious epic, a grave work of genius, the *Gerusalemme Liberata*.

Outside Italy the sap is more vigorous, temperaments more forceful. The Low Countries produce a great spirit in the person of Erasmus, 'Prince of Humanism', author of the *Praise of Folly* and of a Correspondence which may be compared with that of Voltaire.

In the 16th century appear some of the greatest names of French literature. There are the humanists properly speaking, given chiefly to learning — like Guillaume Budé, provost of the merchants of Paris, on whose advice Francis I created the chairs of the Collège de France ; and Henri Estienne, author of the *Trésor de la langue grecque*. Besides these, poets and prose-writers of the first rank arise. The poet of Francis I's court, Clément Marot, is still rather a graceful ballad-maker and imitator of the Latin poets. But with the poets of the Pléiade, Joachim du Bellay and Ronsard, we reach great poetry. Three prose-writers dominate French literature in this century, François Rabelais, Jean Calvin and Montaigne.

Rabelais, author of *Pantagruel*, in which the riotous verve of the Middle Ages and the intellectual intoxication of humanism jostle together tumultuously, is without doubt the most original writer in our history. Jean Calvin, the Protestant Reformer, in his *Christian Institutes* set an exemplary model of style in modern prose. Montaigne — born in 1533, published his *Essays* in 1580 — represents the highest development of a very French kind of mind, cultured and sceptical, consciously at ease in giving himself away and of a diffuse reflectiveness that is later found concentrated in the clear aggressive genius of Voltaire.

Science made rapid progress in this age. The Pole Copernicus revolutionised astronomy. The Swiss Paracelsus influenced medicine largely with his wide-ranging speculations. Andreas Vesalius of Brussels laid the foundations of the modern study of anatomy. The Spaniard Servetus speculated on the pulmonary circulation of the blood. Among Frenchmen, François Viète made improvements in algebra, Jean Fernel and Ambroise Paré were the creators of modern surgery.

The Renaissance is not at all a moral affair. It encourages artifice and ostentation, the decorative arts, representation in colour or design, luxury in extravagant and complex forms. It is all cavalcades, tournaments, 'joyous entries', receptions of princes, pageants : an endless display of inlaid armours, laces, velvets, gold brocades. Learning and art become the fashion. Appetites, however, remain gross ; integrity and decency give way on every side ; the taste for violence is encouraged by the cult of fine gestures. There is a style in the art of killing.

This licence engenders, by reaction from it, first the desire for reform, then religious fanaticism.

CHAPTER IV

The Reformation and the Wars of Religion

❖

*Decadence of the Institutions of the Church — First
Reformers: Calvin, Ignatius Loyola — Attitude of the
Monarchy to the Protestants. Catherine de Medici —
End of the Valois — Henry IV — The Edict of Nantes*

THE Christian religion had acted on men through faith and
through the institutions of the Church. The men of the
Middle Ages — very ready to denounce bad clerics and, like
St. Louis and Joan of Arc, to oppose the secular misdeeds of
individual representatives of the clergy — did not think of
separating their faith in the Gospel from their devotion to
the Church.

But, in the 16th century, in many men's minds and even
among the most religious peoples, a separation was made
between the Christian idea and obedience to the Church.
This movement, which tended at first only to a reform within,
ended later in declared protest against, the Church. Thus the
movement for reform became 'Protestant', breaking with and
in opposition to the authority of the Roman Pontiff.

Many factors conditioned the movement of Protestant
Reform. But the fact that stood out above all others was the
corruption of ecclesiastical institutions and the enfeeblement
of the evangelising spirit in the bulk of the clergy.

From the beginning the Church had been exposed to the
double risk of being engulfed in the material riches which
the piety of the faithful brought it, and of transforming the
cure of souls into the administration of temporal goods, in
direct touch with neither faith nor charity. Almost every
century had known a decline of the Christian ideal, followed
by a reform of the Church. Through controversies and

conflicts often embittered, the spirit of reform in the bosom of the Church had always won, in the end, against the most crying scandals and abuses. Still more, over the course of centuries the Church had always found within herself strength to renew or adapt her mission to circumstances. The history of monastic Orders and religious foundations in the Middle Ages is largely the history of reforms or readjustments of Christian action.

At the beginning of the 16th century the need for a severe reform, for a renewing of the ideal and a moral purifying of the clergy, was evident. Almost everywhere the clergy presented the spectacle of complete indifference to their true mission in life and of greed for material goods. Benefices and bishoprics were distributed as pensions or rewards to people who often did not reside at the place of their ministry, leaving vicars or sometimes 'farmers' there. Many parishes in poor districts had no priest. Abbeys were granted to 'commenda-tory' abbots, clerical or lay, who contented themselves with receiving the revenues to finance the expenses of their worldly life ; these set the worst examples of laxness. For intrigues, for vice and nepotism, as for worldly luxury and patronage of the arts, the court of Rome rivalled the most pagan of princely courts in Italy. The Popes themselves — an Alexander VI (Borgia), Julius II, Leo X, a Paul III — figured as splendid princes, pouring out the treasure of Christendom, promoting favourites, making war and governing according to the pre-cepts of Machiavelli — for their own profit or that of their family — but entirely without any sense of Christian mission.

That a far-going reform was necessary and urgent, believers had felt for nearly two centuries. There was danger for doctrine as well as in practice ; while a fraction of the higher clergy amused themselves by dabbling in profane learning, the lower clergy wallowed in crass ignorance. Since the Councils of Constance and of Basel in the first half of the 15th century, not only had the project of Church reform not advanced, but it seemed to come up against habits more and

more stubborn and increasingly sullen resistance on the part
of the Roman Curia.

The dignitaries of the clergy, insensible to the admonitions
of the elect among the faithful, took account too late of the
danger to the Church of such resistance. Italianised in spirit
and morals as never before, the higher personnel of the Church
judged Europe as a whole by the example of an Italy whose
people found their pleasure in contemplating the new *décor*
of Renaissance palaces and in acclaiming cardinals who gave
fêtes or alms. But Italy was not Europe, and the Europe of
the 16th century was not that of the early Middle Ages, under
the discipline of fear of the Devil. Men had learned to know,
to reason and to judge. The increase of communications, the
frequency of voyages, the circulation of news and the diffusion
of printed books no longer permitted the Church to conceal
her weaknesses from the watchful eyes of society.

Risks threatened on three sides : on that of the most
sensitive believers ; on minds which humanism had trained to
textual criticism ; lastly, on that of lay powers, kings or
princes, ready to possess themselves of the Church's goods.

Among believers, some left the Church to reform themselves, seeking reasons for their faith and a rule for their
conduct in the direct interpretation of Holy Scripture. Others
urged incessantly a reform of the Church and obtained it in
the end at the Council of Trent. Thus the Catholic Counter-
Reformation came into being to oppose the Protestant
Reformation.

Minds detached from belief by humanism attacked, sometimes cautiously, sometimes openly, the doctrinal and historic
position of the Church by means of a more or less radical
criticism. Some joined the Protestant Reform, the individualist essence of which they gradually disengaged and released.
Others became the precursors of free thought.

Lastly, in Northern Europe the kings and princes profited
from the revolt against Rome to annex or confiscate ecclesiastical properties and subject their churches to their authority.

In each nation the Reform movement thus had a particular character of its own. For reasons of temperament and traditional culture, of moral make-up, religious ideas and language, Northern Europe broke away more easily than Latin Europe from the Roman Church.

In France the conflict seemed for some time undecided. But one fact determined the event in the end : the King of France, having the power to confer ecclesiastical benefices in the realm at his pleasure by the Concordat of 1516, had no material interest in favouring the Protestant Reform. Moreover, it threatened to divide the state. The king took the side of Catholicism, in the name of unity rather than of faith : he then had trouble later to resolve the problem of freedom of conscience. Hence the anti-monarchical character that French free thought took on at times.

First Reformers : Calvin, Ignatius Loyola

Before Luther set going the revolt against Rome, a French scholar, Lefèvre d'Étaples — a little feeble old man with a burning faith — proclaimed the sovereign authority of Holy Scripture. He wished for a peaceful reform in the bosom of the Church. His disciples gathered round him at Meaux. His influence extended to the Court, where Francis I's sister, Margaret of Angoulême, adopted his ideas. Towards 1520, however, the writings of Luther began to be spread abroad in France. The Sorbonne denounced the heresy, and the Parliament of Paris persecuted the innovators. Louis de Berquin, translator of Luther, was executed in 1529. In 1534 when abusive libels against the Church were posted up in Paris, in the provinces and even at the gate of the royal palace, Francis I, who had been hitherto indifferent, took alarm and, believing there was a plot, ordered measures of repression.

In 1536 appeared the book that laid down the doctrinal position of the Protestant Reform in France, the *Christian Institutes* of Jean Calvin.

Calvin was then only twenty-seven. Born at Noyon, of

a legal and clerical family, himself at first intended for the Church and the Law, he had studied successively at the universities of Paris, Orléans and Bourges. There he heard the echo of religious disputes and frequented the humanists, listening to the discourse of Lefèvre's disciples and learning Greek and Hebrew from the lessons of a Lutheran, Melchior Valmar. Refusing the benefices offered him, he gave himself up to the new ideas. Francis I's persecution after the affair of the posters forced Calvin to take refuge at Basel, where he published his book. His teaching, more rigorous and radical than Luther's, considered man as naturally corrupt and faith as a special grace, reserved to the predestined elect. It admitted only two sacraments, baptism and the communion or 'supper'. It abolished all religious images, reduced services to prayer and preaching and suppressed all hierarchical order in the Church — pastors and ministers being co-opted and placed under the control of the assembly of the faithful.

A political, followed by a religious, revolution had installed the Protestant Reform at Geneva. Calvin established himself there and, after some conflict, became a sort of dictator in doctrine and morals. He made it an intellectual centre, then a headquarters of propaganda with its influence on France, the Low Countries and Scotland. Many refugees took shelter there from France.

A man of Picardy, of a harsh character and of a disdainful and ruthless logic, with opinions long excogitated and then inexorably fixed, Calvin represented a type of man that 'douce France' rarely produces ; but to whom she gives, when she does produce him, a remarkable rigidity of character. He had the scholar Michael Servetus burned. Up to his death in 1564, the French Reformer was the true incarnation of all the haughtiest and most pitiless that the human spirit could oppose to the weaknesses of the century. After his death, his moral influence penetrated into far-distant countries.

Ardent Catholics and the Church herself, however, began to perceive the formidable danger to which Christian unity was exposed. In fact, already it was impossible to speak of unity. The larger part of Germany and of the Low Countries, and several of the Swiss cantons, had adopted the Protestant Reform. From the time of Henry VIII England had broken with Rome. In France, the king defended Catholicism, sometimes mildly by means of repressive edicts applied spasmodically, sometimes angrily by acts of cruelty like the terrible massacre of the 'Vaudois' in Provence in 1545.

Force was no longer enough. It was essential to recapture men's minds and re-animate their convictions — in short, to build up the Catholic, against the Protestant, Reform. A General Council met at Trent in the Tyrol, for the first time in 1545, for the second in 1551 : each time, its work was interrupted by intrigues or wars. In 1563 it brought its work to a conclusion, reforming the whole discipline of the Church and clarifying its dogmas.

By the time the Council ended, a militia of volunteers — the 'Society of Jesus' or Jesuit Order — had already for nearly thirty years conducted the struggle against 'heresy' with the very arms that the Protestant Reformation made use of : teaching and preaching, writings, missions. The inspirer of this militant reaction, enlightened and very able, was a Basque gentleman, a former officer wounded in the Spanish army, Ignatius Loyola : his resourceful ardour, his burning imagination and sense of the world formed a curious contrast with the concentrated and remote genius of Calvin. Two years before the *Christian Institutes* appeared — on 15 August 1534 — Ignatius and his six companions dedicated themselves to the cause of the Church in a chapel at Montmartre. It was a long time before they could get themselves accepted and recognised by the Church herself. At the death of Loyola in 1556 the Society counted 1,500 members, directed 36 colleges with 6,000 pupils, and had missions in China and Japan. By their teaching of letters and by the careful education that they were almost alone in giving, the Jesuits were to bring the ruling classes of society in part of Europe back to Catholicism.

They gave a new impulse to the art of teaching and helped to form the classical spirit.

Attitude of the Monarchy to the Protestants. Catherine de Medici

When Henry II died in 1559 there was not a province in which Protestant communities were not to be found. Even in Paris, the riot of the Pré-aux-Clercs and other incidents showed the growing success of the Reformed cause. At the beginning of 1562 the number of communities in the realm exceeded two thousand.

The French Reform at this moment was devout, of a still very conservative spirit — it demanded a return to the primitive beauty of early Christianity — and, in spite of official persecutions, faithful to the monarchy. It recruited its adherents chiefly among women of the nobility, in the middle class and the lesser bureaucracy, among the artisans in the towns and villages and among those inhabitants of country districts left unattended by the Catholic clergy. Most of the ministers or pastors were former clerics or monks, notably Augustinians.

Up to the Treaty of Cateau-Cambrésis, gentlemen who were professional soldiers figured only in small number in the Reform movement. One of the greatest families and most highly esteemed at Court, however, the Châtillons — whose leader was Admiral Coligny — openly professed the new ideas. After the peace with Spain, the lesser gentry — without pay, impoverished and discontented — became more and more mixed up in the movement, took direction of it and changed its character.

Henry II's successor was a barely adolescent king, Francis II, husband of Mary Stuart. He died after a reign of seventeen months, leaving the crown to his brother, Charles IX, aged ten. On his accession, the Queen Mother, Catherine de Medici, widow of Henry II, took hold of power. She was to exercise a dominant influence on politics for nearly a quarter of a century.

Florentine on her father's side, Auvergnat on her mother's,

she was robust and very much alive, well educated, a practical mind with a mixture of restrained passion, laborious intrigue, and asserted authority. She was neither vicious, nor ill-intentioned, nor cruel. She bore no hatred for the Protestants, and had no prejudice against anybody. She wanted peace, the safeguard at all costs of the monarchy's prerogatives and of her children's inheritance ; to defend her position, she allowed herself to be troubled neither by sentiment nor scruple. Very broad in matters of belief, but severe towards rebellion, she took constant care to preserve the unity of the realm and to spare the 'poor subjects'. By the standards of the time, she was an able ruler, more humane than her two contemporaries, Elizabeth of England and Philip II of Spain.[1]

Around her, three families fought for political influence : the Bourbons, Guises and Montmorencys. The elder of the Bourbons, Antoine, husband of Jeanne d'Albret and father of Henry IV, was a vain sensualist, without nerve or conviction. The younger, Louis, first Prince of Condé, had the spirit of a poor and ambitious younger son ; he made himself the patron of the Protestants and dragged them into a hopeless enterprise. The Guises were pride itself, with intelligence, *savoir-faire* and a passionate belief in the rights of the Church, which in large part owed to them the salvation of Catholicism in France. François de Guise, the elder, enjoyed the prestige of his earlier victories of Metz and Calais ; his brother, the Cardinal of Lorraine, imposed himself by his ability and his wealth. The Montmorencys were divided. The old Constable recognised only the king's authority and his own interest. But his nephews, the Châtillons, declared themselves Protestants ; the elder, Admiral Coligny, by the sincerity of his faith and his devotion to the Crown, obtained for a time the Queen Mother's esteem.

After the burning of the Protestant Anne du Bourg, councillor to the Parliament of Paris, in 1559, a Périgord

---

[1] This, so far as Elizabeth is concerned, is untrue: one has only to think of the Massacre of St. Bartholomew.— A. L. R.

Catherine de Medici

gentleman, La Renaudie — a tool of the Prince de Condé — fomented a conspiracy to capture Francis II. The conspirators, exasperated squireens who brought along troops of simple folk, made for the château of Amboise in March 1560. The Guises were forewarned and, taking them by surprise, scattered them and had those who persisted hanged or drowned. Catherine de Medici and the new Chancellor, Michel de l'Hôpital, were moved by this episode, however, and for the first time officially recognised liberty of conscience, if not liberty of public worship.

Catherine's idea was to reconcile Catholics and Protestants by a sincere discussion of differences. For this she arranged a meeting of bishops and pastors at Poissy in 1561. The conflict between the two doctrines touching the Eucharist rendered agreement impossible. By the edict of January 1562 Catherine granted the Protestants the right to hold services in the suburbs of towns and in the countryside. Up to this time the monarchy had not definitely taken sides : it claimed to remain arbiter.

On 1 March 1562 the Duke of Guise violated the edict of January and provoked an affray which ended in a massacre of Protestants at Vassy. The Queen Mother and Charles IX hesitated, inclining towards the Prince of Condé who did not respond to their appeal, and were finally carried away by force by the Catholic leaders. Condé then committed the irreparable mistake : he broke into armed revolt and occupied Orléans ; he asked help from abroad and so broke with the authority of the Crown. Thus civil war began, in which the Protestants obtained help from England and Germany, while the Catholics solicited the support of Spain.

Antoine de Bourbon was killed at the siege of Rouen, the Prince of Condé taken prisoner at the battle of Dreux, the Duke of Guise himself assassinated before Orléans. In March 1563 the edict of Amboise, less liberal than that of 1562, established peace for some years. But the realm was on the way to wreck and ruin.

Hostilities began again in 1567. The Constable de Montmorency was killed at St.-Denis. In 1569 the Protestants suffered a double defeat at Jarnac, where Condé fell by an assassin's hand, and at Moncontour. To obtain peace, in 1570, Catherine signed a new edict which granted the Calvinists four places of security with the right to put garrisons in them.

Now that Guise and Condé were dead, it seemed that a reconciliation might last. The young Henry of Navarre, son of Antoine de Bourbon and nominal head of the Protestants, was ready to marry Margaret of Valois, Charles IX's sister. Coligny took his place in the Council again and exerted a growing influence on the young king. He advocated a great design to take Artois and Flanders away from Spain by surprise, in concert with the insurgents of the Low Countries. Catherine was alarmed at the eventuality of a war with Spain at a time when the king was in want of money and troops; she was driven to exasperation by such talk. She lived in fear lest the terrible Duke of Alba, Spanish governor of the Low Countries, should invade Northern France. In order to check Coligny's plan, she came to an understanding with the Guises. Henri de Guise, François' son, believed that his father's assassination was inspired by Coligny. He awaited the opportunity to avenge him. Then, too, all the Guises were exasperated by the way in which Charles IX kept them out of power. Seeing the Queen Mother turn to them, they took courage to strike a shattering blow.

In August 1572 the marriage of Henry of Navarre and Margaret of Valois attracted a crowd of Protestant gentry to Paris. The Guises were furious at the spectacle ; Catherine was in fear that the king would escape her hold. On 22 August an assassin, posted in the house of a servant of the Guises, fired a shot at Coligny, who was seriously wounded. The Court and Paris were in a fever of excitement. On which side would Charles IX come down ? He swore he would avenge Coligny. If he persisted it meant civil war, foreign

war, Catherine's ruin. Beside herself with anxiety, the Queen
Mother laid siege to her son, forced him to change his opinion
and finally extracted from him the order to execute 'those who
intend to rise against the state'. In the night of Sunday
24 August, St. Bartholomew's Day, Henri de Guise himself
directed the assassination of Coligny. Charles IX, driven
half mad, had the Protestants of his court massacred. Then,
the Paris mob having been stirred up, the massacre became
general, and was followed by pillage that made no distinction
of party. The provincial towns, incited by emissaries, soon
followed the example of Paris. For several days there was a
'shameful blood-bath'.

The Calvinist survivors shut themselves up in La Rochelle
and refused to yield. Charles IX ended by granting them
peace. He himself, his conscience tortured, his sleep haunted
by bloody nightmares, died in 1574, at the age of twenty-four
— a sickly, too sensitive boy, whom nothing in his own
intentions predisposed to the frightful rôle that events and
men's passions imposed on his weakness.

End of the Valois

There then succeeded to the throne the best endowed of
the sons of Henry II and Catherine de Medici — Henry III.
In some respects he resembled his grandfather, Francis I : in
intelligence and the gift for words, in the taste for culture and
refinement, and in elegance. But he was corrupt at heart,
under the thumb of his 'mignons', drawn into ill deeds by his
tastes.

Up to then the authority of the Crown, thanks to Catherine's
'game of see-saw', had always some support either among
Catholics or among Protestants. Henry III, neglecting his
mother's advice, committed so many mistakes that he was
disclaimed by both Catholics and Protestants. Caught in this
situation he nearly lost his crown and then lost his life, leaving
his kingdom in open anarchy and invaded by foreign armies.

Since the Massacre of St. Bartholomew the Protestants,

determined to defend themselves at all costs, reorganised their forces and constituted a sort of federal republic within the realm — the 'state within the state' that Richelieu later denounced. With the support of a neutral party which had just come into being and wanted peace — the party of the 'Politiques' — they were strong enough to obtain from the king in 1576 the edict of pacification of Beaulieu, which granted them liberty of public worship (except in Paris), eight places of security for themselves and mixed tribunals in every Parliament to decide their cases.

Thereupon there was formed the same year a 'holy and Christian union' of Catholics, the League, a vast federation set up against both the Huguenots and the royal authority. It took Henri de Guise for its leader. The Protestants, on their side, had the young Henry of Navarre. In 1584 the Duke of Alencon, last son of Catherine de Medici, died. As Henry III had no children, the question of the succession to the throne exacerbated the religious conflict. The legitimate heir was Henry of Navarre, who was a Protestant. The Catholics rejected him and opposed to him the old Cardinal de Bourbon, while Guise prepared the way for his own candidature. Henry III, fearful of the popularity of the Guises, tried to get rid of them. But the Leaguers of Paris revolted against him on the 'Day of Barricades', 12 May 1588, and in order to escape from the outbreak he was forced to draw upon the prestige of his rival, whom he named Lieutenant-General of the realm. Pressed for money, he convoked the States General at Blois in October 1588. Henri de Guise appeared there in the guise of a real sovereign. On 23 December Henry III had him assassinated in the Château of Blois by the gentlemen of his guard, the Forty-Five.

Paris revolted at once and gave power to a 'Council of the Sixteen' which decreed the forfeiture of Henry III and named Guise's brother, the Duc de Mayenne, Lieutenant-General of the realm. The king was reconciled to Henry of Navarre and together they assembled an army to besiege Paris. How-

ever, on 1 August 1589, Henry III was in his turn assassinated
by a Leaguer monk, Jacques Clément. The crown fell to
Henry of Navarre, Henry IV.

Henry IV

Heir, through his father, of the Bourbons — unstable and
pleasure-loving — on his mother's side, of the Albrets —
tough, determined, living close to the people, Henry IV had
spent his unlikely youth between the vicious and bloody Court
of the last Valois, which he himself called 'cut-throat', and the
Biblical exaltation of Huguenot camps. Habituated to bravery
and to cunning, ripened by all kinds of good and ill fortune,
instructed in the secrets of both religions and of all parties,
he was a man in the full sense of the word. A man of
thirty-six, fearless, with knowledge of life, without illusions
but also without resentment, adroit at seducing men's hearts
and good to the people, a virile and human personality :
what a change after three kings going through puberty, sickly
or vicious, under the thumb of an authoritarian but anxious
mother ! Henry IV's bent was all towards health and joy in
living; he was good humoured, shrewd and jovial and loved
the job of being king.

But the time of trial continued. The new king had to
get himself recognised by the Catholics, put an end to civil
war and clear the realm of foreign armies.

He did not fear battle. Already in 1587 he had crushed
the army of the Duc de Joyeuse at Coutras. Soon after his
accession he defeated the Duc de Mayenne at Arques, near
Dieppe, in September 1589. In the following year at Ivry,
near Évreux, rallying his horsemen to his white plume, he led
a furious charge against Mayenne's troops and routed them.
He then moved up to blockade Paris. The Paris League had
inculcated the spirit of martyrdom in the fanatic population.
The siege lasted four months : thousands died of hunger and
privation. A Spanish army under the command of Parma
repulsed Henry IV in Normandy and occupied Paris in

1591. The old Cardinal of Bourbon, the League's 'king', having died, Philip II of Spain tried to get his daughter Isabella, granddaughter of Henry II, proclaimed Queen of France.

The situation was touch-and-go. Catholic opinion was divided. In 1593 the Duc de Mayenne convoked the States General to Paris to elect a king. Philip applied strong pressure in favour of his daughter. In May Henry IV came to a decision : he announced his conversion to Catholicism. At once, he had, if not won the battle, at least gained the strength with which to bargain. On 23 July he abjured the Protestant heresy in the abbey of St.-Denis. In 1594 he at length entered his capital without striking a blow. For three years yet he had to battle against the Spaniards, who held on to Burgundy and Picardy, until, worn down, they signed the Treaty of Vervins in 1598 which liberated the realm.

The Edict of Nantes

The intelligence of Henry IV, at once politic and humane, comes out clearly in the famous settlement he gave to the religious conflict : the Edict of Nantes.

Having made the sacrifice of his religious preferences to the faith of the immense majority of his subjects and thus re-established the position of the monarchy, he could not without baseness betray the memory of his mother, Jeanne d'Albret, the 'Saint of the Reform', nor the claims of his companions in poverty and struggle, the Protestants. By the Edict of Nantes, 13 April 1598, he guaranteed the Protestants freedom of conscience throughout the realm, liberty to hold public services wherever established and in one place at least in every district, absolute equality with Catholics in all employments, the creation in several Parliaments of tribunals composed of judges of both confessions. He left them, for eight years, a hundred places of security. Thanks to Henry IV, France was the first nation in Europe to know religious liberty. Perhaps the Bourbon monarchy later would have saved its fortunes if it had known how to keep faithfully the tradition of its founder.

After thirty years of civil wars, France, according to the word of a witness, resembled 'the corpse of France'. There was great devastation. Many villages and farms had fallen into ruin. Fields went unploughed. The starving peasants took to pillage.

But this very misery assured henceforth the future of a strong monarchy. The people and the middle class felt an immense need of order, authority and internal peace. Men's minds were weary of the subtleties of humanism, of political and religious theses and controversies. What they wanted was practical good sense. The loosening of morals disgusted decent people.

Absolute monarchy, henceforward, was able to establish itself. The civil wars had prepared the way for the adhesion of the people to it.

CHAPTER V

The Work of Henry IV and Richelieu

❖

Henry IV and Sully's Work of Restoration — Louis XIII
— Richelieu's Struggles — The Thirty Years War — Founda-
tions of the 'Grand Siècle'

THREE kings of powerful personality — Philip Augustus, St. Louis and Philip the Fair — built up the Capetian monarchy. Under the Valois the monarchy was weakened, at first almost to the point of perishing, to recover itself later through the awakening of national feeling and to end, under the Valois-Angoulême, in an undefined sort of absolutism where everything depended on the grant of the prince, in the Italian manner. The three great Bourbon kings — Henry IV, Louis XIII and Louis XIV — went on to make of the monarchy a classical construction, at once rational and arbitrary, abstract and yet exacting : power absorbed not only the material resources of the nation, but its very spirit, in a majestic work of synthesis.

The classic monarchy was pleased to invoke Divine Right with Louis XIV. But this deification only became possible after the pathetically human efforts of Henry IV and Louis XIII — two kings who knew how to choose for ministers, the one Sully, the other Richelieu.

Henry IV and Sully's Work of Restoration

Henry IV demanded of his counsellors that they serve the state and not enslave their consciences. He employed the Cardinal d'Ossat, who was a Catholic moderate. He also employed the President Jeannin and Villeroy, who had been Leaguers. He was gracious, very ready to forgive, to flatter, and to thank people for what they did for him. But underneath his jovial good temper, he remained serious, a judge difficult to dupe and very authoritarian. The great lords, during the troubles, had got into the habit of interfering in everything. He put them outside the Council, marooned them in military employments, forbade them to touch finance or justice. One of them, Marshal Biron, an old war-time comrade whom he loved well, dared to plot with the Duke of Savoy, then with the Spaniards: Henry IV pardoned him once, then had him executed in 1602. The towns had usurped liberties, taking advantage of the disorder and giving themselves to one side or the other, looking after their own security and order very badly. The king restricted their franchises.

The essential seriousness of Henry IV may be seen in the fact that he took for his chief minister the person at once the most zealous for the public good and the most unbending in character that he knew, a close-fisted Huguenot, a genius in practical clear-sightedness: Maximilien de Béthune, later Duc de Sully.

Born in 1560 of an old family of the Ile-de-France, of that needy nobility, burdened with children, from which came brigands as well as bureaucrats, Sully was a singular mixture of man of war and man of business, of loyal service and rude pride, of sordid economy and concern for appearances, of bravery and caution, of little schemes and large views, with a solid devotion to the causes he served: that of France and Henry IV. He and his master had met in their youth in the Huguenot army: they understood each other, became attached to each other, had talked over many things together, especially what ought to be done to put the kingdom in good order. In 1598 Sully was put in charge of the finances with the title of Superintendent, then was made Grand Surveyor of France, Superintendent of Buildings and Fortifications, Grand Master of Artillery.

Henry IV had found the Treasury empty and with a crushing debt: when creditors were paid, there remained nothing of the produce of the taxes for the government. By a ruthless management of public revenues Sully succeeded in paying back large sums, in facing the regular expenditure and putting to reserve each year, in the cellars of the Bastille, about a million *livres*.   Taking advantage of an abuse dating from Francis I — the sale of offices — he taxed legal and financial offices with an annual impost, the 'Paulette', from the name of the receiver, one Paulet.

The king had spent his childhood among the peasants and he loved them.   Sully, too, took great care of agriculture : 'Ploughing and pasture', he said, 'are the two breasts that feed France, the true mines and treasures of Peru'.   The countryside suffered from such poverty that, in 1594, 20,000 poor souls attempted a revolt in the South-West.   In order to quieten the peasants, they were let off their arrears of taxes and the poll-tax lowered.   Tax-collectors, nobles, men of war had to bow before the king's determination to protect the labourer in the fields.   'If we are without compassion for the people', wrote Henry IV, 'they must succumb and we all perish with them.'   He detested idle gentry and courtiers.   In his view, the nobility ought to be occupied in managing its lands well and setting the example of zeal for agriculture.   At his request, a gentleman of the Vivarais, Olivier de Serres, published in 1600 a delightful and most instructive book on country life, the *Theatre of Agriculture and Management of Fields*.

A country-man, an old soldier and Huguenot, Sully detested the bourgeois — 'men of the desk', as he called them — their parvenu manners, their ostentation and extravagance.   These bourgeois, inheriting Renaissance habits, brought in from abroad all kinds of luxuries and superfluities which the kingdom paid for by the export of gold and silver. Sully wished to subject them to an austere régime of restrictions. More subtly, Henry IV created French industries to meet the expensive needs of his rich bourgeois, and especially of their wives and daughters.   He founded or subsidised manufactures of carpets, glass, gilt leather and fine stuffs ; he encouraged silk weaving at Lyons and at Tours and introduced the plantation of mulberry-trees and the cultivation of silkworms. He attached an experienced business-man, called Laffemas, to his household.

While Sully as Grand Surveyor had roads repaired, bridges reconstructed, the Briare canal made, so as to revive regular communications between provinces and between towns, the king looked beyond. He was among the first to realise the national importance of big overseas trade and colonisation. He encouraged the founders of the Company for Trade with the Indies, formed in 1603. In 1603, too, a naval captain, Samuel Champlain, having explored the River St. Lawrence to the Great Lakes, established at Quebec what became the capital of the French colony of Canada.

Under the influence of this paternal, authoritarian government France quickly recovered her strength. She was able to lift up her head again before the foreigner. Henry IV had too much experience of war to love it and he was averse to new adventures. A short campaign won from the Duke of Savoy, by the Treaty of Lyons (17 January 1601), Bresse, Bugey, Valromey and the Gex district in exchange for the marquisate of Saluzzo. For a decade there was no more war. But the problem of freeing France from the encirclement in which the union of the houses of Austria and Spain kept her was not resolved. The same peace which had given the kingdom leisure to remake itself gave strength to the ambitions of the Habsburgs.

In the first months of 1610 the renewal of hostilities between France and the house of Austria seemed inevitable. 'Grand designs' were discussed among the king's counsellors. Alarming rumours spread through the realm and reawakened the rancour of some fanatics. One such person with delusions, called Ravaillac, left Angoulême and reached Paris on 14 May ; taking advantage of some carts holding up the royal coach in the Rue de la Ferronerie, he struck Henry two blows with a knife, one of which reached his heart.

In spite of the severity of the taxes he had imposed and

the scandal of his mistresses, the murdered king was lamented by contemporaries, even the less indulgent of them. It has been said that if he had lived longer he would have compromised the benefits of his reign in a 'hazardous and foolhardy' enterprise. One must judge him fairly, not on what he had not the time to do, but on what he did. His short reign sufficed to witness that he possessed a rare political intelligence and that he considered carefully the good of his subjects.

Louis XIII

The new king, Louis XIII, elder son of Henry IV and Marie de Medici, was hardly nine. The Regency fell to his mother. Marie was a large Italian woman, lazy, of little intelligence, credulous, chiefly concerned about her comforts and her toilette, and whom her husband had tried hard, but in vain, to interest in affairs of state. She entrusted power to an adventurer called Concini — husband of her foster-sister, Leonora Galigai — and made him Marquis d'Ancre and a Marshal. The government of France became the wages of a Florentine domestic !

In a dozen years of rule Henry IV had restored quiet and prosperity to his kingdom. But he had not had the time to subdue resistance or extinguish passions to such a point that the royal authority could relax without risk. The bureaucracy, filled with pretensions since offices had been transformed into hereditary property, now followed the example of the Parliaments and meant to take its revenge for the roughness with which Sully had treated it. The great nobility, half foreign by origin or connections, did not resign itself to the subordinate rôle to which Henry IV had relegated it : it considered that the state belonged to it in partnership with the king and that it still had arms enough to support its demands, if necessary by revolt. The governors of provinces put obstacles in the way of the crown's authority instead of serving it. The gentry, accustomed to live by the enterprises of the great and the profits of war, awaited the opportunity for new adventures.

Lastly, Henry IV, reluctant to crush the excessive pretensions of his old co-religionists, had left the Protestants numerous places of security and a military organisation which could serve intriguers to foment new troubles. This autonomous organisation of the Protestants in the bosom of the state retarded the reconciliation of Frenchmen.

Concini at once came up against the demands of the great nobility. To appease them, he distributed among them the treasure Sully had put to reserve. Then in 1614 he called the States General together : the nobility and the middle class quarrelled so merrily over the 'Paulette' and the pensions paid out to gentlemen, that it was easy to send them away without granting them anything.

Soon the troubles began again. The Prince of Condé and the magnates took up arms. The Protestants of the South — disquieted by Louis XIII's marriage to a Spanish Infanta, Anne of Austria (1615) — joined in the revolt. To quieten the malcontents, Concini distributed a few more millions. He pushed the Queen Mother into having Condé arrested. He was, however, more and more detested — most of all by the young king.

Louis XIII had just attained his majority, at the age of fifteen. Very intelligent, but deprived of instruction by the foolishness of his mother, with a sort of modesty that came no doubt from the ignorance in which he had been left — but a defiant modesty, sullen and sometimes brutal — he had a strong personality, repressed and deeply hurt. With his confidant, who looked after his hawks, Albert de Luynes, he plotted against his mother's favourite and Concini was killed, 24 August 1617. Marie de Medici was made to give up interfering in anything. Luynes, promoted to all kinds of honours, was given power. He showed himself hardly superior to Concini. The Queen Mother having fomented a revolt on account of him, he easily overcame it, but failed against the Protestants of the South. He died in 1621, leaving the king humiliated.

The Queen Mother regained influence over her son. In 1624 she got into the Council a man of her entourage whose reputation had been growing for some years : Armand du Plessis, Cardinal Richelieu.

Richelieu's Struggles

On his father's side Richelieu came of a family of Poitevin gentry, violent and quarrelsome, who did not stop short of murder ; on his mother's, Suzanne de la Porte, a woman of application and ability, he was the grandson of a noted advocate at the Parliament of Paris. The two traditions, of arms and the law, are to be seen in this contrast of pride and adroitness, of inflexible will and refinement of spirit, of almost temerarious imagination and cold calculation which, combined with the genius for action, made Richelieu the most famous statesman in our history. He was very highly strung, tortured with headaches and stomach troubles, with all sorts of hidden pains. His proud look, his tall figure, the haughty appearance he made draped in the crimson of a cardinal, the expression of his eyes alight with intelligence and passion, concealed the struggle which he waged ceaselessly with himself and which betrayed itself only at moments in the lines and hollows of his face.

Cadet of a family which had known ruin, without much support, his mother had had him put through a very complete course of study at the College of Navarre in Paris. The obvious superiority of his intelligence and address gained him rapid advancement. Bishop of Luçon at twenty-two, spokesman of the clergy at the States General of 1614, almoner to the Queen Mother, then Secretary of State in 1616, Cardinal in 1622, he was thirty-nine when Louis XIII accepted him as his first minister.

Richelieu was to make France the most strongly governed state in Europe and to gain her supremacy in the West. His work, in which Louis XIII played an important part, served to support the splendours of the *Grand Siècle*. It was he who created the instruments of power for Louis XIV : in the first place, the army and the fleet.

His task was, first, to break the forces within the country which resisted the royal authority. Of these forces, the independent organisation of the Protestants constituted, in his eyes, the most dangerous. The conflict began in 1625. After a truce, it was renewed in 1627. The principal episode in it was the siege of La Rochelle, which lasted nearly a year. The fierce energy of Mayor Guiton, the inexpressible sufferings of the population and the attempts of the English to rescue the city were powerless against the resolution of the Cardinal, who directed operations himself, in helmet and breastplate. The place was surrounded on the landward side by an entrenchment 12 kilometres long, and on that of the sea by a stone dyke 1,500 metres long. The last defenders capitulated on 28 October 1628.

Inflexible on the question of the interests of the state, Richelieu had too perceptive an intelligence to display religious intolerance and violate consciences. By the Peace of Alais, or Peace of Grace, in 1629, he granted Protestants common rights. But he took away their places of security and all that had permitted them to constitute an independent party in the state. They had to content themselves with religious freedom and equality with Catholics.

In fact, the Protestant organisation only appeared so dangerous because it offered a ready support to the intrigues or incessant revolts of the grandees. Against the great (and the unteachable) nobility Richelieu waged an implacable struggle, allowing nothing to deflect him, pursuing the king's brother, Gaston of Orléans, and holding both the Queen and the Queen Mother at bay. A first plot was formed around Gaston in 1626 : Richelieu had the young Count of Chalais executed, whom the intriguer Madame de Chevreuse had drawn in. In 1630 a new conspiracy of the grandees took shape, with the support of Marie de Medici, who nearly forced the adhesion of the king in the 'Day of Dupes' (10 November), but lost the game. The Queen Mother was exiled from court and her accomplices imprisoned or sent away. Marshal Marillac was executed. In 1632 Gaston of Orléans raised a revolt with the Duc de Montmorency, governor of Languedoc: taken prisoner at Castelnaudary, Montmorency — first peer of the realm and godson of Henry IV — was also executed. In 1636 a prince of the blood of the house of Condé, the Comte de Soissons, escaped the same fate only by flight abroad. At last, in 1642, the favourite of Louis XIII himself, the young Cinq-Mars, having attempted to overthrow the Cardinal and signed a secret treaty with Spain, was executed at Lyons, as well as his friend de Thou, who had disapproved of the plot but not revealed it.

Richelieu deliberately kept the great lords out of the king's Council. He replaced and revoked governors of the provinces at his will, without regard to their claims or convenience. For administration he preferred to use agents whom he sent into the provinces on tours of inspection and who were called Intendants, authorised 'to decide, order and execute all that they see good to do'. When the magistrates protested against such powers, he issued a decree forbidding the Parliaments to interfere in matters of state.

Too much absorbed by affairs of high policy to concern himself with the condition of the people, Richelieu did not show the same consideration for the poorer subjects that Henry IV and Sully had shown. The kingdom was burdened with taxes : the wars and foreign enterprises had to be paid for.

The Thirty Years War

From 1618 on, when Bohemia revolted against the Habsburgs with the Defenestration of Prague — two lieutenants of Ferdinand II being thrown out of a window of the castle there — a vast conflict, at once political and religious, had opened in Central Europe. At first simply a civil war among the states of the house of Austria, then a war between the German states, this conflict gradually became, by the intervention of Denmark, Sweden, the United Provinces, Spain and at last France, a European war — the Thirty Years War.

Richelieu saw at once the opportunity it presented to break the chain of possessions with which the Habsburgs had surrounded France for a century, and to give the kingdom its natural frontiers. From 1625 he occupied the Valtelline or upper valley of the Adda, thus cutting one of the principal routes between the Spanish Milanese and Germany. His energetic diplomacy supported all the enemies of the Habsburgs and succeeded in 1630 in throwing the King of Sweden, Gustavus Adolphus, a great soldier, against the forces of Ferdinand of Austria. At the Diet of Ratisbon, the devoted agent of the Cardinal, a Capuchin of noble origin — Francois de Tremblay, Father Joseph, nicknamed 'the Grey Eminence' — ruined Ferdinand's position with the German Electors.

But France did not commit herself deeply till 1635, after Richelieu had assured his position at home against the grandees and strengthened the royal army. That year he declared war against Spain. At the same time he brought his allies, Sweden, some of the Protestant German princes, notably Bernard of Saxe-Weimar, the Swiss, the Duke of Savoy and some of the Italian princes, into the field against Austria.

The struggle was a hard one, for Spain still had the best infantry in Europe and the Imperialists were trained to surprise assaults. In 1636 the enemy besieged St.-Jean-de-Losne, invaded Picardy, occupied Corbie and sent scouts right up to Pontoise. Paris was panic-stricken; but Richelieu with his complete self-control knew how to retrieve a critical situation. Luck soon changed sides. In 1639 the French occupied Alsace; in 1640 they took Arras; in 1642 they conquered Roussillon with Perpignan. Soon the new Emperor, Ferdinand III, accepted the opening of peace negotiations at Münster and Osnabrück.

In the autumn of 1642, after the execution of Cinq-Mars at Lyons, Richelieu had taken the road again for Paris. His body ravaged with ulcers, he could not sit up and had himself carried in a litter draped with purple. Death held him in its grasp. When the curé of Saint-Eustache asked him to forgive his enemies, he answered that he had no enemies other than those of the king and the state. He died on the 4 December. Louis XIII survived him only five months and died 14 May 1643.

Foundations of the 'Grand Siècle'

After the liberties of the Renaissance and the moral anarchy of the Civil Wars, the French spirit, at the beginning of the 17th century, becomes grave, reflective, prone to high thinking and austere meditation. The two currents of Protestant Reformation and Catholic Counter Reformation combine in this reaction which produces Jansenism and the solitaries of Port-Royal, St.-Vincent de Paul and his admirable charity, the Congregation of the Oratory and the Company of the Holy Sacrament.

The deeper spirit of this epoch, which the Italian and later the Spanish fashions of the Court only superficially concealed, manifests itself first in the *Economies royales* of Sully, in the success of books on morals like the *Traité de la sagesse* of Charron and in the refined poetry of Malherbe. It attains, later, the highest and most moving expressions of genius with the philosophy of René Descartes, author of the *Discourse on Method* and creator of analytical geometry ; with the tragedies of Pierre Corneille, whose *Cid* was produced in 1636, the year of the taking of Corbie, and *Polyeucte* in 1643, the year of Louis XIII's death ; in the end, with the agonised researches of Blaise Pascal, who in this same year invented the calculating machine. It appears similarly in the formal painting of Nicholas Poussin, in the high-minded sincerity of Philippe de Champaigne, portrait-painter of Richelieu and Louis XIII. This spirit, formalist and leaning excessively to logic, is yet animated with life, luminous with concrete observation and deeply pondered. Already, however, it has its caricature in the preciosity and artificiality of the *hôtel* de Rambouillet. For the language itself is subjected henceforth to the control of the serious, of reason and even of the state. In 1635 Richelieu founded the French Academy.

Architecture, too, regains in nobility and regularity what it loses in vigour and fantasy. Here all becomes academic or classic. It is the triumph of symmetry, balance, clarity. Each building responds to an integrated design, as each thought to a system. Long façades succeed to the gables, turrets and overhanging roofs. This style of architecture achieves its masterpieces in the palace of the Luxembourg, built by Solomon de Brosse and Lemercier for Marie de Medici, in the chapel of the Sorbonne built for Richelieu, in the houses of the Place Royale and the Place Dauphiné.

In the same way that the 'interest of state' of Richelieu remains the foundation of politics up to our time, the themes of Corneille, the Cartesian method and Jansenist morals, alike with the 'good usage' of the language under the control of the French Academy and neo-classical architecture, continue for three centuries to serve as models.

PART IV

THE CLASSIC MONARCHY

CHAPTER I

From the Fronde to Louis XIV

❖

Anne of Austria and Mazarin — Treaties of Westphalia —
Louis XIV — New Developments of the Monarchy — The
Regulation of the Arts and Letters: Versailles

THE reign of Louis XIV not only surpasses all the reigns of
our history by the splendour and power of the monarchy and
the brilliance of a civilisation dominated by the king, but far
exceeds them in length: seventy-two years. Charlemagne
himself had only reigned half a century.

So long a reign rendered possible the consistent development of a whole phase of political and intellectual history —
what Voltaire was to call the Age of Louis XIV. It gave to
the standpoint and decisions of the king, to his qualities as
well as his defects, the chance of displaying their full effect on
a scope wide enough to bring home both the responsibilities
and the penalties to the same account. Thus it is difficult to
judge such a reign. In admiring it too much we risk doing
an injustice to other reigns which lacked only length. If we
underline too much his share of reverses, mistakes and misdeeds, we are apt not to allow for the fact that Louis XIV, by
the exceptional length of his rule, had to play a rôle and run
chances, for good or ill, of an unprecedented extent and
diversity. What we can fairly say, it seems, is that the reign
of Louis XIV was the greatest of all because of its length,
which encouraged achievement of every kind, and in spite of
its length, which gave mistakes all the more scope to accumu-
late. That Louis XIV never showed himself unequal to the
demands of so long a reign proves at least that he was no
ordinary man.

Anne of Austria and Mazarin

When his father died, he was four years old. His mother, Anne of Austria, was a bigoted Spaniard, passionate, narrow-minded and indolent, but who possessed the pride of authority and a very strong sense of her rights : a nobler nature than Marie de Medici. Louis XIII before his death had constituted a Council of Regency. Anne had this act annulled by the Parliament and took the Regency herself. Of the councillors whom her husband had destined for her, she kept Giulio Mazarini — Mazarin — to whom she gave her confidence, all power and her warmest affection. She ended by losing, with him, even her dignity.

Born of a Sicilian father, of the household of the Colonnas, Mazarin — whom his opponents called 'the Sicilian villain' — was one of those Italians who shine in all trades provided they change them often enough. He could have earned his living as dancer or cook or major-domo. People knew him as student, captain, diplomat, churchman, legate of the Holy See and, though he was not a priest and was not well seen in religion, he did not despair of one day becoming Pope. Richelieu, struck by his astonishing *savoir-faire*, had taken him from the Church to recruit him to the king's service and then brought him into the Council. Mazarin was only forty when he received the cardinal's hat. A year later, in 1643, the favour of Anne of Austria made him the master of France. He had a fine forehead, a look of good humour or of false humility, a physiognomy of disconcerting subtlety and an imperturbable cynicism. His nature was that of a pure nego-tiator. As to governing, he had no conception, since he ignored the general interest and cared nothing for principles. He managed France like the private domain of the great lady, Anne of Austria, whom he had seduced, with more care to aggrandise it than to run it properly.

Without much trouble he disposed of the 'Cabal of the Magnates', a conspiracy of the grandees led by the Duc de

Beaufort, who wished to revenge their humiliation. But he found it less easy to get rid of the financial problem that harassed the state. The revenue from taxes had been anticipated for four years ahead and spent. A European war, however, had to be paid for. Mazarin called in another Italian, a so-called financier, Particelli d' Emeri, whom he appointed controller of finances. For several years every refinement of taxation was resorted to; those who were liable and within range in Paris could not escape it. But in 1648 Mazarin went too far: on the renewal of the 'Paulette', the government decided that the high courts, except the Parliament, should give up four years' salaries.

The lawyers stood together. The Parliament of Paris, proud of having set aside Louis XIII's will at the demand of Anne of Austria, rebelled against the Regency and, by the 'decree of Union', 13 May 1648, invited the other high courts to deliberate with it on the 'reform of the kingdom'. Two months later the magistrates, who had assembled in spite of the royal command, laid down a 'declaration of twenty-seven articles' tending to limit the Royal prerogative. The people of Paris acclaimed those who defended them against the taxes as fathers of the country.

Anne of Austria, on the advice of Mazarin, pretended at first to give way. Then, on 26 August, after the victory of Lens over the Spaniards, she had several magistrates arrested, in particular the councillor Broussel, who was very popular both as a simpleton and an opponent of the new taxes. A dangerous riot took place. It was the 'day of Barricades': all Paris in revolt, the streets barricaded, the Palais-Royal surrounded on all sides. Anne of Austria, indifferent to danger, threatened to strangle Broussel with her own hands; but Mazarin calmed her down and made her release him. Without armed forces she was unable to resist. But as soon as troops were rendered available by the Peace of Westphalia, the Regent escaped from Paris to St.-Germain with the young king and Mazarin (6 January 1649). Then she attempted to suppress the movement, which was to be known as the Fronde.

Thanks to the support of Condé, who remained faithful to the Regent, the parliamentary and Parisian Fronde was speedily subdued. An army of 15,000 men blockaded Paris. Paul de Gondi, later Cardinal de Retz — at that time simply coadjutor to the Archbishop — organised the resistance. It was a sort of mixture of Italian conspiracy and romantic adventure in the Spanish manner. Princes and great ladies played at undermining the state for the pleasure of the spectacle it provided. But the citizens suffered from the blockade and when the intriguers talked of calling in the foreigner, Parliament itself recognised that it was better to yield. Peace was made at Rueil, 30 March 1649.

The real victor was Condé. He certainly showed it by his demeanour and by his demands. He went so far that in 1650 Anne of Austria, her patience at an end, ordered him to be arrested. Thereupon a second civil war broke out, a more determined affair : the Fronde of the Princes. Condé's wife and his sister, the Duchesse de Longueville, raised the four provinces of which he was Governor : Normandy, Guyenne, Burgundy and Poitou. Mazarin, sensing the danger, parried swiftly. It looked as if he were about to suppress the rebellion, when Paul de Gondi, discontented at not yet having received the hat promised him, again raised Paris and the Parliament in February 1651. Mazarin feigned capitulation. He had Condé set at liberty, left the court and departed for Germany.

What was to be expected happened. The Frondeurs, incapable of holding together for anything except disorder, threw the kingdom into anarchy. Condé, having fallen out with the Parisians, allied himself with the Spaniards in September 1651. The misery of it grew intolerable. Turenne, disavowing the Fronde in which he had at first taken part, took command of the royal army. He attacked Condé beneath the walls of Paris, in the faubourg St.-Antoine, and would have taken it, 1 July 1652, if Mlle de Montpensier — the Grande Mademoiselle, daughter of Gaston d'Orléans, then twenty-six

— had not unexpectedly turned the cannon of the Bastille against the king's troops.

With Condé a refugee in Paris, the disorder of the Frondeurs increased in fine style. The populace massacred the magistrates. Condé himself had to quit the capital and rejoin the Spaniards in the Low Countries. In October 1652 the Parliament recalled the Regent and the young king. Mazarin, having let passions subside, returned five months later : everyone toasted his health. Thenceforward he was as 'almighty as God the Father at the beginning of the world'.

After the event, some historians have thought to discover in the Fronde an attempt out of which might have developed some happy formula of constitutional monarchy for the benefit of the people. In fact, the revolt brought together all the elements least qualified to represent the general interest and which had in the past done most harm to France : those cynical grandees, ambitious and venal magistrates, the turbulent mob of the Paris of the Cabochiens, of St. Bartholomew and the League. The nation regarded these people as traditionally responsible for its misery. Far from retarding absolute monarchy, they made it unavoidable, for, in order to escape the nobles and adventurers, France had always invoked the authority of the king.

Treaties of Westphalia

Mazarin, unhappy as a minister, has left a great name as a diplomat. But his diplomacy was enormously aided by the network of alliances and the military system left him by Richelieu. Five days after the accession of Louis XIV, 19 May 1643, the future Prince de Condé, then Duc d'Enghien and aged twenty-two, had crushed the old regiments of Spanish infantry at Rocroi : a victory the merit of which was attributed to the daring of the young general, but which testified also to the valour of his army. In the East, Turenne — son of the Duc de Bouillon and Marshal of France at thirty-two — redressed a dangerous situation. Condé and Turenne together defeated the Imperialists at Freiburg in 1644 and at Nordlingen in 1645. In 1648 Turenne invaded Bavaria with the support of the Swedes, whose army on the other side took Prague by surprise. The Emperor, Ferdinand III of Austria, was forced to sign the treaties of Westphalia, drawn up after long negotiations at Münster and at Osnabrück.

These treaties, which bore the date 24 October 1648, wrecked the Imperial power in Germany. There was no longer one Germany, but several Germanies : a mosaic of principalities and religious confessions, of which each element was independent of the others. The Empire was no more than a title, honorific and elective. France and Sweden had the right to intervene in the affairs of the Empire as guarantors of the peace. France received full sovereignty over the Three Bishoprics (Metz, Toul, Verdun) which had been occupied by her since 1552. As the price of her victories over the house of Austria she acquired Alsace, with the exception of Strasbourg.

The treaties of Westphalia were not so much inspired, from the French point of view, by the direct intention of dividing and weakening Germany ; they were inspired, rather, by the desire to liberate her from the domination of the Habsburgs and, in liberating her, to break finally the chain of Austro-Spanish possessions so dangerous for France. In this case, as ever, diplomacy thought more of the past than of the future. The French negotiators dreamed of completing the ruin of the old empire of Charles V. They did not foresee the unity of modern Germany. Without diminishing their merit, one may even say that, in freeing Germany from the domination of the Habsburgs, they opened the way to the future ambitions of Prussia. In fact the power of Prussia dates from the treaties of Westphalia, which markedly enlarged the domains of the Elector of Brandenburg.

Austria then avowed herself beaten. But Spain was not. Although defeated by Condé a second time at Lens, 20 August 1648, the Spaniards refused to treat. It took twelve more years of hard fighting, imposing cruel sufferings on our frontier provinces, to arrive at an end. In 1651 Condé himself, the victor of Rocroi and Lens, in revolt against the Regent, went over to the enemy. In 1657, to obtain the alliance of Cromwell, Mazarin promised the English the cession of Dunkirk. It was Turenne who, by the victory of the Dunes over the Spaniards and Condé in 1658, forced Philip IV of Spain to come to terms.

The peace between France and Spain, called the Peace of the Pyrenees — after the negotiations which took place on the little island in the Bidassoa, the Isle of Pheasants — was signed 7 November 1659. Mazarin himself had conducted the preliminaries. By this treaty France obtained : in the South, Roussillon and Cerdagne ; in the North, Artois, part of Flanders and a part of Luxemburg with Thionville. Louis XIV was to marry the Infanta Maria Theresa, eldest daughter of Philip IV.

The plans formulated earlier by Richelieu were almost realised, thanks to the forces and alliances left by him to his successor. France thus found herself the preponderant state in Europe. Mazarin, with his *savoir-faire*, had negotiated cleverly. What he had added of his own to Richelieu's plans — that is to say, the Spanish marriage of Louis XIV and the designs on the succession to Spain — might flatter the childhood memories of Anne of Austria, but was to strain irreparably the foreign policy of the Bourbons and then to assure the supremacy of England. Between Richelieu and Mazarin there is all the difference between a statesman of genius and a clever man.

Mazarin died 8 March 1661. By scandalous or simply dubious means, he had amassed an enormous fortune, the equivalent of more than a milliard in our money. He had married his seven nieces to princes of the blood or dukes. He had treated Anne of Austria like a chamber-maid. Everyone had paid court to him, including the king. He left almost nothing in the coffers of the state.

Louis XIV

Louis XIV was then twenty-two years old. The moment Mazarin was dead, he seized the government with surprising decision and declared that he would be his own first minister. In fact, for fifty-four years, he was to exercise his 'craft of king' as the most authoritarian of sovereigns, but also, as the most hard-working and punctual of ministers. The zeal and interest which he never ceased to bring to all the affairs of his kingdom were, at bottom, the secret of his prestige.

A handsome man, tall, inclined to stoutness, a great eater and very sensual, he had an assured bearing, a self-control which went well with the ease of his manners, the physiognomy of a strong and simple personality which impressed without effort. He resembled his father Louis XIII in his inner irritability, his liking for order, the habit of reflection and the obstinacy of his sentiments ; he resembled his mother, Anne of Austria, in his pride, the consciousness of being invested with a title and power more than human, the meticulous care not only for etiquette, but for all the arts by which the monarchy could elevate and refine the cult of itself. Certainly the idea which he held up of this cult was nearer to the Spanish tradition than to the example of his French ancestors. Never had a king so many flatterers : his long reign, his exceptional and unvarying authority, the brilliance of his glory have impressed even witnesses inclined to be critical. We have some difficulty in distinguishing the man from the monarch. He did not shine, it seems, either by originality or vivacity of mind. He judged men well on their plain merits. Without much subtlety or sensitiveness of heart, — because of his pride — he had firmness of character, with a concern for the true and the just. He knew almost always how to moderate himself, save in the passion to be loved, adulated, obeyed and glorified.

Previously the kings of France had lived rather close to their people, travelling about a good deal, in war or peace, visiting the gentry, the towns and their poorer subjects. Except for great occasions, and even under Francis I, their permanent entourage was few in number, composed of their family and their servants, their inner councillors, their favourites and their guard. Louis XIV made the Court a fixed institution and of his own life, from getting up to going to bed, a perpetual display. He figured there himself the star from which all radiated — the Sun-King. He subjected to the service of the Court not only men and women of the world or a body of dignitaries, but made it the microcosm of the values of his kingdom. He succeeded thus in making the authority of the monarch at once the inspirer and the beneficiary of a complete civilisation, in itself admirable. But he did not understand the oldest and deepest characteristic of French kingship : its warm and welcoming aspect, familiar, paternal and above all popular — the character of the king, such as St. Louis had defined it, giving right beforehand to the weak against the strong, to the poor against the rich, friend of the simple, enemy of the great — this character so human with Henry IV and Sully, so terrible with Louis XIII and Richelieu. With Louis XIV become a deity, the multitude bowed down, but felt that the king no longer belonged to them. The French, however, only really love what belongs to them.

The daily routine of the Court and the humiliating demands of the profession of courtier succeeded in undermining the nobility. National unity was made and the power of the monarchy asserted against the great nobles. The kings of France had never had the leisure, the means or the desire to favour the institution of a regular and useful aristocracy. In the 16th century, however, the nobility had still retained enough influence on the people to impose on them its religious and political prejudices in the course of the civil wars. Henry IV and Sully, brought up among the lesser nobility, had had the idea of making out of it a beneficent class to develop agriculture, instruct and guide the peasants. Louis XIV, in obliging all the nobles, great and small, to live only for royal favours, either attached to the Court or looking to it, uprooted the nobility and separated it — save in a few provinces — from the people whom it ceased to know and who ceased to know it. Between the king hidden by the mass of courtiers on one side, and the bulk of the people on the other, there was henceforth a gap. The people fell more and more under the exclusive influence of the lower middle class, naturally hostile to the privileged.

New Developments of the Monarchy

The frequent mistake of historians who have studied the monarchy of Louis XIV in isolation has been to see in it an exceptional degree of absolutism.

In fact Louis XIV did not exercise a power more absolute than his predecessors. His government, bureaucratic and formal, was less subject to the king's 'good pleasure' than had been that of Francis I, for example, and less harsh in some respects than that of Louis XIII. But Louis XIV himself governed, without a first minister, and he found no further resistance to overcome. It has been suggested, after the event, that Louis XIV had compromised the future of the monarchy by the exaggeration of its power. Support for this thesis has been sought in the writings of Fénelon, a rare spirit, but somewhat chimerical and more of a theorist than an observer of the facts. The truth is that Louis XIV compromised the future of the monarchy not in making it absolute — that it had almost always been — but in changing its function in relation to the people and above all in putting it, in spite of itself, at the service of the privileged. The best witness of the reign, who best knew the kingdom in every part — Vauban — was to reveal the real defect of the régime in his famous book : the *Dîme royale*.

This deviation from the rôle of French kingship, under the influence of the spirit of the Court and of modes Spanish in origin, seems all the more surprising since Louis XIV, like his predecessors, distrusted the nobility and kept them out of the government proper even more than they had done. His reign, according to St.-Simon, was 'one long reign of the old middle class': in other words, a reign in which bourgeois 'book-keepers' and not great lords assisted the king in government and administration. Almost all the ministers or secretaries of Louis XIV — like Michel Le Tellier, Hugues de Lionne, Arnauld de Pomponne, Colbert, Louvois — were men of small beginnings, ennobled in the course of their employment.

It was men of this sort who filled the king's Councils: the Council of State which treated great affairs, peace, war, diplomacy; the Council of Finance; the Council of Despatches, where the correspondence from the provinces was examined; the Council of Suitors, a sort of supreme court. It was men of the same class, most often masters of requests in the Council of Suitors, whom the king sent to the provinces to exercise the functions of Intendants, with powers such that the title of Governor, reserved for members of the great nobility, represented only — Mme de Sévigné wrote — 'noise, trumpets and violins'.

But however attentive he was to his government of 'book-keepers', the king remained none the less, above all, the star of the Court, the prisoner of the religion of courtiership which he had established. In the end, the Court was to outweigh the government.

The Regulation of the Arts and Letters : Versailles

What Louis XIV knew how to do in the service of his glory — as none of his predecessors had succeeded in or even dreamed of doing — was to bring together under his patronage almost all the intellectual and artistic forces of France then in full flower. The greatness of the monarchy, which became the target for the competition of the best minds, gave them discipline, unity and the motive to create. Louis XIV neither invented nor formed the French genius of his age. But without

Louis XIV and the spirit of emulation which he drew round him, that genius would not have produced the consummate and coherent culture that was to be the classic model for Europe.

From then on intellectual life constituted, so to say, a department of the monarchy. The king became the born protector of writers and artists. He paid them regularly. To organise them he instituted privileged 'companies'. Besides the French Academy which Richelieu had founded, and the Academy of Painting and Sculpture founded under Mazarin, there were the Academy of Sciences, the Academy of Architecture, the French Academy at Rome, the Academy of Inscriptions, the Academy of Music. From this organisation naturally flowed principles, discipline, the prestige of regular order. The classical spirit is, in essence, invention subordinated to rule.

The most original triumph of Louis XIV appears, perhaps, in the fact that he patronised almost all the great writers of his time without enslaving or limiting their inspiration. The king treated Molière with marks of esteem that astonished contemporaries, and it was the king who commanded that *Tartufe* should be performed, in spite of the prohibition of the Parliament. Racine had close access to the king, just like a favourite. Boileau, La Fontaine, Bossuet, Mme de Sévigné, La Bruyère, Fénelon thought, wrote and talked, in very diverse ways and with very different temperaments, in the circle of the royal entourage and of the Court. Some of them, like La Bruyère and Fénelon, did not refrain from criticising what they saw. Their criticisms — those at least of Fénelon — were ill received. They prove nevertheless that Louis' reign did not render them impossible.

The influence of Louis XIV dominated the arts even more than it did letters. The buildings of his reign, the Louvre, the Invalides, Versailles, Trianon, Marly, constitute a famous part of our national scene — the classical aspect of it, that which has been imitated everywhere. He himself examined the plans of the works, directed the artists, imposed his taste. From his reign and by his will — which the Academies subserved — dates the triumph in France of an architecture in which all is sacrificed to order, regularity, the majestic : an abstract architecture that defies even the climate, the old roofs with steep slopes being replaced, contrary to all good sense in our country of frequent rain and snow, by flat surfaces or roofs in the Mediterranean style.

The painter Le Brun was Louis XIV's principal adviser in the Fine Arts, and in particular directed the decoration of Versailles. Mignard, admirable portrait-painter, decorated the dome of Val-de-Grâce. The sculptors, Puget, Girardon and Coysevox, sculpted the principal groups in the park at Versailles. A doctor who became an architect, Claude Perrault, suggested to the king the plan of the grand colonnade of the Louvre, the work that has been most admired and reproduced abroad. But the perfection of classical art was attained in the Hôtel des Invalides, built by the architect Bruant, and in the palace of Versailles.

Versailles sums up the whole splendour of the reign of Louis XIV. It is in a sense a collective work, on which great artists and a crowd of artisans worked for more than thirty years, under the direction of the king himself. Louis XIII had had a simple hunting-box built there. Louis XIV, whom the memory of the Fronde kept away from Paris, had new buildings begun at Versailles by the architect Le Vau. Then, from 1676 to 1695, Hardouin-Mansart, the ablest architect of the team, directed the works. These works cost a milliard of our money. The builders' yards employed up to thirty thousand men ; several thousand of these men died there. The palace and its outbuildings were conceived to hold ten thousand persons. The vast work, theatrical and a trifle cold, became a marvel of harmony and grace owing to the genius of Le Nôtre, who designed the perspectives of the park and made of the whole the most glorious dwelling in the world.

The glorious dwelling of that one among our kings who, not content with achieving glory, wanted it without measure.

CHAPTER II

The Rise of Louis XIV

❖

*Fouquet — Colbert, his Achievements and his Genius —
Louvois and the Army: Vauban — Victories and Conquests: Peace of Nijmegen*

THE first acts of Louis XIV were to assert his personal
authority and to restore order in the government.

One man insisted, if not on disputing the government
with him, at least on playing a dominant part beside the
throne : this was Fouquet. Sprung from a family of Paris
lawyers, Fouquet had rendered useful services to Mazarin and
obtained in exchange the superintendency of finances, that is
to say, the means of getting rich quickly. By means which
the Cardinal's own example justified, he had acquired an
enormous fortune, which he spent, sumptuously and with
intelligence, but with a display inflated by ambition. His
country house of Vaux-le-Vicomte, near Melun, built by
Le Vau and decorated by the great artists of the time, was a
Versailles before Versailles. Fouquet lacked neither intellect
nor, it seems, charm. But he lacked tact, or at least finesse.
In fact his enriching himself was not more scandalous than
that of his predecessors in the same office. What finished him
was to lay claim to too much power, after having gained too
much money. Usually ministers began by toiling before
enriching themselves. He had enriched himself first. In
addition, he did not understand that the new king meant to
shine alone.

Louis at first concealed his irritation, then suddenly had
Fouquet arrested in September 1661. The royal displeasure
weighed heavily upon the Superintendent's trial, which lasted
three years. Fouquet was condemned for malversation of

funds to a sentence of banishment, which the king commuted to life-long imprisonment.

Fouquet's chief enemy, who had done most to undermine him with Louis XIV, was another creature of Mazarin's, Jean-Baptiste Colbert, then aged forty-two, a former Intendant of the Cardinal and son of a draper of Rheims. This newcomer understood finance very well, but he had not yet made his way and his bearing was of the most modest. Louis XIV found in him the man in whom he put his trust. He named him Controller-General of Finances in 1665, then in 1669 Secretary of State of the Royal Household and of the Navy; in fact he had the management of the whole administration, except for war and foreign affairs.

Colbert, his Achievements and his Genius

Colbert represents, at the side of the Sun-King, the down-to-earth bourgeois : not the big bourgeois of Paris, but the petit-bourgeois of the provinces with his relentless toil, his practical sense, his harsh avarice, his rather servile dodges and — beneath the somewhat repellent crust of preoccupation with interests — at bottom a certain sentimentality and naïf zeal. Of his kind, this petit-bourgeois had surprising genius. An expression at once tenacious and uneasy, a hard line of forehead upon deep-set eyes, a determined yet at the same time humble look, an aspect of morose devotion, a freezing personality — Mme de Sévigné called him 'the North Wind' — made of him a person without grace or charm. He had a powerful imagination and an extraordinary gift for unravelling affairs, for bringing them into order, for work and organisation. He had also an exalted idea of France.

Since the end of the 15th century, since Louis XI had made France a great state, she had lived on her own resources, those of her soil and those which the trade along her routes brought her. She had lived on her resources, sometimes sparingly, but more often wastefully, without thinking systematically of increasing them. She had thought of war rather than of commerce. The Italian wars, then the civil wars, had hindered her from taking any continuous part in the development of the new currents of trade. She was left behind in the general development, economic, maritime, colonial, in which Portugal and Spain had preceded her and England and Holland were now asserting their success. The good sense of Henry IV and Sully had tried to broaden the bases of French wealth. Louis XIII and Richelieu also had intended to tackle it. But political activity at home and abroad had absorbed almost all the energy of the illustrious Cardinal. In 1661 France, victorious over the house of Austria, freed from all external fear and now become the preponderant state in Europe, could consolidate her power in two ways : either in developing her resources and going in for commercial expansion, or in trying to impose her political hegemony on Europe.

Louis XIV had the choice. In the first period of his reign he was to pursue the two ends at the same time, with success. In the second, he was to sacrifice everything to political and military prestige and, ruining the realm, to leave it weakened and demoralised.

The first period corresponds to the administration of Colbert.

The leading idea of Colbert was that in the end the wealth of a state determines its power. He wanted to make France richer, to assure her abundance of money, to stop currency leaving the realm, to attract foreign currency to it, to develop industrial and commercial activity of every kind, to place the finances on a sound footing and regularise their operation, in the end to apportion political undertakings to the resources available.

Whatever may have been Louis XIV's later mistakes, one must admire him — given his education, his arrogant temperament, his passion for glory — in that he did adopt Colbert's policy and follow it for so long.

By a 'chamber of justice' Colbert first had some hundreds of peculators compelled to restore to the state the sums stolen from it. He then undertook to set the administration of the finances in order. He set himself in the first place to institute exact accounts of the revenue and expenditure of the state, serving as basis for a kind of budgetary estimates. This prime work of financial rehabilitation was the real foundation of the greatness of the reign. If the disorder of the expedients of Mazarin's time had continued, both the undertakings and the authority of Louis XIV would have encountered dangerous obstacles.

Colbert wished to develop industry according to plan so as 'to make the whole country abound in goods, having need of nothing and able to dispense everything to other countries'. He maintained that France should sell to the foreigner and buy nothing back : a doctrine which, in an absolute form seems to us chimerical, but which, in the circumstances of the time, represented a sensible reaction against the old habit of Frenchmen of impoverishing themselves to buy all kinds of things from abroad : a habit that Sully had already tried to combat.

Old industries were extended and new ones created. Abbeville, Arras, St.-Quentin, Elbeuf, Sedan, Carcassonne became great centres of cloth-weaving. Gobelins at Paris, Aubusson and Beauvais made tapestries. Lyons won an incomparable name for its production of silks and gold stuffs. The faubourg St.-Antoine made mirrors to replace those that were bought in Venice. The laces of Alençon, Chantilly, Rheims were set in competition with English lace and Venetian. St.-Étienne manufactured Swedish steel and arms.

Colbert attracted to France foreign specialists, manufacturers and workmen, and had capital advanced them to install their factories and to buy raw materials. He created privileged concerns and gave them the title of royal manufactures.

With rare foresight he perceived that French industry could only impose its products and conquer a lasting market by the quality of its work. To regulate or inspect the products, he issued 38 regulations and 150 edicts and instituted inspectors of manufactures. Later, such a degree of regimentation became a nuisance. All the same, it founded the prestige by which our luxury industries still live and which ensures a market for our special products. In 1668 the Venetian ambassador wrote : 'What is best in all parts of the world is manufactured today in France'.

Colbert, the son of a tradesman, knew that, in order to sell goods, it was not enough to produce them. He knew, too, that trade only develops with freedom of circulation. He made an effort to break the economic and customs-compartmentation of the realm. Already twelve provinces, among them the Ile-de-France, Normandy, Picardy, Champagne and Burgundy, formed a customs union, called the 'Five Great Farms'. He tried to simplify the customs. He could not unify the extraordinary diversity of weights and measures, a unification which is still not fully realised today. But he had roads repaired, began the Orléans canal and accepted the project, suggested by Riquet, of joining Atlantic and Mediterranean by the Canal du Midi.

Against the competition of foreign goods, particularly Dutch, he established a protective system of very high tariffs, 'crutches for infant industries', he said. But his greatest work, and also the least known, was the creation of a powerful fleet, both mercantile and naval. Alone, with Richelieu, of all ministers in the history of France, Colbert understood the decisive importance of the sea for the fortunes and liberty of a great state.

He founded the prosperity of our mercantile marine by the system of bonuses to French shipbuilders and owners and by imposing limitations on commerce under foreign flags. He gave the country new means for engaging in distant trade by founding five joint-stock companies : those of the East Indies, the West Indies, the Levant, the North and Senegal. Taking up Richelieu's programme and enlarging it, he made the French Navy the first in the world. In 1661 the king possessed only 18 unseaworthy ships. Twenty years later the fleet

numbered 276 vessels : galleys, ships of the line and frigates.
To recruit crews, Colbert established the system of maritime
conscription, which has remained in force up to our time. He
had arsenals constructed and schools for sea-officers set up ;
he founded the 'Bureau for Naval Pensioners'.

He dreamed of giving France the vast colonial empire
which was one day to fall to England. His mind had grasped
the stages along the famous imperial route : St. Helena, the
Cape, Mauritius, Ceylon, Singapore. He had 4,000 peasants
from Normandy, Brittany, Anjou and Poitou transported to
Canada, where they gave birth to the French-Canadian people.
The French West Indies attained their chief wealth by the
growth of sugar-cane. In 1673 two Frenchmen — Louis
Jolliet, a Quebec merchant, and a Jesuit, Father Marquette —
discovered the Mississippi (which they called the Colbert
River) and reached as far as Arkansas. Some years later,
in 1684, an inhabitant of Rouen, Cavelier de La Salle, took
possession of the lower course and delta of the Mississippi and
gave the territories discovered the name of Louisiana in honour
of Louis XIV.

Colbert applied the same policy and methods of vigorous
organisation to agriculture : he established studs and improved
the breeding of cattle ; he encouraged the planting of mul-
berries and vines and the reclamation of marshes ; he laid down
new regulations for the exploitation of water-resources and
forests.

His immense achievement was legislative as well as political
and administrative. He simplified procedure, and issued a
number of codes, civil and criminal, for commerce and the
navy, and a code for the colonies which England made use of
later.

Finally, one should emphasise the original and fruitful
part Colbert played in directing Louis XIV's patronage. It
was Colbert who founded the Academy of Sciences, the Paris
Observatory, the *Journal des Savants*, the School of Rome for
young artists. It was he, too, who enriched the collections of

the Royal Library, later the Bibliothèque Nationale, and created the Cabinet of Medals.

With Richelieu, Colbert was the principal founder of modern France. The two men resembled each other little, except in creative imagination, a prodigious capacity for work and a sort of feverish passion in the service of their country. They represent in this phase of history, in which the idea of the state triumphed finally over local particularisms, the sudden up-thrust of French ambition. The economic, administrative and intellectual fabric of our nation still bears many significant imprints of Colbert's genius, as our policy still obeys certain impulses that date from Richelieu.

Still, however large and lasting has been the influence of his work, Colbert seems not to have been wholly understood. For the relative check administered to his great designs, one must not look solely to the humour of Louis XIV. On the contrary, it is a wonder that for more than twenty years a king so proud should have subjected his will and his dreams to the arid and tiresome labour that such a minister imposed on him. Louis XIII had not had to support such a restraint at the hands of Richelieu. In the end, Louis XIV let himself be drawn on by other ambitions and be distracted dangerously by the temptation of more palpable triumphs, nearer to hand and less morose than those Colbert offered. But the secret of the historic contradiction incarnate in the figure of the son of the draper of Rheims is not concerned with the rôle of Louis XIV.

The truth is much larger and more important. From the moment that France, by the defeat of the Habsburgs of Austria and Spain, became the preponderant state in Europe, she found herself borne on towards the rôle of empire. But the character of France, the underlying cause alike of her balance, her strength and the fluctuation of her ambitions, resides in this : that she is a continental power open to the seas. Between the pressure of continental necessities and the attraction of outer expansion, France remained divided and undecided.

Colbert bore in his mind the aim of achieving the imperial rôle of France by trade and industry, technical knowledge, maritime supremacy, colonies — all the means which were to make the British Empire. But France is not England. France's strong continental attachments forced her to seek empire first on her own continent. From Henry IV to Louis XIV, from Louis XIV to the Revolution, to Napoleon I, to Napoleon III and the Third Republic, France, after seeking fortune on the sea, has always in the end sacrificed the sea to the continent — without being able, precisely for lack of mastery on the sea, to achieve her designs on the continent. The failure of Colbert is the inherent contradiction in the French destiny made by the very divergence of her geographical opportunities.

In the 18th century, in a supreme effort, France achieved a dazzling compromise of empire, continental and maritime, in the realm of the intellect and the arts. She achieved it thanks to the work accomplished by the great men of the 17th century. But it was only for a short time. Soon policy had to choose between the continent and the sea: a painful choice and one that the French imagination has never accepted.

Louis XIV himself would have wished to associate for good, in his own glory, the ideal of Colbert with the ideal of Louvois.

Louvois and the Army: Vauban

Louis XIV loved glory too much not to seek that kind before which peoples bow most readily: military glory. 'The character of a conqueror', he observed himself, 'is regarded as the noblest and highest of titles.'

At first with an old political secretary of Mazarin's, Michel Le Tellier, then with his son François Le Tellier, Marquis of Louvois, Louis XIV created an entirely new army, the instrument of French preponderance. Louvois filled the office of Secretary for War for nearly thirty years, from 1662 to 1691. His influence on the king, less strong at the beginning than Colbert's, who was his senior by twenty-two years, did not cease to grow with his flattery of his master's pride.

Louvois had not a fine character. Always careful to have himself thought well of and to remove those who did not serve his ends, he showed himself obsequious and complaisant enough to the powerful; but he was so harsh, arrogant and offensive towards others that Louis, himself very courteous, was sometimes shocked by it. Like all the great makers of the 17th century, he was a tyrant for work, with a lucid and orderly brain, able to see the whole picture and every detail of a task, to prepare and carry through a reform with the most rigorous vigilance. He won the favour of the king, who loved toil, by his method of work. As he grew old, he came to look like a smug bureaucrat, small and fat, with his body held rigid, his face brimming with self-sufficiency, with grey-blue eyes, without scruple or pity.

Being only an administrator and without the imagination that made the genius of Colbert, Louvois had the good luck to receive the advice of the greatest soldier of the time, Turenne, raised in 1660 to the dignity of Marshal-General of the camps and armies of France.

Louis XIV increased the army on a permanent footing. Peace-time effectives reached 125,000 foot and 47,000 horse. The army was made professional throughout, with the same discipline for all the troops, the same rules of manœuvre and the same step — the 'Louvois step'. A system of commissariat was constituted, furnished with special equipment and re-victualling magazines: an innovation which at once ensured a marked advantage to the French army. The health service was improved by the creation of hospitals and ambulance-units. In 1674 the Hôtel des Invalides was opened for maimed old soldiers. In the training of officers and the recruitment of men, in arms, each war brought new improvements.

Louis XIV conducted, above all, wars of sieges. Hence the creation of a special corps of engineer-officers, whose chief was Vauban, appointed Commissioner-General of fortifications in 1678. A first-class engineer, as much by virtue of his science as by the gift he had—like all the great spirits of his age—of shaping into order both the whole and the details of a work, Vauban marked the frontiers of France with a series of fortresses of which the remains move us still by the beauty of their design.   He too was a glutton for work, an indefatigable creator, director and inspector of works, a technician of powerful imagination.   Beneath his roughness and frankness, this child of the Morvan concealed a devoted and sensitive soul. Louis XIV was fond of him and then, as happens, dismissed him because Vauban was not a flatterer.

Victories and Conquests: Peace of Nijmegen

In 1665 the King of Spain, Philip IV, died leaving a sickly son to inherit — Charles II — who seemed incapable of living for long, but who in fact reigned forty years.   In January 1668 Louis XIV signed with his brother-in-law, Leopold of Austria, a secret treaty partitioning the Spanish inheritance. Already, invoking the 'right of devolution' — a custom of Brabant in virtue of which the children born of a first marriage (in this case Maria Theresa, Queen of France and eldest daughter of Philip IV) were the sole heirs of their parents — Louis had ordered Turenne to invade Flanders and occupy Lille in the spring of 1667.   A little later, in February 1668, another army, commanded by the Prince of Condé, took possession of Franche-Comté.

In fact, Louis was determined to break the power of Holland, the Calvinist republic of 'cheese-merchants'.   Colbert himself, for commercial motives, drove him on.   Large-scale diplomatic preparations were made by the Secretary of State, Hugues de Lionne, then by his successor, Arnauld de Pomponne.   Louvois assembled an army of 150,000 men, amassed equipment and planned the stages of the future campaign.

In May 1672 the French forced the passage of the Rhine at the ford of Tolhuys and invaded Holland, whose fate soon looked desperate.   But, in an heroic uprising, the Dutch, sacrificing part of their territory and their towns, opened the sluices and broke down the dykes which protected the low country from the sea. The French had to stop at the edge of the inundated territories. Holland sued for peace ; but Louis XIV's demands were such that a revolution broke out in Holland, bringing the fanatical party of Orangists to power, whose leader was the young Prince William of Orange, who was named Statholder of the Republic. William succeeded in forming a European coalition against France, including the Elector of Brandenburg, the Empire and Spain.

Louis turned at once against his most vulnerable enemy, Spain. In 1674 Franche-Comté was conquered anew. Vauban forced the strong places of the Low Countries to surrender one by one. By a rapid winter campaign, which was a masterpiece of manœuvre, Turenne drove the Germans out of Alsace. The illustrious Marshal was killed by a cannon-ball near Salsbach on the right bank of the Rhine, in July 1675. Colbert's fleet achieved great things. The French fleet, commanded by Abraham Duquesne, beat the Dutch off Syracuse in 1676 : the famous Dutch Admiral, Ruyter, perished there.

The adversaries of France resigned themselves to signing the peace of Nijmegen in 1678. Spain paid the price : she had to cede to Louis XIV Franche-Comté and a dozen places in Flanders — Valenciennes, Maubeuge and Cambrai among others.

The gains obtained by the peace of Nijmegen were increased by the annexation to the realm of those lands that had at any time belonged to the newly acquired territories. France thus annexed Montbéliard, the Saar towns, Deux-Ponts, the greater part of Luxemburg, and Strasburg. The Emperor and the King of Spain recognised these annexations by the truce of Ratisbon in 1684.

On the morrow of the Peace of Nijmegen Louis XIV received from the town of Paris the name of Louis the Great.

The first twenty years of the personal reign of Louis XIV mark not only the apogee of the monarchy, but the high-point, perhaps, of the qualities, intellectual and moral, of our people. The men of the time and the king himself, the more or the less gifted, exemplify a maturity that is both vigorous and finished, a culture of mind and character that supports a splendid ambition to create and build. It is the result of a long process of controversies, reflection and education, that dates from the Renaissance and the religious struggles of the 16th century.

The tradition in schools and above all in literature has accustomed us to view the men of Louis XIV's epoch as persons on a fascinating stage, but too deliberate and a trifle artificial. In reality they were men of an ordered, but powerful and passionate, life. The artificiality was only in the trappings of their work. In the 18th century the trappings gained upon the characters.

This first period of Louis XIV was also an epoch of great prosperity, as even the accounts of rural families show.

CHAPTER III

The Exhaustion of Glory

❖

*Madame de Maintenon — The Jansenists — Revocation of
the Edict of Nantes — Europe against Louis XIV —
Spanish Succession: Treaty of Utrecht — Miseries and
Humiliations*

TURENNE had been killed in 1675. Colbert died in 1683.
These two men belonged to the generation that had known
the monarchy brought low and ruined by the misfortunes of
the Fronde, before it mounted to a degree of incomparable
power.

With them gone, Louis XIV submits to the influence of
the men of his own generation, of those who, since their
twentieth year, have participated in the success of a king whom
they could not flatter enough. The person who represents
this presumptuous generation best is Louvois, Minister of War
and, in consequence, of glory : the young rival whose growing
favour with Louis poisoned the last days of Colbert.

From now on, the policy of Louis XIV no longer pursues
only results : it seeks satisfactions of prestige. Self-love, the
worst enemy of good sense, blinds the eyes of the monarchy.
The king becomes his own god.

The first Louis XIV was human, sensible and sensual,
accessible to life, ambitious for greatness, but not hiding his
weaknesses ; exacting for himself and others, but not closed to
the idea of a society outside his approbation. Even his
scandalous liaisons with Mlle de La Vallière and especially with
Mme de Montespan took away from his spirit the formidable
mixture of pride and rigour. The new Louis XIV, the Louis
of the fifties, while retaining his qualities of application, high
conception of duty and courtesy, gradually loses, by reason of

thinking himself above human beings, the measure of the human. Politics, however, is the art of the human.

In 1683, after the death of the Queen, Maria Theresa, he married Mme de Maintenon, granddaughter of the poet Agrippa d'Aubigné, a woman of real worth, Catholic and serious-minded, intelligent and well-educated, but who knew nothing of the business of reigning and governing and thought that one managed the greatest kingdom in the world as one managed a family of the lesser nobility.[1] She rendered invaluable service to the person of her illustrious husband. But by the rather servile cult she paid to him, as by the influence which her moral rigour had on him, she completed the process of enclosing him in the prison awaiting princes who are subjected to too much adulation : artifice and artificiality.

The Jansenists

The political mistake that sovereigns who have too much pride always commit is to violate men's consciences. It was not his religion, but his pride that impelled Louis XIV to use force in matters of religion.

He began by embroiling himself with the Pope in reopening an old dispute of the Middle Ages on the subject of the 'right of regality': the right which the sovereign claimed of administering a diocese during the vacancy of the see and of enjoying the revenues. This right did not exist in the dioceses of the South. In 1678 Louis XIV claimed to apply it indifferently to all bishoprics, and Rome took offence. In 1682 the king invited an assembly of the French clergy to pronounce against the Pope and to uphold the 'liberties of the Gallican Church' against ultramontane pretensions. Bossuet drew up the 'Declaration of the Four Articles', affirming the independence of the temporal power in regard to the Church, the superiority of universal Councils over the Holy See, the unchangeable character of the liberties of the Gallican Church

---

[1] This is a little unfair to this remarkable woman, who is now known to have interfered in government less than has been supposed.—A. L. R.

and, finally, the relativity of the Pope's judgments. This dispute made a great disturbance and lasted till 1693. The Pope obtained a complete retraction of the doctrines called Gallican, but gave way on the right of regality. A simple negotiation and some bargaining would have gained the king the same result, without plunging the dioceses into trouble for more than a decade. The Pope possessed, to defend himself against the presumption of Louis XIV, means of which neither the Jansenists nor the Protestants disposed.

Mazarin, little versed in religion but very vengeful, could not abide the Jansenists, whose relations with Cardinal de Retz, his enemy, and whose uncompromising doctrine equally displeased him. Before his death he had advised the young king to suppress them. On the other side, the Jesuits, who felt the moral influence of Jansenism on the middle class growing, kept up an open war of controversies and accusations against the people of Port-Royal and their school — a war illuminated on the Jansenist side by the publication of the *Lettres provinciales* of Blaise Pascal in 1656. Louis XIV had always shown aversion to the 'sect'. When he fell under the influence of Jesuit confessors, Père La Chaise and then Père Le Tellier, aversion changed into persecution. In 1709 twenty-two old nuns of Port-Royal des Champs were expelled from the convent by the lieutenant-general of police assisted by three hundred soldiers. Then the convent was razed to the ground, and even the cemetery destroyed. In 1713 Pope Clement XI condemned Jansenism anew by the bull 'Unigenitus'. In consequence of which, to make recalcitrants submit, the king had more than two thousand persons imprisoned.

By these useless brutalities, which offended a whole school of thought — the nobility of whose attitude had impressed many people — the monarchy broke with intellectual and moral forces which were soon to turn against it. Repressed Jansenism is to be found at the bottom of the 18th-century opposition to the monarchy and the Jesuits.

Revocation of the Edict of Nantes

Still more grave were the consequences of the famous act, the Revocation of the Edict of Nantes, by which Louis XIV abolished liberty of conscience.

After a century of blood-stained conflicts from Francis I to Louis XIII, France had arrived at a state of religious peace which gave satisfaction both to private consciences and public order. She had arrived at this, thanks partly to the position taken by the monarchy in not confusing questions of public order and questions of conscience. From 1560 on, a century before Louis XIV took over the government of his kingdom, Francis II had formulated the distinction : recognition of liberty of conscience, limitation of the public activity of dissidents. Two years later, in 1562, Charles IX and Catherine de Medici had proclaimed not only liberty of conscience, but liberty for the Protestant form of worship so far as compatible with the maintenance of public peace. The thirty years of so-called religious war had not changed the monarchy's point of view. In granting the Edict of Nantes to his old co-religionists, Henry IV maintained the position of his predecessors : reconcile the principle of religious freedom with the Catholic rule of the majority of the nation. Even Louis XIII and Richelieu, little inclined to tolerate promoters of indiscipline, had been careful not to combine religious intolerance with political repression : by the Peace of Alais they had confirmed liberty of conscience and freedom of worship to Protestants. Since then the Protestants, relieved from the agitation of restless spirits among the nobles who used their cause to trouble the realm, lived peaceful and industrious — peasants, merchants, bourgeois — concentrated chiefly in the West and South. They had in no wise participated in the Fronde. Mazarin himself said : 'If the little flock feed on bad grass, at least they do not stray'.

The pride of Louis XIV committed the sin that all the authoritarian tyranny of Richelieu had carefully avoided : the

use of force against consciences. In his excuse it has often
been recalled that spirits like Bossuet, Racine, La Bruyère,
La Fontaine, Mme de Sévigné approved. But writers at all
times are ill judges of politics, which they judge by surface
appearances or their own personal contacts ; and those, living
close to the Court, little knew the country. La Bruyère
understood nothing of the people. The only writer who
knew all parts of the country, Vauban, condemned Louis XIV's
obsession against the Protestants. What one can say to
excuse the king is that his entourage and his agents deceived
him as to the consequences of his intolerance and that his
mind, gifted in some respects, lacked the practical sense that
protects heads of states against their flatterers. Among the
bad advisers of the king in this matter were to be found former
Protestant converts, like the historiographer Pellisson.

Up to 1680 they confined themselves to applying the
Edict of Nantes in the narrowest and most vexatious manner.
At the same time they brought about conversions and even
bought them for money. In 1681 a decree permitted children
to abjure the Protestant religion from the age of seven on,
in spite of their parents' wishes. Then Protestants were
excluded from all offices, from employment in the royal
household, and from the legal and medical professions. Soon
after, to hasten conversions, recourse was had to 'dragon-
nades' : soldiers, dragoons transformed into 'booted missionaries', were quartered on Protestants, who, to escape such an
abuse often accompanied with brutalities, hastened to abjure.
It must be said to Louis XIV's credit that he condemned these
violences when he heard of them. But by the order of Louvois,
who encouraged the zeal of the Intendants, the process was
extended. At last, 18 October 1685, persuaded by his entourage that there remained in France only a few hundred obstin-
ates, the king signed the revocation of the Edict of Nantes.

The first consequence of this act was to force two or
three hundred thousand Frenchmen to emigrate, renouncing
their country and their goods to save their faith. It was not

only tradespeople, business-men and tillers of the soil who left. It was 9,000 of the best sailors, 600 officers and 12,000 soldiers. Provinces like Saintonge, Poitou, Touraine, the Lyonnais, experienced a real disaster. The emigrants went to England and Holland, to Brandenburg and above all to Berlin, carrying their skill and their unforgettable grievance with them. The revocation of the Edict of Nantes at once wrested the whole of foreign policy out of its course, by raising against France the Protestant states which had been her traditional allies since Francis I. Louis XIV himself felt the consequence almost at once, when in 1688 he had to face the formidable League of Augsburg.

At home, in regions like Languedoc and the Cévennes, where the peasants had not the means of emigrating, it was civil war. In 1702 the Calvinist peasants of the Cévennes, the Camisards or Whiteshirts, rose in rebellion. They had their heroes, like the young baker, Jean Cavalier. For three years they held their ground against a large number of troops and even against Marshal Villars, the best commander in the royal army. Louis XIV had finally to offer them an amnesty : French Protestantism survived.

The revocation of the Edict of Nantes is, without doubt, the gravest error that the Bourbon dynasty committed. This error weighed right up to our time on the internal politics, the foreign policy and even the reputation of France abroad. It created divisions and lasting grievances in our country. It is at the bottom of the peculiar passion that the religious question arouses with us. With a great number of free spirits, it has broken the reputation of the ancient monarchy for justice. It engendered, among the old nations of Northern Europe and among the new overseas, strong prejudices against French civilisation. . . . It was a folly that one can only explain by the unreality in which Louis XIV lived, victim of the cult of his own majesty — in fact, of his education by a Spanish mother.

Europe against Louis XIV

The revocation of the Edict of Nantes turned the Protest-ant states of Europe against Louis XIV at the very moment when the Emperor Leopold of Austria, victorious over the Turks, could bring his forces west and when William of Orange, France's enemy, became King of England. The League of Augsburg, formed in 1686 and augmented by new recruits up to 1690, laid France under the menace of a coalition which included nearly all the forces on land and sea of the rest of Europe.

A general war began in 1688. It was then seen what power and what means the country had acquired, thanks to the work accomplished in the first years of the reign. Louvois had the Palatinate invaded and laid waste in 1689. Marshal Luxemburg defeated the Germans at Fleurus in 1690, the Dutch at Steinkerk in 1692 and at Neerwinden in 1693. Marshal Catinat conquered the states of the Duke of Savoy by the victories of Staffarde and La Marsaille. At sea the tough privateers Duguay-Trouin and Jean Bart won renown. The royal fleet, commanded by Tourville, brought off a brilliant success at Beachy Head, but was beaten by the Anglo-Dutch at La Hogue in 1692.

In this glorious resistance France used up her reserves. In the cruel phrase of Voltaire, 'they were dying of misery to the sound of Te Deums'. At last, after nine years, everyone was exhausted. Peace was signed at Ryswick, near the Hague, in 1697. Louis XIV had to give up the greater part of the territories he had occupied since the Peace of Nijmegen and to recognise William of Orange as King of England. He obtained the definitive renunciation of Strasbourg by the Germans and the Emperor.

Spanish Succession: Treaty of Utrecht

Under the influence of a clever minister, Torcy, Colbert's nephew, Louis XIV perceived that he must make his diplomacy more flexible. He made an agreement with the maritime powers, England and Holland, to prepare the eventual regulation of the succession to Spain. A very sensible treaty was signed in London in March 1700 : French diplomacy renounced the claim to the throne of Spain and reserved simply a bargaining counter to obtain Lorraine and Savoy.

On 1 November 1700 Charles II of Spain died, naming as his sole heir the Duke of Anjou, Louis XIV's second grandson, on condition that the two crowns of France and Spain were not to be united. After some hesitation Louis XIV accepted the will. The Duke of Anjou became King of Spain under the name of Philip V and was recognised by all sovereigns, the Emperor excepted. England and Holland raised no objection. But suddenly Louis XIV changed his tack. He guaranteed Philip V his eventual rights to the crown of France, alarmed the Dutch by occupying the Spanish fortresses or 'barrier towns' of the Low Countries, exasperated William of Orange by recognising James II as King of England. William, before his death, succeeded in raising against France a new coalition of England, Holland, the Emperor and the greater part of the German princes. This was the Grand Alliance of the Hague, formed in September 1701.

So began the War of the Spanish Succession which lasted thirteen years and exhausted the country's strength. It had to defend both the frontiers of France and the possessions of Spain.

At first the French had some success. In 1702 the Duke of Vendôme beat the Austrians under Prince Eugene at Luzzara. For his part Marshal Villars was victorious over the Germans at Friedlingen in 1702 and at Höchstätt in 1703. But from the next year on, a series of disasters overwhelmed the royal armies. Marlborough and Prince Eugene won the battle of Blenheim in 1704. At the same time the English, who were allies of the Portuguese, captured Gibraltar. Two favourites of Louis XIV, Villeroy and La Feuillade, got their forces crushed : the one at Ramillies, losing the Spanish Netherlands, the other at Turin losing Piedmont, in 1706. Two years later the French were beaten again at Oudenarde. The Allies invaded France and took Lille.

The country was at the end of its resources and suffered terribly. In 1709 it endured the horrors of famine. Louis XIV consented to 'forget his glory' : he asked for peace. But the Allies replied with such demands that he had to break off. Then, turning to his subjects, he appealed to their devotion 'to the French name'. France, grievously weakened, responded to the appeal of her king. Marshal Villars, the successor of Turenne, fought a desperate battle at Malplaquet against Marlborough and Eugene, who had 23,000 casualties. Louis XIV asked again for peace and still could not obtain honourable conditions. At the end of 1710 the Duke of Vendôme crushed the Anglo-Austrian army at Villaviciosa in Spain. But soon, Prince Eugene, having carried almost all the fortresses of the North, prepared to march on Paris. Villars hurried forward and surprised the Austrian camp at Denain in 1712. After that it was possible to negotiate.

Two treaties signed, one at Utrecht in 1713, the other at Rastadt in 1714, put an end to the War of the Spanish Succession. Philip V kept Spain and her colonies, but solemnly renounced all rights to the crown of France. The Austrians got the Spanish Netherlands, the Milanese and the kingdom of Naples and Sicily. The Duke of Savoy obtained Sardinia and the title of king. As for England, she had ceded to her Gibraltar, Minorca, Newfoundland, Acadia and the entrance to the St. Lawrence, with commercial and maritime privileges that gave her limited intercourse with the Spanish colonies. She exacted the closing of the port of Dunkirk upon the North Sea.

France saved, more or less, her position on the Continent. But she had exhausted herself without any compensation, had lost the political benefits of a century of victories and rendered her maritime and colonial future precarious.

Miseries and Humiliations

During the first twenty-five years of Louis XIV's reign, in spite of the increase of taxes, France had prospered. Colbert's initiative and even his projects merely, awakening the economic energies of the nation, had brought about a rapid increase of wealth. Without this expansion of wealth — of which one should seek the signs in public and private accounts rather than in the narratives of writers — the splendour, the works and the reforms even of the reign would have been impossible, as the resistance to the disasters of the last period would have been inexplicable.

Up to the war with Holland the old imposts, the 'taille' (a direct tax), the 'gabelle' and the 'aides' (indirect taxes), hardly sufficed for the payment of annual expenses. But afterwards, it was necessary to have recourse to loans. From 1685 when the capitation tax was established — a personal and vexatious imposition — government fell into all sorts of fiscal, credit and monetary expedients, sale of offices and even lotteries. At the end of the reign, the most honest and capable of Louis XIV's last ministers, Desmarets, nephew of Colbert, considered bankruptcy inevitable. Industry had contracted. From financial ruin and dearth only a few speculators profited, like 'Turcaret', whom the comedy of Le Sage exposed before public opinion.

Want, and then famine, took on a fearful character in the countryside. The time of Henry IV and Sully had certainly gone. The king, surrounded by a Court of noble flatterers, lived remote from the people. He was absorbed by war and diplomacy, by religious affairs, buildings, the care of the *décor* which never seemed to him too expensive for his glory. The almost incessant war on land and sea left less and less opportunity for trade, and consequently smaller and smaller revenues from commerce. It was necessary to look for money, in St.-Simon's phrase, 'right in the bones of the subjects'. The peasant, victim of the lowering of prices due to the scarcity of currency, had no other defence than flight or revolt against the demands of taxation and the lords. Peasant revolts broke out in several regions, notably in Brittany. In 1707 Vauban estimated the number of beggars whom 'hunger and want had driven from their homes' at two millions. In 1709 troops had to be brought to the bridge of Sèvres to stop the market-women of Paris from marching to Versailles to demand bread. The lackeys of the king himself, it was said, begged at the gates of the palace.

At the end of August 1715 his leg was attacked by gangrene. Louis XIV watched death draw near with that self-control, that majestic imperturbability which were the admirable sides of his character. He repented of his love for buildings and for war. He confessed himself 'unhappy' in not having been able to bring comfort to his people. He died on Sunday morning, 1 September, seventy-seven years old.

Louis XIV is the most illustrious of our kings, the one who, with his distant ancestor St. Louis, contributed most to the prestige of the French name. But he was never popular. He obtained almost all his desire for glory of every kind, except that legendary kind that the people had not refused to the most unsatisfactory kings of former times, like John the Good. According to St.-Simon, whose judgments are otherwise suspect, Louis XIV's death caused the provinces to 'thrill with joy'.

He had incomparable gifts for the craft of king : a very high conception of his rôle and not only the passionate ambition for fame and glory, but the desire to be a good prince. He was the hero and the victim of a conception of monarchy in which the strong nationalism of the French in his age was overlaid with artificiality borrowed from the Spanish tradition. Heir to the work of Henry IV, of Louis XIII and of Richelieu, he carried it to the summit of its greatness and at the same time used it up and, so to say, exhausted it. He misunderstood or strained some of its

Louis XIV

principles, both at home and abroad.   Certain historians
maintain that the abuses and mistakes of his reign rendered the
French Revolution inevitable a century later.   A tendentious
case : no revolution is inevitable and a revolution is not
prepared a century beforehand.   In the past the monarchy had
undergone far more dangerous trials than those it suffered from
the sort of lassitude in which Louis XIV left it.

What is true is that beneath the appearance of absolutism
on the surface, Louis XIV allowed the ties which bound the
king to the nation to be relaxed.   He isolated the sovereign
from his subjects.   He put royalty into a prison of courtiership.
He made it one with an idle and hated nobility.   By the sale
of forty thousand new offices he lost grip of the real administration and immeasurably increased both the pretensions and
the powers of a sort of bureaucratic feudalism.   Finally, by
his religious policy, going beyond the rôle of guardian of
public order to violate beliefs and ideas, he raised up a vast
movement of intellectual criticism against the French monarchy
at home and abroad.

After him the monarchy needed at the same time to come
back to its true traditions and to renew them.   During the
18th century it tried to reconcile the irreconcilable : the
sumptuous artificiality of a Court monarchy and the function
of popular arbiter.   After Louis XIV it needed a Charles V,
a Louis XI, or a Henry IV.   What it got was a spoilt child,
Louis XV.

CHAPTER IV

The French Monarchy at the Crossroads

❖

*The Regency — The Banker, Law — The Administration
of Fleury — Louis XV and his Character — The War of
the Austrian Succession*

THE first half of the 18th century represents an historic crossroads. Louis XV, an orphan five years old, who succeeded
to his great-grandfather Louis XIV, assumed a heritage as
burdened with difficulties as with prestige. The regency fell
to the late king's nephew, Philip of Orléans, the famous
Regent of the libertine stories. A man of lively intelligence,
brave and good-humoured, Orléans lacked only those qualities
that are indispensable to government: the bent for work,
serious-mindedness and a certain decency in behaviour.

Just as Louis XIII's will had been annulled formerly, so
was Louis XIV's now. The latter, uneasy about his nephew's
character, had provided that power should belong to a council
and reserved the most important charge for the Duc de
Maine, one of his legitimised children by Mme de Montespan.
The Parliament of Paris was only too happy to show itself
once more the arbiter of royal affairs: it recognised all
authority to be in the Regent.

The Regency

The Regency lasted eight years, from 1715 to 1723. It
was a régime of relaxation, the apogee of elegant anarchy,
of ingenious disorder in morals, politics and finance, a sort
of escapism into licence and fantasy. They thought they had
reserves to consume, when the nation was exhausted and the
moral credit of the monarchy impaired.

Louis XIV had been converted to piety under the influence of Mme de Maintenon : all the courtiers had turned devout to flatter the king. After twenty-five or thirty years of obligatory piety, the Court, at last free, gave itself up to demonstrations of unbelief and debauchery. It was the time of the 'roués', of late suppers, balls and masquerades which people quitted drunk at dawn. The Regent himself set the pace and danced at public balls.

In government, the slackening produced a 'real beargarden'. The Regent, in gratitude, at first gave back to Parliament its right of remonstrance : remonstrances flew so fast and furious that a blunt stop had to be put to them in 1718. The old secretaries of state or ministers were replaced by six councils recruited from the higher nobility, a régime of arrogant 'polysynodie' which ended by making government impossible : three years later the system of secretaries of state was restored. Louis XIV's confessor, the Jesuit Le Tellier, was sent away and the Jansenists set at liberty. Then, as their retaliation degenerated into public agitation, the strong hand was imposed on them again in 1720.

The Banker, Law

The most astonishing episode of the Regency took place in the realm of finance.

Louis XIV had died practically insolvent, leaving 800 million livres of debts immediately due, a budget deficit of 77 millions, all the revenues already anticipated. The amusements of the Regency could not very well go far in such poverty.

The Council of Finance, presided over by the Duc de Noailles, consulted the bankers, particularly the brothers Pâris. They tried to get restitution out of contractors and munition-makers. All that did not produce much. Then appeared a sort of financial faith-healer, the Scotsman, John Law.

This Scot knew banking well : he had learned it in London and Amsterdam, in Genoa, Florence and Venice. He was very intelligent. He possessed that kind of faith in the virtues of speculation which Frenchmen, inclined to miserliness, regard with a mixture of fear and envy. As money was needed without any means of finding it, Law easily won over the Regent. His system consisted in transposing the methods of banking into the domain of public finance. The state should be banker, to receive the money of individuals and to make it yield returns in all sorts of enterprises more or less privileged. By means of which, bank-bills payable at sight would be issued, and their number would be increased according to the needs of credit, the development of business and the amount of trade or speculation. Out of the profits the state would pay its creditors.

Law was authorised to start a private bank in 1716. In 1718 this became the Royal Bank, the state bank. The bank's bills succeeded at the same time as its commercial connections grew. Law had founded the Company of the West or Mississippi Company. Then he bought back the monopoly of the old Companies, of the East Indies, China, Africa, etc. He formed the Company of the Indies. The capital of all these concerns was put into stock, like that of the bank itself, payable a quarter in specie, three-quarters in bills.

As might have been foreseen, a formidable boom ensued, based on the new abundance of means of payment, on the commercial privileges that the bank enjoyed, and on the announcement of the riches, gold-mines and precious stones which it was to exploit in the colonies, particularly in Louisiana. . . . In less than two months, thirty thousand people rushed to Paris from the provinces or abroad to profit from stock-jobbing and the rise in the price of shares. After that, it was easy to borrow. In 1719 Law issued a loan of 1,600 millions in the name of the Companies, to pay the debts of the state, of which they became sole creditors. Some months later, stocks of companies issued at the price of 500 livres, rose to 20,000. This was the peak, and soon after the fall began. The rate of return on stocks diminished in proportion to the speculative rise in

value of the capital. The interest distributed being thus
reduced to 1 per cent, it was to the advantage of holders to
realise their holdings. They began to sell. Selling gathered
speed. The Duc de Bourbon, a prince of the blood, realised
60 millions at one blow. Everybody took fright. That meant
bankruptcy. In 1720 the bank suspended payments.

'Law's system' has left, in the minds of the French, the
memory of a sort of guilty adventure, mysterious and yet
somehow possessing genius. The fact is that our thrifty people
have never had the feeling for banking. Actually, the Law
episode is one of the classic cases in the art of banking. It
has been repeated thousands of times through history, on
large or small scale, among commercial and colonising peoples.
The fundamental idea consists in multiplying the capital and
making it mobile in the form of bills and discounting their
eventual productivity. Law's errors appear banal today. They
were above all to confuse a deposit bank with a commercial
one, to misunderstand the rule of liquidity and not to know
how to avoid the crash at the peak, that is to say, the out-
running of possible returns on the shares by speculation on
capital appreciation.

The state emerged from this experience with its debt a
little lightened. The Company of the Indies and the prosperity
of the port of Lorient, on which its trading operations were
based, survived. But the French support the alternation of
speculation and bankruptcy less well than others. All confidence was killed for a long time. Low morals and venality
had won, from crossing-sweepers to princely families. The
bitterness of those who were ruined and their rancour
against the lucky stock-jobbers poisoned public opinion. The
monarchy appeared more or less responsible for the shattering
shifts of fortune.

The Administration of Fleury

The Regent died of an attack of apoplexy, 2 December
1723. Louis XV, now thirteen, had attained his majority, but

remained docilely under the influence of his tutor, Fleury, Bishop of Fréjus. Fleury got power handed over to the Duc de Bourbon, great-grandson of the great Condé. Bourbon was known, above all, as having realised an enormous fortune in the dizzy speculation that preceded Law's fall. He governed for two years, married Louis XV to Marie Leczinska, daughter of a dethroned king of Poland, then was abruptly exiled in June 1726 for intriguing against Fleury.

This time Fleury decided to take power himself : he was named minister of state and received the cardinal's hat. He was to govern France for seventeen years. A man of good sense, with a great deal of practical sagacity and subtlety, a man of order and decision, he would have been a great minister if he had not been so old : he was seventy-three and only relinquished power to die at ninety. After the terrible trials that had marked the end of Louis XIV's reign, followed by the eccentricities of the Regency, this old ecclesiastic, with a face of peasant cunning, understood very well that the country needed to breathe again. His policy of peace without and economy within kept off the accidents that threatened.

In finance and trade his government, guided by the financier Orry, Controller-General since 1730, came back to the principles of Colbertism. A balanced budget, stability of the currency, construction of roads for internal trade, encouragement to maritime commerce. Thanks to these means, France rapidly regained a prosperity which was to support the brilliant civilisation of the 18th century proper. It was the heyday of the Atlantic ports, Bordeaux, La Rochelle, Nantes, Le Havre. France's external trade doubled in a few years.

Under Fleury's administration there was no serious trouble except on the score of Jansenism. The Jansenists remained numerous mainly among the middle class of Paris and in the Parliamentary world. Fleury was suspected of being the man of the Jesuits, but in reality he aimed only at stopping religious agitation which threatened public order, and for that purpose to impose respect, at least outwardly, for the Bull 'Unigenitus'.

But, instead of yielding, resistance grew.   Men's minds were over-excited.   In the cemetery of St.-Médard miracles were seen at the tomb of a Jansenist deacon called Pâris, with a saintly reputation.   The sick flocked there and fell into convulsions. In January 1732 the police drove out the 'convulsives of St.-Médard' and closed the cemetery.   The Parliament of Paris ostentatiously upheld the Jansenists.   Some of its members having been arrested, it resigned in a body.   Fleury exiled them, then recalled them shortly after.   In the end the old minister succeeded in calming things down for the time.

Fleury was as wise in his foreign policy as at home.

Under the Regent, an old tutor of his, the Abbé Dubois, subsequently Cardinal, had conducted foreign policy.   This little man of low origin, lean and with a foxy look — whom St.-Simon represents as the incarnation of all the vices — possessed certain gifts as a diplomat.   He set himself to save the treaties of Utrecht against the projects of the Italian Alberoni, a curious and designing brain, whose dream was to throw the Austrians out of Italy and restore the Spanish ascendancy.   Alberoni had become head of the Spanish government through the favour of Elizabeth Farnese, second wife of Philip V.   To stop the dangerous enterprises of Alberoni, Dubois did not hesitate to come to an understanding with Louis XIV's old adversaries, England and Holland, which was joined later by the Emperor of Austria.   Thanks to which Spain, having started war, gave way and Alberoni was sacrificed by Philip V in December 1719.

Out of that, in order to seal the reconciliation of France and Spain, came a project of marriage between Louis XV and the Infanta Anna Maria, Philip V's daughter, a child of three, which would have condemned the young king to wait a long time for the chance of having an heir.   In fact, after the death of Dubois and the Regent, the Duc de Bourbon hastened to marry Louis XV to Maria Leczinska.   Philip V was angered and opened negotiations with the Emperor.   A new war seemed about to break out.

With the concurrence of the English minister Walpole, who was also of a peaceable disposition, Fleury succeeded in averting the conflict. He even succeeded in concluding, in 1729, a Franco-Spanish alliance which freed France from too close a dependence upon England.

In February 1733 the death of Augustus II rendered the elective throne of Poland vacant. Thirty years earlier Charles XII of Sweden had had Stanislas Leczinski elected King of Poland. After the crushing of Swedish power at Pultava, under the attack of Peter the Great of Russia, Stanislas had been dethroned. But on the death of Augustus II, Stanislas, now the father-in-law of Louis XV, pitted his candidature against Augustus III, who had the Austrians and Russians on his side. The Austro-Russian armies entered Poland. After six months' resistance, Stanislas escaped only with great difficulty from Danzig.

Louis XV could not ignore his father-in-law's misfortune, and France could not disinterest herself from Poland, her traditional ally. Yielding to the pressure of Chauvelin, Secretary of State for Foreign Affairs, Fleury allowed him to declare war on Austria in October 1733. An alliance was concluded with the Duke of Savoy and the King of Spain. A French army, commanded by the old Marshal Villars, crossed the Alps and, reinforced by the Duke of Savoy's Sardinians, conquered the Milanese in 1734. Villars died during the campaign, but the French defeated the Austrians at Guastalla, near Parma, while the Spaniards entered Naples.

After these first successes Fleury hastened to seek peace. In October 1734 he concluded preliminaries of peace with the Emperor Charles VI. In 1738, the final treaty was signed at Vienna. Stanislas Leczinski renounced Poland, but kept the title of king and received the duchy of Lorraine and the county of Bar, which were taken from Francis Duke of Lorraine, Charles VI's son-in-law. At the death of Stanislas, duchy and county were to come to the King of France. Don Carlos, son of Philip V and Elizabeth Farnese, was recognised king of the two Sicilies. So the War of the Polish Succession ended in the establishment of a third Bourbon royal house, the Bourbons of Naples, and in the perfecting of French unity on the east with Lorraine, annexed from the Empire.

It was an important success. The secretary Chauvelin piqued himself too much on it : Fleury had him dismissed.

A Russo-Turkish war had broken out in 1736. The Russians, supported by the Austrians, drove back the Turks who were in great danger. Turkey appealed to France. The French ambassador, Villeneuve, and an adventurer of talent, the Comte de Bonneval, encouraged the Turks' resistance. The Turks defeated the Austrians and by the treaty of Belgrade regained almost all the territories lost. In return the Sultan accorded to France the renewal of the 'Capitulations', that is to say, religious and commercial privileges conceded to Frenchmen in the Turkish Empire since Francis I. The Capitulations of 1740 assured the predominance of French commerce in the Levant.

The year 1740 marks the beginning of one of those periods in our history when French policy, between its continental traditions and its maritime ambitions, wavers, then, having sacrificed the sea, exhausts itself on the Continent. This is the long period of the War of the Austrian Succession (1740–48) and of the Seven Years War (1756–63) : a decisive period, in which France lost her position of indisputable pre-eminence.

The revival of Colbertism, the expansion of the maritime and colonial trade of France, the place taken by her merchants in the Levant and the West Indies, the development of the French marine which had greatly increased by 1730, the challenging prosperity of the ports of Bordeaux, La Rochelle and Marseilles, the prestige of French products which were much sought by the English themselves — all those things irritated England. England felt herself the more affected as at the same moment her traders, smugglers and sailors saw the market of the Spanish colonies, which the Treaty of Utrecht had opened to them, gradually close. In 1739 war broke out between England and Spain. Soon after, two French squadrons left to co-operate with the Spanish fleet. The peaceful Fleury himself was willing to seize the occasion offered to affirm the power of the king at sea and to bring down English pretensions.

The dream of Sully, of Richelieu and Colbert — the mercantile, naval and colonial supremacy of France — seemed about to be realised. But to achieve that, it would have been necessary to think only of the essential conflict, that at sea, against England who staked her future there.

It so happened that on 20 October 1740 the Emperor Charles VI died. So, suddenly, the problem of the succession to Austria opened up. At once a powerful party at Court and in Paris rose up to bring French policy back into the beaten track of continental ambitions and dynastic disputes. Here was the chance, they said, to achieve the ruin of Austrian power. The leader of this party, which invoked tradition, was a grandson of Fouquet, Marshal Belle-Isle. He and his friends argued as if Richelieu had not freed France from the constraint of the Habsburgs and as if Louis XIV himself had not paid grievously for his imprudence in continental affairs. It often happens that diplomacy, under the influence of mediocre men, thinks of the past instead of foreseeing the future. Fleury, who was very old and enfeebled, allowed his hand to be forced by the anti-Austrian party, the party of continental adventurers.

By a decree called the Pragmatic Sanction, of 1713, the Emperor Charles VI had laid down that in default of male heirs the succession to Austria should come to daughters. Later, it had become an obsession with him to assure the succession to his daughter Maria Theresa, born in 1717. When her father died she was twenty-three years old : she possessed rare qualities of mind and character. Frederick II, her worst enemy, was to recognise that she was 'a great woman, doing honour to her sex and to the throne'.

It was against this young and heroic woman that France

exhausted her strength for the benefit of the King of Prussia.

Four princes disputed with Maria Theresa all or part of the succession to Austria : the Elector Charles Albert of Bavaria, Philip V of Spain, Charles Emmanuel King of Sardinia, and lastly the most intelligent, the most determined and the most unscrupulous of all, the new King of Prussia, the famous Frederick II of Hohenzollern, who claimed Silesia. With regrettable lack of foresight, French diplomacy was to aid the superior genius of Frederick II to make the Prussian state one of the most enterprising and formidable forces in Europe.

Frederick invaded Silesia in December 1740. Four months later, the Prussians defeated an army of Maria Theresa at Mollwitz. A coalition of aspirants to the succession soon formed. Marshal Belle-Isle, who had departed for Germany, brought about an agreement between the Elector of Bavaria and the King of Spain. In June 1741 a Franco-Prussian alliance followed, to which the Elector of Saxony adhered. Without declaring war on Maria Theresa, Belle-Isle got the king to approve the sending of two French armies into Germany. The French, commanded by Belle-Isle, joined the Bavarians and occupied upper Austria ; they then invaded Bohemia and captured Prague by a daring assault, in which Colonel Chevert and Maurice de Saxe distinguished themselves. In 1742 the Elector of Bavaria was elected Emperor at Frankfort as Charles VII. It was Belle-Isle's triumph.

But by astonishing energy and political tact, Maria Theresa retrieved the situation. In 1741, responding to the desperate appeal of their young sovereign, the Hungarians swore that they would die for their *king* Maria Theresa and voted her a levy of 100,000 men. Upheld, on the other side, by the diplomatic support and subsidies of England, she succeeded in buying the King of Sardinia and then, in July 1742, by the cession of Silesia, in detaching Frederick II from the coalition. The Austrians returned everywhere to the offensive : they forced Belle-Isle to make a clever but costly retreat through the Bohemian mountains ; they invaded Bavaria and occupied

Munich ; they advanced to the Rhine and threatened Alsace.

In 1743 Maria Theresa raised against France a great coalition comprising, with Austria, England, Holland, Hanover, Saxony and Sardinia.

Victim of the ambitions of her continental diplomacy, France again found herself — as in the last years of Louis XIV — in peril both on land and sea with a decadent Spain for sole support.

In the meantime the aged Fleury had died : Louis XV at last began to reign.

The Character of Louis XV

Most historians have been so severe on Louis XV and he himself served his reputation so ill among his own subjects that one is almost inclined to rehabilitate him, if only out of a sense of just proportion. In reality, from the point of view of the public interest, the vices with which he is reproached were his least weakness. More serious was his inability to feel the gravity or even the importance of his position. With an air of elegant distraction he lived through his own reign, which he conducted as if bored by it all. He was the child too soon invested with this courtly royalty, dazzling, enchanting, creating fashions propitious to the arts — of which Louis XIV had set the splendid model — but foreign to the French people, whom its earlier kings had accustomed to a more human simplicity.

Actually France at that moment was in need of a king whom she could approach and prize and love as she wished. She stood in such need of it that it was enough for Louis XV to fall ill at Metz, in the course of the campaign against the Austrians in 1744, for men and women throughout France to throng the churches to pray for him and for him to be surnamed 'Louis le Bien-Aimé'. The following year his presence at the victory of Fontenoy gained him unheard-of popularity. All he had to do was to strengthen the monarchy, instead of enfeebling it. 'The French', noted d'Argenson, 'are the people most given to the love of kings that there ever will be.'

By temperament Louis XV was indolent. The exaggerated care that had been taken to spare him the least risk or the least unpleasantness in his childhood, then the succession of tutelages that had constituted the ministry of the Duc de Bourbon and the government of Cardinal Fleury in his youth, had made him lazy. Never having suffered at all, nor experienced anxiety or any opposition, having acquired the taste of living for what might turn up, he found himself free and responsible for governing at thirty-three, an age when it is too late to found a character. Hence his seemingly 'inscrutable' personality, in turn shy and capricious, silent and cynical, witty and flatly egotistical, disdainful of the business of kingship and fond of contacts of a low character, incapable of sustained effort and ceaselessly in quest of change, of distraction, travelling about, and having little adventures : a fine young man, neither ill-natured, nor stupid, nor cowardly, but whose too pampered existence, with everything made easy, destroyed his energy.

Married quite young to Maria Leczinska, older than he by seven years, he had ten children by her, of whom seven survived, six daughters and one boy. As the tutelage exercised over him by the old Fleury relaxed, he took to having mistresses. After Fleury's reign began that of 'favourites, mobcaps and petticoats'. The Duchess of Châteauroux was the first of these favourites to play a part in politics. She died in 1744. A bourgeoise, astute, ambitious and well-educated, Jeanne Poisson, soon named Marquise de Pompadour, succeeded in 1745 : she was to 'reign' for nearly twenty years, clever at making clients among artists and writers, directing ministers according to her humour, suspected of ruining the finances and perverting politics, and, finally, detested by the people.

Many kings had had mistresses or favourites in centuries that made more exacting demands on virtue than the

18th century. The particular scandal of Louis XV's conduct, for the public opinion of his time, was not that it outraged morals : the scandal was that it showed political weakness in the king, a sort of abdication. Louis XV made his mistresses figures of political importance. Accustomed to live under the tutelage of someone, he gave the government to the Pompadour as he had left it to Cardinal Fleury. The rôle of mistress became a public employment. Even under the most debauched kings, one had never seen quite that.

From then on there was neither 'personal government' as in the time of Louis XIV, nor 'principal counsellor' or first minister as in the time of Louis XIII. There was a series of ministers whose choice depended upon the views of the favourite, on the influences that acted upon her and through her, on the sentiments of the king. Among these ministers some were men of merit : it is possible to know how to play the courtier and be a good administrator. For example, the Comte d'Argenson, who remained Secretary of State for War for fourteen years, from 1743 to 1757. So too the Controller-General of Finances, Machault d'Arnouville, who, after the War of the Austrian Succession, tried to re-establish the financial situation by the imposition of the 'vingtième' or twentieth, on all incomes, including those of the privileged, in 1749. The privileged, the Parliaments, the provincial Estates, the clergy, resisted this so successfully that the main burden of it fell on the ordinary citizen, the Third Estate. Machault left the Ministry of Finance for that of the Marine in 1754.

A weak king never has his finances in order, because he does not know how to restrain his expenses. After Fleury's death Louis XV became wasteful and disorderly, drawing from the resources of the Treasury larger and larger sums to pay for his journeys, his buildings, his fêtes and those of the Pompadour, the pensions to courtiers and the debts of great nobles. The Court, by its demands, its prodigality and its follies, became, according to d'Argenson's phrase, the 'tomb of the nation'.

Louis XIV had thought to make it the shrine of the monarchical cult : Louis XV made it the object of the people's hate.

From 1750 onwards, popular hatred makes its appearance. It has a new character : it is anti-royal ; the Pompadour is insulted in the streets. D'Argenson writes, 'One sees an extraordinary antipathy growing up between the king and his people'. A riot breaks out in Paris and 'shocking things are bandied about against the king' ; soon, 'people talk only of the necessity of an immediate revolution . . . to remove the intolerable influence of the Court on the government'. The people demand a return to the system of first ministers 'wise and respected', or indeed the calling of the States General. The Court — an invention of Louis XIV's pride — having broken with the old memories of a kingship near to the people and hostile to the nobility, separates the king more and more from his subjects.

The War of the Austrian Succession

Up to the end of the War of the Austrian Succession, however, the people have the impression of being associated with a successful reign. Although Frederick II of Prussia deserts France a second time to treat with Maria Theresa, Louis XV's armies triumph under the command of a great soldier, Maurice de Saxe, a naturalised Frenchman, son of Augustus II, King of Poland. Three victories — Fontenoy in 1745, Rocoux in 1746, Laufeld in 1747 — enable the French to invade Holland and lay siege to Maestricht in 1748. These successes dissipate, for a time, the anxieties caused by the holding up of the Franco-Spanish armies in Italy, the invasion of Provence by Anglo-Sardinian forces, the growing superiority of the English navy and the loss of the fortress of Louisbourg which covered Canada. In India, it is true, the chief English station, Madras, was taken, thanks to the enterprise of Dupleix seconded by La Bourdonnais.

The Treaty of Aix-la-Chapelle, signed in October 1748,

was a truce.   Louis XV gave up all his conquests.   French
and English restored what they had taken from each other in
the colonies.   Frederick II kept Silesia.

It was a truce before the great test that everyone felt was
coming and for which a moral discipline was required that
the French monarchy could no longer command.

CHAPTER V

The Régime Borne Down by Society

❖

The Spirit of the 18th Century — Wealth and the Arts —
The Passion for Criticism — Applied Science — Anti-
Religion — Maritime and Colonial Disaster

IT was certainly less difficult for Louis XV to provide for the
well-being of his realm, the most powerful in Europe, and
the prestige of his crown, the most glorious in Christendom,
than it had been for Charles V to repair the follies of John the
Good, for Charles VII to recover France from the English,
or for Catherine de Medici to save the authority of the Crown
and the integrity of the kingdom in the Wars of Religion. . . .
But the task was not just to exploit the heritage of Louis XIV :
the new demands and dangers of the century had to be faced.

For the 18th century resembles the 17th only in quite
superficial appearances — the appearances, in particular, of a
Court tradition and of a royal *décor* which no longer correspond
to the deeper spirit of the time. The spirit is no longer the
same : in the 17th century movements of thought converge
towards order, authority, unity ; in the 18th, the spirit moves
away, movements of thought diverge in all directions, towards
criticism, discussion, doubt and change. France is no longer
the same : there is no longer the old bourgeoisie that upheld the king against the nobles ; there is a new bourgeoisie,
itself privileged, which uses the popular discontent to
attack alike nobility, clergy and king, henceforth regarded as
one. Finally, Europe is no longer the same : there is little
danger from Austria or Spain ; the decisive threats in future
come from England, whose mastery on the sea is growing,
and from Prussia which resurrects the continental danger in a
new form.

Circumstances called for one of those energetic, realistic, cunning kings, such as France had known in the past. We can say of Louis XV that he was better than his reputation. We cannot say that he in any way dominated the problems or the men of his century. Rather, he submitted to them or misunderstood them.

Wealth and the Arts

It is from the beginning of the 18th century that the social and worldly importance of money dates in France. And it is the ease with which profits are made in certain classes that permits the incomparable refinement of the arts of all kinds as well as of the life of society. The greatest spirits, like Voltaire, are possessed by the idea of money. Money becomes a preoccupation of literature. The immorality of the 18th century that has been so much denounced, or else so easily pardoned, was at bottom only the penetration of the social and intellectual *élite* by money. The 'reign' even of the Pompadour covers money matters.

The new importance of money in society comes from several causes. It comes, first, from the great number of people who suddenly become rich — from the beginning of the century on — by war-contracting, by speculation of all kinds on the realm's necessities and the monetary expedients of the king, on the banking adventures of the Regency and on colonial prosperity, and by farming the taxes. There is thus a pullulation of financiers, contractors, sub-contractors, bankers and business-men, which forms the base of this aristocracy of money, of which the body of big farmers of the taxes, the 'farmers-general'—patrons who well rewarded flatterers or the fixing of informed opinion — occupy the summit. The court nobility, to meet its expenses, and the higher bureaucracy (*noblesse de robe*), to lighten its burdens, seek the society of financiers and ally themselves to them. The development of international trade, relations with the mercantile states, England and Holland, the new prestige of banking and industry in a country where the majority of fortunes were up till then to be found on the land, the discovery by France of the laws of wealth and of the science of the 'economists' — everything turns men's minds to money. Finally, as a result of contacts with foreign countries, the diffusion of Court fashions, the relaxation of morals and the multiplication of pleasures, people's needs grow as well as their expenses. The very instability of fortunes, in consequence of the Law episode, which affected thousands of people, changes the morale of society. . . . All through the 18th century one senses the operations, open or occult, of the bankers. After Law, the banker Pâris-Duverney was for a moment a sort of secret first minister. One of the last ministers of the monarchy was to be the banker Necker.

We must pay attention to this change. The power of money creates a whole network of new servitudes. But at the same time it liberates mind and manners from their ancient bonds. What could only be done formerly under the control or the patronage of the Church or the monarchy, of the professions or official bodies, of regular and recognised forces, is henceforth accomplished more and more freely, thanks to the dispersed and individual connections that money gives. Money permits every insolence, except against itself. Thus money and no longer royalty animates luxury and fashionable life, the salons and the arts, literature, science, philosophy and politics.

The financier Crozat is the patron of the young Watteau. The financier Helvétius pours out 300,000 livres a year to artists and men of letters and in his wife's salon gather 'the States General of European philosophy'. At Madame de Lambert's and Madame de Tencin's, then at Madame Geoffrin's and the Marquise du Deffand's, men of intellect and learning, the philosophers, meet the *parvenus* of speculation and the tax farmers.

Under the influence of private patronage, which greatly surpasses that of official patronage, art attains a finesse and grace without parallel. But it becomes finicking, and loses in force what it gains in elegance. Small suites, intimate rooms, concealed staircases succeed the vast buildings of hitherto. Robust and massive furniture is replaced by light pieces, round tables, work-tables, card-tables, commodes, chiffoniers, secretaires, chaises-longues and easy chairs. Painters triumph in subjects witty, libertine or, on the other hand, intimate. Decoration on the grand scale is dead. Overdoors or pier-glasses are made gay with small scenes, *fêtes galantes*, picnics, pastoral episodes. Watteau, Lancret, Boucher paint not to teach, but to charm. Portraits become the fashion among the middle class as in the aristocracy. The middle class finds its artistic expression in the pictures of Chardin, while the master of the art of pastel, La Tour, catches the spirit of celebrated contemporaries. Official art continues in some fine examples of planned lay-outs, of which the most famous is the Place Stanislas at Nancy. But the taste of the time is dominated by rich connoisseurs and private commissions. From 1737 on artists present their works to the public at an exhibition called the 'Salon'. And art criticism appears — for criticism is the main tendency of intellectuals in a period when one has no longer to be careful of discipline or prove oneself worthy of respect.

The Passion for Criticism

We have difficulty today in estimating the full novelty of the intellectual attitude of the 18th century, because it has become, in a way, part of the routine of our education. Up till then the French mind in general respected principles, the sense of discipline, the dominating preoccupation with order and construction. In the 16th century the Renaissance had given a first impulse that was naturalist and critical, but this had been only a fashion of the learned or 'humanists', limited to restricted circles and, moreover, soon repressed by the tragic debate on religious reformation, a debate between believers. Then the 17th century had marked the extension

Voltaire

of serious reasoning, basing itself on observation and experiment, to elaborate conceptions or systems so ordered that they confined things to the abstract. The 17th century, by the genius of Galileo in Italy, Descartes in France, Hughens in Holland, Leibniz in Germany, Newton in England, had shed new light, but on the summits. In the 18th century the luminaries descend to the public, they are dispersed among a multitude of coteries, salons, clubs, meetings of those interested. Science is popularised ; it arouses enthusiasm lower down by its practical applications. From that time the notion gains credit that everything can and ought to be questioned. For the idea of permanent principles is substituted that of relative circumstances and changing data. The mind defends itself against the past by incessant criticism and reassures itself for the future by a new faith : faith in illimitable progress.

Traditions, beliefs, institutions, were passed through the sieve of critical reason. It was a woman, Mme de Lambert, who wrote in 1715, defining the programme of her century : 'To philosophise is to render to reason all its dignity and to give it back its rights ; it is to shake the yoke of opinion and authority'. Such an attitude of mind, coinciding with the refinement of culture and indeed of language that the age of Louis XIV had produced, helped to bring about the success of two writers who represent the perfection of the new rationalism : Montesquieu and Voltaire — Montesquieu, whose doctrines have passed into our political constitutions; Voltaire, whose spirit has become a part of the French spirit.

This passion for criticism has both a national source and a foreign one. The national source is the intellectual opposition brought about, under Louis XIV himself, by the excess of a system that had ended, less perhaps in political absolutism than in a sort of absolutism of ideas, manners and sentiments. The last writings of Fénelon and Vauban heralded the 18th century, whose method of discussion is already found fully formed in the *Dictionnaire historique et critique* which the Protestant Pierre Bayle, refugee in Holland, published in 1697.

After Louis XIV's death the intellectual opposition boiled over with all the more force since it had been so long repressed or inhibited, and since the Regency itself gave an official and cynical contradiction to the principles hitherto respected.

The foreign source was England. The 16th century had made Italy the fashion, the 17th Spain. In the 18th century English influence became the dominating one upon our intellectual trends. Starting from 1715 a long period opened in which the political alliance of France and England encouraged a double current of personal and intellectual relations between the two countries. French writers discover England, while the English visit the salons of Paris. Montesquieu and Voltaire speak enthusiastically of the political liberty England enjoys. 'We should love England', writes Voltaire. And Montesquieu is eloquent : 'England is at present the freest country there is in the world'. . . . It is from England that the prestige of the idea of revolution comes, supported by the famous theories of Locke on the rights of man, the sovereignty of the people and religious toleration.

Applied Science

The critical spirit drew its strength — even more than from the influence of foreign ideas — from the results of science. The 18th century was carried away, not with high speculation, but with experiments and discoveries. It had a passion for astronomy, physics, chemistry, natural sciences. It was the age of Fahrenheit, Réaumur, James Watt, mechaniser of industry, of Franklin, Lavoisier, Buffon. Thenceforward, people began to live in the expectation of material inventions, of the 'marvels' of progress, with the certitude that the power of human reason was henceforth without limit. How could the prestige of discoveries and the incessant increase of knowledge fail to make the traditional positions of politics and religion appear decrepit by contrast?

Finally, the expansion of commerce and of European settlements throughout the world, in the 17th and 18th centuries, brought other finds, other contacts, other comparisons, upsetting faith in the absolute value of old principles and habits. Five great colonial powers counted then : Portugal, Spain, the United Provinces, England and France. Thus all Western Europe felt the influence of a certain exoticism. A vast new geographical experience was built up, challenging peoples and their customs, in a way not less dangerous than scientific experiment for the stability of prejudices. Since Colbert, since Law, the great trading companies attracted their shareholders' interest towards the world overseas. The French possessed Canada, Louisiana, the Antilles, stations in Senegal, the Mauritius in the Indian Ocean. They founded trading stations in India, at Mahé, Yanaon, Karikal. Dupleix made Chandernagore the centre of Indian commerce. Soon after, he took Madras, with the aid of La Bourdonnais. In 1754 countries under French influence occupy the whole breadth of the Indian peninsula, from the Gulf of Bengal to the Gulf of Oman, covering an area twice that of France and peopled by thirty million inhabitants.

A flux of new ideas was produced in the French mind, in the course of the first half of the 18th century, while society itself was being modified both in its structure and in the balance of forces. It is this double movement of intellectual and social transformation that those writers who have been named the *philosophes* were to erect into a system.

The open attack of the *philosophes* on the old order breaks out at the very moment when the weakness of Louis XV provokes popular discontent. Montesquieu's *L'Esprit des lois* appears in 1748 ; the first volume of Buffon's *Histoire naturelle* in 1749 ; the first *Discours* of Jean-Jacques Rousseau in 1750 ; the first volume of the *Encyclopédie* in 1751.

Anti-Religion

In a world thus in motion Louis XV reigns, advised by the Pompadour, without a solid basis of support in the nation, without any appearance of will or consistency, without a prime minister. Hence come indecisions and clashes that rapidly exhaust not only the personal popularity of the king, but the authority even of the monarchy.

In this century in which beliefs and fanaticisms are declining through the very progress of the critical spirit, Louis XV allows a new exasperation in the way of religious quarrels to grow — quarrels in which the monarchy had always had the greatest trouble in safeguarding both its position as arbiter and its moral credit.

The Archbishop of Paris, Christophe de Beaumont, had forbidden the sacraments, in particular extreme unction, to be given to anyone who refused to sign a certificate of confession making complete submission to the Bull 'Unigenitus'. That was to refuse Jansenists burial in Christian soil, in the cemetery. Parliament, favourable to the Jansenists, but incompetent in spiritual matters, found itself competent enough, on the other hand, to regulate burials. In March 1752 the curé of St.-Étienne du Mont refused the sacraments to a Jansenist priest. Parliament replied by ordering the arrest of the curé. The king stopped the arrest. The Parisians took sides and demonstrated against the king for the Parliament. The affair and its complications lasted no less than five years. Paradoxically, it was the Pope who, to arrange matters, suppressed the exaction of a certificate of confession, in 1756. But so long a struggle brought the Parliament of Paris, supported by the dozen provincial Parliaments, to deploy against the royal authority a whole arsenal of arguments which amount to the doctrine — henceforth affirmed by the magistrates — of the superiority of the nation over the king. And passions remained so high that in 1752 an excitable valet, Damiens, struck Louis with a cane, an outrage for which the culprit paid the penalty in frightful tortures.

From these troubles the Pompadour, for a moment anxious, emerged more powerful than ever. She contrived the disgrace of the two best ministers, Machault d'Arnouville and the Comte d'Argenson. In 1758 she had the first place in the councils of the king given to a former general, now ambassador, the Duc de Choiseul, an adroit courtier and, in addition, an energetic mind, son-in-law of the financier Crozat, one of the richest men of the time. Choiseul flattered the *philosophes*, favoured the publication of the *Encyclopédie*, sought to get back some popularity for the régime. His foreign policy was at times happy. After the king had raised against himself the hatred of the Jansenists, Choiseul gaily sacrificed the Jesuits.

The Society of Jesus, considered as the militia of the Roman Church, had numerous enemies — the Protestants, the Jansenists, the Gallicans, the *philosophes*, the free thinkers of all shades. It was held responsible both for the excesses of absolutism in the Church and for the relaxation in morals. In 1759 the Jesuits were expelled from Portugal. This example encouraged their enemies in France. A French Jesuit, Father Lavalette, inspired by the colonial fever of the time, founded a trading-house in the West Indies and went bankrupt for several millions, inflicting heavy losses on the commerce of Marseilles. The business-men of Marseilles obtained from the Parliament of Aix a decree condemning the Society as responsible. The Jesuits committed the mistake of appealing to the Parliament of Paris, the citadel of Jansenism, which not only condemned the Society to pay but in 1761 declared its constitutions contrary to the laws of the realm. The General of the Jesuits refused to modify the constitutions — 'Sint ut sunt, aut non sint', said he; next year most of the Parliaments ordered the suppression of the Society in France. After two years of hesitation Louis XV issued a decree conforming.

Maritime and Colonial Disaster

The incidents of politics at home would have had less importance if the public mind had not been disturbed on the other hand by the king's reverses abroad.

The Seven Years War, lasting from 1756 to 1763, marks

the partial collapse of the great work of French supremacy which the first three Bourbons built up: Henry IV, Louis XIII, Louis XIV, under the inspiration of counsellors of genius like Richelieu and Colbert. It marks also the decisive advance of two powers which were henceforth to check our people's advance and periodically threaten its security: England and Prussia.

The immediate fact that determined this external catastrophe, which errors of judgment or conflicting policies had been preparing over a long period, was the famous manœuvre that has been called the Reversal of Alliances. It seems that Louis XV had a wish to prevent it, but weakly gave way to the preferences of the Pompadour, who was cleverly managed by Kaunitz, the celebrated ambassador and minister of the Empress Maria Theresa. Frederick II, perceiving correctly that he would gain more with English than with French support, precipitated matters by allying himself with England. This alliance at the moment when Franco-English rivalry turned anew to open war, automatically made France the ally of Austria, which was joined besides by Russia, Sweden and certain German states. Once again continental influences drew France away from the decisive field of battle: the sea.

At first there were successes. In 1756 the English Admiral Byng was not able to prevent the French from taking Minorca. In June 1757 the Austrians defeated Frederick II at Kollin and some months later a Hanoverian army capitulated at Klosterseven. Prussia was invaded by Russians, Swedes and Austrians. But Frederick II retrieved the situation with astonishing mastery. With one blow after another, on 5 November and 5 December 1757, he crushed a Franco-German army at Rossbach in Saxony and an Austrian army at Leuthen in Silesia. Thenceforward England put forth her full effort. The French forces, sometimes ill commanded, more often ill supported, were held in check everywhere on land and sea.

The navy experienced a double defeat in 1759 at Lagos

on the coast of Portugal and at Belle-Isle on the Breton coast. In Canada a real leader, the Marquis de Montcalm, without effective support from the mother country and with a small army, defended the magnificent possessions and the noble achievements of the French in America. Attacked at once on the Ohio, on the St. Lawrence and on Lake Champlain, Montcalm successfully resisted the English for three years. In July 1758 his band of 4,000 men defeated superior numbers at Fort Carillon on Lake Champlain. But some weeks later, for lack of troops, he had to give ground and let his communications with Louisiana be cut. In the following year the English, reinforced under the command of a young general of valour, Wolfe, drove straight on Quebec. On Thursday, 13 September 1759, on the heights of Abraham, not far from the famous citadel of New France, French and English confronted each other in a desperate battle. Montcalm and Wolfe both fell, like heroes. Quebec was occupied. Montreal was soon blockaded and surrendered a year later. . . . In India the commander of the small French force, Lally Tollendal, hard pressed by an Anglo-Indian army of 22,000 men supported by a squadron of fourteen ships, was forced to sign the capitulation of Pondicherry, which marked the end of our domination.

In Germany the arbitrament of arms swung to and fro. Marshal Broglie held up Ferdinand of Brunswick, Frederick II's best lieutenant. Frederick, at one moment threatened on every side, thought himself lost, but — aided by the dispersed tactics of his enemies and provided with regular subsidies by England — succeeded in defeating the Austrians anew in Silesia and in Saxony. In 1762 the death of the Empress Elizabeth and the accession of Peter III resulted in Russia's passing over to Prussia's side. Choiseul belatedly obtained the alliance of Spain, which had no other result than the cession of French Louisiana to the Spaniards.

By the Treaty of Paris, signed 10 February 1763, Louis XV surrendered Canada, the valley of the Ohio and all the left bank of the Mississippi to the English. He renounced India,

where the French were to keep, without garrisons, only the
trading stations of Pondicherry, Chandernagore, Karikal,
Yanaon and Mahé. The English kept, in addition, a part of
the Antilles and the French stations on the coast of Senegal,
which dated from Richelieu and Colbert. In Europe our
continental enterprises ended in a triple check, military,
political and moral. Frederick II acquired Silesia definitively.
Prussia became a great power. France's old allies, Sweden,
Poland, Turkey, soon suffered from the change of equilibrium
produced by the Seven Years War. In 1772 Prussia, Russia
and Austria proceeded to the first Partition of Poland.

All the same, in the last period of Louis XV's reign,
France gained Lorraine (which was annexed in 1766 after the
death of King Stanislas) and Corsica — its cession obtained
by Choiseul from the Genoese in 1768, in spite of the opposition of the partisans of independence, led by Paoli and favoured
by England.

The Treaty of Paris closes, with a sudden downfall of
French prestige, what was perhaps the most brilliant period
of our history. Since Voltaire it has become customary to
speak of the 'siècle de Louis XIV' and the 'siècle de Louis XV'.
The truth is that the radiating influence of French culture and
politics was continuous in various forms but with ever greater
range from Henry IV to Louis XV, from Richelieu to Choiseul.
At the same time, in spite of wars, temporary losses and
the abuses of power, the French nation benefited from the
internal order and reforms, the new equipment and new
impulse which had been given it by men like Colbert ; and it
was enriched too by the maritime and colonial trade which
remained prosperous up to the middle of the 18th century.
It became a prolific, ambitious nation, brimming over with
material and intellectual activity. Even the administration
made considerable progress : Louis XV's reign, so poor in
statesmen, had excellent administrators.

This France, in the full flow of its vitality, experienced in

1763 an external disaster which was the result both of an old and artificial misdirection of its diplomacy and of the immediate incoherence of its government. On the other hand, its internal régime moved towards an impasse, resulting from the fact that the monarchy, prisoner of the Court spirit, no longer having its support in the people, had allowed a rebellion to mature in the class that had become socially predominant : the middle-class bureaucracy, transformed by the sale of offices into a new feudalism commanding not only material and political force, but the greatest intellectual influence.

In the last quarter of the 18th century, the monarchy attempted to restore its position abroad, but failed tragically at home.

CHAPTER VI

Attempts at Recovery

❖

Louis XV's Last Reaction — Louis XVI: Turgot —
Vergennes: The War of the American Revolution —
Conflict of Court and Nation — Financial Impasse

THE end of Louis XV's reign reveals the raising of two great reefs against which the monarchy later is broken: the irreducible insubordination of the bureaucracy — holders of offices or magistracies — and the refusal of the nation to pay the expenses of the Court. We are at the juncture when the profound mistakes of Louis XIV's system — the institution of a religion of courtiership which is only the consecration of a more or less decorative parasitism — push the monarchy on to an almost desperate course.

Louis XV's Last Reaction

The conflict between royal power and the Parliaments broke out anew over the affairs of Brittany. The Attorney-General at the Parliament of Rennes, La Chalotais, an opponent of the Jesuits, opposed the military commander, the Duc d'Aiguillon. The duke having imposed a supplementary tax, the Parliament of Rennes rejected it on the ground that the Estates of Brittany had not consented to it. Louis XV had La Chalotais arrested. Upon which the Parliament of Rennes resigned in a body, supported by the other Parliaments of the kingdom. The king, descending unexpectedly 3 March 1766 on the Palais de Justice at Paris, ordered the parliamentarians to obey. 'It is in my person only that sovereign power resides.' But soon after this disciplinary session, royal authority flinched. The Parliament of Rennes came back and d'Aiguillon departed. In 1769 the members of the Parliament even brought a suit against d'Aiguillon, accusing him of abuse of power and of attempting to poison La Chalotais.

The Pompadour died in 1764. In 1769 Louis XV took for favourite a shop-girl of light morals, whom he made Comtesse du Barry. This beautiful but ignorant creature, following the traditions of her profession, interfered in politics. Thanks to her, the 'pious party' succeeded in getting Choiseul out of power in December 1770. After which, power passed to a triumvirate of the Chancellor Maupeou, the Abbé Terray, Controller-General of Finances and the Duc d'Aiguillon himself, who became Minister of Foreign Affairs. It was an energetic government, quick to react, and it lasted just long enough to arouse immense unpopularity against its policy.

Chancellor Maupeou, a man of decision, who knew what went on behind the scenes of parliamentary opposition all the better for having been a president of the Parliament of Paris, wished to subdue this opposition, if necessary by force. When the Parliament went on strike, musketeers were sent in the night of 19-20 January 1771 to each of its members to order them back to their duties. Most of the magistrates refused : the refractory were exiled and their places filled. At once Maupeou began to reform the administration of Justice. He created six 'higher councils' in the jurisdiction of the Parliament of Paris, to make justice more easily available ; he abolished the sale of offices on these councils and the fees which formed their principal source of revenue. The reform was extended to the provincial Parliaments. In spite of bitter resistance and a regular pamphleteering campaign, in which Beaumarchais distinguished himself, the reform seemed in a good way to succeed.

The Abbé Terray had to ward off a bankruptcy which seemed inevitable after the Seven Years War. He showed himself even harsher than Maupeou against the privileged and the financiers. He converted the paper money put into circulation by the farmers of the taxes, raised the terms for the lease of these farms, cut interest rates, imposed indirect taxes and tried like Machault to establish an equitable and general income-tax. The numerous and powerful interests he threatened raised themselves against him. His enemies held him responsible for all ills, including the bad harvests, and even accused him, during the dearth, of speculating in corn.

Louis XV died in 1774, decried, ridiculed, almost hated, at the very moment when his ministers were trying to restore the royal authority.

Louis XVI: Turgot

He left the throne to his grandson, Louis XVI, a great boy of twenty, backward in development, awkward, struck by a sort of stupor at the fate that made him king, but anxious to fulfil his duties honestly: a personality of mixed stock, in which were mingled the Germanic heaviness of his mother's family with a certain dignity that took after the Bourbons. His wife, Marie-Antoinette, daughter of the Empress Maria Theresa, was then nineteen: she showed the charm, vivacity and all the seductiveness that could be found in a decent woman who lacked seriousness of mind or any real fineness of perception.

Conscious of his inexperience, Louis XVI called to his side to help him govern, Maurepas, an old courtier of sixty-three, who had been Minister of Marine in the time of Fleury. This man, well-intentioned but with no fight in him, at once gave the new reign a character of weakness by restoring the Parliaments and replacing Louis XV's reforming ministers. In their place the king chose good 'honest fellows': Vergennes, a clear-sighted diplomat who received the Ministry of Foreign Affairs; Turgot, economist and administrator, that of Finance; Malesherbes, appointed secretary of the Royal Household; the Comte de Saint-Germain, the Ministry of War.

Turgot had the heaviest responsibility, that of finding money. In entering upon his task, he formulated his doctrine as follows: 'No bankruptcy, no increase of taxes, no loans'.

He thus proclaimed his resolve to seek resources in the lowering of expenditure, equalising burdens and developing public
wealth. He set the example of economy by renouncing half his
own salary, suppressed numerous jobs and improved the levying and collecting of taxes. But he could not conquer the bad
habits of the Court, the corrupt pensions, the ruinous luxury,
the disorder of 'discharged for cash down'. As a good classical
economist, by the celebrated decree of 13 September 1774, he
applied the principle of complete freedom of trade in corn.
He thus ran up against powerful interests. A bad harvest
supervened : the price of bread went up. Riots broke out
in Paris and outside. In May 1775 twenty-five thousand
troops had to be brought in to maintain order. In 1776
Turgot abolished the gilds and the system of forced labour :
in place of forced labour, which the peasants detested, a tax
upon all property owners was substituted.

The same man, clear-sighted, courageous and sincere, planned
other reforms of great importance, such as the suppression of
internal customs, the unification of import duties, the establishment of representative assemblies based on the municipalities. All that was lacking to carry through his excellent
projects was the support of a strong and steady authority.
Louis XVI soon let himself be got hold of by his courtiers,
irritated by the restrictions on expenditure, and by all the
people whose interests and habits were interfered with by
the minister. The Queen, Marie-Antoinette, made herself the
determined champion of Turgot's enemies. He was abruptly
dismissed 12 May 1776.

The same day as Turgot, Malesherbes went too—secretary
of the Royal Household, who had tried to put an end to
arbitrary imprisonments by 'lettres de cachet', and who
favoured the return of civil rights to Protestants.

The Comte de Saint-Germain, a very active reformer as
Minister of War, was also a victim, shortly after, to the
opposition of the courtiers. In two years he had brought
about decisive reforms in the army : restored discipline,

regularised promotion, reduced the sale of military offices, created preparatory schools for the sons of poor gentry, doubled the number of effectives and given France the best of artillery equipment. These reforms made possible the victories of the Revolution and the Empire. At the Ministry of Marine, Sartine, who held on some years longer, equipped the ports and arsenals and increased the size of the fleet : thanks to his work, France could oppose to England 264 vessels, 78 of them ships of the line.

Vergennes: The War of the American Revolution

As Minister of Foreign Affairs, Vergennes, supported by the king against the courtiers and Marie-Antoinette herself, was able for thirteen years to pursue a work worthy of the great traditions of historic French policy. Son of a president of the Parliament of Dijon, he had had a long career as diplomat : he had distinguished himself as ambassador in Turkey, then in Sweden and had been Secretary for Foreign Affairs from the end of Louis XV's reign, on the recommendation of Maupeou. He was a man of great application, severe, clear-headed and firm in his views.

Vergennes understood at once that, as against the errors committed since 1740 — which had cost France dear — what was necessary was to keep away from dynastic intrigues and adventures, get out of the hornet's nest of Austrian affairs, safeguard the peace in Europe and, through the tranquillity maintained on the Continent, try to check the growing power of England. In spite of the solicitations of the Emperor Joseph II, supported by his sister Marie-Antoinette, he refused to intervene in a new Austro-Prussian war which broke out in 1778 over the Bavarian succession. He let Joseph II exhaust his forces in Germany, on the Danube and in Eastern affairs. On the other hand, he delivered a master-stroke against England in lending the support of France to the revolt of the English colonists in North America.

In 1775 the thirteen English colonies in North America,

scattered along the Atlantic coast from Massachusetts to
Georgia, had revolted against the English government, which
claimed the right to impose taxes without their consent.   On
4 July 1776 the Congress of delegates from the colonies,
assembled at Philadelphia, voted the Declaration of Independence of the United States of America.   War had already
begun ; it promised to be long and difficult.   It was at first
to be expected that the Americans, ill-armed, lacking regular
troops and divided by local jealousies, would be defeated.
They won through finally owing to the tenacity and prudence
of their leader, a Virginia planter, a man of commanding moral
prestige :   George Washington, the Republican general.   And
thanks also to the support of France.

    At once Vergennes advocated intervention, and in this he
was supported by public opinion.   Benjamin Franklin, the
most celebrated of Americans, arrived in France in the month
of November 1776 and was received there with enthusiasm.
Already, astute traders — among them the writer Beaumarchais — were engaged, in connivance with the government,
in sending money, cannon, tents, uniforms to America.   In
1777 young officers of the French army, led by sons of the
great nobility, the Marquis de La Fayette, the Duc de Lauzun,
the Duc de Noailles, the Comte de Ségur, left as volunteers
to put themselves under the orders of Washington.   Then,
6 February 1778, Vergennes signed with Franklin a treaty of
commerce, friendship, and alliance between France and the
United States.   Free of continental entanglements France
could take her revenge on England.   Vergennes succeeded in
getting Spain and Holland to intervene against her ; while,
to resist the 'right of search' which the English claimed to
exercise upon neutral ships, Russia formed with Sweden and
Denmark a League of Armed Neutrality.

    In America the English had just occupied Georgia and the
capital of South Carolina, Charleston, when France sent to
the insurgents a corps of 6,000 men, commanded by Rocham-
beau, with the squadron of Admiral de Grasse.   With this aid,

Washington was able to lay siege to Yorktown in Virginia, where lay the English army of Cornwallis, which surrendered 19 October 1781. This victory assured the independence of the United States. At sea, the French squadrons, reorganised and well led, held the English fleet at bay, in the Mediterranean and the West Indies, as well as in the Indian Ocean where Suffren distinguished himself.

Peace was signed at Versailles, 3 September 1783. The English recognised the independence of the United States, ceded Minorca and Florida to Spain, gave up to France Senegal, the island of Tobago in the West Indies, the islets of St.-Pierre and Miquelon and the right to fortify Dunkirk.

France recovered her prestige. She had co-operated decisively in achieving the independence of the first European state outside Europe. Her ideas, those of her writers and philosophers, had encouraged the American Revolution : they came back fortified by the prestige of a great victory overseas.

Unfortunately, on the other hand, the war had meant an enormous expenditure — more than a milliard and a half.

Conflict of Court and Nation

In October 1776 Maurepas had entrusted the country's finances to a Protestant banker of Geneva, Necker, a man more clever than profound, imbued with the ideas of the day ; for whom his wife, by the brilliance of her salon, had made a great reputation with the *savants*, philosophers and men of letters. Necker sailed with the wind : instead of levying new taxation, he borrowed. Then he started reforms in the direction desired by public opinion : he reduced assignments to the farmers of taxes and introduced state administration for the national domains, the aids and feudal rights — the origin of our system of indirect contributions ; he improved hospitals and reformed prisons, suppressed 'third degree' methods by which accused persons were man-handled, and abolished serfdom on royal domains. Taking up an idea of Turgot's, to associate the educated classes in the administration of

the country, he tried out provincial assemblies in Berry and
Guyenne.

As a Protestant he was suspect to the clergy. The Parliaments felt themselves threatened or insulted by his reforms.
The old Maurepas saw the advance of his former protégé with
impatience. Necker in his turn was subjected to a whispering
campaign, pamphlet attacks, defamatory libels. In February
1781 he replied with a bold counter-attack : the publication
in the form of a 'Report to the King' of a Budget statement.
It was the first time in our country that a public statement of
the royal finances was made, in the English manner. The
public was aroused by the Report, above all because it revealed
the expenses of the Court and the pensions poured out on
the courtiers. They decided he should go. Necker forced
Louis XVI to choose, by demanding of him the title of Prime
Minister and new provincial assemblies. The king, influenced
by Maurepas and fearing the opposition of the Parliaments,
allowed Necker to resign, 19 May 1781. Public opinion
concluded that the privileged were strong enough to obstruct
the reforms it demanded. Maurepas died the same year.

From then on, the Court ruled, with the growing influence
of Marie-Antoinette and the Comte d'Artois, the king's
brother. The queen exposed herself thus to popular hatred :
her frivolity was no longer forgiven ; her imprudences were
exploited as scandals. In 1785 the affair of the Diamond
Necklace made her appear in a very questionable light.[1]

Necker's immediate successors, Joly de Fleury and
d'Ormesson, could not check the disorder in the royal
finances. At the end of 1783, on the suggestion of people at
Court, the king called Calonne to office, former Intendant at
Metz and at Lille — an ingenious man, cheerful and optimistic,
who set out to arrange everything by good humour. For
three years he succeeded in maintaining the illusion of financial
ease by borrowing incessantly. Suddenly, faced with the

---

[1] This celebrated affair, too complicated to go into here, is the subject of a famous
essay by Carlyle, 'The Diamond Necklace'.—A. L. R.

excess of his prodigality, credit took flight. Then Calonne changed his course : he proposed reforms more severe than those of Necker : he took up the rôle of Turgot. On 20 August 1786 he submitted his plan of reforms to the king, who was dumbfounded by it.

Financial Impasse

This plan of reforms reopened immediately the conflict between the public interest, represented by the government, and the privileged — the question was how to get them to pay. At the moment of taking up the struggle, Calonne committed a great blunder that was to bring about his defeat. He thought of bringing together an Assembly of Notables, to which he would submit his plans. It furnished the privileged, forming the majority of the 'notables', with the opportunity to gather together to defend their privileges and at the same time to pose as representatives of the nation against royal power. The Assembly, sitting at Versailles 22 February 1787, refused to discuss plans for taxation so long as it did not know the origin of the deficit, and appealed to public opinion. Once more, defamatory libels supported the manœuvre of the privileged. Once more, Marie-Antoinette took part against the minister attacked. Calonne had to resign in April 1787.

The queen had power given to one of the notables who had led the opposition, Loménie de Brienne, Archbishop of Toulouse. Becoming minister, he realised the necessity of reforms, but ran up against the same resistance as his predecessor. He dismissed the notables and decided to present the proposed reforms directly for registration by the Parliament. Parliament refused to register the fiscal decrees and, taking the offensive, on 16 July 1787 declared that only the nation assembled in its States General could consent to permanent taxation. So the privileged, taking advantage of an equivocation, took refuge behind the nation.

Brienne exiled the Parliament to Troyes. But he was too

late : riots broke out ; the idea of a great revolution spread in all classes. The queen was publicly insulted, nicknamed 'Madam Deficit' and 'the Austrian Woman'. Brienne negotiated with the Parliament and abandoned his proposals for taxation. On 19 November 1787 the presence of the king and a sitting of nine hours were necessary before Parliament would register a decree for a loan ; then, after the king's departure, the registration was declared illegal.

It was henceforth a struggle to the end, between the Parliaments and royal power. The Parliaments had the intellectual circles and popular opinion for them — both of which they flattered with consummate skill. The royal authority had only slight impulses of energy left, betrayed by the Court and by a great part of the nobility itself. The Parliament of Paris gave a judgment which was a declaration of the rights of the nation, in which it presented itself as the defender of liberty. At the beginning of May 1788 Brienne hit back, by ordering the arrest of two leaders of the opposition, the magistrates d'Épremesnil and Montsabert. Then the king imposed six ordinances drawn up by the keeper of the seals, Lamoignon, who transferred the registering of the decrees to a plenary court, and to forty-seven chief bailiwicks the greater part of the cases hitherto coming within the jurisdiction of the Parliaments. Procedure was improved and torture abolished.

But royal authority no longer had any solid support in the nation. Movements of revolt broke out in Paris, in Brittany, in Béarn. On 21 July 1788 the Estates of Dauphiné, assembled at the castle of Vizille — six hundred deputies of Nobility, Clergy and Commons — addressed an appeal to all the provinces to resist despotism, to refuse taxes and demand the calling of the States General. Under the pressure of this agitation, the crisis mounted rapidly. Brienne demanded an advance of funds from the Assembly of the Clergy. It refused, and also demanded the calling of the States General. Bankruptcy was imminent. The king accepted the summoning of the States General for 1 May following. It was none the less necessary to suspend payments.

Against his will, Louis XVI on 26 August recalled Necker, who obtained from the bankers and the great merchants a loan of 75 millions. The Parliaments were victorious. But they had opened wide the gates to Revolution.

THE REVOLUTION

It is a temptation for historians to reconstitute concatenations of events after they have happened. Thus the Revolution has been represented as the ineluctable end of the movements, political, intellectual and social, of the 18th century. In fact, revolutions are never ineluctable. They result from the feebleness and the immediate mistakes of the rulers. A régime is not overthrown : it falls. The old régime could have changed, transformed itself and lasted. Its fall came, not from a push from below, but from failure at the top. Under John the Good, under Charles VI, under Catherine de Medici, at the beginning of Louis XIII's reign and during the Fronde, the monarchy had encountered difficulties perhaps graver than in 1789. It had triumphed by a constant effort to identify itself with national unity and the interest of the people. It was lost at the end of the 18th century not because of the obstacles it encountered, but because of the double equivocation in its position in regard, first, to the interest of the people and then towards national feeling. This two-fold ambiguity in the attitude of the monarchy was to make the crisis of the Revolution both long and tragic.

To understand such an equivocal situation one must recall how the monarchy and the nation were gradually separated.

Absolute power is not given or inherited easily : it is won. Almost all the kings, up to and including Louis XIV, had more or less to conquer their authority before they could exercise it. Almost all were men of war or men assured of the strict devotion of their army. On the other hand — for no régime, even an absolute one, is lasting without an element of popular faith — all the kings had justified their authority and force by their service, doing justice, defending the weak against the privileged — according to the old idea of the knights, then of the lawyers, of the Middle Ages. Finally, all had held up territorial and legal unity as an ideal to the nation. It is the doctrine that was developed in the *Grand Siècle*, under Henry IV, under Louis XIII and in the first half of the reign of Louis XIV.

From the end of Louis XIV's reign, the sovereign loses the sense of difficulty and struggle. He is only symbolically the head of the army and in war. He is, above all, the prince of the Court. Kingship becomes soft, Louis XV and Louis XVI are just successors, who have not the slightest obstacle to overcome, do not need to exert the slightest will or effective authority before exercising plenary power. Since the beginnings of the French monarchy, no king had installed himself with less trouble than the last two Bourbons. The ease they experienced did not detract from their good intentions. But it deprived them of that experience of being tried and tested, of that memory of risks run, which made the surest political education for their predecessors. They do not know how to defend themselves; they do not know, in fact, how to prevent, thwart or break resistance. They depend on their counsellors, their entourage, their affections : the weakness of the virtuous Louis XVI in relation to Marie-Antoinette is not less dangerous politically than that of Louis XV before the Pompadour. One cannot imagine Louis XVI forbidding his wife to interfere in affairs of state, as Saint Louis did ; or condemning his best friend to death, like Henry IV ; or waging war against his mother and exiling his brother, like Louis XIII.

From the time of Louis XIV the king appears no longer as the justiciar, born defender of the little against the great, but on the contrary as the greatest of the great, the master of the privileged. He is separated from the people doubly : by the Court nobility, which exploits the realm in one manner, and by the official bourgeoisie, monopolisers of magistracies and offices, which exploits it in another. Even the clergy is hardly anything other than the emanation of royal power, which it makes use of but does not always serve. So the distant figure of the king, elegant and bored like that of Louis XV, good-natured like that of Louis XVI, becomes in the eyes of the people the symbol of all the abuses from which they suffer. And when the king wishes to correct these abuses, they no longer understand him : he has lost contact with his subjects.

Finally, from the last years of Louis XIV, the monarchy has alienated almost the whole intellectual movement of the nation. The misunderstanding dates from the revocation of the Edict of Nantes. It is aggravated by the persecution of the Jansenists. It gains new scope with the propaganda of the admirers of England and of the *philosophes*. Even the lower clergy soon declare themselves against the régime.

The truth is that the king has no longer any sure basis of support. No sure support in the army, which serves him without knowing him. No longer any sure support in the Court, which is the butt of public opprobrium, and which, far from defending him, seeks in him a protector. No longer any sure support in his own functionaries, whom the sale of offices has rendered insubordinate and presumptuous. Nor any sure support in the people. . . . The rôle of Louis XVI during the Revolution is that of a search, pathetic and in vain, for lost bases of support.

That, at a moment when everything is being renewed and remade—ideas, the sciences, applied arts, industry—and when the nation, conscious of unity achieved, of its greatness, of the increase of wealth, of the progress of mind, intensely longs for a renewal ; at the moment when, in the whole of Europe, all the talk is of reform ; at the moment when despots declare themselves 'enlightened' and the American insurgents are giving a glorious inflection to the word 'Liberty'.

In such conditions, even for a king less hesitant than

Louis XVI, to confront the States General would have been a formidable challenge. For the States General, by virtue of the control they represent from the moment that their consent is needed for taxation, are naturally opposed to absolute power and had put it in peril in the past every time that they had been summoned.

Louis XVI thus exposes himself to the greatest risk with the feeblest chances in his favour. However, impatient France, which aspires to every kind of novelty, does not dream of overthrowing the monarchy. She does not disown the monarchical principle and does not wish any evil to the person of the king. It takes an unexpected series of personal failings on the part of Louis XVI, of political blunders and psychological misconceptions — it takes, above all, the panic provoked in the people by invasion and the fury of patriotic reaction for the misunderstanding between king and people to end in a tragic break.

An astonishing history, that of the Bourbon dynasty ! It gave France an incomparable prestige and her definitive unity; it fell under the reproach of combining with the foreigner, of opposing itself to the nation 'one and indivisible' ! It produced three sovereigns who most of all sacrificed personal affections to necessity of state, Henry IV, Louis XIII and Louis XIV ; it allowed itself to be led to disaster by the levities of a queen. It started from the people with Henry IV, the playmate of the little villagers of Béarn, the king of 'a chicken in everybody's pot' ; it ends with the lamentable spectacle of the flight to Varennes, of flight in the face of its own people ! It is accused of every abuse and every scandalous vice in the person of the one king, Louis XVI, whose private virtues no-one can dispute, nor his sincerity for reform. In the end it falls as the incarnation of privilege, when, for more than half a century, it tried to break down the resistance of the privileged. . . . In truth, it perished as the victim of the isolation its glory inflicted upon it and of that inability to act upon the people which gradually grew from such isolation.

PART V

THE SIX REVOLUTIONS: FROM THE ANCIEN RÉGIME TO DEMOCRACY

CHAPTER I

The Constitutional Revolution

❖

States General and Constituent Assembly — Taking of the Bastille — Conflict of King and Nation — Legislative Assembly — Threats of Counter-Revolution and Foreign Invasion — Fall of the Monarchy

THE 18th century had immensely enlarged the middle class. Above the people, who complained of the abuses and the poverty from which they suffered, many people had enriched themselves not only by speculation, but by the expansion of industry, international or colonial trade, the diffusion of applied sciences and techniques. Even in small towns the middle class had acquired new strength and self-confidence. The progress of administration, the growth in the number of offices of every kind, the multiplication of legal jobs had greatly increased the opportunities of influence for whoever possessed some property and could learn.

There was, then, an immense middle class, from the haughty world of the Parliaments, which administered rebuffs to the king's ministers, to village attorneys who sought to advance themselves ; from the great financiers of Paris to the small *parvenus* of the provinces. This class was 'enlightened' : it read books, adored intellectual — or, as they termed it — 'philosophical' novelties, was imbued with prejudice against traditions and filled with that combativeness of mind which was not going to be duped by anything — of which Voltaire, who died in 1778, had been the untiring promoter. Enlightened, it was also given up to sensibility, liable to enthusiasms and emotions ; like an adolescent discovering the marvels of life — hidden up till then, believing in the easy realisation of the good, and running with head lowered into every kind of optimistic hypothesis. Voltaire had taught it to laugh at the past. Jean-Jacques Rousseau — who also died in 1778 — had taught it to confide tenderly in the natural goodness of man. Once liberated from political or social inequality, man was free to practise virtue and uphold a just order. Enlightened and full of sensibility, it was not less the child of the religious conflicts and ethical disputes that had been going on in France since the Reformation. In spite of Voltaire's irony and Rousseau's imagination, it retained the liking for systematising, for abstract reasoning that easily led to fanaticism.

It is this enlightened middle class, given to reasoning and sensibility, that overturns the French monarchy without wishing it. It first rises up against a king who was without any political sense, and then lets loose a revolutionary dynamic it cannot stop, itself overwhelmed by passions at home and dangers from abroad. But in the end the great Revolution — the work of the middle class — reaches its term to the benefit of the middle class. The nobility loses all its privileges ; the people gain almost nothing ; the middle class becomes master in our society for a whole century.

States General and Constituent Assembly

Louis XVI did not wish to move away from Versailles 'because of the hunting'. The States General then were convoked at Versailles — only a few leagues from the Paris which, in all times of trouble from John the Good to Louis XV, had been a menace to kings. Louis XVI showed thus his ignorance of the history of his ancestors and that he had no notion of the elementary safeguards of his authority. As soon as the sovereign and the States General can no longer get away from the demands of Paris, the Revolution is made. To push it to the extreme, the agitators have only to arouse the Commune.

At Versailles, in the great hall of the *Menus*, the king

solemnly opened the States General, 5 May 1789. He asked the deputies for money to re-establish his finances, but said not a word of the projects for a constitution of which everybody was thinking. They felt disillusioned. Next day a quarrel arose among the three orders — Nobility, Clergy and Third Estate (the Commons) — on the point whether deliberating and voting should be in common — that is to say, by counting heads, which would give the majority to the Third Estate ; or whether each order should meet separately. The quarrel lasted more than a month without reaching any agreement. On 10 June the Third Estate decided to go further. On 17th, considering that it represented '96 per cent at least of the nation', it declared itself the National Assembly. On 20th, finding the hall of the *Menus* locked and guarded, the deputies of the Third Estate met in the Tennis-Court ; they swore an oath not to disperse 'until the constitution of the realm was established and settled'. On the 22nd, at the church of St.-Louis, the majority of the deputies of the Clergy and two from the Nobility joined the Third Estate. At a royal session on the 23rd, Louis XVI annulled the deliberations of the Third Estate and proclaimed the maintenance of the three distinct orders. But when the king had gone and the Marquis de Dreux-Brézé, Grand Master of Ceremonies, tried to make the deputies of the Third Estate leave, Mirabeau cried out : 'We will not go out of here till bayonets drive us out'. 'Oh well', said the king when warned of it, 'if they won't go away, let them stay.' On 27th, he himself gave the order to the Clergy and the Nobility to join the Third Estate. On 9 July the States General proclaimed themselves a Constituent Assembly. The king having given way to a simple refusal to obey, there was no longer an absolute monarchy.

Taking of the Bastille

The Court, in fact, was thinking of using force : regiments were on the move round Paris and Versailles. On 11 July the king dismissed Necker and handed government over to two men known for their 'Turkish despotism', Breteuil and Marshal de Broglie.

What could have succeeded at Orléans or Blois could not succeed only a few leagues from Paris. Stirred up by the malcontent middle class and by Necker's partisans, the people of Paris began to rise. A foreign regiment, the Royal German, tried to curb them. But the French Guards passed over to the people. On 13 July a revolutionary municipality was formed ; a committee levied a militia of 12,000 men in the city. On the morning of the 14th the crowd pillaged the Hôtel des Invalides for rifles and guns. They wished to do the same at the Bastille, another arms-depôt; but the Governor de Launay resisted. As negotiations dragged on, towards midday the people, reinforced by French Guards, rushed to the attack. After four hours of fighting, the Bastille was taken. Governor de Launay and Flesselles, provost of the guilds, were put to death as traitors. Among the assailants 200 men were killed or wounded.

The king capitulated a second time. On 16 July he recalled Necker, while the princes and courtiers in alarm began to go into exile. On 17th Louis XVI gave the people's victory his blessing by going to the Hôtel de Ville to visit Bailly, head of the revolutionary municipality and received from Lafayette, commander of the Paris militia, the tricolour cockade, in which the colours of the capital, blue and red, framed the king's colour, white.

The example of Paris at once became infectious. All over France people set about creating municipalities to resist the encroachments of absolutism, that is to say, the king's officers. Disturbances broke out everywhere, which, joined to the exaltation and the fears caused by such novel events, brought about the 'Grande Peur'. Men armed themselves and pillaged ; Jacqueries began ; peasants burned châteaux, title-deeds and above all rent-rolls and accounts of dues.

The Assembly began to be disturbed, when several deputies of the liberal nobility, notably the Vicomte de Noailles and the Duc d'Aiguillon, themselves proposed to give up their privileges. In an emotional session, 4 August, feudal and seigneurial privileges were abolished, but rights of property retained. On 26 August, to give principles to the new order, the Assembly voted the Declaration of the Rights of Man.

Conflict of King and Nation

The king and the Court, however, far from taking direction of the movement to guide it, sought secretly to break it. On the other side, the disturbances disorganised trade and increased unemployment and want. In Paris there were thousands of poor people, without work or resources, whom anger or hunger predisposed to riot. At Versailles on 1 October, during a banquet given by the Lifeguards to the officers of the Flanders Regiment, insulting speeches were made about the Revolution. On 5 October seven or eight hundred women from the capital, drawing guns, marched on Versailles, invaded the Assembly and blockaded the Palace. Next day the mob forced one of the gates, killed the guards and got as far as the apartments of the queen. Lafayette and his National Guards stopped them; but the king had to consent to quit Versailles. That afternoon Louis XVI and his family came to Paris escorted by the mob. They installed themselves in the Tuileries — prisoners, in fact, of the people. On 16 October the Assembly established itself in Paris, at the Riding School near the Tuileries, henceforward not less subject than the king to the pressure of popular movements.

The people in the provinces thrilled at the news from Paris. To the 'Grande Peur' there succeeded an emotional surge towards brotherhood and fraternity. It was the origin of the movement for 'federations', which expressed the impulse towards a more complete union of classes and regions of the realm, now freed from absolutism. The name of 'patriot' became the fashion: it signified that the nation existed outside the king and should be served for its own sake. On the initiative of Paris the Constituent Assembly decided to organise a fête of the National Federation on 14 July, anniversary of the taking of the Bastille. About 14,000 delegates from all parts of France were present. Talleyrand, Bishop of Autun, celebrated a solemn mass on the altar of the Country raised on the Champ-de-Mars. Then Lafayette, in the name of all the National Guards, swore fidelity 'to the Nation, to the Law and to the King'. Louis XVI himself swore an oath to maintain the Constitution. The people cried, 'Long live the king!'

The Revolution could easily have stopped there, keeping the supremacy of the national idea, the abolition of privileges and a constitutional monarchy. But for the Revolution to stop, the Assembly would have had to sit elsewhere than in Paris and not remain under the pressure of the people. Popular pressure was from this time systematically organised by the new clubs, particularly the Jacobin Club which had ramifications all over France, and the club of the Cordeliers which stirred up the poorer quarters of the capital, setting in motion the rough workers of the faubourgs St.-Antoine and St.-Margeau. To disengage the Assembly and the king's authority from the embrace of insurrectionary Paris would have needed another man than Louis XVI.

To give the Gallican and Jansenist spirit of the French middle class its revenge — since it had been rather brutally repressed for a century — the Assembly voted the Civil Constitution of the clergy, 18 July 1790. It reduced the number of dioceses from 134 to 83, corresponding to the number of newly created departments; it subjected the choice of metropolitans, bishops and curés to election and took away the investiture of bishops from the Pope to charge the metropolitans with it. This was to transport the Revolution from the realm of politics into that of religion and open up one of those conflicts between conscience and the law that cannot be resolved by force. Resistance was at once aroused. To overcome it, the Assembly decreed that functioning ecclesiastics should take a civil oath. All the bishops, except seven, and almost half the clergy refused the oath. Thenceforth there was a 'Constitutional' clergy who had taken the oath and a non-juring or refractory clergy. The moral union of citizens was broken. Very Catholic regions — the West, the North, Alsace — broke away from the revolutionary movement. Thenceforward there was a Counter-Revolution not only at Court and among the privileged, but among religious people.

In the spring of 1791 the Pope condemned the Civil Constitution of the clergy. It was certainly not the first time that the Pope had asserted his authority against the civil power. In the past condemnations had led to negotiations. But, in the past, the civil power had been defended against Rome by the kings themselves. Louis XVI, who was very pious, at first sanctioned the Assembly's initiative ; when Rome's condemnation came, he was distraught. Instead of offering to negotiate with the Pope, he took flight.

For six months his entourage pushed him towards committing the supreme mistake : to seek help and protection abroad against his own people. He solicited his brother-in-law, the Emperor of Austria, to send troops to the frontier. A French army at Metz, commanded by the Marquis de Bouillé, appeared on this side to promise eventual support. But revolutionary Paris was suspicious : the mob watched the king and guarded the Tuileries.

In the night of 20-21 June 1791 Louis XVI, disguised as a valet, with the queen, his two children and his sister Elizabeth, fled — believing themselves protected by loyal troops posted along the route to Metz. The heavy coach, in which the royal party travelled, went too slowly. Recognised at St.-Menehould by the son of the postmaster Drouet, the king was stopped at midnight on 21 June at Varennes, then brought back to Paris by the commissioners of the Assembly. He reentered the Tuileries beneath the hostile and contemptuous gaze of a crowd which had been forbidden to shout. Up till then the people had been attached to the monarchy : from that day, for want of a king whom they could trust, France found herself in fact a republic.

On the very day of Louis XVI's return, the Cordeliers' Club, interpreting the anger of the faubourgs, demanded the abolition of monarchy. The majority of the Constituent Assembly, exhorted by Barnave, tried to protect the king and the monarchical principle. The Jacobins were divided: the moderate fraction formed a new club: the Club of the Feuillants. But the Republican agitation grew among the people of Paris. On 17 July, to restrain demonstrators, Lafayette ordered the National Guards to fire on them. This and other repressive acts intimidated the popular leaders; Danton and Marat went into hiding. On 14 September the Assembly submitted the final form of the Constitution to the king, and Louis XVI solemnly swore to it. This Constitution established the sovereignty of the people and the separation of powers. It was essentially middle-class in character, in the sense that only citizens paying a rather high rate of taxation received the right to vote. The king remained 'inviolable and sacred', but was no longer 'the hereditary delegate of the nation to the executive'; no order from him could take effect unless countersigned by a minister who would be responsible for it. All the same he had the right to refuse his sanction to laws voted, for two consecutive legislatures: it was the right of a suspensive veto.

After granting a general amnesty, the Constituent Assembly declared its mission fulfilled and its sessions ended, 30 September 1791.

It had made the Revolution and established the principles of an 'enlightened' political and social order. But its work remained in great part theoretical; exposed on one side to violent reactions and, on the other, to all the dangers that came from demagogy. Far from solving the financial problem, it had started the fatuous system of selling national property and issuing immense numbers of 'assignats' (paper money)

against it : a system that was to exasperate the Revolution, constantly subject it to anxieties for the morrow and the pressure
of economic and social anarchy.   It had created a religious
conflict that broke the national impetus and prepared the way
for civil war.   It had left foreign affairs to drift with the
currents, and let the country in for war.

Surprised by the very ease with which the Revolution
was made, to some extent disconcerted by the astonishing
incapacity of Louis XVI, composed of doctrinaires and fed
on abstractions, the Constituent Assembly left a structure ill
supported and unstable.   Its omissions, like its rashnesses,
rendered unavoidable the two dictatorships that were to forge
— through terrible trials — the framework of the new state :
the Reign of Terror and the Bonapartist dictatorship.

The first Revolution, disorganising the king's power and
his diplomacy, paralysed France's political activity abroad.
Foreign sovereigns seemed at first to scorn the revolutionary
movement.   In May 1790 the Constituent Assembly, induced
by the pacifism that the intellectuals had sown among the
middle class, declared 'peace to all the world' : it voted a
decree by which the nation renounced ever undertaking a war
of conquest or employing its forces against the liberty of any
people.

But pacifism did not prevent propaganda, both that of
example and that of ideas.   The greatest state in Europe
could not change its régime and overturn its old institutions
without its neighbours, and then the whole continent, being
disturbed.   In October 1789 the Belgians had risen against
Joseph II.   The agitation soon gained the Rhineland states,
Savoy, Piedmont ; in the spring of 1790 Avignon revolted
against the Pope.   In 1791 Poland changed its constitution.
Thenceforth the European sovereigns, anxious and mutually
encouraging each other, sought an opportunity to interfere
in the affairs of France.

Opportunities of conflict sprang from the new principle

proclaimed by the French Revolution that 'peoples could henceforth dispose of themselves'. The German princes with estates in Alsace saw themselves dispossessed of their feudal rights by the will of the Alsatian people, which the Constituent Assembly soon legalised.

On 12 September 1791 Avignon and the county of Venaissin were annexed to France 'in conformity with the freely expressed will of the people'. In consecrating the right of peoples to revolt, the Revolution threatened to make pacific conquests, less costly but not less real than those of force.

The sovereigns prepared for armed intervention. The *émigrés* among the French nobility who had taken refuge at Coblenz and Worms around Louis XVI's brother, the Comte de Provence, and the Prince de Condé, intrigued to unleash foreign intervention, promising it an easy success. Driven on by Marie-Antoinette, Louis XVI himself was in constant negotiation with Austria to rescue him. On 27 August 1791 the Emperor and the King of Prussia published the Declaration of Pillnitz, proclaiming the re-establishment of order and monarchy in France to be 'an object of common interest to all sovereigns'. At this news national sentiment ranged itself on the side of the Revolution. The clubs announced a crusade of the peoples 'against the tyrants'. Pacifism changed into patriotism ; the king appeared more than ever suspect.

It was in these circumstances that the Legislative Assembly was elected to succeed to the Constituent. The new Assembly contained no member of the old, which had itself decided on this measure.

Legislative Assembly

The Legislative Assembly met 1 October 1791. The new deputies were for the most part unknown. They represented almost the same currents of opinion as their predecessors, but with a certain deviation. The majority thought neither of pushing the Revolution further nor of overthrowing the king. On the right sat 264 deputies who were members of the moderate Club of the Feuillants ; on the left, 136 deputies who belonged to the Jacobin Club ; in the centre, a mass of Independents without any precise leaning. The Assembly was to be led from outside by the clubs. At the Jacobin Club, the journalist Brissot, an active and supple politician, and the advocate Robespierre, former deputy for Arras at the States General, were rivals for influence.

Disturbances continued in the country from different causes, religious and political, economic and social, exasperated by administrative disorder and the growing dearness of victuals. A firm and clear-sighted authority, a disciplined Assembly, could doubtless stabilise the new régime. There were intrigues, discords, war. Worse advised than ever, the king and his entourage, awaiting rescue from abroad, followed an extreme course, secretly supporting the violent faction against the moderates. Thus, thanks to the manœuvres of the Court, the government of Paris was handed over to the Jacobin Pétion and the people's tribune, Danton.

The Court awaited a foreign war as a deliverance. The clubs also began to wish for it : the Feuillants because war would serve as an excuse for a brutal repression of the factions at home ; the Jacobins, or at least Brissot's following among them — the 'Girondin' faction [1] — because war, they thought, would heighten revolutionary passions and put the monarchy to the test. Robespierre, on the contrary, opposed it as long as he could, foreseeing with singular lucidity that war would ruin the nation and lead, sooner or later, to the dictatorship of a Caesar.

At the end of 1791 the Assembly, impelled by the orators of the Girondin Left, voted several decrees against the émigrés — naming the king's brother, the Comte de Provence — against refractory priests and the Rhineland Electors : all accused of designs hostile to the country. Louis XVI refused to give his sanction to the decrees against the émigrés and non-juring priests. On 25 January 1792 the Girondins got

[1] So called because their leading deputies came from the Gironde district.

a regular ultimatum to the Emperor Leopold voted. Red
bonnets and pikes were distributed to the people. Louis had
to constitute a Girondin ministry, formed of Brissot's friends.
An enterprising and unscrupulous man was installed at the
Ministry of Foreign Affairs ; at that of the Interior an honest
bureaucrat, Roland, whose wife — Madame Roland — by her
intelligence, grace and her convictions exerted a great influence
on the Girondins.

Threats of Counter-Revolution and Foreign Invasion

The Emperor Leopold, it seems, was loth to war. But he
died suddenly, 1 March 1792. His son Francis II, 'militarist
and absolutist', replied to the Legislative's ultimatum by
summoning the French government to re-establish the princes
with lands in Alsace in their feudal rights and to restore
Avignon to the Pope. In reply, 20 April 1792, on the proposi-
tion of the wretched Louis XVI himself, who was preparing
his own downfall, the Assembly declared war on Francis II.

The French army was composed, in fact, of two armies :
the old troops of the line, much weakened by the emigration
of 6,000 officers and the desertion of 30,000 men ; and the
battalions of volunteers recruited in June 1791 from the
National Guards, full of patriotic spirit, but without experience
or training. These two armies got on badly and, moreover,
the troops had no confidence in their generals. An offensive
into Belgium was ordered ; at the first shock the invasion
columns turned back in panic ; General Dillon was killed by
the men in flight. The frontier was left open. The Court
and the generals themselves were accused of rejoicing at this
check, while the religious revolt took a menacing turn in the
West and South. From that moment danger pushed the
Revolution on to supreme deeds.

The Assembly voted three new decrees, ordering the
deportation of refractory priests, the licensing of the constitutional guard of the king and the formation below Paris of
a camp of 20,000 volunteers. The king refused to sanction

the first and third of these decrees, dismissed the Girondin ministry and appealed to the Feuillants. A violent *coup* on his part was feared.

Fall of the Monarchy

At once the Commune was set in motion by Pétion. On 20 June a mob of several thousand patriots, the men armed with pikes and wearing red caps, invaded the Assembly, then pushed back towards the Tuileries and forced the gates. The king was jostled into a window embrasure, but bore himself with courage. He donned the red bonnet and drank to the health of the nation ; but he maintained his veto on the decrees.

This attempt on the king's person provoked keen resentment among the moderates. Lafayette left the army to come to Paris and offer his help against the 'factions'. But Marie-Antoinette, more than ever determined on an extreme course, detested the Constitutional moderates and had their offer rejected. Some days later the news arrived that the Prussians and the *émigrés* threatened the frontier. On 11 July the Assembly, ignoring the king, on its own authority decreed the country to be in danger, commanded all officials to be on permanent guard at their posts, mobilised the national guards and called for 50,000 volunteers. A growing agitation followed. The 'federates', come up from the provinces for the fête of 14 July, were infected by the fever of the Clubs. A band of 500 from Marseilles entered Paris singing the hymn composed at Strasbourg by a young officer of the Army of the Rhine : the Marseillaise. The Jacobins, among whom Robespierre distinguished himself, prepared an insurrection to overthrow the monarchy.

The Duke of Brunswick, commander of the Prussian and Austrian armies, put out on 25 July a manifesto — inspired by Marie-Antoinette — the terms of which were a senseless provocation of the French people. On 10 August, in reply, the popular sections of Paris rose at the sound of the tocsin. An insurrectionary Commune installed itself at the Hôtel de

Ville under the influence of the leaders Danton and Santerre. The king and the royal family, threatened in the Tuileries, with difficulty reached the Assembly to take shelter. The Swiss Guards fired on the Marseilles Federates and for two hours a battle was fought around the Palace, which was sacked. The Swiss had some 600 out of 900 killed ; the insurgents 376 killed or wounded. The king had sent the order to cease fire too late. . . . The Legislative Assembly had to submit to the victory of the people : it decreed the king's suspension and the internment of the royal family. While awaiting the election of a new Assembly — the Convention — which would establish a régime founded on the sovereignty of the people, it named a provisional executive Council, whose real chief was Danton, promoted Minister of Justice. It completed the abolition of feudal rights and decreed the sale of *émigré* property. In fact, the Assembly was henceforth subject to the Commune of Paris. The constitutional Revolution was soon to give way to the terrorist Revolution.

CHAPTER II

The Terrorist Revolution

❖

*The Convention. Louis XVI's Execution — Girondins
and the Mountain — Danton and Robespierre — Dictatorship of Public Safety by Terror — The 9th Thermidor —
Relaxation and Reprisals — Work of Reform — National
Defence and Conquests*

AFTER 10 August 1792 the idea of 'Constitution' loses its
prestige. The idea of 'Public Safety' takes possession of
the Revolution : an idea that sweeps away scruples, exalts
violence, puts the people into a permanent condition of
anxiety and anger, and gives victory to the aggressive over
the intelligent. Thence began the duel between the Girondins,
orators of the Assembly, and the Mountain,[1] agents of the
Commune. Under pressure from these last, the Assembly
authorised the municipalities to make house-to-house searches
and filled the prisons with suspects who were dragged before a
criminal Tribunal.

However, the country was invaded. Blow followed blow :
between 15 August and 2 September came Lafayette's desertion,
the enemy entry into Lorraine, the capture of Longwy, the
investiture of Verdun. The Commune and Danton called on
the people of Paris to rise and rescue the country in danger.
The tocsin was rung, alarm guns were fired. The mob, in
a fever of suspicion, denounced conspirators and sought for
traitors. Marat, made a member of the Watch Committee of
the Commune, pushed the people on to execute its own justice
before marching against the enemy from without. On 2 September bands of cut-throats began to massacre non-juring
priests imprisoned in the Abbaye. For four days and four

---

[1] So called because they occupied a block of seats high up in the Assembly.

nights till 6 September the massacre of suspects continued in all the Paris prisons, at the Abbaye, La Force, the Châtelet, the Conciergerie. This ferocious butchery claimed 1,100 victims, priests, old men, women — among others the Princesse de Lamballe, friend of the queen. Danton did not deign to stop the fury of the 'men of September' until the moment when Marat wished to turn it against the Girondins.

While Paris suffered these massacres, the Prussians and Austrians advanced into the Argonne. Fortunately the cool heads of the French generals Dumouriez and Kellermann enabled the revolutionary troops to repulse the Prussians in the famous encounter of Valmy. It was the first military success of the Revolution: the Republican army felt itself ready for greater ventures.

The very day of the victory of Valmy, the Legislative Assembly made way for the Convention, a new Assembly elected in principle by universal suffrage and dominated by the Jacobins.

The Convention. Louis XVI's Execution

From its first public session, 21 September 1792, the Convention — by a unanimous vote of those present (300 out of 749 elected)—abolished the monarchy. Next day its acts began to be dated 'the first year of the Republic'; Danton had the Republic decreed 'one and indivisible'.

It remained to settle the fate of Louis XVI and his family. For two months the authorities delayed. But at the end of November, a secret cupboard at the Tuileries was opened and proofs were found of the king's appeals to the émigrés and the foreigner against the Revolution. The young Saint-Just, deputy for the Aisne — inspired by cold passion, the interpreter of Robespierre — made his début at the tribune by demanding that the former sovereign should be treated not as a man on trial, but as an enemy: 'He is a foreign prisoner of war'. The trial began on 11 December before the Assembly. Louis was defended by his former minister Malesherbes and two advocates, Tronchet and de Sèze. He showed great dignity, but confined himself to denying everything charged against him. The trial lasted till 20 January. The king was declared guilty of 'conspiracy against public liberty and of an attempt against the security of the state' by 707 voices; the others abstained. He was condemned to death, after two doubtful scrutinies, by 387 votes against 334. Two Girondin amendments attempting to delay the execution were rejected: one by 424 votes to 287, the other by 380 votes against 310. On Sunday, 21 January, Louis XVI mounted the scaffold with courage, and was guillotined on the Place de la Révolution (today the Place de la Concorde) facing the Tuileries, after trying to address to the people a few words that were drowned by the beating of drums.

What the men of the Mountain — Robespierre, Danton, Marat — had wished was accomplished: henceforth the Revolution could neither go back nor compromise, for it had to conquer its outraged enemies by any and every means, or perish. In February and March Austria, Prussia, England, Spain, Holland, the States of the Empire and Italy formed a coalition against France. In March Catholic La Vendée rose. On 5 April General Dumouriez, after having prepared a *coup d'état*, passed over to the enemy. Agitators, known as the 'Enragés', denouncing the dearness of victuals — already the 'assignats' had lost half their value — tried to raise the people against the Convention.

The Convention decreed successively a levy of 300,000 men, the sending of commissars into the departments, the setting up of a revolutionary Tribunal, of a watch committee in each commune, the death penalty against rebels and *émigrés*, the hunting-down of refractory priests, an impost on the rich and the creation of a Committee of Public Safety.

Girondins and the Mountain

Marat demanded the arrest of the Girondins. They had him brought before the Revolutionary Tribunal, who acquitted

him 24 April.   On 4 May the Mountain gained the adhesion
of the 'Enragés' by decreeing a maximum price for grain.
The Girondins tried to defend themselves by appealing to the
departments.   But on 31 May the Commune rose under the
command of a former collector of tolls, Hanriot, and invaded
the Convention.   In spite of the outrage and Robespierre's
threats, the Assembly refused to vote for putting the Girondins on trial.   On Sunday 2 June came a new and more violent
outbreak :   80,000 men with arms and sixty guns surrounded
the Convention.   It still tried to resist and even to fly.   Then,
under the threat of the guns, it ended by delivering up twenty-
nine of its members to the insurrection.

The Mountain were then masters in Paris.   But sixty
departments were in rebellion against them : the Counter-
Revolution had raised Bordeaux and Lyons; La Vendée, the
South-West and Normandy ;   the Rhône Valley and Provence.
On 13 July, in the middle of Paris, Marat was assassinated in
his bath by a young woman, Charlotte Corday.   On 16 July
Chaslier — one of the Mountain — was guillotined at Lyons.
The foreign armies themselves announced that they would
force the frontiers and conquer the Revolution by terror.

Danton and Robespierre

Such a situation was fated to call dictatorship into being.
Robespierre, the leader of the Mountain — assisted by two
fanatical disciples, the young and rigid Saint-Just and the
invalid Couthon — defined the policy of dictatorship and
erected terror into a doctrine.   He was a man of thirty-five, a
bleak logician, gifted with a lucidity, sometimes prophetic, in
whom the cult of 'virtue' and deism in the manner of Rousseau
had developed an inexorable faith in his own rightness and in
the use of violence to bring about the triumph of the ends
that his mind imposed on the Revolution : a cold dreamer,
without intuition or sense of life, a pettifogging attorney,
careful in habits and without any vices, stilted in his formulae,
and who soon left so little way out to humanity that he fell a

Marie-Antoinette

victim to the revolt, not of those opposed to his course but of the most cowardly of those profiting from it.

Facing Robespierre was Danton, a sort of bully of the Clubs risen to the leadership of the great forces of the Revolution, with a powerful eloquence touched by the breath of genius, bursting with vitality, sentimental, given up to and at last corrupted by his pleasures : he thought himself a Titan, but for lack of order in his spirit and of real strength of mind, he let things go their own way even to his own downfall.

From April to July 1793 Danton dominated the Committee of Public Safety, the organ of revolutionary dictatorship. In July Robespierre had the Committee renewed and became its master. From then on the instruments of the active Revolution fell gradually under the dictatorship of Robespierre and his men. Police, Revolutionary Tribunal where the former advocate Fouquier-Tinville sat as public prosecutor, representatives of the Convention on mission, local committees and popular societies, national agents in the districts and the communes : all were so many tools for a violence that no scruple or pity held back any longer from imposing the ideology of Robespierre in a vast country which had to defend itself at once from being split up and invaded.

Dictatorship of Public Safety by Terror

On 27 July 1793 the Convention voted the death penalty for profiteers. On 23 August it ordered the conscription of citizens against the foreigner and the rebels ; on 3 September a forced loan of a milliard on the rich. On 29 September it decreed the 'law of the maximum', limiting the price of essential goods ; on 22 October it set up a commission of supplies to control all agricultural and industrial production. Under the pressure of a new outbreak, organised by the violent Hébertists, the Assembly declared the Terror to be in permanent being. On 17 September the immediate arrest of all suspects was decreed. Marie-Antoinette was guillotined, 16 October. Next fell the heads of the Girondins, of the Duke of Orléans (Philippe-Égalité), Bailly, former mayor of Paris, Mme Roland, Barnave. In one year a large number of people all over France were victims of individual or mass executions ; in Paris alone the number of victims reached 2,627.

The most violent revolutionaries, the Hébertists, pressed for total 'dechristianisation'. The institution of a revolutionary calendar, the pressure put on the Bishop of Paris to cast off his orders, the celebration of a feast of Liberty and Reason at Notre-Dame on 10 November 1793 and, soon after, the closing of all the Paris churches — these marked the stages of the campaign. Danton protested against the 'anti-religious masquerade' and Robespierre himself got the Convention to pass a decree against 'all violence and acts against liberty to practise religion'. This did not succeed in stopping anti-religious excesses, which turned a section of the people away from the Revolution.

However, the revolts inside the country were beaten down, broken, drowned in blood : the Convention's troops re-entered Lyons in October, Toulon in December and destroyed the army of La Vendée at Mans and Savenay. The Austrians and Prussians were defeated at Wattignies and Wissembourg and retreated across the frontier.

Robespierre sought to get rid of his rivals of the Mountain — the ultra-revolutionaries or partisans of Hébert on his left, the moderates or followers of Danton on his right. In September he had Jacques Roux, the leader of the Enragés, thrown into prison.

The Hébertists exploited the people's poverty and want, and threatened the Convention. They were arrested with Hébert at their head on 14 March 1794, brought before the Revolutionary Tribunal and guillotined ten days after. Danton demanded the end of the dictatorship. He and his friends, notably the horrible Fabre d'Eglantine and the eloquent Camille Desmoulins, were arrested on 30 March, declared 'outside debate', judged summarily and guillotined 5 April.

The 'incorruptible' Robespierre remained at last sole

chief of the Revolution — or, more exactly, of a dictatorship that confused the personal ideas of the dictator himself, political, social and religious, with the object of a people's revolution.   This personal dictatorship — though parliamentary in appearance, thanks to the votes more or less imposed on the Convention — lasted four months, from April to July 1794.   It was an attempt without precedent in our history to subject the life of a whole people by force to abstractions invoking the antithesis of force — reason.

From 16 February to 3 March Robespierre's lieutenant, Saint-Just, had the decrees of Ventôse voted, ordering the confiscation of the goods of many thousands of suspects and the distribution of these goods to the 'poor patriots'.   On 7 May Robespierre obtained a decree instituting a new official religion, the worship of the Supreme Being, a religion of deism, morality and patriotism.   The first feast of this cult took place 8 June, presided over by Robespierre who himself set fire to a statue representing atheism, while choirs sang a hymn to the 'Father of the Universe, Intelligence Supreme'. Next day the famous law of the '22 Prairial' was passed, which suppressed all guarantees of justice for those accused of political offences and gave the Revolutionary Tribunal power to send people to death simply on 'moral' proofs without hearing witnesses.

Then heads 'fell like tiles' — according to Fouquier-Tinville's phrase.   Every day the Tribunal sent cart-loads to the guillotine : in forty-five days in Paris alone 1,285 persons. So perished the famous chemist Lavoisier and the young poet of genius André Chénier.

The 9th Thermidor

At this rate the Terror went beyond its mark and produced a reaction.   The least significant was no longer sure of escaping the guillotine :   fear which made men cowards made them revolt.   A conspiracy was formed within the Convention by the very members most suspect of combining plunder with

bloodshed : Fouché, Tallien, Barras, Fréron. Blind with
pride, Robespierre thought it easy to crush them with the
support of the Jacobins and the Commune. On 26 July
(8 Thermidor), mounting the tribune, he committed the error
of denouncing as rascals and traitors not only the less scrupulous of his opponents, but men of some prestige : Vadier,
Billaud-Varenne, Cambon, Carnot. The Convention
applauded at first and voted that the speech should be printed.
Then, forced out of its weakness by a vehement protestation
from Cambon and Billaud-Varenne, it took back its vote and
rebuffed Robespierre.

Too sure of himself, Robespierre lost time and went off
to be acclaimed at the Jacobin Club. During the night the confederates gained the floating vote in the Convention. The
President, Collot d'Herbois, agreed with them. On Sunday
27 July (9 Thermidor), in overpowering heat, Saint-Just had
hardly mounted the tribune when he was interrupted by
Tallien. He and Billaud-Varenne denounced Robespierre as
'the new Cromwell'. The 'incorruptible' wished to speak.
The President drowned his voice with the sound of his bell.
Angrily Robespierre insisted : 'For the last time, President of
assassins, I demand of you that I may speak'. He was too
late. The Convention decreed the arrest of Hanriot, commander of the National Guard, Robespierre himself, Couthon
and Saint-Just, to the cry of : 'Long live the Republic'. But
in the evening the Commune, rising in insurrection, had the
prisoners set free. The Convention replied by declaring
Robespierre and his partisans outlaws — a decree which
authorised execution without judgment. At two in the morning
of the 28th (10 Thermidor) Robespierre and his friends took
refuge at the Hôtel de Ville. As the Convention's soldiers
penetrated into the hall to arrest the 'tyrant', Robespierre fell
down with his jaw shattered, wounded either by his own hand
or by a gendarme. He was carried away. He and his brother,
Saint-Just, Couthon, Hanriot and his chief partisans were
guillotined in the course of the day.

The crowd and the workers themselves applauded as the tumbrils went by. The Terror had not only sown fear, but increased the miseries of the people.

Relaxation and Reprisals

With Robespierre beaten, the Convention continued : the Terror was not ended. But the terrorist dictatorship, having lost the man who inspired and embodied it, slackened and then gave way. A month after the death of the 'incorruptible', the Committee of Public Safety was stripped of its exceptional powers, the Revolutionary Tribunal purged and rendered less brutal, the Commune subjected to the Convention. The Jacobin Club was closed 12 November 1794. The law of the Suspects and the law of the Maximum were revoked, trade became free again, the prisons were opened and the most hated terrorists — Carrier and Fouquier-Tinville — condemned to death. Liberty of worship was re-established by a decree of 21 February 1795 and on the 30th the Convention restored the churches to the faithful.

This reaction encouraged the Royalists and exasperated the Jacobins. The Royalists demonstrated daily. The Jacobins took advantage of the rapid rise in prices, as a result of the debasing of the paper-currency, to organise insurrections of the poor. On April Fool Day 1795 a mob of people, chiefly women, invaded the Convention and demanded bread. The Assembly's majority expelled the mob and as a reprisal voted the immediate deportation of former members of revolutionary committees. On 20 May workers from the faubourgs penetrated into the Convention and killed the deputy Féraud, whose head they presented to the President, Boissy d'Anglas, at the end of a pike. The last remnants of the Mountain expected to get their revenge. But in the evening the National Guards and Royalist demonstrators recaptured the hall. The workers or accomplices of the outbreak were declared under arrest. Surrounded by an army of 20,000 men the people of the faubourgs were forced to give up their pikes, guns and cannon — the arms that for six years had materially made the Revolution.

The Royalists pushed home their advantage in the provinces, especially in the departments of the South-East where a new Terror, the 'White Terror', began to rage. During May 1795 Royalist bands cut the throats of former Jacobins at Lyons, Aix-en-Provence, Tarascon and Marseilles. On the death in prison of Louis XVI's young son — called Louis XVII — the Comte de Provence took the title of Louis XVIII and put forward a manifesto to the French people. The rising in La Vendée started up again. At Quiberon the English fleet landed some hundreds of *émigrés*, whom General Hoche defeated and captured.

The Convention lived as much in fear of Royalist reprisals as of Jacobin fury. It defended itself with violent measures : it reinforced the laws against the *émigrés*, had 750 prisoners from Quiberon shot, and — to stop Royalist returns — decreed that two-thirds of future deputies should be chosen among its members. This last decree ended all possibility of a legal restoration of the monarchy. The Royalists then tried to overthrow the Convention by force. They assembled 20,000 National Guards to attack it. There were only 4,000 soldiers and a thousand *sans-culottes* volunteers to defend it. The Assembly was in grave danger. But on the day of the attack, 13 Vendémiaire (5 October) 1795 Barras, the member in charge of the defence, took as his adjutant a young Jacobin artillery officer, Bonaparte. The latter with forty cannon broke the double attack of the insurgents by the Rue St.-Honoré and by the quays along the left bank. After that the people were disarmed.

Some days later, 26 October, the Convention ended its labours.

Work of Reform

In 1793 the Convention voted a first Republican Constitution — called that of the Year I — democratic and decentralising, permitting in certain cases the direct vote of laws by the people, or the referendum. This Constitution, which never came into effect, was replaced in 1795 by the Constitution 'of the Year III', drawn up by Daunou. In place of direct universal suffrage it gave the vote only to citizens with an income equal to 150 days of work. The Legislative body was divided into two assemblies, the Five Hundred and the Ancients, renewable by one-third annually. A Directory of five members was to exercise executive power ; delegates of this executive were to control the elected local administrations. It was a return to the middle-class Revolution ; for fear of dictatorship, the principle of separation of powers was applied so rigorously that the different powers became independent of one another and could only be made to give way mutually by the application of force.

In August 1793 the Convention created the Great Book of the Public Debt ; this was drawn up by its Finance Committee presided over by Cambon, a former merchant, rude and upright. It tried to institute a progressive tax on luxury and wealth. But it was impossible to carry through a serious financial operation when the currency went on losing its value : the taxes, like the loans, vanished with the value of the assignat. From December 1793 to July 1795 the paper money lost more than nine-tenths of its value. The inflation got completely out of hand, prices rose dizzily, a large part of the population went hungry. But the peasants gained : the total abolition of feudal rights without indemnity and then the sale at low prices — and often on credit — of the confiscated property of émigrés, clergy and suspects made the peasants masters of the soil. One of the most lasting consequences of the Revolution was the redistribution and dividing up of rural property.

The Legislative Committee of the Convention, presided over by Cambacérès, elaborated a first draft of a Civil Code, inspired by the principle of equality within the family, particularly in the division of inheritances. On the Committee of Public Instruction Lakanal — a former brother of the order

of Christian Doctrine — laid the base of a wide system of
education by the creation of primary schools in each canton
and central secondary schools in the departments.   Most
remarkable of all was the Convention's work in the realms
of higher education and science : it reorganised or created the
School of Oriental Languages, the Bureau of Longitudes, the
Museum of Natural History, the Conservatoire of Arts and
Crafts, the National Library, the National Archives, the Louvre
Museum, the Conservatoire of Music, the School of Health,
the École Normale, the Institute of France, and for the Army —
St.-Cyr.   Reacting at last against the destruction of religious
buildings, it voted a law for the care of public buildings and
had the survivals of the art of the Middle Ages brought under
the Museum of French Monuments.

National Defence and Conquests

Recalling the wars of the Revolution, the celebrated
Royalist advocate, Berryer, said in 1825 : 'I shall never forget
that the Convention saved my country'.

After Valmy, in the last months of 1792, French armies
had occupied Savoy and the county of Nice ; Speyer, Worms
and Mainz ; and, by the victory of Jemmappes, driven the
Austrians out of Belgium.

From the end of 1792 the Convention had moved from a
pacifist policy to one of conquest of the 'natural frontiers'
upheld by Danton himself.   At the beginning of 1793 it had
decreed the annexation of Nice, Belgium and the left bank of
the Rhine.   The annexation of Belgium led to an inevitable
struggle between France and England, since England from the
time of the Middle Ages had never accepted the installation of
a rival power opposite the mouth of the Thames.   The policy
of the English minister, Pitt, succeeded in drawing together
against France a vast coalition comprising, with England,
Holland, Austria, Prussia, Spain, Portugal, the States of the
Empire, the kings of Sardinia and Naples and even Russia.

On 18 March 1793 Dumouriez' army was defeated at

Neerwinden. On 23 July the French garrison of Mainz capitulated. On 27 August Toulon was delivered to the English. All the frontiers were giving way. The Austrians took Valenciennes and the strong places of the Scheldt and were besieging Maubeuge. The Committee of Public Safety, re-formed, in some months accomplished the feat of reorganising the whole of national defence : they succeeded in reconstituting effectives, amalgamating disparate units, re-establishing disci-pline, assembling arms, material and provisions, and at last in finding real leaders and employing effective tactics. Two men were the organisers of this great work : Lazare Carnot, deputy for the Pas-de-Calais, and Prieur, for the Côte-d'Or, both members of the Committee of Public Safety and both officers of genius, inheritors of the tradition of Vauban and utilising the means created by the military reforms of Louis XVI.

From the end of 1793 the French armies, led by young officers from the ranks — Jourdan, Hoche, Pichegru — re-gained the advantage. The frontiers on the North and East were liberated. On 26 June 1794 the Austrians were crushed at Fleurus. Soon the French were to occupy Antwerp, Cologne, Coblentz, and to invade Holland. Corsica was lost, but the French fleet, reorganised by Jean Bon St.-André, put up a resistance against the English at sea.

In 1795 the states affected or directly threatened by the French victories withdrew from the Coalition. The chance of a new partition of Poland attracted the attention, moreover, of Russia, Austria and Prussia. The treaties of Basel and of the Hague (April-July 1795) sealed the triumph of the Convention's armies. France obtained the left bank of the Rhine, Dutch Flanders and Maestricht, the setting up of a Batavian Republic which would be her ally, and the island of St. Domingo. Only England and Austria refused to treat.

Even so, the Convention had had to break various revolts at home, maintain a cruel and long struggle, particularly against the rising in La Vendée. Begun there to defend the priests and resist military service, the rising had spread to Poitou, Anjou, Brittany, mobilising many thousands of men — 'Vendéens', then 'Chouans' — under leaders from both people and nobility, Stofflet, Cathelineau, d'Elbée, La Roche-jacquelein. After having taken Cholet, Saumur and threatened Nantes, the Vendéens were beaten before Cholet, 17 October 1793. They tried to gain the Cotentin and seize Granville but, thrown back on the Loire, they suffered a double defeat at Le Mans and at Savenay in December. The survivors formed bands hiding in the woods and marshes. They finally obtained an amnesty and liberty of worship in 1795. General Hoche then succeeded in pacifying the West.

CHAPTER III

The Military Revolution: Bonaparte

❖

*The Directory's Disorders and Coup d'État — The 18th
Brumaire — From Consulate to Empire*

WITH the Convention gone, the Commune disarmed, the
Royalists and the Mountain equally repulsed, what remains
of the Revolution is chiefly the interests it served, the responsibilities its agents have taken on, and the fear people feel of
seeing its excesses return.   Interests that do not wish to lose
what they have gained, responsibilities that desire oblivion,
fears of the past that resign themselves to the present : all
that makes for a state of mind propitious to the *status quo*, at
once mistrustful and weak, a taste for living for the moment,
with the maximum of pleasure and the minimum of ideals
or curiosity.   It is the state of mind of society under the
Directory — and called after it — in which the easing of the
nerves compensates for the cynicism of the characters : a
sort of plebeian Regency which endeavours to forget the
virtue of Robespierre, as earlier, after Louis XIV, people
forgot the piety of Mme de Maintenon : the same license,
the same indecency, the same facilities for corruption and
speculation.

But the régime, having no other support than men's
egoisms, is precarious.   Intrigue and voracity devour it.
Secretly it feels itself incapable of defending for long the
position it has acquired against the monarchical reaction on one
side or the disillusionment of the people on the other.   It
lives by trickery, expedients, changes of front.   It seeks a constitutional formula to protect it, while waiting to invoke
force, the soldier — Caesar.

The Directory's Disorders and Coup d'État

The five Directors elected in October 1795, Barras, Reibell, La Revellière, Le Tourneur and Carnot found themselves confronted by an empty treasury. The milliards of assignats were worth nothing. Officials received in real value less than carters. The state, reduced to mendicity, seemed all the poorer when a whole world of *parvenus*, speculators and corrupt politicians dazzled Paris with its fêtes, junketings, the eccentricity of its fashions. It was the world of the 'Merveilleuses' and the 'Incroyables', filling the show-gardens, the Tivoli or the Frascati, where Mme Tallien shone with Barras, ex-Vicomte, ex-terrorist, now Director.

Soon they had to repress a Communist plot, headed by a certain Gracchus Baboeuf, a former land-surveyor, who wanted to suppress private property and found the 'Republic of Equals'. This plot had affiliations among all the fanatics of Revolution. Betrayed, the conspirators underwent a trial which lasted a year, from May 1796 to May 1797. Baboeuf was executed.

At the elections of April 1797 for the renewal of a third of the Ancients and of the Five Hundred, the fear of Communism inspired by the Baboeuf trial produced a majority of the Right, almost Royalist, against the Conventionals and the Directory. Three of the Directors, to defend themselves, did not hesitate to foment a military *coup d'état*, favoured by the two most popular generals, Hoche and Bonaparte. The *coup d'état* was put through by General Augereau on 18 Fructidor (4 September) 1797. The elections in forty-nine departments were annulled. The Directory, returning to Terrorist methods, had suspects or returned *émigrés* executed, priests deported, the attack on religion renewed. . . . But they fell from one danger into another. At the elections of April 1798 the majority almost passed to the former Jacobins. The Directory proceeded to a new resort to force, this time against the Left : the elections were in part annulled.

The Directory, however, floundered in unprecedented financial and monetary difficulties. In September 1797 it had had to declare two-thirds of the national debt cancelled, ruining *rentiers* and the state's credit. The most lasting reform the Directory accomplished was to institute the regular recruitment of the Army by conscription. This measure, which assured an annual levy of 200,000 men, prepared the nation for military rule.

From 1789 to 1795 the revolutionary process reflected the periodic and irresistible pressure of the armed bands of the Commune of Paris, which dominated all the assemblies, Constituent, Legislative, Convention. After 9 Thermidor the Convention found itself between two material threats, that of the Commune which had lost its leaders and that of the Royalists, who were hesitant and ill-directed. From that time the Convention made use of the Army and the generals to protect itself. After 13 Vendémiaire Bonaparte disarmed Paris. At the end of two years the Directory managed to exist only by the complicity of the generals. The use of force which was formerly a means of revolutionary propulsion, then of defence of the *status quo*, was henceforth to be brought into play for the benefit of force itself, that is to say, military dictatorship. Too often one forgets the material conditions of the historical process. Bonaparte subsequently confessed it himself: military dictatorship was inevitable, either by him or by someone else.

Napoleon Bonaparte was thirty years old. This little Corsican with the skin drawn fine over the bones, the dry countenance, expressive mouth, avid nose and chin, with the high forehead and eyes of a fascinating intelligence, hair that fell down '*à la chien*', gestures curt and rapid walk in his worn uniform, was the type of the designing man, avid for action. A scion of the poor gentry of Ajaccio, for whom conquering France represented only an outlet, he held a bursarship from the king at the college of Brienne, then became a pupil at the École Militaire in Paris, was hardworking and thoughtful. Sub-lieutenant at sixteen, he was twenty when the Revolution began. Nothing attached him to the Ancien Régime. His age and his ambition bound him to the Revolution. Captain in the South, a patriot in the Jacobin manner, contemptuous of the Girondins, he awaited his opportunity. At the siege of Toulon in 1793, he took a fort that commanded the roads and thus decided the taking of the town : Robespierre the younger, commissar with the Army, had him named brigadier at twenty-four and commander of the artillery in the Army of Italy. After 9 Thermidor he was nearly broken as a Robespierrist. He had been earmarked for the Army of the West ; he did not rejoin his unit but worked at the topographical bureau of the Committee of Public Safety, and allowed himself to be removed from his regiment. He was going to leave for Turkey to reorganise the Sultan's artillery when Barras asked him to defend the Convention against the rising of 13 Vendémiaire. The gratitude of the Conventionals and Carnot's high opinion made him Commander-in-Chief of the Army of the Interior, then Commander of the Army of Italy at twenty-seven.

What did he stand for ?

First, the Army : that army which had become, by successive reforms since the end of Louis XV's reign, a corps both modern and scientific ; that army whose lower officers were disgusted with the Ancien Régime, on the very eve of the Revolution, by a decree made under the influence of the Comte d'Artois, re-establishing priority in promotion for the nobility — an abuse that had gradually been diminished since Louis XIV and Louvois ; that army in which a whole youth fired with ambition found a career, a refuge, the promise of adventure and opportunity for enthusiasm outside of revolutionary atrocities ; an army for which the fusion of old regulars and companies of ardent volunteers achieved, after five years of varied campaigns, an incomparable quality ; that army which, having saved the Revolution by its victories abroad and at home, was conscious of embodying it better than anyone.

Bonaparte represented also what was most solid in the spirit of the 18th century : education and the cult of precise knowledge ; quickness of judgment, the sense of initiative, an audacity freed from prejudices ; the liking for novelties and taking risks, the practical handling of human energies ; a bias towards rationalism that reduced scruples and obstacles alike to the simplest. Bonaparte represented the 18th-century spirit magnified in action by astonishing gifts : an imagination that analysed, brought together and combined the elements of a battle, of an action, of a political and social order as in a flash of lightning ; a nervous system geared to work, to physical and intellectual mobility, to the direct control of men and things, that transcended all common measure. His defects were the ordinary defects of the mathematician in action : impatience and sometimes, by contrast, hesitation or cheating when confronted with what is not rational, the misappreciation of forces not defined in advance and contempt for what eludes calculation, pride feeding on success and gradually ceasing to take account of resistance, of expediency and even of ridicule. Bonaparte's great weakness, when responsible for the destiny of France, was to look forward and act as if France ought to serve him, not he France. In this way he lost much : first of all, the sense of limits to his own career and fortune.

In 1796 the Directory launched against Austria two Army groups — the one, which was to cross Germany and play the main part, under Generals Jourdan and Moreau ; the other, which was to conquer the Milanese and make a diversion, under the command of Bonaparte. In Germany there was defeat and failure ; in Italy a series of dazzling victories. Bonaparte defeated the Austrians at Montenotte and Dego (12-14 April), crushed the Piedmontese at Millesimo and Mondovi (13-22 April) and forced the latter to ask for an armistice. He then invaded the Milanese, forced the bridge of

Lodi, and entered Milan in triumph (15 May). He defeated the
Austrians again at Lonato, Castiglione, Bassano (August-
September), threw back an army of enemy reinforcements at
Arcole (15-17 November), brought off a decisive victory on
the plateau of Rivoli (14 January 1797) and entered Mantua and
imposed the peace of Tolentino on the Pope (19 February).
He then forced the passes of Tarvis and Neumarkt and arrived
less than a hundred kilometres from Vienna, when the Austrians
resigned themselves to accepting preliminaries of peace at
Leoben (18 April). He had taken over 100,000 prisoners and
600 cannon. All this was the work of forces numerically
inferior to the enemy, but manœuvred with crushing rapidity.
On 17 October 1797 Austria signed the Treaty of Campo
Formio : she recognised the Cisalpine Republic created by
Bonaparte out of the Milanese, Modena and Romagna, and
agreed to abandon part of the left bank of the Rhine to France.

But continental victories changed nothing of the decisive
problem before which French greatness had miscarried from
the time of Louis XV and where even the genius of Bonaparte
seemed to hesitate : the problem of conquering England,
which controlled the secret working of European coalitions and
claimed maritime and colonial supremacy.

After Campo Formio, Hoche having died, Bonaparte
received the command of the army against England. Would he,
following the earlier plans of the ministers of the monarchy —
Choiseul and Vergennes — attack the bull frontally, try to
leap across the Channel ? No. This Corsican, victor of the
battlefields of Italy, this Mediterranean figure, saw the English
problem in Mediterranean terms. He mounted an expedition
as ingenious as it was romantic, which dispensed him from
confronting the problem directly : an expedition to conquer
Egypt and cut the English trade-route with India. The
expedition won him glory but solved nothing. On 19 May
1798 Bonaparte embarked at Toulon ; 10 June he took Malta,
30 June Alexandria ; 21 July the victory of the Pyramids
made him master of Cairo. But on 1 August the English

fleet under Nelson surprised the French fleet at Aboukir, near
Alexandria, and almost entirely destroyed it. Bonaparte's army
was imprisoned in its conquest. Against it the Sultan, at the
instigation of the English, massed troops in Syria. Bonaparte
moved ahead of the Turks, occupied Gaza and Jaffa, and
defeated the enemy at Mount Tabor. He failed for want of
artillery before Acre and returned to Egypt to throw back at
Aboukir another Turkish army that tried to land. Finally on
22 August 1799, after sixteen months of adventure, he embarked secretly for France, leaving the consequences to
General Kléber.

England, however, had raised a new coalition against
France of Austria, Russia, Turkey and Naples. Jourdan was
defeated in Germany and the Archduke Charles threatened
Alsace. Under the blows of the Russian Suvaroff, the French
armies gave up the whole of Italy except Genoa. General
Brune failed to stop the English and Russians from landing in
Holland. Only General Masséna held fast in Switzerland : he
succeeded in crushing the Russians at Zürich 25-26 September.
This victory dislocated the Russo-Austrian front and saved
our frontiers.

The 18th Brumaire

On his return to France Bonaparte found the Directory discredited by defeat abroad and violence at home, by repression
and brigandage, administrative disorder and excesses of every
kind beginning again, not to speak of financial ruin. The
most capable of the Directors in office, Siéyès, and his
friends wanted a new Constitution and a general to impose it.
He thought previously of General Joubert, who promised him
to finish the job 'with twenty grenadiers'. But Joubert had
just been killed at Novi.

The nation talked only of Bonaparte, the conqueror of
Italy, the hero of Egypt. A plot was formed into which
entered, with Siéyès, another Director, Roger-Duclos ; the
former bishop, Talleyrand ; Cambacérès, Minister of Justice ;

Lucien Bonaparte, the General's brother and President of the Council of Five Hundred. The plan was to overthrow the Directory and get the Assemblies to accept an executive committee of three Consuls provisionally to revise or change the Constitution.

On 9 November — 18 Brumaire — the Council of the Ancients, whose President had been won over to the plot, named Bonaparte commander of the Paris troops and transferred the two Assemblies to St.-Cloud, away from the Commune. One of the Directors, Barras, consented to resign. Two others, Gohier and Du Moulin, refusing to give up, were kept out of the way. At St.-Cloud next day, 10 November (19 Brumaire), the Five Hundred, warned of the *coup* being prepared, greeted Bonaparte with cries of 'Down with the Dictator', 'Outlaw him'. Bonaparte lost his head under the threat of outlawry, which was equivalent to a sentence of death without trial. But his brother Lucien, President of the Assembly, succeeded in delaying the vote for some minutes. The grenadiers invaded the hall in time to stop the vote and expel the deputies, while outside the troops acclaimed their General. At nine o'clock that evening the Ancients and some members of the Five Hundred gathered in session and voted the suppression of the Directory, the adjournment of the Assemblies and the handing over of executive power to three consuls : Siéyès, Roger-Duclos and Bonaparte.

The greater part of the population approved of the *coup d'état*, which represented the return to order and security without the return to the Ancien Régime. Military dictatorship was the régime that least alarmed newly acquired rights.

On 15 December 1799 the Constitution of the Year VIII was promulgated : it was confirmed two months later by a plebiscite. Legislative power was given to two Chambers neither of which could initiate laws : the Tribunate of 100 members, the Legislative House of 300 members. These two Chambers could accept or reject the proposals of the government without amending them.   A conservative Senate of sixty members, nominated at first by the Consuls then by co-optation, was to choose the members of the Assemblies among notabilities designated by a vote on three levels—communal, departmental, national.   Executive power was conferred on three Consuls installed for ten years.   The first Consul, Bonaparte, is in fact dictator : he decides peace and war, proposes and promulgates laws, nominates ministers and officials.   A Council of State of dignitaries, chosen by the First Consul, assists him in preparing, drafting and interpreting laws ; it constitutes also a supreme court of administrative justice.

Bonaparte's government as First Consul is a translation of the spirit and methods of military command into the exercise of civil power : a chief who conceives and decides, offices or staffs to study and prepare, agents to execute.   The essential work of this government consists in raising a structure ample, orderly and solid out of the projects or materials left by the revolutionary Assemblies.   Most of the men employed by the new régime also come out of the Revolution.   The government of the Consulate represents in our history the maximum of efficiency and the minimum of liberty.

Administrative centralisation became absolute : the departmental prefect, the sub-prefect of the district, the mayor of the commune, the local councils, were nominated by the central power.   Similarly with the judges of every category. The choices were excellent, within the limits of political docility. 'I like honest men of all colours', says Bonaparte — provided that they rallied to him.   So he was able very quickly to re-establish quiet, abolish emergency laws and impose his police. The *coup d'état* had the result of sending up stocks to almost double.   A technician of repute, Gaudin, called to the Ministry of Finance, reorganised the budget and brought order into fiscal returns with the aid of direct taxation.   A Bureau of Redemption, administered by Mollien, began to lower the Debt.   In February 1800 the Bank of France was created, which three years later received the monopoly of the issue of bank-notes and put an end to the fearful monetary insecurity left by the system of assignats. In less than a year the budget was balanced, the currency cleaned up and credit restored. The pacification of interests guaranteed submission of spirit.

Occupied in consolidating his power, Bonaparte had need of external peace. He sought it by a letter addressed to England and Austria on 25 December 1799. It was refused him. The Austrian forces were dispersed ; one body besieged Masséna in Genoa, another invaded the Var, another let itself be pushed back on the Danube by General Moreau. Bonaparte secretly concentrated an army of 60,000 men between Dijon and Lyons, got it across the St. Bernard Pass in five days (15-20 May 1800), descended into Lombardy and entered Milan 2 June. On 14 June at Marengo, after a very hard battle, for long undecided, he threw back the Austrian army of General Melas. After which he returned to Paris in triumph. But he had not got peace. It needed the crushing victory of Moreau over the Austrians at Hohenlinden in the valley of the Inn, 2 December 1800, and the successes of General Brune in the plain of the Po, to force the enemy to negotiate.

On 9 February 1801 the Treaty of Lunéville was signed : it confirmed the cessions of territory made at Campo-Formio, recognised the existence of the Batavian, Helvetian, Ligurian and Cisalpine Republics — all dominated by France — and extruded all Austrian domination in Italy, except for Venice. In the Kingdom of Naples, a special treaty permitted French troops to occupy Taranto, Otranto and Brindisi. Russia accepted the peace on 11 October 1802. England, whose fleet was mistress of the Mediterranean, had taken Malta ; she held also the French and Spanish West Indies, the French factories in India, Guiana, Ceylon and the Dutch Cape. She had forced the French army in Egypt to surrender. She consented at last to the Peace of Amiens, 27 March 1802, which left her Trinidad and Ceylon. The French, in exchange for the return of their colonies, gave up the places conquered by them in the Mediterranean.

From Consulate to Empire

During the relative respite that the new treaties afforded him, Bonaparte — now become in the eyes of the masses the 'genius of war' and the 'angel of peace' — established his authority over the state as a general prepares the way for victory, by exploiting the elements in the situation as they presented themselves to him.

A child of the 18th century, indifferent to religion, one of his first cares was to capture for the benefit of his power the Catholic revival manifesting itself in France. After long negotiations, he signed a Concordat with Pope Pius VII, 15 July 1801. The 'Catholic, Apostolic and Roman' faith was officially recognised as that of the majority of Frenchmen and the government pledged itself to assure its free and public exercise. The First Consul was to nominate the bishops, who would then receive canonical investiture from the Pope. The bishops would choose the parish priests with the agreement of the civil power. Bishops and parish priests were to receive a salary and swear fidelity between the hands of the First Consul or the prefect. But those who had acquired Church goods would not be disturbed. An official *Te Deum* was sung at Notre-Dame. The young Chateaubriand distinguished himself with his *Génie du christianisme* (1802). A law and a police regulation, entitled 'Organic Articles', completed the process of turning the clergy into a graded and centralised body of functionaries. The Protestants, Calvinist and Lutheran, received analogous advantages and submitted to similar discipline. Thus Bonaparte acquired the support of religion at the same time as he domesticated it.

After religion — property. The Convention had already tried to codify the elements of a new civil law. In March 1804 the Civil Code was voted — the work of the Council of State — over the drafting of which Cambacérès and Bonaparte himself had presided. The Civil Code confirmed, with clarity and style, the social conquests of the Revolution ; it guaranteed property and organised the family in the Roman manner : it was at once anti-feudal and conservative.

After religion and property — education. By the institution of *lycées*, whose teachers formed a body of closely-watched functionaries and whose studies were minutely regulated from Paris, the central power gained complete authority over the education of youth. The higher schools and those to which admission had to be applied for were more or less militarised, on the model of the École Polytechnique.

Lastly, the creation of the order of the Legion of Honour, breaking with the egalitarian principles of the Revolution, constituted a sort of hierarchy of merit, military and civil, beside the regular grades or employments and in the direct service of the régime.

For what and for whom did Bonaparte work ? He himself said later that he seized the immediate opportunities that offered without preconceived plan. In the conduct of his career as of his armies, he is the general who conquers his positions successively, without setting a term in advance to his success.

He re-established order and the administration ; regularity in affairs and in the finances ; confidence ; religion. He installed a practical and sovereign authority, which carried out his orders at his wish. His name was popular and had great prestige. What would be the upshot of it all ? Return to the régime of the Directory or to the formulas of a revolutionary Constitution ? Either of these would reopen all the wounds, put all the reforms in question once more, throw the nation back into anarchy or foreign adventures. Recall the *émigré* dynasty, restore the monarchy and give the crown to Louis XVI's brother and heir, the former Comte de Provence who called himself Louis XVIII ? The latter naïvely counted on it and wrote Bonaparte a letter claiming the crown. The

way to a restoration of the monarchy seemed ready. But
Bonaparte understood clearly that a great part of the nation
feared the return of the Ancien Régime and the Bourbons :
such a return would threaten too many acquired or usurped
rights, reawaken too many passions, put too many positions,
material or moral, in danger. Since a monarch was wanted
and many people wanted no more Bourbons, why not fill the
post himself ? . . . To prepare the ground, he would check-
mate Royalists, Republicans and Liberals alike. And he would
make use of the plebiscite.

On 8 May 1802 a popular plebiscite, afterwards ratified by
the Senate, then by the Constitution of the year X, gave him
the title of Consul for life with sovereign powers. Two
years later he put between him and the Bourbons a corpse,
that of the Duc d'Enghien, arrested by a surprise move and
executed at Vincennes, contrary to all justice. On 18 May 1804
an organic *senatus consultus*, which a new plebiscite sanctioned,
proclaimed Napoleon Bonaparte Emperor of the French.

CHAPTER IV

The Epic Revolution: Napoleon

❖

*Imperial Rule — Trafalgar — Austerlitz — Tilsit — The
Peninsular War — The Grand Empire — The Russian
Campaign — Leipzig — The Campaign in France —
Waterloo*

AFTER a constitutional revolution, and then a terrorist and a
military one, France from 1804 to 1814 experienced an epic
revolution : an imperial adventure of the most astonishing
kind in our history — but an adventure without limit, out of
all traditional proportions and calculations, an adventure that
had no reason or end except itself. Carried away by his
imagination and by the habit of domination which his successes
gave him, Napoleon's mind was divided between two ambitions : one that was difficult to bring off, demanding great
practical sense, calculation and decision — that of creating
a dynasty ; the other ambition — that of the conqueror,
intoxicated with his own genius, who dreamed of subjugating
the whole of Europe. After a dazzling experience of glory,
these two ambitions miscarried, leaving France full of pride
and heroic legends, but effectually diminished. Napoleon had
all the gifts in the highest degree — except political sense,
properly speaking.

Imperial Rule

The Imperial government accentuated the characteristics
of the Consulate. Tribunate, Council of State, Legislative
Body, Senate, ministers became the instruments of the Imperial
will. After 1807 even the laws were replaced by Imperial
decrees.

With a mixture of calculating adroitness and romantic

Napoleon

pretension, Napoleon constituted a potentate's Court, distributing pompous titles galore. All his family were elevated to princely rank. He instituted a Grand Elector, two Archchancellors, an Arch-treasurer, a Constable and a Grand Admiral ; he created fourteen Marshals of the Empire, six civilian grand officers, a legion of prefects of the palace, chamberlains, equerries, pages. Each member of the Imperial family had a household. He re-established the nobility, conferred fiefs, was prodigal of titles — princes, counts, barons, knights. In all he created 31 dukes, 500 counts, 1,500 barons. Gradually he seduced the old nobility, to amalgamate it with the new. Ten years after Bonaparte was arrested as a Robespierrist one would think one was dreaming.

In fact, in a France by no means healed of the doctrines of the Revolution or of the passions, enthusiasms and rancours let loose by it, the Imperial adventure could only develop under cover of a police system, rigorous, interfering and often arbitrary. The Press was reduced to almost nothing : four newspapers, the directors of which were nominated by the government. A similar control was exercised over printing and publishing. Liberal writers were suspect. In reorganising the Institute, Napoleon suppressed the faculty of moral and political sciences. He exiled Mme de Staël and disgraced Chateaubriand ; he instituted the Imperial University from which the critical spirit was banished. He ended by entering into conflict with the Pope himself, Pius VII, whom he had seized by his soldiers from the Quirinal in July 1809 and shut up at Savona, near Genoa. Catholics and the clergy gradually detached themselves from the Empire.

Napoleon could doubtless have dispensed with establishing such a tyranny, if he had had the leisure and freedom of mind necessary to give himself to the subtleties of civil government. But he was at war with all Europe, and his epic adventure abroad demanded that nothing should move or resist him at home.

Trafalgar

Threatened by the Consulate's policy of commercial, maritime and colonial expansion, alarmed by France's encroachments in Holland, Switzerland and Italy and by Napoleon's claim to close the Mediterranean, exasperated by French demands in regard to Malta, England — sure of winning the game at sea — renewed the war in 1803. In a few weeks she blockaded Toulon, Rochefort and Brest and cut France off from her colonies. In return Napoleon took up an old project again and made his dispositions to cross the Channel : he assembled 150,000 men at the camp of Boulogne and had transports and landing craft built. But, in order to cross, he needed the mastery of the Channel for at least some days. The Emperor became impatient and tried strategic combinations. Admiral Villeneuve — the defeated commander at Aboukir — on returning from the West Indies, instead of coming to relieve Brest from blockade, sought refuge at Cadiz. Napoleon ordered him to put to sea. The French fleet was completely crushed by Nelson off Cape Trafalgar, 21 October 1805. Henceforth, England dominated the sea.

Austerlitz

On the Continent, through the efforts of England, a Coalition was formed against the territorial aggressions of France : it was led by Alexander I of Russia, and included Austria, Sweden and Naples. From Boulogne Napoleon raced with his Grand Army ahead of the Austrians, who were advancing on the upper Danube, and overwhelmed them. After a series of engagements he forced their General Mack to sign the Capitulation of Ulm, 20 October 1805. From Ulm he descended on Vienna, which he occupied without resistance. Then he turned north again to encounter the joint armies of Alexander I and Francis II of Austria. On 2 December, upon ground chosen by himself, he gave battle to his enemies, the famous 'model' battle of Austerlitz : the Allies lost 26,000 men (against Napoleon's 7,000) and 180 guns, the bronze of which served for the Vendôme Column. On 26 December the Austrians signed the Treaty of Pressburg: they ceded to France, Venice and Istria, except Trieste and Dalmatia; to Bavaria, Tyrol and the Trentino; to Württemberg, Suabia.

The victory of Austerlitz made Napoleon Emperor of the West, a new Charlemagne; he dominated all Italy, Holland, and South and West Germany. In the spring of 1806 he took the Kingdom of Naples away from the Bourbons to give it to his eldest brother, Joseph; a younger brother, Louis, was crowned King of Holland. Imprudently he destroyed the Holy Roman Empire, which ensured the fractionalisation of Germany, and constituted a Confederation of the Rhine comprising vassals whom he thought to attach to himself by titles: the Dukes of Bavaria and Württemberg whom he made kings, the Dukes of Hesse-Darmstadt and Baden promoted to be Grand Dukes, and Murat, his brother-in-law, made Grand Duke of Berg. He gave Hanover to the King of Prussia. The head of the Habsburgs became no more than Emperor of Austria. It meant the open road to German unity.

Some months later Prussia, roused against the Napoleonic domination over Germany, took up the rôle lost by Austria: she entered into Coalition with England and Russia. A new war began on 7 October 1806. Napoleon was then at Bamberg with his troops. On 14 October the Prussian armies were crushed at Jena and Auerstädt. Prussia foundered; the French occupied Magdeburg, Spandau, Stettin, Küstrin, and entered Berlin. King Frederick William no longer had a province in which to take refuge.

Tilsit

Then Napoleon advanced across the bad roads and marshes of Poland against the Russians; he gave battle first at Eylau 8 February 1807, but he finished with them only four months later at Friedland, where he won a decisive victory on 14 June. The Russians asked for an armistice almost immediately.

Alexander and Napoleon met for several days in the middle of Lake Niemen. On 7 July they signed the Treaty of Tilsit : Prussia was dismembered and reduced to four provinces with five million inhabitants ; Russia left Cattaro and the Ionian isles to the French ; the two Emperors formed a secret alliance against England and Turkey.

Napoleon then created the Kingdom of Westphalia for his youngest brother Jerome, gave the Grand Duchy to the Elector of Saxony promoted to be king, and made the new states enter the Confederation of the Rhine, which comprised now all Germany, except the provinces left to the King of Prussia.

The Peninsular War

But this astonishing series of continental victories did not shake the essential adversary : England was neither conquered nor ready to give up. She was mistress of the seas ; her fleets remained aggressive. Napoleon, not being able to reach her directly, tried to ruin and starve her. By the Berlin decree of 21 November 1806 he had already declared the British Isles in a state of blockade. By the Milan decree of 17 December 1807 he tightened the blockade 'at sea as on land'. But to render the blockade effective the coasts of Europe had to be watched, and, to watch the coasts, he had to occupy more and more territory. Napoleon ordered Swedish Pomerania, Bremen, Hamburg, all Holland, Tuscany and the Papal States to be occupied and Portugal invaded. The invasion of Portugal drew him into the hornets' nest of Spain.

The Spanish Bourbons, discredited, lived in fear of their people. In the spring of 1808 the rising of Aranjuez forced Charles IV to give up the crown to his son Ferdinand. Father and son appealed to Murat's French troops, who entered Spain on the pretext of reinforcing Junot's corps who were occupying Portugal. Napoleon summoned the Spanish sovereigns to Bayonne. At this news a rising broke out in Madrid and French soldiers were massacred there. The Emperor seized the opportunity : he wrung from Ferdinand and Charles an

abdication shameful for those who consented to it, immoral
for him who exacted it — as he himself confessed later. In
June Joseph Bonaparte was promoted to be King of Spain.
Murat succeeded him as King of Naples.

But Spain refused to give up her independence. She rose
up against the 'trap of Bayonne' : thousands of Spaniards took
up arms. The revolt drew in peasants and workers ; Joseph
Bonaparte had to fight a battle to reach Madrid. On 20 July
a disaster shook French prestige : General Dupont, surrounded
by rebels at the entry to the defiles of the Sierra Morena, surrendered at Baylen. King Joseph fled from Madrid. Under
the blow of this defeat Napoleon gave way to Prussia, whose
territory he evacuated, and demanded in vain of the Tsar,
whom he met at Erfurt 'before a *parterre* of kings', to show his
teeth to Austria which was becoming hostile again. He
himself left for Spain and, after some victories in November
and December, thinking he had re-established the position for
his brother, left Soult and Ney to continue the war. But this
war, maintained by bands of guerrillas,[1] became inexorable ;
at once national and religious, cruel and incalculable. The siege
of Saragossa was to leave thousands dead. A war unpopular
in France itself, where the Emperor had to deal with the
intrigues of Talleyrand and Fouché. A murderous war which
held up and exhausted the best troops, at a time when recruits
began to desert and the people showed themselves weary.

The Grand Empire

In these conditions Napoleon would have liked to recover
breath. But he could not. A new Coalition — the fifth —
bringing together England, Austria and the insurrectionary
government of Spain, was formed against him in 1809. The
Spanish example became contagious : it was no longer
dynastic spirit, but national spirit that henceforward inspired

---

[1] To say nothing of Wellington's army, whose achievements in the Peninsular
War are one of the glories of the British military tradition — an odd, and significant,
omission.—A. L. R.

the Emperor's adversaries. However, by the incredible activity he imposed on everybody and which he imposed on himself, by the speed which was his favourite medium, he succeeded in winning again. After the victory of Eckmühl, then the hard and indecisive struggle of Essling, he succeeded in pushing back, if not defeating, the Archduke Charles's army in the plain of Wagram, near Vienna. It was high time. National movements made their appearance in several places in Westphalia, in Bohemia and the Tyrol. But the Austrian Court gave way. On 14 October 1809 the Emperor Francis signed the Treaty of Vienna, handing over Salzburg and the Engadine to Bavaria; a part of Galicia to the Grand Duchy of Warsaw, another part to Russia; Trieste, Fiume, Carinthia, Carniola, Croatia to France, which joined them to Dalmatia to form the Illyrian Provinces.

The Emperor felt the need of stabilising his fortunes and his dynasty. He separated from his wife, Joséphine de Beauharnais, by whom he had no children: a *senatus consultus* of 16 December 1809 pronounced the divorce and the Empress retired to the château of Malmaison. On 1 April 1810, having asked for the hand of the Tsar's sister in vain, Napoleon married the Emperor Francis of Austria's daughter, Marie-Louise, aged eighteen. On 20 March 1811 the new Empress of the French gave birth to a son, the 'King of Rome'.

With the exception of Russia, Austria, Turkey, Scandinavia and the Prussian provinces, the whole of continental Europe was under the domination of Napoleon in 1810, either directly or by means of vassal states. The French Empire proper comprised 130 departments: France up to the Rhine, Holland, North Germany, Swedish Pomerania, the Valais, Piedmont, Genoa, Parma, the Papal States and beyond the Adriatic, the Illyrian Provinces. Napoleon was suzerain and protector, by right or in fact, of the Confederation of the Rhine, of the Helvetic Confederation, of Italy, the Kingdom of Naples, Spain. France represented hardly a quarter of this total — an immense construction, improvised and brittle. France even recognised herself to be exhausted and hardly hid her discontent : she wished for a régime of peace, relaxation of effort, of tranquil work. The peoples outside France, inspired by the ideas of the French Revolution and learning from it lessons of national pride, would not resign themselves to being the subjects or vassals of a passing conqueror. The old dynasties awaited their revenge.

Napoleon enjoyed two years of respite from 1810 to 1812. He could have readjusted the lines of his system and his fortune, rendered the régime at home milder, and offered pledges, compensations or concessions abroad. But he had neither political sense nor a sense of moderation. Soon he committed the supreme mistake : that of embroiling himself, over the Grand Duchy of Warsaw, with the only sovereign who could in some respects draw advantage from the overturns he had brought about — the Tsar Alexander of Russia.

The Russian Campaign

The war started again in June 1812, this time against Russia, naturally supported by the English, and Sweden, which had taken Bernadotte, a former Marshal of France, as king.

Napoleon had assembled a colossal army, 675,000 men, in which the contingents of 'twenty nations' served. The French were only 200,000 of it. This army passed the Niemen at Kovno on 26 June. The Russians fell back, leaving an empty space behind them, withdrawing the inhabitants and destroying food supplies. At Smolensk on 17 August Napoleon tried to hold them, but after a hard struggle they escaped and set fire to the town. Gradually the army exhausted itself and melted away through privations and desertions. When some leagues from Moscow, it had already lost 150,000 men. But the Russian general, Barclay de Tolly, author of this tactical retreat, was replaced by old Kutusov, incarnation of resistance. Kutusov awaited Napoleon south of Borodino on the Moskwa. A furious battle was fought on 7 September, in which the Russians lost 40,000 men, the French 30,000 — but without decisive result. On 13 September the French entered Moscow. They hoped to make peace there, but the town was almost empty. Next day — on the initiative, it is said, of the Russian governor — an immense fire broke out which destroyed three-quarters of the city and aroused European opinion against Napoleon.

The Emperor's projects were thrown out of gear. He hesitated. Should he pass the winter in Moscow? At length he gave way and gave the order to retreat. On 19 October the French began their retreat across country rendered desert, menaced by surprise attacks of the enemy and defenceless against the exceptional rigours of an early winter (37 degrees of frost at the beginning of December). On the banks of the River Beresina the retreating army, surrounded by three Russian corps, was saved only by the heroism of the sappers who threw two bridges over the river in thaw. But almost all the sappers were killed and Kutusov collected 9,000 stragglers. When it reached Kovno on 18 December, the Grand Army counted only 18,000 men.

The disaster called forth conspiracy. On 5 December Napoleon left Vilna in haste for Paris, where the state of morale was disquieting. On the news of the retreat from Russia, General Malet attempted a *coup d'état*. He was shot ; but the fact that he could arrest the Ministers of War and of Police and install a provisional government, betrayed the fragility of the régime.

Napoleon had no time to readjust his political course. Regenerated and trained by German patriots like Stein and Hardenberg, Prussia declared against him. In February she allied herself with Russia and in March imposed conscription. Napoleon himself hurried to recruit a new army : he conscribed beardless boys — the 'Marie-Louises' — who would be trained in action. He committed the gross error of not recalling the 250,000 men, his best troops, who were in Spain, and the cavalry whose absence cost him his last battles.

Leipzig

However, the campaign of 1813 began with successes. The Emperor succeeded in beating the Russians and Prussians at Lützen in Saxony on 2 May, and at Bautzen on 19-21 May. But the situation remained critical. Austria could intervene at any moment with forces intact. Metternich, the Austrian Chancellor, profited by this opportunity to raise the prestige of his country. He proposed conditions to Napoleon which would buy Austria's neutrality by restoring to her the Illryian Provinces, abolishing the Grand Duchy of Warsaw, and giving up all domination over Germany. The bargain proposed was a hard one, but it would enable time to be gained. Napoleon refused, in spite of the counsels of his entourage and although the news from Spain announced the defeat of his troops at Vittoria and the entry of Wellington into Madrid.

In the month of August 1813 France found herself facing a general coalition and had to struggle against three armies containing half a million men. Napoleon succeeded in defeating the Austrians again at Dresden on 26 and 27 August. But for fear of being overwhelmed, having only 155,000 men against 300,000, he retired on Leipzig. There during three days, 16-18 October, he resisted a formidable onslaught that the Germans celebrate as the 'Battle of the Nations': in the end, the defection of the Saxon and Württemberg troops forced him to give way. It was his first great defeat. Retreating on the Rhine, he had only 40,000 men left. At the same time he learned that Wellington, having thrown the French out of Spain, was invading the south-west of France.

The Campaign in France

At the end of December the armies of Russia, Austria, Prussia and Sweden crossed the Rhine. The Prussians and Austrians made towards the valley of the Seine. Bernadotte's Swedes came through Belgium. The great invasion was on. But at the sight of the invader, the people rushed to arms : a war of *francs-tireurs* took shape. Napoleon himself, pressed in on all sides, put up a magnificent display of genius. He beat Blücher's Prussians at Champaubert, Montmirail, Château-Thierry, Vauchamps from 10-13 February and threw them back ɔn Châlons; then, from 16-18 February in the engagements of Mormant, Nangis, Montereau, he drove back Schwarzenberg's Austrians on Troyes : seven victories in eight days. After some hesitation the Allies, having promised each other not to conclude a separate peace, advanced again. Napoleon had only a skeleton army. He succeeded in throwing Blücher back on Laon, but he could not stop Schwarzenberg at Arcis-sur-Aube. Then there came to him the audacious idea of marching on Lorraine to cut the enemy's communications and force him to retreat. He thus uncovered Paris. By ill-luck his despatches revealing this plan were intercepted. Paris was unfortified; after a courageous resistance by the garrison, National Guards and students of the École Polytechnique, the Allies entered the capital on 21 March. Ten days earlier the Austrians had occupied Lyons. Wellington took Toulouse 10 April.

The Royalists, for long supported by England, succeeded in gaining the consent of the Tsar, Austria and Prussia to a restoration of the Bourbons, for which Talleyrand's intrigues prepared the way. On 31 March 1814 the Allied sovereigns proclaimed that they would not treat with Napoleon or any member of his family. Next day Talleyrand had himself designated head of a provisional government by a few dozen senators. On 3 April the Senate and Legislative Body voted the deposition of the Emperor and his family.

Napoleon, however, had returned in haste to Fontainebleau. He still wanted to give battle. The soldiers remained faithful to him; but the Marshals refused and some deserted. On 4 April he signed a first abdication in favour of his son, the King of Rome. On 11 April he was forced to abdicate unconditionally. The Allies consented to leave him the title of Emperor and the sovereignty of the isle of Elba with a pension of two millions which the French government was to pay. On 20 April he said a moving farewell to the soldiers of his guard in the courtyard of the palace at Fontainebleau and departed for Elba. On the 6th the Comte de Provence was proclaimed by the Senate King of France as Louis XVIII.

The Treaty of Paris, signed 30 May 1814, brought France back within her national frontiers, but left her Annecy and Chambéry, Avignon, Montbéliard, Mulhouse, Philippeville, Marienbourg, Sarrelouis and Landau.

Landing at Calais, 24 April, suffering from the gout, Louis XVIII found himself rather out of his element in a France he had left more than twenty years before, of which the social foundations had been overthrown and in which minds and manners bore an imprint very different from the Ancien Régime. On his arrival he had some difficulty in understanding the need to make certain concessions. He rejected the tricolour cockade and restored the white flag. However, on 4 June he resigned himself to granting his people a Charter which established constitutional monarchy after the English model, with a Chamber of Peers and a Chamber of Deputies. At least he succeeded in liberating the territory from foreign occupation.

The nation, terribly exhausted and weary of war, was at first grateful to the Bourbons — whom it knew only as a symbol — as representing peace. But a few months were enough for disagreement to become acute between public opinion and the demands or claims of certain returned *émigrés* who besieged Louis XVIII. The most dangerous conflict was over the 'national properties'. Although the Charter declared the sale of these irrevocable, the *émigrés* reclaimed their old properties, and even tried to take them back. The clergy in the West denounced those who held on to them; many peasants and bourgeois were afraid of losing their acquisitions. Moreover, the royal government, not having to make war any more, reduced effectives and dismissed 12,000 officers on half pay, while reintroducing *émigrés* into the army and giving them promotion. Soon Liberal criticism grew bold in speech and writing. Peasants refused to pay taxes. In the garrisons the temper was conducive to conspiracy. The regiments of Lille and Cambrai had to be dispersed when marching on Paris.

Waterloo

Informed of all this, Napoleon gained new hope in his fortunes. He was restless in the isle of Elba, where neither wife nor son had joined him and where he awaited his promised pension in vain. On 26 February 1815 he left the isle and on 1 March landed near Antibes. He gathered 700 soldiers and took the road for Grenoble. Troops barred the way to him at the defile of Laffrey ; he harangued them and they threw their guns down crying, 'Vive l'Empereur'. Thenceforward nothing stopped him. Colonel La Bédoyère handed over his regiment. Grenoble surrendered to him and Lyons acclaimed him. On 17 March at Auxerre Ney went over to his service and on 20th Napoleon re-entered the Tuileries. Louis XVIII had left the night before for Belgium. The France of the peasants and the people had given the throne back to the little Corsican.

But there was Europe. In vain Napoleon proclaimed that he wanted peace and tried to negotiate to obtain it. The Allies were resolved to have no more of him. The English army under Wellington and the Prussian under Blücher advanced across Belgium. To the 210,000 soldiers of the enemy Napoleon opposed 124,000. He was in contact with the Prussians on 16 June at Ligny, near Fleurus, beat them and ordered General Grouchy to pursue them with 30,000 men. Then he turned to face the English entrenched on the height of Mont-St.-Jean, near the village of Waterloo. Held up by the saturated soil, the French attacked too late on 18 June at midday. At two o'clock, when Napoleon was hoping for the return of Grouchy's army corps, the Prussians who had deceived him began to appear on the French right. By seven o'clock infantry assaults and cavalry charges alike had failed against the English squares ; the reserves were engaged against the Prussians. At half-past seven the Emperor launched the Imperial Guard against the English : they lost two-thirds of their men. At this moment a new Prussian army corps arrived. Panic broke the French army. Only the survivors of the old Guard remained unbroken in the disaster, refusing to give themselves up ; they beat a retreat only at nine in the evening.

Returning to Paris, Napoleon found almost everyone there against him, first of all his own Prefect of Police, Fouché. On 29 June he left Malmaison for Rochefort where he intended to embark for the United States. A capitulation of 3 July opened Paris to the English and the Prussians. Louis XVIII re-entered the capital 8 July.

At Rochefort Napoleon found the port blockaded by an English squadron. He then decided to give himself up as a prisoner of war. He embarked on 15 July in the English ship *Bellerophon* which took him to the island of St. Helena.

Interned and strictly watched in this island of the South Atlantic, in a climate that aggravated the melancholy of his exile and the sickness of his inaction, he died there 5 May 1821, aged fifty-two, already transfigured by legend.

A second Treaty of Paris, 20 November 1815, took sanctions for the Hundred Days and the disaster of Waterloo. France was brought back to narrower limits than before the Revolution ; her frontiers remained open on the North and East. She had to pay an indemnity of 700 millions and maintain a foreign army of occupation of 150,000 men on her territory at her own expense ; she was excluded from the councils of Europe.

The Napoleonic saga was the supreme — and senseless — exaltation of the policy of continental expansion.

First, after Colbert, then under Louis XV, this policy deflected France from her maritime opportunities, which alone could assure her the rank of first power. The fall of the Empire marks the decisive triumph of the new mistress of the seas — England — and her arrival at the position of arbiter in Europe. Occupying Malta, the Ionian Isles and Gibraltar, the English hold henceforth the keys of the Mediterranean. Masters equally of the maritime highway to the Indian Ocean and the Far East by the Cape, they acquire, in America, Trinidad, Tobago and Santa Lucia. Their trade, compensating the effects of the Continental Blockade by expansion overseas, dominates the markets in overseas commodities.

A Congress of Allied plenipotentiaries and diplomats, assembled at Vienna from November 1814 to June 1815, ended in the treaties of 1815. These treaties rearrange the forces of continental Europe among four powers — Russia, Prussia, Austria, France — in such a way that the last is under constant guard by its neighbours and none of the other three becomes preponderant. Buffer states — the Netherlands, Switzerland, the Kingdom of Sardinia — strengthen the solidity of the edifice. Germany and Italy remain divided : the latter under Austrian dominance, while Austria and Prussia share influence over Germany.

It is peace, but a peace that leaves the future completely free only to England. Hence the ease with which in the course of the 19th century the greatest empire in history is built up : the British Empire — something of which Colbert formerly dreamed for France.

The Napoleonic adventure shows that glory is no substitute for political sense. One must admire it for the renown it gave to our arms. It must be deplored not only for the irreparable defeat with which this renown was purchased, but for the sterile expenditure of energies that, better managed, could have accomplished a work both great and enduring.

CHAPTER V

The Restoration: A Compromise that Failed

❖

Disequilibrium of the Nation — Louis XVIII — From
Conciliation to Reaction — Charles X — Revolution of 1830

IT is a France very much alive, but unbalanced, that comes out of the upsets of the Revolution and the glories of the Empire. Unbalanced in energies, in mind, social and economic constitution, in political aspirations.

In spite of terrible loss of blood, the population has appreciably increased : it reaches 29 millions in 1814. Since the end of the Ancien Régime Paris has gained about 150,000 souls. It numbers 650,000 inhabitants. Except for the sea-ports, which have suffered from the consequences of the Continental Blockade and the misfortunes to our colonies, almost all the towns are growing, helped by the attraction that their mobility, ideas and even politics exert on people's imagination, by the development of administrative institutions and still more by the expansion of economic life.

In the country, great material progress has been accomplished. In several regions the peasants have greatly profited from the sale of national goods, Church or *émigré* properties : the class of small independent proprietors has everywhere grown and constitutes the most stable element in French society until the end of the 19th century. The suppression of tithes and feudal rights has been for the mass of country people a decisive sign of an emancipation, an incentive to work. Under Napoleon, the construction of roads, the strengthening of the police, the spread of a system of uniform measures, the stabilisation of the currency — not to mention the Civil Code — give order and security in the countryside. The Continental Blockade, while restricting imports of luxury products, encourages fruitful agricultural experiments. In 1801 the banker Delessert starts the manufacture of sugar from beetroot : an industry grows up in the North and East. Growing tobacco, chicory, plants for dyeing is encouraged. Special schools are set up for agricultural research. The government grants subsidies and awards decorations to producers. The expanding needs of the armies and the towns increase the flow of products. The small towns are growing. In villages or hamlets, small proprietors, farmers and labourers live relatively comfortably, fed and maintained by cultivating the soil without having to spend anything.

With the Continental Blockade and the conquest of Europe which enlarges the market, industry enters into a new age — the Industrial Age. The use of machinery spreads widely. Spinning-machines come in from England. Under the Empire, Philippe de Girard invents a machine for spinning flax. Oberkampf brings rollers for printing stuffs into use. Jacquard sets up his famous factory for silk-making. Cotton-spinning and -weaving develop in Normandy and Alsace, woollen-weaving at Sedan. The brothers Didot improve printing processes. In 1814 France produces, notably in the furnaces of Lorraine, twice the quantity of raw and cast iron made in 1789. In 1801 the first iron bridge across the Seine — the Pont des Arts — is built. Chaptal, Berthollet, Vauquelin open up new fields to industrial chemistry. At the end of the Empire the value of industrial production almost equals that of agriculture. Napoleon returns to the vigorous methods of Colbert : any and every means, diverse and sometimes contradictory ones, are used to encourage or support industries.

To this industrial expansion is added a large and rapid development of public works. The deepening of the port of Antwerp, the building of the great breakwater of Cherbourg, reclaiming the marshes of the Cotentin and Aunis ; making the canals of the North, North-East and from Nantes to Brest ; the remaking, widening and extension of the network of main roads, opening of carriage ways over the Simplon and Mont-cenis passes and along the Corniche ; the embellishment of towns, particularly of Lyons, Turin, Rome, but above all of Paris, where several quarters are graced by monuments of the Empire : such are the principal public works of the Napoleonic 'epoch.

Intellectual life experiences a shock and a stimulus as strong as that in politics and economics. Ideas, the sciences, literature — all the movements of the mind feel new impulses. Contacts are multiplied, communications widened. The social range reached by writers, scholars, popularisers of knowledge is much wider than ever before. The great schools founded or reorganised by the Convention — the Musée, the Ecole Polytechnique, the Ecole Normale Supérieure — provide the middle class with a greatly expanded staff, more open-minded and critical in their education, more ready for change and experiment than hitherto.

The first professors of the Ecole Polytechnique — Lagrange, Monge, Laplace and their successors, Cauchy and Galois — make advances in the realm of astro-physics. The engineer Fresnel founds modern optics. Sadi Carnot, son of the great Carnot, studies the motor power of fire and steam. Volta invents the electric pile about 1800. Ampère, shortly after, establishes the mathematical laws of electro-magnetic phenomena. In 1804 the Cornishman Trevithick tries out the steam-locomotive ; in 1807 the American Fulton launches his steam-boat ; in 1828 the Frenchman Séguin invents the tubular boiler. Chemistry and natural history make as rapid progress. At the Museum, Lamarck, Cuvier, St.-Hilaire distinguish themselves. From 1800 to 1805 Cuvier gives his famous demonstrations of comparative anatomy and creates palaeontology or the science of extinct species.

In 1781 the great philosopher Kant published his *Critique*

of Pure Reason. The principal French metaphysician, Maine de Biran, remains unappreciated. But a brilliant populariser, Victor Cousin, by his eclectic teaching, spreads ideas from all quarters among the middle class. Later Auguste Comte puts forward his Positive Philosophy.

In the realm of letters a wide breach appears between the last writers of the classical tradition and a generation which, undergoing the influence of Germany and England — following Mme de Staël and Chateaubriand — exalt Romanticism and liberate the poetic sensibility of our people.

Disequilibrium of the Nation

But this France, vibrant with new experiences, dominated by urban influences, is in disaccord, is soon to be in conflict, with the other France which by its mentality, its memories or simply by material conditions, remains attached to the past : the old rural France, in which the returned *émigrés* seek their support. In spite of the progress made by centralisation under Napoleon, the flow of communications and contacts is still very slow. There is a marked difference of degree and rhythm between the material, cultural and political life of the country and that of the towns, a difference more marked at the beginning of the 19th century than in previous centuries — and one that lasts till the completion of the railways. Hence the political and social disaccord that marks France for a half-century and diminishes only with the diffusion of urban ways by the penetration of the railways into the most remote provinces.

For this nation in disequilibrium, exacting and restless, full of regrets and for ever seeking something — a nation in which the men of thirty do not understand the men of fifty — what is needed is a new régime, at once reassuring and constructive, open and popular, a régime Capetian in spirit. The Bourbons only offer it an attempt at restoration, a well-intentioned compromise, though hardly sincere, between the cult of the Ancien Régime and reluctant acceptance of the

more moderate gains of the Revolution. This compromise —
which offends both sides in turn and brings them back to
their quarrels instead of distracting them from them — does
not fortify itself with any visible prestige. The Bourbons
lose the game. To win it they would need a political genius
and a brilliance in action that they do not possess.

Louis XVIII

Louis XVIII was now an old man, amiable and intelligent,
dignified in his general bearing and attitude, to whom experience
had brought wisdom and *savoir-faire*, but who remained the
prisoner of memories from which his temperament in no ways
predisposed him to free himself. Obese and gouty, unable to
mount a horse, he had refined and out-of-date tastes, a man of
wit who was keen on etiquette and genealogy.

He returned to France after the Hundred Days in the
midst of the agitation and reprisals provoked by Napoleon's
downfall. Royalist bands took their revenge by killing and
pillaging in the South: it was the White Terror that was
responsible for bloodshed in Marseilles, Avignon, Nîmes,
Toulouse, the Rhône valley and Aquitaine.

The Charter envisaged two legislative chambers: the
Chamber of Peers whose members were nominated by the
king on their hereditary title, and the Chamber of Deputies
elected on a restricted suffrage by electors no more than
100,000 in number. The elections of August 1815, held
immediately upon the disastrous blow of the Hundred Days,
produced a Chamber of ultra-royalist deputies, the 'Chambre
introuvable'. At once the king's moderation and prudence
were overwhelmed by the demands of the Ultras, who wanted
their revenge. Emergency laws abolished guarantees of
liberty and instituted a legal terror. The accomplices of the
Hundred Days were brought before special tribunals and
Marshal Ney was shot on 7 December. Some former members
of the Convention were proscribed; Monge, Lakanal, Siéyès
and fifteen other Academicians had to quit the Institute. The

administration was purged. Louis XVIII's brother, the Comte d'Artois, encouraged these excesses. Committees of Ultras combed officials in the departments. Under colour of reawakening faith, a pious association, the 'Congregation', compromised religion and especially the Jesuits (re-established in 1815), in this policy of aggressive reaction. Getting rid of Talleyrand and Fouché, ministers with no authority, the king gave power to a former *émigré*, the Duc de Richelieu, a good man but out of touch.

After the reprisals the 'Chambre introuvable' went in for demagogy: it had to be dissolved, 5 September 1816. Then a group of moderate and abler Royalists, forming the Constitutional party, took control of affairs. The brains of this party, who wanted to see the loyal application of the Charter, were the Comte Decazes, Pasquier, Molé, Royer-Collard, Guizot, the Comte de Serre, Lainé. The October elections gave the Constitutionals a majority. A serious effort became possible.

Financial difficulties had first to be solved, the state's credit and budgetary methods re-established. In this respect the work of the Restoration was remarkable for its honesty, technical excellence and brilliant results, thanks to the management of Baron Louis, then of Comte Corvetto; thanks too, in the Parliamentary domain, to the leadership of Royer-Collard and Villèle, the leader of the Right. The budgetary laws of the Restoration remain models. In military affairs, Marshal Gouvion-St.-Cyr showed himself a reformer of the first rank: he reorganised the Army, enlarged and made its units more flexible and provided it with a system of recruitment which it retained up to 1872. In 1817 a law reforming the electoral system in a liberal sense substituted direct vote by list for the department, in place of elections by several stages. In 1819 the Comte de Serre re-established liberty of the press and newspapers began to multiply. Thus liberal ideas gained foothold. A party of 'Independents', hostile to everything that recalled the Ancien Régime—including the dynasty—was

formed with men like Lafayette, Benjamin Constant, General
Foy, the banker Laffitte, the advocate Manuel ; its spirit was
propagated and popularised by the pamphlets of Paul-Louis
Courier and the songs of Béranger.

Meanwhile, on the night of 13-14 February 1820, the Duc
de Berry, the next heir to the throne after the Comte d'Artois,
was assassinated at the door of the Opéra by a workman,
proclaiming his hatred of the Bourbons. 'The dagger that
killed the Duc de Berry is a Liberal idea', cried Chateaubriand.
Faced with the reaction provoked by this crime, Decazes and
the Constitutionals yielded power again to the Right, represented first by the Duc de Richelieu, then from 1821 by the
Comte de Villèle, who remained Prime Minister for seven
years.

From Conciliation to Reaction

The assassination of the Duc de Berry broke the attempt
at marrying tradition to liberalism. In 1820 the system of
direct election and the departmental list was replaced by a
system of double voting which assured predominance to the
large landowners. Liberty of the Press was suppressed in
1822. Opposition took refuge in secret societies, notably the
'Charbonnerie' (a name borrowed from the Neapolitan
Carbonari), all the more given to conspiracy since secrecy
obliged their members to bind themselves by oath.

Charles X

Louis XVIII, disillusioned with politics, let things take
their course till his death 6 September 1824. His brother, the
Comte d'Artois, sixty-eight years old, succeeded as Charles X.
He was the incarnation of the two-fold spirit of the Ancien
Régime and the émigrés : a grand seigneur, formerly elegant
and frivolous, now very religious, with much more self-
conceit and much less sense than his elder brother.

The Chambre of 1824, elected by double vote, was a
'Chambre retrouvée', recalling the 'Chambre introuvable'.

A beginning was made of purging the administrative services. Religion provided occasion for committing blunders and interferences which did not correspond with any monarchical tradition at all. The University was put under the clergy, higher teaching suppressed or interfered with, sacrilege punished with death. Thus there seemed to hang over this society avid of ideas, new discoveries and sentiments, a sort of menacing spectre that the Liberals called the 'parti-prêtre'. Worse — a decisive mistake — the government attacked the interests, the positions gained and the social achievements, of the Revolution. Villèle gave an indemnity to the *émigrés*, the 'milliard des émigrés', obtained by a conversion of stock which hit the middle class. He tried to get a law passed re-establishing primogeniture. His projects against the Press aroused a protest from the French Academy itself. The régime became one that even the Chamber of Peers resisted. Demonstrations of discontent increased : in 1825 the funeral of the Independent, General Foy, was attended by a hundred thousand Parisians. In 1827 the National Guard, recruited from the middle class, had to be dissolved. Fractions of the Right, even, and of the Catholic world rebelled with Chateaubriand, then with the Comte de Montlosier. In spite of the rigour of the government, the opposition finally swept it away. The elections of 1827 gave a crushing majority to Villèle's opponents and obliged him to resign in January 1828.

Before a new Chamber with a Liberal majority Charles X at first hesitated. He gave power to the moderates of the Right under the leadership of a clever Parliamentarian, the Comte de Martignac. This minister tacked between the king, the majority of the Chamber and the exigencies of opinion. He tried to check the encroachments of the clerical party, but fell on the question of administrative reform and was dismissed in August 1829.

Then Charles X came out on the side of the Ultras. He called on the fire-eaters for a fighting government : Jules de Polignac, who represented the memories of the old Court

and the 'Chouans'; La Bourdonnaye, one of the leaders of
the White Terror; Bourmont, an old Vendéen who deserted
Napoleon on the eve of Waterloo. This government could not
be accepted by the Chamber, which voted an address of defiance
as soon as it assembled, the 'Address of the 221', drawn up
under the inspiration of Royer-Collard. The Chamber was
dissolved 16 May 1830. Indifferent to the brilliant capture of
Algiers on 5 July, the electors confirmed the Liberal majority
with an increase of fifty-five members.

Revolution of 1830

Henceforth the dynasty was in peril. The Republican
party reconstituted itself with Cavaignac, Garnier-Pagès,
Hippolyte Carnot; the rich bourgeois, Baron Louis, the
banker Laffitte detached themselves from the Bourbons and
looked to the Duke of Orléans. The young historian Thiers
directed public opinion into the same channel by his articles
in the *National*.

Far from giving way, Charles X attempted a sort of
coup d'état. On 25 July he signed four decrees, suspending
the liberty of the Press again, restricting the vote to owners of
land, annulling the last elections and fixing the date of new
ones. It was a partial violation of the Charter. It was above
all a blow to the middle class of the towns.

After a moment of stupefaction the opposition accepted
the struggle. Newspapers, bills, placards appeared in protest.
Secret societies and improvised committees aroused the
working-class districts of Paris. On 27 July demonstrations
of the mob began; on 28th Marshal Marmont failed in
repressive measures and lost the faubourgs. On 29th the
people drove the Royal army out of Paris; the Louvre was
taken by force, everywhere the capital brought out the tricolour
flag. The same day Charles X consented to withdraw the
decrees. But he was too late: the people wanted no more of
the Bourbons and more and more inclined to the Republic.
A prompt move of the Orleanists induced them to accept the

Duke of Orléans, the future Louis-Philippe. On 16th August Charles X embarked for England.

Like the Ancien Régime, the Restoration was overthrown by the middle class and for the same reasons : the failure of the king to understand the historic law which in the past always associated the monarch's authority with the defence of the commons against the nobles ; the failure to understand, too, the position of the king as arbiter, which forbids the head of the state to take sides, unless to maintain national power, public order and justice. The Restoration was a difficult enterprise in a country that had undergone such great changes. But it was not impossible. One fault could compromise it irretrievably : that the king should behave as a partisan. Charles X fell into it completely unaware. His presumption left behind it much more hatred and mistrust than the tragic incapacity of the unhappy Louis XVI.

The Restoration, however, rendered services which it would be unjust not to recognise. It re-established the public finances and reconstituted the army ; it introduced some of the fundamental rules of Parliamentary government ; it freed France from foreign occupation, gradually restored the prestige and influence of our foreign policy and conquered Algiers. Its mistakes were made above all against itself.

CHAPTER VI

An Attempt at Middle-Class Monarchy: Louis-Philippe

❖

The Original Misunderstanding — Movement and Resistance — Triumph of the Conservative Middle Class : Guizot — External Success : Conquest of Algeria — Social Aspirations — Revolution of 1848

THE Restoration was an abortive effort at compromise between the Ancien Régime, aristocratic in spirit, and the new middle-class society that had benefited from the Revolution. The reign of Louis-Philippe is another such attempt at compromise between the monarchy, middle-class in spirit, and the aspirations of the people. It is again the same failure, deriving from the same profound cause : the deviation of the monarchical idea since the 18th century, a deviation that made the king the preserver of a certain state of affairs and the associate of certain class-interests, and no longer the incarnation of impartial justice. To understand the reason which alienated France in the 19th century from its most ancient institution — the monarchy — one has only to measure the distance that separates not only the conduct, but above all the principles of government, of a St. Louis, a Catherine de Medici, a Henry IV, a Louis XIII and even Louis XIV from the principles of government of a Charles X and a Louis-Philippe : the distance of a supreme Justiciar, more or less faithful to his mission but not surrendering it, from the more or less adroit representative of party interests, political and social.

Louis-Philippe was nevertheless completely adapted to his function and his time. Very intelligent, liberal minded, clever, with great self-control and a certain dignity in his attitude, of irreproachable morals, he knew life and men and was the dupe neither of ceremonial which he despised nor of partisan- ship for Right or Left.   He walked about Paris happily on foot, with a grey hat on and umbrella under his arm.   His weakness — and that too a middle-class one — was to think himself too cunning, to take others too easily for nit- wits and to take too many blind chances on his superior *savoir-faire*.

Movement and Resistance

Set going by the Republicans, the July Revolution in fact benefited the Orleanists.   The new régime had at first to get itself accepted by popular opinion — which was not easy.   It was all the more difficult in that Louis-Philippe modified the constitutional basis of the Restoration very little and refrained from submitting the revised Charter to a plebiscite.   The working-class agitation continued, strengthened, moreover, by the rigours of an economic crisis which gravely affected industry and commerce in Paris.   Riots threatened constantly and disturbances broke out in October and December 1830 over the trial of Charles X's ministers.   Then in February 1831, on the occasion of a memorial service for the Duc de Berry, the mob sacked the church of St.-Germain-l'Auxerrois and destroyed the Archbishop's palace.   The new régime seemed to hesitate : would it lean towards 'resistance' and conservatism, or towards 'movement' and progress ?

The party of movement carried the day in November 1830 with the ministry of Laffitte and Dupont de l'Eure, relying on the popularity of Odilon Barrot, prefect of the Seine, and of Lafayette, commander of the National Guard.   But the economic crisis got worse, the agitation redoubled and bankruptcy threatened.   On 13 March 1831 Louis-Philippe entrusted power to Casimir Périer, leader of the party of 'resistance', and recalled Baron Louis to the finances.

Industrialist and banker, Casimir Périer was a man of action, a tremendous worker, an organiser with definite, clear views, dictatorial and passionately desirous of order. He got the basic laws of the new monarchy voted. The municipal, district and departmental councils were henceforth to be elected by the largest tax-payers. The National Guard was to be recruited exclusively among those tax-payers rich enough to pay for their own equipment and arms. The elections to the legislature was by single vote for the district list; the qualification for the vote was slightly lowered. For the rest, street disorders were repressed and agitators rounded up.

The régime asserted its authority brutally against all seditious movements. In November 1831 the silk-workers of Lyons, impelled by terrible want, rose and took possession of the town. The government despatched 20,000 troops there and disarmed the population; it then took back the concessions already made to the workers. Some weeks later the partisans of the Bourbons organised a conspiracy to overthrow Louis-Philippe. The Duchesse de Berry landed in Provence and secretly reached La Vendée. The government procured the betrayal of the Duchess in June 1832 and shut her up in the château de Blaye; it released her when discredited by the birth of a daughter, fruit of a clandestine marriage with an Italian count. About the same time, 5 June 1832, a Republican insurrection broke out in Paris on the occasion of the funeral of General Lamarque, and the districts in the east barricaded themselves off. But the rebels were blockaded, then crushed in the cloister of St.-Merry by regular troops and the National Guard.

Casimir Périer died 16 April 1832, victim of a cholera epidemic which claimed 20,000 victims in Paris.

From this time the Conservatives, under different labels and with men of different shades of opinion, governed for sixteen years, supported by the bulk of middle-class electors.

Kept out of power and without hope of coming back, the 'dynastic Left' or progressive fraction of the middle class soon joined the Republicans to attack the régime. The Republican propaganda — led by Cavaignac, Garnier-Pagès, Cabet, Louis

Blanc, Armand Carrel, supported by societies public or secret, by papers like the *Tribune* and the *National*, by pamphlets and caricatures in which Daumier, Grandville, Gavarni, Henri Monnier made their name — gradually destroyed the prestige of the July Monarchy. In April 1834 a Republican rising broke out in Paris and attempts were made to extend it to St.-Étienne, Clermont, Grenoble, Marseilles, Chalon-sur-Saône. It failed before ruthless repression. Attempts were made against the king's person : on 28 July 1835 the Corsican Fieschi killed eighteen persons of Louis-Philippe's escort, among them Marshal Mortier. The government tried to break the opposition by emergency laws ; it succeeded in stopping daylight demonstrations. But opposition never ceased to be active in the younger generation, in literary circles and among groups where the Radicals encountered another stream of propaganda, that of the Socialists, disciples of the Comte de St.-Simon, of Fourier, and then of Proudhon. Lyons, Toulouse, Dijon, Nancy, Alsace, above all Paris were the centres of the revolutionary spirit.

Triumph of the Conservative Middle Class : Guizot

The conservative middle class now in the saddle counted in its ranks many intelligent men and sensible reformers who would doubtless have stabilised the régime if Louis-Philippe, determined to govern personally, had not employed his cleverness to divide it. The Duc de Broglie, Thiers and Guizot remained together in the same Cabinet from 1832 to 1836. It was under this ministry in 1833 that Guizot brought in his law creating primary schools. But in 1836 the Conservative leaders separated. Thiers became President of the Council and leader of the Left Centre ; Guizot symbolised the Right Centre ; a third party, with Dupin, represented the middle Conservatives. This disunion favoured the king's game, who soon dismissed Thiers and directed affairs himself from 1836 to 1839, under the name of his friend Count Molé. In 1839 Molé, attacked by a Parliamentary coalition, dissolved the Chamber. He was defeated in the elections and Thiers returned. Public opinion was excited and found the king too conciliatory towards England; it was irritated over the Egyptian affair and smitten by nostalgia for the past on the return of Napoleon's ashes from St. Helena. Louis-Philippe, disagreeing with Thiers, entrusted power to Guizot on 29 October 1840. Guizot and the king understood each other perfectly in putting across a policy of order and increasing wealth for the middle class at home, which took too little account of the ideal needs of the nation and the demands of the people.

The materialist spirit of the régime encountered opposition not only in republican rancour and in the growing body of socialist thought, but in the Catholic movement of social charity whose voices were Montalembert, Ozanam and Lacordaire. From this movement a new party was born which demanded liberty of teaching, in the name of the Charter, against the University's monopoly.

Too conservative, the wealthy middle class held up even economic advances. The total power of steam-engines in France was one-sixth of that possessed by England. Our merchant marine of sailing ships increasingly lost the trade of our ports to foreign steamships. As to telegraph-lines we were even behind Russia. The first railway line, from Lyons to St.-Étienne, was built in 1826. But it was only in 1842 that the state undertook legislation for the construction of railways. And in 1848 France still had only 1900 kilometres of railway against England's 6350 and Prussia's 3500.

The middle class of Louis-Philippe's period got rich chiefly owing to protective tariffs, which had the result that a ton of iron, for example, cost 325 francs in France against 125 in England; and by the facilities afforded for borrowing, which encouraged departments and communes to borrow. Five per cent stock went up to 125 francs. Property in land was very much sought after. This form of increasing wealth gave little employment to manual labour, while increasing the price of goods. Hence the striking contrast between want and low wages on one side and the comfortable circumstances of the middle class on the other. It was the source of the current of the revolt that overturned the July monarchy.

External Success: Conquest of Algeria

Louis-Philippe's great merit was to have been able to spare France all foreign war and to have understood that, to succeed in this, it was necessary — in spite of the unpopularity of such a policy — to patch up disagreeable incidents with England as well as he could : such as the fuss over the 'right of search', the Pritchard affair or that of Tahiti, the question of Morocco. Since Louis XIV, England had not ceased — except under Fleury — to pursue the abatement of France.[1] To give our people a certain scope for expansion, after the disasters of the Napoleonic adventure, it was necessary to calm English hostility and mistrust.

Partly owing to this prudence, the independence of Belgium was assured and guaranteed, which finally freed our northern frontier from the old threat of the Low Countries, a threat carefully re-established by the Allies in 1815.[2]

Peace with Europe being maintained, French expansion

[1] In the text the original word is *abaissement*, which might more usually be translated 'abasement'. But it would not be just to say that this was the object of English policy. Europe had had a long experience of the aggressions of Louis XIV, as it had again — on a still more spectacular scale — with Napoleon. From a European point of view the aim of containing and restraining the aggressiveness of French policy from Louis XIV to Napoleon had only too much justification ; and England in making this the aim of her policy was not only protecting her own interests — as any state does and must do — but pursuing a course in keeping with the interests of Europe. Hence the readiness of the rest of Europe to join with her in coalition to restrain French aggression from Louis XIV to Napoleon. This long record of aggression had laid up a good deal of hatred, not only in England, but even more elsewhere. The mistrust was therefore justified. Fleury saw this and pursued a policy of moderation — until he was forced out of it by the aggressive trends of French policy — as Romier admits, *v*. above, p. 280.—A. L. R.

[2] 'Menace' is Romier's word. As if the Low Countries in themselves had ever been a 'menace' to France! They had stood in the way of French expansion — that was their chief offence ; and they had several times suffered as victims of French aggression — notably in Louis XIV's criminal invasion of Holland in 1672 and again under the French Revolution and Napoleon. The Allies in 1815 were again only too much justified in trying to erect a defence against French aggression : this was the purpose of their union of Holland with Belgium.—A. L. R.

could turn itself towards Algeria. After the capture of Algiers, French troops occupied Oran in 1830, Bône and Bougie in 1832, Mostaganem in 1833. But in 1835 the young Emir of Mascara, Abd-el-Kader, a famous warrior among the Moslem tribes, defied the French at the defile of the Macta. General Clauzel, appointed governor, in the attempt to extend the conquest, failed before Constantine and was recalled. General Damrémont prepared a new expedition against Constantine and the town was taken by assault at the point of the bayonet by Lamoricière's soldiers on 13 October 1837. In 1839 Abd-el-Kader invaded the plain of Algiers, pillaging and massacring. General Bugeaud, nominated governor in 1840, had to undertake a wholly new war, mobile, dispersed, incessant, against this redoubtable adversary. The Emir, after the capture of his 'smala' by the Duc d'Aumale, fled into the mountains, then into Morocco. He came back with the army of the Sultan of Morocco, which Bugeaud routed at the battle of Isly, 14 August 1844. Abd-el-Kader surrendered to the Duc d'Aumale in 1847. From 1840 onwards the settling of French colonists began in the plains of Algiers and Oran, and in the neighbourhood of Sétif and of Bône. Thus a French colonial empire was born. Under Louis-Philippe, France also established herself in Guinea and in Tahiti.

Social Aspirations

While an authoritarian middle class, strictly adhering to its own interests, governed France, Romanticism won the day in the realm of feeling and taste, literary and artistic forms, philosophical and historical ideas, in manners and social aspirations. Victor Hugo, Lamartine, Vigny and Alfred de Musset, George Sand and Balzac, Michelet and Lamennais expressed new ways of feeling and emotion. They only disturbed those who loved reading. But the disciples of Saint-Simon and of Fourier claimed to remake the whole of society. Proudhon gave an economic and social direction to popular idealism. The harsh contrast in conditions between employers and workmen, which the development of industry produced in the absence of any corporate organisation, encouraged sympathy for socialism, not only among workmen but among many intellectuals and philanthropists.

There was then a latent conflict between the too materialistic conservatism of mind of the July monarchy and the great regeneration of feeling and generous sentiment of a large number not only of the people, but of the *élite*. This conflict proved fatal for the régime.

In 1846 and 1847 a series of economic misfortunes ruined prosperity at one blow. The harvests were bad; seven departments had disastrous floods. In industry orders were falling; scarcity and unemployment produced riots and bloodshed. There were deficits on the Budget. The Bank of France lost part of its cash reserves; people were hoarding their money. On top of this a scandal broke: some years earlier a minister called Teste, since promoted President of the Court of Cassation — the supreme court of appeal — had taken a bribe for a mining concession. The prestige of the régime crumbled on all sides. Guizot's authority over a docile Chamber deprived the Left Centre, led by Thiers, of the hope of obtaining reforms and taking power.

Revolution of 1848

So the Left Centre made an alliance with the Left, the Radicals and Republicans and, secretly with the revolutionaries, undertook to rouse public opinion. On 9 July there began in Paris a 'campaign of banquets' to demand Parliamentary and electoral reform. Seventy banquets took place in the provinces before the autumn. The Left Centre was rapidly overwhelmed in this campaign by the elements that were hostile to the dynasty.

Since the death of his eldest son, the Duc d'Orléans, killed in a carriage accident in 1842, Louis-Philippe lived without any close contact with public opinion: he read only the foreign newspapers. He let himself be taken by surprise.

After the last banquet, which took place in Paris, 22 February 1848, the National Guard joined the demonstrators against the government. The king, seeing himself suddenly deserted by the middle class, dismissed Guizot. That would perhaps have calmed the agitation, if the guard posted at the Ministry of Foreign Affairs had not, in the course of a brawl on the night of 23 February, fired on the crowd and killed sixteen people. All night the mob drew the corpses through the streets on a wagon lit by torches, and then took to building barricades. Marshal Bugeaud took measures to restore order. But the king hesitated and preferred to be clever : he announced that he would give power to Thiers and Odilon Barrot. The insurgents took the Hôtel de Ville and invaded the Carrousel. The National Guard greeted the king himself with cries of 'Down with the ministers'. On the advice of Thiers, Louis-Philippe abdicated in favour of his grandson, the Comte de Paris, and fled in his carriage. In the afternoon of 25 February, Lamartine, Dupont de l'Eure and Ledru-Rollin, accompanying the insurgents to the Palais Bourbon, had the Republic proclaimed.

PART VI

UNIVERSAL SUFFRAGE

CHAPTER I

The Republic of 1848. Napoleon III

❖

Defeat of the Revolutionaries — Reaction from Universal Suffrage — Louis Napoleon — Coup d'État of 1851 — Internal Régime of the Second Empire

THE Revolution of 1848 is the decisive turning-point in the internal history of France in the 19th century, because it marks the coming of universal suffrage, that is to say, of democracy. The great Revolution had certainly proclaimed the principle of universal suffrage ; but the principle had received no real application. All the revolutions from 1789 to 1848 had been the work of minorities backed by the force of the people of Paris and some great towns. The establishment of universal suffrage in 1848 had not only the result of giving, for the first time, a regular application to the principle of democracy ; it enabled the people of the provinces, of the countryside, of the small towns to enter into the movement of politics which had hitherto excited only townspeople and working-class centres. In the long run, universal suffrage, the outcome of Parisian revolutions, turns against Paris through the growing influence it gives to the provinces.

Established by the provisional government almost immediately after the proclamation of the Republic, universal suffrage at one stroke brought the number of the electors from 200,000 to more than nine millions.

Thus the underlying evolution of politics would henceforth express not a pre-established conception of government nor an ideology formed by clubs, groups or militant minorities, but the preferences, fears and average interests of the population. Universal suffrage itself, in a country where the bulk of the population retained a horror of disorder, was not long in producing a reaction against the improvised attempts of those who talked of changing the whole of society without indicating precisely what changes or where the changes would stop. Universal suffrage became alarming at the very moment when it was at last allowed to express itself. Further, if democracy presupposes universal suffrage, universal suffrage is not necessarily to be confused with the Republican idea, which is a liberal idea. By virtue of its very sovereignty, it remains master of the constitution, able to conserve or modify it, or simply to resign itself to its fall. The Republican faith — however ardently formulated and propagated it may be by certain groups of the Leftist lower middle class and by active militants of the working-class cause who mingle socialist aspirations with it — remains an unfamiliar idea and subversive in character in the eyes of many people, even poor people, especially in the country. It evokes the memory of the Terror, makes old men shudder in recounting the horrors of the past. It is only in the last third of the 19th century, the Terror forgotten, that the Republican idea conquers the country.

The fulsome rhetoricians of journalism, literature or the soap-box, fertile in sonorous and imaginative phrases like their fathers of the great Revolution — but much less solid since Romanticism made feeling predominate over reason — these 'men of 1848' display immense illusions, little political sense and hardly any experience of the problems they wish to solve. Most of them do not even know what are the real miseries of the people whose cause they represent.

The Republic of 1848 seems like an impulse of renewal, soon enfeebled by the politicians' calculations, then breaking itself against conservative realities. But this impulse leaves an ineffaceable imprint on the political and social imagination of the 19th century.

Defeat of the Revolutionaries

With universal suffrage established, restrictions on the liberty of the press and of assembly abolished, the provisional government — in which figured Dupont de l'Eure, Lamartine, Arago, Ledru-Rollin, Louis Blanc — was faced with an economic and financial crisis. It had to fix by decree the market price of bank-bills and increase the burden of direct taxes by almost a half, which was bound to arouse country people. Then the government was divided between the Liberal majority and the Socialist minority. A conflict at once broke out, between the revolutionary elements of Paris led by Cabet, Raspail, Blanqui, partisans of the red flag, who organised demonstrations almost daily, and the moderates, faithful to the tricolour which Lamartine had acclaimed. Universal suffrage assured a crushing victory to the moderates. The elections of April 1848 sent to the Constituent Assembly 500 moderate Republicans, 300 Conservatives, Catholics and Royalists and an infinitesimal number of Socialists. The provisional government transformed itself into a restricted executive Commission, excluding the advanced elements.

The revolutionaries tried to regain their lost position by force. But their attempt strengthened the reaction more and more. 'National workshops' had been opened for the unemployed. This organisation, badly run perhaps on purpose, wasted millions. Under the pressure of the Assembly, the government suppressed them on 21 June, deciding that young unmarried workmen without work should be enrolled in the army, the others were to return to the provinces. Foreseeing a rising, General Cavaignac, Minister of War, received dictatorial powers. The quarters in the east of Paris rose : 400 barricades were put up. The street-fighting lasted four days, the most murderous Paris had known. It claimed several hundreds of victims, including six generals and Monsignor Affre, Archbishop of Paris, struck down when trying to intervene. The defeat of the insurgents left 11,000 prisoners on the government's hands ; 4,000 were deported to Algeria by decree of the Assembly. Restrictions on the liberty of the press and of public meeting were reimposed. The middle classes and country people — frightened by this insurrection

and the threat of socialism communising property and by
seeing taxes go up and stocks go down — held the Republic
responsible. As for the working class, under the blow of
repression, their social romanticism changed to class-hatred.

Faced with the frightful drama provoked by the clash of
ideologies with real life, the conservative reaction was to
revoke all the liberties.

Reaction from Universal Suffrage

A new constitution was promulgated in November 1848.
It admitted the sovereignty of the people, that is to say, universal suffrage, the separation of powers, national representation
by a single assembly, the delegation of the executive to a President of the Republic who would nominate the ministers and
officials, dispose of the armed forces 'without commanding in
person', negotiate treaties and be responsible before the
Assembly. The President was to be elected by universal
suffrage. This constitution, in which the desire for democracy
and that for strong government were paradoxically mingled,
prepared the way for a conflict.

Cavaignac, a moderate Republican ; Ledru-Rollin, a more
extreme Republican ; Raspail, socialist ; Lamartine, idealist :
all presented themselves as candidates for the Presidency to
a vote by universal suffrage. But it was a personality very
different from those who carried it off : Louis Napoleon, head
of the Bonaparte family, son of the former King of Holland
and nephew of Napoleon I. Re-entering France after the
February Revolution, deputy in the Constituent Assembly, he
was elected President on 10 December 1848 by 5,400,000
votes against 8,000 for poor Lamartine, 36,000 for the socialist
Raspail, 370,000 for the Left Republican Ledru-Rollin,
1,400,000 for the 'moderate' Cavaignac.

This election revealed, from the very beginning of the
operation of universal suffrage, the predominance of negative
considerations in determining the people's vote. Louis
Napoleon was elected by the middle class *against* both

monarchy and socialism; by the peasants *against* feudal landowners and *against* communists; by the Catholics *against* the anti-clerical revolutionaries and free-thinking liberals; by the 'patriots' *against* the conciliatory foreign policy of the Bourbons and of Louis-Philippe; finally by the legitimists and Orleanists themselves *against* the disorder that threatened their social position. And all this under the halo of the Napoleonic legend.

Louis Napoleon

Yet, in fact, Louis Napoleon's personality did not correspond to the wishes of any of the factions in question. He aspired to absolute power, he had socialist tendencies and had conspired with the Italian Carbonari against the Church; he had the soul of a dreamer and the habits of an adventurer; he knew nothing of the elementary principles of foreign policy; he was dissembling and authoritarian, but a gambler and without forcefulness. Paradoxically, the generous side to him was his love of the workers and of romantic conspirators — against whom he had been in fact elected. Had he not been a conspirator himself, exiled once, then on his second offence imprisoned in the fort of Ham under Louis-Philippe? Was he not the author of a tract on *The Extinction of Pauperism?* He was now forty. Universal suffrage had guarded itself only against its own fears, without studying the man it had elected. But the person elected, if he lacked all political profundity, was, on the other hand, an astonishing politician.

The new President called to power the 'party of Order' that had got him elected, represented by Odilon Barrot and the Comte de Falloux. In May 1849 a new Chamber, the Legislative Assembly, replaced the Constituent: the party of Order formed the majority in it with 450 elected; the Left opposition, called the Mountain and led by Ledru-Rollin, comprised 150 members. The doubt about the personality of Louis Napoleon having played no part in the legislative elections, the elected body was divided according to the two old tendencies : Resistance and Progress. But the relatively large number of 'Reds' in the Assembly, in accentuating the conflict between the two tendencies, provoked a more marked reaction of the majority towards the Right.

On the occasion of an expedition of French troops to Rome to forestall the Austrians in helping the Pope against the Roman Republic, Ledru-Rollin and his friends protested vehemently. On 13 June 1849 the Republicans of Paris, in contradiction to the principle of universal suffrage which they had borne to triumph, resorted to a new attempt at insurrection and raised barricades around the Arts-and-Crafts building. The result is what one might have expected : ruthless repression and restrictions on the liberties of the press and of public meeting ; the arrest of thirty deputies on grounds of complicity and the flight of Ledru-Rollin ; a proclamation of the President reassuring the 'good' and denouncing the 'bad'. Thenceforth the majority of the Assembly did not have to consider the minority any more.

On 15 March the famous Falloux law was voted, which gave any Frenchman provided with a qualifying certificate or any recognised minister of religion, the right to open an elementary school or — if he held a degree or certificate — a secondary school. The clergy had the right of inspecting the public schools and of becoming members of the academic councils. The Falloux law permitted the free development of Church schools in competition with university teaching. On the other hand, by removing Catholics from the official teaching, it gradually assured lay and Protestant influence upon it. Without the Falloux law, French schools would not have become the issue in a regular war of parties. Another law, of 31 May 1850, restricting universal suffrage, reserved the right to vote only to citizens domiciled in a commune for three years. Lastly, in July 1850, liberty of the press was practically abolished.

It became evident that 'fear of the Reds' favoured those of the members of the party of Order who wanted to re-establish the monarchy. In view of this, attempts were made to reconcile the Comte de Chambord and the princes of Orléans. General Changarnier, commander of the army of Paris, was to give his support to a restoration. But Louis Napoleon did not intend to yield place to others. A consummate politician, he manipulated opinion in his favour, cultivated popularity, and got himself acclaimed. He got rid of Changarnier and put men he could trust at the head of the army of Paris and the police. His friend, General St.-Arnaud, became Minister of War. Further, to gain the sympathies of the people, the President proposed the full re-establishment of universal suffrage against the conservative majority of the Assembly. As he was not able to obtain the three-quarters of the votes in the Assembly in favour of a revision of the Constitution to permit him to be re-elected on the expiry of his mandate, he decided to force matters.

Coup d'État of 1851

In the night of the 1st-2nd December 1851 — the anniversary of Austerlitz — under the direction of Morny, Louis Napoleon's half-brother, and of Persigny, his personal friend, a *coup d'état* was carried out by Maupas, prefect of police, St.-Arnaud, Minister of War, and Magnon, commander of the army of Paris. To allay suspicions, the President gave a reception at the Élysée. Meanwhile the police arrested inconvenient persons, Cavaignac, Changarnier, Thiers; troops occupied the Chamber. Two decrees were posted up : one dissolved the Assembly, re-established universal suffrage and proclaimed a state of siege ; the other called on the French people to maintain Louis Napoleon's authority by a plebiscite, and to delegate to him the power to remake the constitution.

During the day, 300 deputies of the party of Order, under the direction of Berryer, met to organise a legal resistance. Some deputies of the Mountain — Baudin, Jules Favre and Victor Hugo — exhorted the suburbs to revolt. But the 'legal resistance' soon yielded to the troops, who arrested the recalcitrant deputies. As to attempts at armed revolt, which the workers supported poorly enough, Morny put an end to it on the 4th by taking the offensive in a repression, of which the 'shooting on the boulevards' formed the bloodiest episode. In the provinces, the Republicans provoked movements in the Yonne, Nièvre, Allier, Hérault, Drôme, Var, Basses-Alpes. The insurrection was quickly suppressed by mass arrests, the extension of the state of siege to thirty-two departments, the deportation of nearly ten thousand political prisoners to Algeria and the expulsion of sixty-six deputies — among them Victor Hugo. On 21 December a plebiscite sanctioned the *coup d'état* by 7,349,000 votes against 646,000.

On 14 January 1852 a new constitution assured the Presidency to Louis Napoleon for ten years, with consular powers. A legislative body was, however, retained, composed of deputies elected every six years by universal suffrage, to vote taxes and discuss projected laws, but within a rigorously limited framework of deliberation. Still the Prince President, travelling about a great deal, had himself acclaimed to the cry of 'Long live the Emperor!' The complaisant Senate decided to invite the electors to pronounce on 'the re-establishment of the Imperial dignity in favour of Louis Napoleon'. A plebiscite gave 7,839,000 in favour, 253,000 against. On 2 December 1852 Louis Napoleon received the title of 'hereditary Emperor of the French' and took the name of Napoleon III.

By a sequence of reactions which betrayed above all the fear of disorder and the horror of revolutionary threats, universal suffrage itself had overthrown the Republic! To understand the event, one must look less at the sincerity of the plebiscites of 1851–52 than at the meaning of the preceding elections, which demonstrated a conservative reaction against the 'red' bogey.

Internal Régime of the Second Empire

The Second Empire practically suppressed internal politics and subjected the press to a system of censorship; it organised

legislative elections by decree and in such a way as to favour
official candidatures. The mayors of communes were chosen
by the government. The police controlled everything, even
teaching. An opposition subsisted, sullen with the legitimists
and Orleanists, satirical and mocking with the Republicans but
hunted by the police. It secretly circulated the *Châtiments* of
Victor Hugo. In 1853 the workers of Paris demonstrated
in silence behind the coffin of Raspail's wife. In 1857 Paris
elected five Republicans out of ten deputies. On 14 January
1858, an Italian — Orsini — to pay out Napoleon III for
having betrayed the cause of the Carbonari, threw bombs at
the Emperor's carriage and wounded 156 people in front of the
Opéra. All this only gave new pretexts to the police, which
led to the methods of the 'authoritarian Empire'. But from
1859 Napoleon's foreign policy, supporting Italian liberty
against the Pope and agreeing to a commercial treaty with
England, irritated the conservatives. Henceforth the Emperor
sought support on the left, and hence the substitution of the
'Liberal Empire' for the 'authoritarian Empire'. Political
prisoners benefited from an amnesty and those who had been
deported might return to France. By a decree of 24 November
1860 Parliament was revived : the Chambers got the right to
vote an address to the throne concerning general policy, to
discuss in public projected laws brought before them by
ministers without portfolio, to give a complete report of their
debates to the newspapers. The opposition could thus make
itself heard throughout the whole country. It was not long
in profiting by it. Bringing together a number of the Catholics,
protectionist industrialists, monarchists and republicans, it
became dangerous. At the elections of 1863 it obtained two
million votes and completely captured Paris, which elected
eight republicans. Through the voice of Thiers, it demanded
new liberties.

Held back by the Empress, a Spanish noblewoman
— Eugénie de Montijo, whom he had married in 1853 — by
men who had aided or flattered his fortune, like Morny and

Persigny, and by those who had rallied to an authoritarian régime, like the orator Billault and the advocate Rouher — the Emperor, whose health was being exhausted in pleasure, was in the end unable to choose between right and left. He entrusted education to the historian, Victor Duruy, who reorganised the University and laid the foundations of secular education for the people. The Emperor had a law passed granting the workers the right of combination and the right to strike. But at the same time he refused the political concessions demanded by Thiers. And in 1865 he gave effective power to Rouher, the exponent of authoritarian methods.

These oscillations in internal politics aggravated the painful impression caused by the failures in foreign policy. A new party was formed, the Third Party, bringing together liberal Bonapartists and republicans who had rallied to the Empire. Its leader was an advocate, Émile Ollivier, who had been a member of the republican opposition of the 'Five' in the legislative body and whom Morny had brought over. From 1867 to 1870, Rouher and Ollivier disputed the 'vacil-lating soul' of Napoleon III. On 19 January 1867 a brief of the Emperor gave Parliament the right of interpellating ministers and promised liberties for the press and public meetings. These concessions encouraged the republican opposition. The newspapers, more free, became also more biting. Henri Rochefort edited a weekly, famous as the *Lanterne*. The young lawyer Gambetta made his name in defending one of these republican journals, the *Réveil*.

As the Republicans sharpened their offensive, they fright-ened the Catholic or moderate opposition. The elections of 1869 took place amid these divisions. However, the Third Party had 116 deputies, the Republicans 30 — among them Gambetta, elected in Paris on a radical programme called 'the programme of Belleville'. The partisans of authoritarian methods lost their majority. Rouher handed in his resigna-tion. By a *senatus consultus* of 6 September 1869 Napoleon almost completely re-established the parliamentary régime, still reserving the 'personal power' of choosing the ministers. A parliamentary ministry was formed, 2 January 1870, under the presidency of Émile Ollivier. A new *senatus consultus* of 20 April made of the Empire a sort of constitutional monarchy with two Chambers, the head of the state being recognised as responsible only to the people to whom he could always appeal. In fact, to reply to the republican agitation revived by the murder of the journalist Victor Noir by Prince Bonaparte, Napoleon III demanded a plebiscite for or against the Empire. This plebiscite, which took place 8 May 1870, gave 7,538,000 for and 1,572,000 against. Republican propaganda had only shaken opinion in the big towns. The mass of universal suffrage remained, above all in the country, anti-revolutionary.

The attachment to, or acceptance of, the Empire by the great majority of Frenchmen is explained not only by the anti-revolutionary feeling — the word 'Republic' being then associated with the memory of revolutionary violence — but by the material prosperity which marked the régime of Napoleon III. Maladroit, vacillating and at times odious in its conduct of home affairs, astonishingly blind in its foreign policy, the régime was most successful on the economic and financial side. The people were all the more grateful since they remembered the misery that had marked the end of Louis-Philippe's reign and the troubles of 1848. In this respect the Second Empire had luck : it benefited from the world-wide expansion of trade with the development of industrialism, the building of railways, the opening up of new gold-mines in America and Australia, the application of many more discoveries in industry and the fertilising effects of new and popular forms of credit. But the influence of Napoleon III himself on the economic progress of France was considerable. This man who could never be other than a manœuvrer and a 'conspirator' in politics, without foresight

or logic in general, had, on the other hand, an economic and
social sense much in advance of the conventional ideas of the
France of his time. If it had not been for the disaster brought
upon it by its foreign policy, the régime would perhaps have
resisted the attacks of the Republican minority for a long
time, by offering the people material and social improvements
inspired by the percipient views of the Saint-Simonism of
which Louis Napoleon had been the disciple.

Taking up the tradition of the first Empire, Napoleon III
instituted great works of display, in particular for the transformation and embellishment of Paris. Baron Haussmann,
prefect of the Seine during almost the whole reign, gave his
name to this immense undertaking, the boldness and intelligence of which have been only feebly imitated since. Paris,
which was the centre of opposition to the régime, yet profited
by it immensely. The capital owes to it the opening up of
the great boulevards of Saint-Michel, Sébastopol, Strasbourg,
the completion of the Rue de Rivoli and the tidying up of the
Faubourg St.-Antoine, the joining up of the Louvre and the
Tuileries, the clearance around the Etoile, the creation of
the parks of the Bois de Boulogne, of Vincennes and the
Buttes-Chaumont, the annexing of small towns — Auteuil,
Passy, Montmartre, Grenelle, Vaugirard, etc., which doubled
the capital's extent. It owes also the Opéra, the Châtelet,
St.-Augustin, the Trinité, the Hôtel-Dieu, the Halles and
numerous other markets, barracks, railway stations and the
sewerage system. Lastly, it owes to it a social prestige, a pre-
eminence in the world of taste and the arts which attracted all
the fashion of Europe.

Similar works were carried out or begun in the great
towns of the provinces.

It is from the Second Empire that the main development
of railways dates. In 1852 the railway system, ill-run, covered
about 3,000 kilometres; in 1870 it reached 18,000 kilometres
and the six big companies that ran it achieved remarkable
results. The Montcenis tunnel was begun in 1858 and

finished in 1870. Thanks to another disciple of Saint-Simon, Ferdinand de Lesseps, strongly supported by Napoleon III, France achieved the greatest work of the century : the Suez Canal, opened in 1869.

The teachings of Saint-Simon and his school also encouraged the expansion of credit. In 1852 the 'Crédit Foncier' and then the 'Crédit Mobilier' of the brothers Péreire were founded, the commercial bank which permitted big enterprises to be launched ; in 1863 the 'Crédit Lyonnais'; in 1864 the 'Société Générale'. The Bank of France began to open branches in the provinces. The Paris Exchange became one of the financial centres of the world.

In industry, the period of the Second Empire marks the rapid substitution of machines in place of work by hand, the concentration of factories, the increasing output of metallurgy owing to the coking-oven and to the Bessemer process in steel-making and the appearance of industrial groups like the 'Comité des Forges', founded in 1864. The sugar industry quadrupled its output in ten years.

Agriculture benefited by great drainage schemes which notably improved and made healthier the Landes and the Sologne. New roads were made in country districts. New manures improved cultivation, above all in the North. Wheat production rose by a fourth. But more than anything else, peasants and farmers made money by the good investments they found for their savings.

The prosperity of the reign gave a dazzling brilliance to the life of Paris, not to mention the fêtes of the Court. The universal Exhibition of 1855, and especially that of 1867, drew the leading figures of Europe to Paris and many thousands of visitors. They applauded the opéra-bouffe of Meilhac and Halévy and the irresistible music of Offenbach.

Inspired by Saint-Simonian ideas and English example, the commercial policy of Napoleon III took a bold turn and came back to free trade. Commercial treaties lowering duties were concluded first with England in 1860, then with Belgium,

Italy, the German States, Sweden, Switzerland, Austria, Spain and Portugal. This course of policy aroused among certain sections of industry and agriculture an opposition to the Emperor which contributed more discreetly, but not less effectively, than Republican attacks to undermine confidence in the régime. Yet, in ten years, external trade had doubled. And though the Empire borrowed a great deal for its grand projects, it always found plenty of lenders, owing to the nation's rapid increase of wealth.

From the social point of view, Napoleon III undeniably took care to improve the material lot of the workers, which the absence of all collective organisation since the Revolution, the unregulated influx of people into the towns and the rigid individualist ideas of the Civil Code had made deplorable. The Empress gave her patronage to works of charity and rescue-work, orphanages and convalescent homes, maternity welfare. Subscriptions for homes for old people were started, for insurance against accidents and for advances to poor workers ; to subsidise the building of workmen's dwellings and encourage 'approved' mutual benefit societies.

On the other hand, all propaganda of a socialist or revolutionary character was suppressed. Nevertheless the working-class movement made progress under the impulse this time, not of middle-class politicians, but of manual workers like the carver Tolain, a follower of Proudhon. From this movement came the 'Manifesto of the Sixty' in 1864, a charter of purely working-class demands. But soon 'Marxism', a body of doctrine developed by a German Jew, Karl Marx — an exile in London — claiming a systematic philosophy of history and preaching an international revolution, overwhelmed the reformist demands of the French working-class movement.

A socialism Messianic and collectivist in character triumphed over the mutualist ideas of Proudhon at the Congress of workers' associations at Brussels in 1868, and Basel in 1869.

At the end of the Second Empire the French population

reached 38 millions, while the population of England did not exceed 30 millions. France was still the leading state in Europe and, it seemed, the most solid. Her good fortune was to founder in a disaster brought on by the follies of a foreign policy without tradition or foresight.

CHAPTER II

Diplomacy of Optimism. The Disaster of 1870–71

❖

Crimean War — Italian Unity — Mexican War —
Franco-German War — Loss of Alsace-Lorraine

NAPOLEON I yielded the mastery of the seas to England, prepared the way on the Continent for the formation of nationalities dangerous for the future balance of peace and left the territory of France diminished and open to invasions. Napoleon III was responsible for France's fall to the rank of third European power, and put her under the direct menace of a new German Empire, against which she was able to defend herself only by allying with Russia and giving way to England. This humiliating downfall, aggravated by the loss of Alsace and Lorraine, deeply disturbed the morale of the French people, who henceforth never ceased to doubt their position of greatness and security.

With the two Napoleons the cause of the disaster is the same : the optimistic confidence of the lucky adventurer in his star — an optimism mingled in the first with the pride of a genius who has lost the sense of opposing forces and, in the second, with a sort of outlook that was sometimes dreamy, sometimes sly and cunning : both one and the other distrusting or not recognising the old tried rules of empirical politics.

Napoleon III by temperament was not bellicose : his nerves ill supported scenes of warfare, and his upbringing in ideas inclined him towards a vague pacifism. But Imperial fortune went with the name of Bonaparte ; it stood for the revenge of the Napoleonic legend upon the timidity of the

Bourbons and the squalid calculations of Louis-Philippe ; it fitted in with the need for epic that the defeated emperor at Waterloo had left in a whole area of the French imagination ; it could not, without denying itself, refuse to recognise the feelings and demands of the Bonapartist party.

It was, then, essential to seek glory and opportunities of gaining it. Napoleon III sought them and seized on them a little haphazardly, in the conspiratorial manner which appealed to the sense of 'secrets' of which he thought he alone held the thread ; and he followed, not a reasoned design, but the impulses of an imagination fed on romanticism. Romanticism in foreign affairs meant the idea of nationality. Unfortunately for him, and for France, he had to deal with the two greatest realists in European politics of the 19th century : Cavour and Bismarck.

Crimean War

Paradoxically, Napoleon III's foreign policy began by making France 'England's soldier' in an undertaking of which the real purpose was, in defending Turkey, to weaken the Russians in the Near East and to prevent their access to the Mediterranean.[1] From that came the expedition to the Crimea. Following a series of incidents in connection with the Holy Places — which were skilfully exploited against Russia by Stratford Canning, the English ambassador at Constantinople — France, as protector of the Christians in the East, found herself in alliance with England and Turkey. This coalition was joined by the little Piedmontese and Sardinian state, represented by Cavour, in order to create a claim upon the gratitude of the Western powers. The war with Russia lasted two years, from March 1854 to March 1856.

---

[1] This paragraph provides a characteristic example of the unfairness of Continental historians towards Britain. Great Britain did not *want* the Crimean War. She had, unlike the Second Empire, no need to 'seek glory or opportunities of gaining it'. Romier allows, immediately before, that Napoleon III had. So far from France being the soldier for England's purposes, England found herself muddling into a war which served chiefly to give the Empire its baptism of glory.— A. L. R.

Repelled from Silistria by the Turks, then forced to evacuate the Roumanian principalities, the Russians were attacked in the Crimea, at the instigation of England who wished to destroy the maritime arsenal of Sebastopol. Beaten at the Alma River by the Zouaves 20 September 1854, the Russians hurriedly fortified Sebastopol. It took the Anglo-French army almost a year to capture the town. The famous Malakoff bastion, the key to the defence, was carried on 8 September by General MacMahon's division. This expedition cost 20,000 English and 95,000 French lives. A treaty signed at Paris 30 March 1856 neutralised the Black Sea, proclaimed the autonomy of the principalities of Moldavia, Wallachia and Serbia, guaranteed freedom of navigation on the Danube and affirmed the independence and territorial integrity of the Ottoman Empire. France drew from it increased prestige, England the security of her interests in the Orient. The Christians of Asia Minor were not any the more protected from violence. In 1860 and 1866 France had to intervene in Syria to stop massacres of Christians by thousands.

Italian Unity

The Treaty of Paris was not signed before the Piedmontese minister Cavour had obtained the secret support of Napoleon III in favour of Italian unity against Austria. Still the Emperor delayed for two years before launching into a new war. But the Italian patriot Orsini's attempt upon him — he addressed moving letters to the Emperor before dying — inclined the balance. In the course of a secret interview with Cavour at Plombières in July 1858 Napoleon III — unknown to his ministers — fixed the conditions of the war against Austria : in exchange for the liberation of the Lombardo-Venetian states, the duchies of Parma and Modena and a portion of the Papal states, France would receive Savoy and the county of Nice.

The Italian war, begun in May 1859, was marked by the Franco-Italian victories of Magenta and Solferino in June.

In July, the armistice of Villafranca gave Lombardy to the King of Sardinia. Popular risings, followed by a plebiscite, enabled the Sardinian kingdom to annex pacifically, between August 1859 and March 1860, Tuscany, Modena, Parma and Romagna. Six months later, the two-fold intervention of Garibaldi's Redshirts and the Sardinian army brought about the adhesion of the Umbrian marches and the kingdom of the Two Sicilies to Italian unity. The first Italian Parliament, which met at Turin, proclaimed Victor Emmanuel King of Italy, 14 March 1861. There remained outside the kingdom, Rome and Venice. The Italians profited by the defeat of the Austrians by the Prussians to obtain Venice, thanks to the mediation of Napoleon III, in October 1866. As to Rome, Garibaldi tried to occupy it in 1867 in spite of the agreements to the contrary and the resistance of French troops : he was beaten at Mentana. The result was to turn Italian resentment against France, which had made Italian unity. Victor Emmanuel's Italians entered Rome in 1870, after the crushing of Napoleon III's armies by Prussia.

The Italian episode brought France Nice and Savoy, which voted their annexation by a plebiscite in April 1860. It was the only foreign enterprise of Napoleon III that left a positive advantage. On the other hand, it overthrew the conditions of European equilibrium, installed on our frontier and on the Mediterranean a great power in rivalry with our interests. While in pushing Germany to unify itself under the authority of Prussia against Austria, it prepared the disaster of 1870 and a life of insecurity for us.

The dispersal of effort and lack of tradition which were the dangerous characteristics of the foreign policy of the Second Empire could not harm colonial enterprise : on the contrary. So on this side the achievement of the reign was happy. French troops completed the conquest of Algeria by the submission of Kabylie and the occupation of the southern oases, while our influence began to penetrate into Tunisia.

But Napoleon III, wishing to apply the principle of nationality to the Arabs, slowed down European colonisation in
Algeria. Owing to the merits of a great leader, Colonel
Faidherbe, the Second Empire extended our possessions in
Senegal and set going the improvement of the vast domain
of French West Africa. A still richer domain was opened up
to France by the conquest of Cochin-China and the establishment of the protectorate over Cambodia. Frenchmen made
themselves masters of Saigon in 1859 ; from 1863 they held
all the outlets of the valley of the Mekong. The opening of
the isthmus of Suez led France to seek a port at the mouth of
the Red Sea : thus Obok on the Somali coast was acquired
in 1862. Ten years before, New Caledonia in the Pacific
Ocean had been occupied, unknown to the English.

Mexican War

Unhappily this dispersion of ideas and efforts drew the
Emperor into the romantic and lamentable Mexican adventure.

The Mexican Republic—under its Liberal President Juarez
— having suspended the payment of interest due to its
European creditors, England, Spain and France decided on
intervention in 1861. Ships and some troops were sent to
Vera Cruz. Soon England and Spain withdrew their forces.
Instead of following them, Napoleon III pushed forward the
enterprise : he had conceived the project of founding a
Catholic Empire in Mexico, under French influence, the crown
to be given to the Archduke Maximilian, brother of the
Emperor of Austria. Thus France would have a strong foothold in America and at the same time attract in Europe the
support of Austria and the Pope. A first French detachment
failed in 1862. But a new army of 28,000 men, sent under
the command of Generals Forey and Bazaine, took Puebla in
1863 and occupied Mexico. A national assembly of yes-men
proclaimed Maximilian Emperor, who arrived in his capital in
1864. Still Mexican resistance, maintained by the guerrillas,
continued. In 1865 the United States, their Civil War over,

declared their opposition to the French enterprise. Napoleon III, judging the game lost, recalled his troops. Maximilian, who had fallen into the hands of Juarez' partisans, was shot in 1867.

This disaster, on the morrow of the Austrians' defeat at Sadowa, strengthened Prussia in the idea that from henceforth she could try her hand against the principal continental state, France.

Franco-German War

The Hohenzollerns had founded Prussia's fortunes on the army. Since 1813 the Prussians had been subjected to military conscription. From 1859 William I — first Regent, then King of Prussia — assisted by General von Roon and by a minister of brutal genius, Otto von Bismarck, had no other pre-occupation than to forge a new instrument of war to realise German unity by force, against Austria and against France.

Prussia's manœuvres against Austria began with the affair of Schleswig-Holstein, duchies peopled mainly by Germans but which were attached to the Danish crown.

Bismarck succeeded in drawing Austria into a war with Denmark ; then, Denmark defeated, in getting Lauenburg, Kiel, the military control of the future canal and the administration of Schleswig for Prussia, while Austria was to administer Holstein. From then on the struggle for prestige and power was virtually joined between Austria and Prussia for the domination of Germany.

France's interest was clearly to hinder the constitution of German unity under Prussia's aegis, which would at once menace our frontier on the Rhine. In prudence, then, France should not have let Austria be crushed. But Bismarck knew his craft. He came to seek Napoleon III at Biarritz in 1865, flattered his dreams and obtained from him a sort of free-pass for Prussia's enterprises and even France's patronage for an alliance between Italy and Prussia. Thus freed and supported, Bismarck felt himself strong enough to launch a tremendous campaign against Austria and the German states which resisted Prussia. He abruptly re-opened the question of Schleswig-Holstein. The Prussians defeated the Hanoverians, then the Bavarians. On 3 July, at Sadowa in Bohemia, the two armies of Prince Frederick Charles and the Crown Prince of Prussia crushed the Austrian army reinforced by the Saxons. Was Prussia — led by von Roon, Bismarck and her chief of staff Moltke — going to drive Austrian influence out of Germany and achieve German unity?

The future was menacing for France. Everybody felt it. There was only one means of removing the danger : by French mobilisation to impose armed arbitrament upon Prussia, Austria and the German states. Napoleon III, embarrassed by his promises, hesitating and physically enfeebled, could not act. He allowed himself, once more, to be manœuvred by Bismarck. On 26 July 1866 the preliminaries of the Peace of Nikolsburg were signed : Austria practically withdrew from Germany in favour of Prussia ; Prussia got Schleswig and Holstein, the leadership of a federation of German states north of the Main and the right to annex all these states except Saxony. Three hundred years of precautions, struggles and successes for the security of France were rendered null and void.

To allay his people's irritation, Napoleon III tried to wrest consolation prizes from Prussia. He went to work as maladroitly as possible, and pushed imprudence to the point of asking from Bismarck the right for France to annex Luxemburg and Belgium.

Thenceforward Bismarck thought only of profiting from the weakness and incoherence of French policy to achieve, by a war against France, the work of Prussian hegemony and of German unity.

In 1867 war nearly broke out over Luxemburg, which in the end was declared a 'neutral state under the guarantee of the powers'. Both sides continued to prepare for the conflict. In Germany, Moltke and Roon brought up forces, already better trained and armed, to the highest pitch. In France,

Marshal Niel, inadequately supported, tried to bring about military reforms creating a front-line army composed of regulars and reservists, and an army in reserve formed of those exempt from regular service. Niel died in 1869 and his successor, General Lebœuf, gave himself up to illusions. The marvels of a new rifle, the 'chassepot', and of another invention, the 'mitrailleuse', were talked about. The organisation of an army in reserve, the 'garde mobile', was, however, left a mere project.

Napoleon III improvised once more in diplomacy. He got into touch secretly with Austria and Italy to gain their alliance. He obtained nothing precise, but was deluded into thinking that peace was assured. Then, in spite of the long-declared opposition of France, in June 1870 Bismarck brought forward Prince Leopold of Hohenzollern as candidate for the throne of Spain, vacant by revolution. The struggle was on. French policy woke up.

France's ambassador, Benedetti, obtained from King William of Prussia the withdrawal of the Hohenzollern candidate. But Bismarck was to get his revenge : French blunders gave him his chance. Pushed on by his entourage, the Empress and her cronies, the Emperor wished to add to his political success one of prestige. The minister of Foreign Affairs, the Duc de Grammont, demanded the King of Prussia's written guarantee of Leopold of Hohenzollern's renunciation. On 13 July 1870 the ambassador Benedetti demanded this of William at Ems. The king, irritated, took refuge in a polite refusal. Bismarck who was at Berlin, learning of the refusal from his master's telegram, the 'Ems telegram', published it in a curt résumé transforming the polite refusal into a blunt rejection. Grammont took this publication for a slap in the face. On 15 July the head of the government, Émile Ollivier, announced a state of war and was applauded, in spite of the reservations of Thiers who asked that they should wait for the facts to be confirmed. On 17 July France declared war on Prussia.

European opinion, at first hostile to Prussia, did not understand why France decided so rashly. It considered that we were in the wrong. Bismarck divulged Napoleon III's project aiming at Belgium, which influenced England against us. Austria and Italy, solicited by Grammont, took refuge in bargaining which was humiliating to our dignity. The South German states, worked on by Bismarck's agents, rallied to the 'German crusade'.

Completely isolated, France had to pay very dearly for the mistakes of her ill-considered diplomacy and the gaps in her military organisation.

War began on 2 August. The German front-line armies totalled more than half a million men, forming three groups — Steinmetz, Prince Frederick Charles, the Crown Prince of Prussia — under the general command of King William, but directed in reality by Moltke. In France, General Lebœuf concentrated barely 265,000 men in a fortnight, forming a single army, that of the Rhine. The German troops, far superior in numbers and cohesion, were concentrated on a front of 150 kilometres, facing Northern Alsace and Lorraine ; the French troops, dispersed over a front of 250 kilometres, from Bâle to Thionville.

On 4 August a French division was surprised at Wissembourg. On the 6th MacMahon's army corps, moving up hurriedly, was surrounded and defeated at Froeschviller, in spite of the desperate charges of the Reichhoffen cuirassiers and the Algerian sharp-shooters, the 'Turcos'. The Germans at once occupied Alsace. On the 9th they laid siege to Strasbourg, which was bombarded for thirty-nine days and surrendered on 29 September.

In Lorraine, on August 6, General Frossard allowed himself to be defeated at Forbach by a German army which had got itself engaged rashly.

Napoleon III, demoralised and wavering, hesitated between three or four possible courses. On August 12, recognising

his incapacity to direct the war, he gave the command-in-chief
to Marshal Bazaine, an officer who had been a man of courage,
but who did not feel himself intelligent enough to take a line of
his own, and who was overwhelmed by the responsibilities.
Not daring to take the initiative, nor indeed knowing how to,
Bazaine was to submit blindly to the enemy's pressure.

To avoid battle, Bazaine resolved to bring back his troops
intact under the fortress of Metz. The Germans followed
him there, themselves disconcerted. On 14 August an indecisive battle took place at Borny. On the 16th at Rezonville,
the Germans were nearly crushed, lost 16,000 men, but to their
astonishment saw the ground given up to them by Bazaine's
retreat. On the 18th a terrible but confused battle took place
from Gravelotte to St.-Privat, between 200,000 Germans and
140,000 French. The French resistance was magnificent, but
the right wing commanded by Canrobert, subjected to the
fire of 180 cannon and left without support, gave way. The
French lost 13,000 men, the Germans 20,000. Bazaine's army
found itself henceforth blockaded round Metz.

Another French army was re-formed at the camp at
Châlons, made up of troops escaped from the defeats in Alsace
and badly trained recruits, under MacMahon's command :
about 130,000 men. Bazaine being heavily engaged, the army
of Châlons became the chief resource. What to do with it?
Napoleon III wished it to protect Paris. The Empress and
the ministers insisted that it should try and make contact
with Bazaine. It set out from Châlons on August 12, leaving
nothing to speculation as to its movements. When it
arrived ten days later towards Montmédy, Bazaine's army was
blockaded and immobilised round Metz, while the forces of
the Prussian Crown Prince and of the Prince of Saxony,
accompanied by a powerful corps of artillery, turned towards
the North to forestall the turning movement of the French.

At Sedan, on September 1, MacMahon's army, overwhelmed, surrounded and mown down by 700 cannon, could
not break out of the circle of fire, in spite of desperate charges.

An unprecedented disaster befell it. On the 2nd it capitulated, leaving the enemy 100,000 prisoners including the Emperor himself who, on the eve before, had had the flag of surrender run up.

In Paris on Sunday 4 September, under the blow of the news of Sedan, the Legislative body was invaded by the mob and Gambetta proclaimed the downfall of Napoleon III. Soon after, Gambetta and Jules Favre went to the Hôtel de Ville and there proclaimed the Republic. A provisional government was constituted, with Gambetta, Jules Favre, Jules Ferry, Rochefort, under the presidency of General Trochu. Its purpose was to organise the 'Defence of the Nation'. Jules Ferry had a secret interview with Bismarck at the château of Ferrières on September 18 to learn the enemy's conditions of peace. Alsace and Northern Lorraine were demanded. Faced with that, the provisional government decided to struggle on. It would prepare Paris for resistance, while a 'delegation' established at Tours would mobilise the forces of the provinces. Gambetta, at first remaining behind in besieged Paris, reached Tours by balloon on October 9.

The Germans had invested Paris on September 19. A circle of ramparts and sixteen detached forts protected the capital. Troops of very mixed kinds — some of them first class, like the crews from the fleet and soldiers of the line, some 75,000 men — others called up in a hurry, without training or discipline, 'gardes mobiles' and national guards, more than 400,000 men — were to assume the defence under General Trochu, who doubted his own capacity for the task. Paris resisted till 28 January 1871, at the cost of much suffering. The population had to undergo every kind of privation, and in the last weeks of the siege the bombardment claimed 500 victims.

Gambetta, however, aided by the engineer de Freycinet and Colonel Thomas, succeeded in levying, assembling and arming 600,000 men with 1,400 cannon in the provinces. Such an effort, which took the German command by surprise, might have been decisive in spite of its having been improvised, if it had been able to link itself with a corresponding effort on the part of the army of Paris and above all of Bazaine's army, which would immobilise on their side the bulk of the German armies. But Bazaine's incompetence, already largely responsible for the catastrophe of Sedan, was to lead to utter betrayal and disaster. After two months of suspect negotiations, on 27 October 1870, Bazaine handed over to the Prussians Metz and all his army: 173,000 men, 1,570 cannon, 56 flags. Henceforth free to move, the forces of Prince Frederick Charles descended upon the Loire, where they broke the attempt of the 'army of the Loire', led by d'Aurelle de Paladines, to support the sorties of the army of Paris. Already d'Aurelle de Paladines' army, with a victory at Coulerimiers, 9 November, had freed Orléans. But it came up against Frederick Charles's Prussians at Loigny, 8 December, and was beaten. Then the army of Paris, 100,000 men strong and commanded by General Ducrot, after having reached Champigny, re-entered the capital exhausted and decimated.

Gambetta did not give up. A new army of the Loire under Chanzy, that of the north under Faidherbe and of the east under Bourbaki attempted a supreme effort. After holding up the German advance with his sharp-shooters, Chanzy was defeated at Le Mans, 12 January 1871. Faidherbe employed similar tactics and won a success at Bapaume, but was beaten at St.-Quentin, 19 January. As for Bourbaki, ordered (with 130,000 men) to deliver Belfort and harass the enemy's lines of communication in Alsace, he allowed himself to be forestalled by the Germans, who stopped his march at Héricourt, 17 January; afraid of being surrounded, he threw his troops into Switzerland, where they were disarmed.

Loss of Alsace-Lorraine

On 28 January 1871 Jules Favre signed an armistice with Bismarck at Versailles : the fortifications and troops of Paris were to be disarmed, except for the forces necessary for the maintenance of order, all the forts to be occupied by the Germans and an immediate contribution of 200 million francs paid. Already on 18 January, in the Gallery of Mirrors of the palace of Versailles, Bismarck had achieved German unity in proclaiming the German Empire, with the King of Prussia as Emperor.

There, on 26 February — after painful negotiations and in spite of the solemn protest of the inhabitants of Alsace-Lorraine — Thiers, head of the executive, and Jules Favre, Minister of Foreign Affairs, signed the peace preliminaries which were confirmed by the Treaty of Frankfort, 10 May. The conditions were : cession of the whole of Alsace, of Metz and northern Lorraine — two departments and a half, 1,600,000 inhabitants ; the payment of an indemnity of 5 milliard francs. To keep Belfort, the entry of German troops into Paris had to be accepted. Profiting from an option clause, 60,000 Alsace-Lorrainers quitted the lost provinces for France.

Four centuries of efforts for the security of France were brought to nothing. France lived from now on mutilated, restless, in search of a new equilibrium abroad and at home.

CHAPTER III

Beginnings of the Third Republic

❖

*The Paris Commune — Return of Confidence — Struggle
for Power: the Republic wins — Internal Reconstruction —
Colonial Empire: Lyautey*

ON 8 February 1871 immediately after the armistice and
before any other negotiation, universal suffrage had had to
pronounce either for war to the end or peace, and to elect a
National Assembly. It had pronounced for peace and elected
400 Royalists, 30 Bonapartists, 200 Republicans for the most
part moderates — except in Paris where the Left Wing had
triumphed with Louis Blanc, Victor Hugo, Gambetta, Garibaldi, Edgar Quinet and Rochefort. The Assembly met at
Bordeaux 12 February and designated Thiers as 'head of the
executive of the French Republic'. Until the institutions of
France should be settled by statute, Thiers and the Royalist
majority agreed to postpone those questions which divided the
parties. The object was, first, to make peace and liberate
French territory. On 10 March the Assembly moved to
Versailles, distrusting Paris and its risings.

The Third Republic began, then, in a France two-thirds of
which had just voted against the Republicans. Doubtless the
'war to the very end' preached by Gambetta and his friends
had frightened the people, who wanted peace. But in fact the
political map of France remained the same as in 1848. The
real Republicans were numerous only in the great towns and
working-class centres. Besides, the word 'republic' appeared
synonymous with 'revolution': it inspired and brought about
a conservative reflex. To misunderstand that would be to
misunderstand the internal history of the new régime during
nearly forty years : the nature of the struggle between the
real Republicans and the others, the former being obliged at

first to spar with universal suffrage, then to conquer it painfully
to preserve the Republic, defend it and make it secure.

The Paris Commune

Without the popularity of Thiers, who had tried to prevent
the war and who announced his decision to be active head of
the state, and without the political inexperience of the conservatives, the Republic would perhaps have foundered at
once in the reactions provoked by a new revolutionary explosion of the old insurrectionary Paris. For there was the
ordeal of the 'Commune'.

The physical privations and moral tension imposed on the
people of Paris by a long siege had rendered it irritable, ready
to be aroused. Unemployment was general, money lacking,
poverty gave an edge to anger against the humiliation of the
disaster and the armistice signed by Thiers. The people of
Paris considered it an affront that the National Assembly
established itself at Versailles. The Assembly itself made the
mistake of reducing the number of those benefiting from the
pay of national guards and of suppressing the moratorium
on debts and rents. These grievances were all the more
dangerous in that Paris was still armed. The national guards
drew 200 cannon from the Champs-Élysées to Montmartre
and Belleville. A Central Committee of revolutionary groups
was formed, 3 March, to take charge of the workers'
rising. Soon it was master of the munitions depôts and of
450,000 rifles. When Thiers arrived in Paris on 18 March, he
thought he could recover the cannon. Soldiers of the line,
sent to Montmartre under General Lecompte to seize the guns,
came up against the resistance of a mob of national guards,
women and children. They refused to fire on the mob and
arrested their commander. The insurrection gained the whole
capital. Thiers withdrew the government and the loyal troops
to Versailles, while in Paris a band of insurgents shot General
Lecompte and Clément Thomas, the former commander of
the national guards.

Thiers, who knew his history, put into practice what had always succeeded with the kings of old : he isolated Paris, while relying on the belief of the provinces in law and order.

After the election of 26 March by which 230,000 Paris voters thought to confer sovereign power on the new 'Commune of Paris', the revolutionaries at once divided into groups, each one of which had its own aims and suspected the others. They had no time to agree upon a practical programme. They had, with real effectives of some 20,000 or 30,000 combatant 'Federals', to withstand a new siege imposed on them by Thiers, who had reconstituted an army of 100,000 men under Marshal MacMahon.

This new siege lasted two months, April and May 1871. A sortie of the Federals upon Versailles, 3 April, resulted only in their leaders being captured and shot. The Commune then seized hostages. Rigault, delegated to the Prefecture of Police, had numerous people imprisoned, from the Archbishop of Paris, Monsignor Darboy, and the President of the Court of Appeal, Bonjean, down to simple gendarmes. On 21 May the army of Versailles entered the undefended gates of the capital. For a whole week, from 21 to 28 May, street fighting laid waste the city. The 'Federals' burned the Tuileries, a part of the Louvre, the Cour des Comptes, the Hôtel de Ville and many houses. On 24 and 26 May, realising they were lost, they massacred their hostages. On the other side, the Versaillese troops, driven to desperation, killed nearly 20,000 insurgents. The repression which followed resulted in the arrests of some 50,000 persons. Brought before courts-martial, 110 were condemned to death, 275 to forced labour, 6,000 to be deported. The revolutionary groups were not to raise their head again for a long time.

Return of Confidence

Thiers' energy, reassuring the provinces, gave somewhat more credit to the republican idea. The elections of July

1871 showed an increase of confidence in the new régime. Thiers hastened to get a provisional constitution voted by the Assembly, leaving him the responsible head of the government but with the title of President of the French Republic. A law voted in August laid down the framework of departmental administration, the powers of provincial councils and prefects. This law, in spite of the Assembly's secret wish, directed the régime along the Jacobin and Bonapartist way of centralisation.

By the Treaty of Frankfort France had been granted three years in which to pay the Germans the indemnity of five milliards which would liberate the soil from foreign occupation. Two loans, the first in June 1871 — which was covered more than twice — the second in 1872, covered fourteen times over, enabled the indemnity to be paid well before the date fixed. By 16 September 1873 the soil was freed from German troops. The Second Empire had led France to disaster, but had left her rich ; the Germans were astonished and regretted that they had only demanded five milliards.

The country's wealth facilitated the prompt re-establishment of the public finances and hence that of national defence. An increase of indirect taxes was voted, a tax on revenue from movable property, additional centimes on patents — which yielded the receipts expected. A military law, of July 1872, established the principle of conscription tempered by exemptions, the duration of service being fixed at five years in the active army, four years in the reserve, eleven in the territorial.

Still the Republic remained a provisional régime. As soon as Thiers sought to give it a definitive organisation, he came up against a majority of the Assembly. In May 1873 open conflict between him and the Right broke out. He was beaten in the Assembly by a majority of 24, on an order of the day by which the Royalists and Bonapartists demanded a 'resolutely conservative policy'. He resigned.

With Thiers gone, it remained for the conservatives to agree on what they wanted. They elected as President of the

Republic Marshal MacMahon, a man of courage but with no experience of politics. The government was entrusted to the Duc de Broglie, head of the Right coalition which was preparing the way for a restoration of the monarchy. It was first necessary to reconcile the two branches of the royal family in order to bring about an agreement between legitimists and Orleanists: the Comte de Paris, Louis-Philippe's grandson, went to Frohsdorf in Austria in August 1873, to salute the heir of the elder Bourbon line, the Comte de Chambord, as head of the house of France. The 'fusion' being made, the Royalists got ready to welcome the Comte de Chambord to Paris and to recognise him as king under the name of Henry V. But they could not reach agreement on the flag. MacMahon himself deemed it impossible to renounce the tricolour. The Comte de Chambord, regarding the tricolour as the symbol of revolution, made it a question of principle: he wished to bring back the 'white flag of Henry IV', symbol of the sovereignty of divine right. That brought everything down.

For want of anything better, the law of the Septennate was voted in November 1873, reserving the question of the future. This law conferred the presidency on MacMahon for seven years and charged a commission of thirty members to consider constitutional laws. The Broglie Cabinet applied a policy of 'moral order', as it was termed: combating Republican propaganda and demonstrations, restricting liberty of the press and bringing the clergy to the defence of conservative ideas. However, the Republican party worked zealously. Gambetta travelled all over the country, holding numerous meetings and making himself the 'commercial traveller of the Republic'. The municipal elections of 1874 rewarded this effort: at least in the towns, they registered the marked progress of Republican opinion.

In the Assembly divisions reappeared among the conservative fractions. A part of the Orleanists drew near to the moderate Republicans. In January 1875 the laws of the constitution were debated. On the first vote, the majority

rejected the word 'Republic'. But on the second vote, the
Wallon amendment — Wallon was a Republican of the Right
— fixing the mode of election of the 'President of the
Republic', was adopted by 353 votes to 352. From February
to July the Assembly voted three laws relating to the organisation of the Senate, the organisation and relation of public
authorities — the whole going to form what is called the
'Constitution of 1875'. Thus was established a parliamentary
régime more or less inspired by English practice : the head of
the state non-responsible, the ministers responsible to the
Chambers, a Chamber elected for four years by universal
suffrage and a Senate comprising 75 permanent members and
225 elected for nine years, renewable a third at a time, by
colleges of electors from the departments and communes. The
Chamber had the right to vote primarily the budget and the
laws ; the Senate, the power to constitute itself a High Court
to judge attempts against the state. A régime which was to be
plied in very different ways: according to circumstances, the
spirit of the dominant parties and men's practical sense.

Struggle for Power: the Republic Wins

The Republic was voted, but it was not assured. Not even
its title was fixed. It was to be subjected to repeated threats,
bend to all sorts of compromises, draw support from widely
different quarters, attack opposition of various kinds or divert
it, win over the new middle class and appeal to the interest, as
much as to the idealism, of the masses. From that came
its character of conflict, a troubled mistrust and a spirit
of reprisals which long marked the Republican advance.
Within the régime the 'true Republicans' found difficulty
in believing in those who had come over. From that, too,
came the splitting up of politics into numerous fractions,
according to the precise shade of Republican adhesion. Thus
our parliamentary system, founded not on two great parties
but on fluctuating coalitions of groups, soon began to suffer
from an excessive frequency of ministerial crises, which resulted

in instability of government and in reforms being slowed up or improvised.

The Assembly dissolved 31 December 1875. The elections of February-March 1876, by single-member constituencies — which favoured local influences — gave a resounding victory to the Republican principle : the Royalists and Bonapartists elected were only 155 against 340 Republicans. For the first time the word 'Republic' no longer appeared to prudent people as synonymous with 'Revolution'. Thiers had grafted on to it the idea of public order. But between public order and 'moral order' there was a sufficiently strong difference for the lower middle class to be smitten anew with the charms of liberty. Having ceased to be disturbing to order, the Republic looked again to its liberal support. It was against the intervention of the clergy in politics and Ultramontane intrigues that the alliance between liberals and radicals was made. And this anti-clerical alliance found discreet support among the peasants, gradually undermining the solid strength of the conservatives in the countryside. In May 1877 Gambetta launched the slogan : 'Clericalism — there is the enemy !'

President MacMahon accepted Republican ministers in order to conform to parliamentary rules. But he did not approve of their policy. He considered dissolving the Chamber to 'make the country judge between Parliament and me'. On 16 May 1877 he withdrew his confidence from the head of the government, Jules Simon, who resigned. MacMahon called the Duc de Broglie to power against the majority. A month later the majority, by a vote of 363, condemned MacMahon's policy and the formation of the new ministry. The President then obtained a dissolution of the Chamber from the Senate. This meant open conflict. MacMahon took a personal stand against Republican propaganda and brought pressure to bear upon officials. Gambetta was prosecuted and condemned for contempt of the President. The general election took place in October : the Republicans carried 327 seats, the Royalists 208. MacMahon tried to form a ministry from outside Parliament, but the Chamber refused to recognise the ministers. In December the President gave way and called a ministry of the Left Centre to power with Dufaure and Freycinet. A little later partial elections gave the Republicans a majority in the Senate. MacMahon himself gave up the struggle : he resigned 30 January 1879. In his place the Chambers elected a Republican of 1848, Jules Grévy. Then they decided to leave Versailles to sit in Paris, fixed the national fête on 14 July and voted an amnesty for those condemned for taking part in the Commune.

The Republicans had won. But among them two tendencies were already strongly opposed : the cautious or opportunist tendency, and the radical tendency.

Internal Reconstruction

The opportunists were patriotic, quietly anti-clerical and strongly attached to property. The radicals were also patriotic, but violently secularist and in favour of democratising the economic and social life, as well as the institutions, of the state.

The opportunists governed, with figures like Freycinet and above all Jules Ferry, without the Republic changing its social aspect much during a decade. To them are owed the laws or decrees which profoundly influenced the character of the new régime : the decrees against the religious congregations engaged in teaching (1880), the education acts, notably that establishing compulsory primary instruction, free and secular (1881-82), the laws on the freedom of the press and freedom of public meeting (1881), those on trade unions and municipalities (1884) and the law revising the constitution in a more republican direction by enlarging the electoral college for choosing the Senate and abolishing permanent senators (1884).

To them equally is owed the great military law of 1889, creating a democratic army, with compulsory service for all, the period being reduced to three years for the mass of young people and to one year for certain special cases.

We owe them, too, a vast plan of public construction of railways, navigable waterways and ports, of which the chief author was Freycinet, who was both a minister and an engineer. In 1883 conventions were signed handing over the running and construction of railways to six railway companies — except for a small network in the South-West run by the state. Works were set on foot to enlarge the ports and connect up waterways. Bounties were granted for shipbuilding and navigation, to enable our merchant marine to survive against our English and German rivals.

The period of opportunism greatly encouraged the growth of mobile wealth, of savings and capital. Internal trade profited by the development of general consumption, the diffusion over the countryside of goods which had never before penetrated into it, the rise in middle-class incomes, the spread of comfort and even of luxury. But the sense of saving is so powerful in France that a part of this wealth, not consumed, and too abundant to be absorbed in subscribing to state loans, began to be directed towards foreign investment. Soon Russia, Turkey and South America were to equip themselves with the disposable surplus of French capital. Our great banks organised themselves more and more with a view to these loans.

The opportunist Republic was not indifferent to social questions. To it was due not only the Waldeck-Rousseau law of 1884, which allowed trade unions to be constituted and grouped into federations, but the law of 1898 dealing with accidents incurred at work — one of the turning-points in social legislation — and the creation of the body of factory inspectors and of the General Council of Labour.

On the other hand, from 1871 on, the population of France continued to lose ground relatively to that of her neighbours. Reduced from 38 to 36 millions by the loss of Alsace-Lorraine, the French population took nearly forty years to recover this loss. Various causes contributed to this : the parallel progress of thrift and habits of well-being in the middle classes, under the influence of regular incomes; the terrible impoverishment of certain agricultural and wine-growing regions — the former affected by the competition of new countries, the latter by the scourge of phylloxera — which made the inheritance of land in families precarious; the constant uprooting of young people from the countryside, drawn to the towns by the railways and by compulsory military service — an uprooting far from propitious to family spirit; finally the substitution of small retail trade or the workshop for handicraft : the whole thing aggravated by the Civil Code's law of inheritance and the breakdown of religious belief.

Colonial Empire : Lyautey

Abroad, the period in which opportunism inspires, if not always parliamentary oratory and debates, at least the deeper levels of Republican policy and administration — a period which lasted from the electoral defeat of MacMahon to the crisis of the Dreyfus affair — was marked by a vigorous effort of colonial expansion and by a slow restoration of France's diplomatic position. In spite of considerable differences, one notes a sort of resumption by the Republican middle class of the methods of the July monarchy.

In four years, from 1881 to 1885, under the two ministries of Jules Ferry, France acquired Tunisia, Annam and Tonking, and prepared the way for the conquest of the Sudan, the Congo and Madagascar. According to the ideas put forward by Jules Ferry, the object of this colonial drive was to offer outlets to French exporting industries threatened by the protectionism and competition of new industrial powers, Germany and the United States; to secure ports of call for our shipping and protect our influence and trade in the world; finally, to procure for our civilisation, language and cultural ideals a field of influence not too inferior to that of other nations, particularly of our old rival, England. But also, it must be said, it offered a chance for Frenchmen to recover their morale, which had been deeply affected by the catastrophe of 1871, and a means for the Republic to win prestige without too many risks. In this respect as in others, did not the opportunists show, in difficult circumstances, that they had political sense?

In 1871 100,000 hectares of Algerian lands had been granted to Alsace-Lorrainers opting for France. Ten years later the European population in Algeria exceeded 450,000. A law of 1889 automatically naturalised children of foreign parents born in Algeria. The administrative services of North Africa, following the Republican doctrine of 'assimilation', were attached to ministries in Paris. This policy, pushed too far, caused mistakes and abuses in regard to the natives themselves, and from 1896 onwards brought about a reaction in the direction of administrative, economic and financial autonomy.

Tunisia was brought under French protection by the Treaty of Bardo, imposed on the Bey 12 May 1881, to prevent its conquest by the Italians and to put an end to the incursions of Tunisian tribesmen into Algeria.

Then French detachments began to occupy the oases of the Sahara. In West Africa a forward policy was pushed on in Senegal and in the Congo. In 1898 an important episode took place that had detonating consequences: a brilliant young soldier, Colonel Marchand, led a French expedition from the west right across Africa to take possession of the Sudan. The success of his mission would have had the effect of cutting the possibility of a North-South link-up for Britain. Unfortunately for him, though perhaps fortunately for France, he arrived on the upper Nile at the very moment when Kitchener had defeated the Mahdi and was moving south to occupy the Sudan. After a great deal of tension France gave way: which produced an explosion of Anglophobia among the Paris mob. But the incident of Fashoda produced very different conclusions in the mind of the remarkable Foreign Minister, Delcassé (1898–1905): it determined him on a planned course of clearing up all disputes with Britain and achieving an understanding, with all the possibilities that might flow from that for France and for Europe.

The first important consequence was that Britain recognised France's paramount concern in Morocco, gave her a free hand there and firm diplomatic support. It was inevitable that the European powers should be drawn into the vacuum created by the feeble Shereefian régime in Morocco. Disorder and anarchy prevailed ; the tribesmen were uncontrolled ; France was drawn in by the necessity of her position in Algeria, by the investments and interests of her nationals — while her concern with North Africa goes back to the special privileges granted her there by Francis I's treaty with the Sultan. In fact, there was an historic opportunity at hand for the career of the greatest of French colonial administrators, Lyautey — 'the Royalist who gave an Empire to the Republic'.

Lyautey was a man in the tradition of Bugeaud, the conqueror of Algeria, and of Galliéni, with whom he served his apprenticeship in Indo-China and Madagascar. French interest in Madagascar goes back to Richelieu and Louis XIV ; but not till 1884 was the island brought under a French protectorate. There followed a war, English influence was extruded, and then came outright annexation. Meanwhile, in French North Africa, commercial development, railways, cultivation of the soil, missionary work, military roads and security measures went forward by leaps and bounds, under the guiding minds of two remarkable spirits : Cardinal Lavigerie, Archbishop of Tunis and Carthage, a great prince of the Church, founder of schools and hospitals, builder of cathedrals and churches, organiser and ruler of missionary orders ; and Lyautey.

Lyautey, a Royalist and man of the Right by origin, was to spend the whole of his life collaborating with the men of the Third Republic. He was much influenced by the ideas of the nobleman — in both senses of the word — Comte Albert de Mun : to favour social reform and to live his life under the ideal of service. A leading idea of Lyautey's was the absolute value of stability in government — 'En France on fait toujours de l'inachevé'. This led him to look abroad, to service in France's growing Empire. He pondered whether the Colonies might not become a school of training for the home country ; his insistence on social duty was partly to deliver France from the Republic's tendency to fractionalisation and decomposition.

In the penetration of Morocco, in its conquest largely by persuasion and moral force, in organising and maintaining an indirect rule there, in direct construction and building in Algeria, he found a vast outlet for his creative energy and his genius for government. He waged a long contest between his almost independent paternal despotism in North Africa and the departments in Paris. But, in the event, standards of colonial administration and service went up, the quality of the personnel improved. In 1894 the creation of a Ministry of the Colonies was forced upon the central government. The French population in Morocco multiplied by ten in three years. The test came with the war of 1914–18, when Lyautey had done his work so well that he could practically denude North Africa of troops for metropolitan France, and peace and security were still maintained. Before the French occupation Morocco had never been homogeneous or stable ; Lyautey achieved its pacification and fruitful organisation with the minimum of force.

By 1914 France was the second colonial power in the world : a position largely achieved by such men as Ferry, at home, against the virulent opposition and unjust accusations of the Left in the Chamber, and the indifference of the country ; and carried out by such men as Galliéni, Lavigerie and Lyautey. Lyautey held before his countrymen the conception of 'a France of a hundred million inhabitants'. The brilliant achievement of the French Colonial Empire was the best *revanche* for the defeat and disaster of 1870–71.

CHAPTER IV

Internal Politics: Radicals in Power

MEANWHILE, the internal state of affairs was far less satisfactory, though not without interest and excitement — indeed
too much interest and excitement to be good. Frenchmen were
at (what Paul Morand calls) their purely indigenous sport —
internal politics. Far too many ministries succeeded each
other at far too frequent intervals. From 1871 to 1914 the
Third Republic had some fifty Prime Ministers; during the
same period Britain had seven. Impossible to plan anything
in such circumstances : the wonder is that anything was carried
through at all. It was this instability of government that was
mainly the explanation of the various financial scandals that
rocked the Third Republic, from Panama to Stavisky.

The pity was that Gambetta's aim of a great united
Republican Party should not have succeeded, for he had a
grand instinct for leadership. He was defeated by the small
men of the Third Republic, and shortly after died. It was no
less a loss that Clemenceau in these decades should have
devoted his talents to destruction. The leader of the Radical
Left, he bitterly attacked Ferry's colonial policy, rejected any
idea of conciliation with the moderate Republicans and so
building up a strong Republican party. Jaurès thought this
the capital error of Clemenceau's life : the conflict between
the Republicans naturally weakened the Republican régime
itself, it undermined what might have been a strong govern-
mental tradition in the hands of such men as Thiers, Ferry,
Gambetta — or Clemenceau himself. It opened the way to
such a dangerous assault on the Republic as Boulanger's. When
President Grévy was forced out of office on account of the
electoral bribery of his son-in-law, Ferry as the outstanding

figure should have been elected. But Clemenceau gave the
cue to the electors, 'Vote for the stupidest'. They did. The
office of President, which might have been a rallying point
for the Republic, was systematically lowered. History has its
ironies : when in 1919, at the apogee of his fame — and of
his services to France — Clemenceau should have become
President, he too was turned down as too big a man.

What wonder that this kind of thing gave an opening to
the enemies of the Republic itself? All the rancour and resentment of the Right, the hysteria of the Paris mob, the disgust
and disillusionment of many politically innocent, the money of
the Duchesse d'Uzès, crystallised round the figure of a popular
young general, Boulanger, who was expected to overthrow the
Republic. Educated at the *lycée* at Nantes with Clemenceau,
with a Breton father and a Welsh mother — with the charm
and the weakness of the Celtic temperament — he was a kind
of bogus Hitler : not wholly bad, but wholly weak and vain.
The campaign he waged against the Republic was rendered
dangerous by its external situation and by its internal weakness.
By their support of such a candidate the French aristocracy
revealed once more their criminal folly and levity — the same
that, going back through their conduct under the July
Monarchy and the Restoration to the 18th century, had
produced the great Revolution.

France needed a stable régime — a constitutional government at once dignified, representative and flexible. This its
governing class would not provide : idiotically divided
between Legitimists and Orleanists they opened the way for
the misfortune of 1848 and the disastrous adventure of the
Second Empire. Presented with another chance after 1871,
they muffed it. This — a Boulanger — was their last chance,
their last sputter. But at the ultimate moment Boulanger
flinched from marching on the Élysée (instead, some time
later, the amorous Celt shot himself on his mistress's grave).
Jules Ferry was a man of will : he was not such a fool as to
allow democratic *doctrine* to be misused on behalf of a dictator.

Scrutin de liste — the system of multiple constituencies that had given Boulanger his chance — was abolished : Paris was never again to impose a dictator on the country. As for the people — they had to be saved from the consequences of their own folly : the real, though unexpressed, work of all government.

Henceforth, the aristocracy were on the defensive, after the pitiable exhibition they had made of themselves. It was for the middle class, and of them the lower middle class, to govern. Regarding the period as a whole, in long-term perspective, to their triumph with the Treaty of Versailles, they made a good job of it. They achieved the reversal of 1871 ; they built up a great empire ; they maintained France in prosperity, the most agreeable country in the world to live in — along with a freedom of mind and spirit that enabled prodigious achievements in culture to flower, in literature, painting, music and science.

Underneath the surface effervescence of politics, the enjoyable scandals, financial or sexual (of a Boni de Castellane or a Madame Caillaux), the lubricious details of a President found dead in bed with his mistress, the duels and suicides, there were deeper strains and conflicts. To the struggle between Monarchists and Republicans over the nature of the régime itself that occupied the first decade, there succeeded the struggle between Left and Right over the Church and the Army, that was resolved by the victory of the Radicals at the turn of the century. Still deeper issues were involved in the emergence of the working-class movement — the Socialist party in the Chamber, the Trade Unions in industry — into the foreground of politics ; while all the time the growing danger of the wars that were to break Europe and end her ascendancy in the world drew nearer. These two movements were inextricably connected. The horror ahead lay heavy on prophetic spirits like Péguy ; the danger from Germany was apprehended by men of common sense like Poincaré ; it was tragically denied by the great tribune of the working class, Jaurès, who was the first and greatest victim of 1914.

The internal struggle found characteristic expression in a number of crises and scandals. The revenge of the Right for the defeat of Boulanger came with the outburst of the Panama scandal in 1892. It would have been a great thing for the Third Republic if it could have accomplished the Panama Canal as the Second Empire had done the Suez. But the Saint-Simonian entrepreneur, Lesseps, was old and doctrinaire : he insisted on the impossible, on the Canal being at sea-level, and refused to recognise the necessity for locks. The estimates were from the first far too low, and as the work was held up and began to fail, the dominant political parties became involved in a vast mesh of bribery to keep the truth from the public. When the crash came, thousands of small investors lost their savings, and the parties any reputation they had for Republican virtue. One minor consequence was that the Radical leader, Clemenceau — suspect not only financially but, what was worse, thought guilty of English contacts and sympathies — was driven out of politics for the next ten years.

The Left had its revenge in the course of the Dreyfus affair, the *Affaire par excellence* of the Third Republic, for in it so many characteristic issues came together : it formed a water-shed in modern French life. Its importance was alto-gether greater than the occasion itself : that provided merely a case over which rival ideologies could fight it out. In 1894 Captain Dreyfus, a staff officer of good Jewish family, was condemned by a military court for betraying military secrets to a foreign power, *i.e.* to Germany, the perennial enemy. Without doubt military secrets were betrayed — but not by him : he was entirely innocent, a rather null man with the air of a *marchand de crayons*, as Clemenceau said, and he was condemned unjustly to a long term of imprisonment. It makes an immensely complex story of a kind that some people find fascinating but has become sickeningly familiar in our time. Let us concentrate on the salient facts : not once, but again and again the rulers of the French Army showed that they were determined justice should not be done to an innocent officer who was a Jew. All the forces of the Right were behind them in this, the influence of the Church, and the militant polemics of certain religious orders. In the Affair the beastliest elements in modern politics come together : the use of anti-Semitism by the Right, the fomenting of national and racial prejudice, the bribery and prostitution of the Press, the poisoning of opinion, sensationalism, suicides, the systematisation of lying — of which last Charles Maurras became the most distinguished exponent.

For long justice was withheld, in spite of the suspicions that were spreading as to the fabricated evidence upon which Dreyfus had been condemned. It was a great day when Clemenceau was convinced of its falsity and gave Zola's article in his paper the famous heading *J'accuse !* French society was split from top to bottom by the Affair : it lined up the intellectuals, Déroulède, Barrès, Maurras on the Right, Zola, Anatole France, Péguy on the Left. Borne forward by its impulse, Clemenceau fought his way back into politics and the Radical leadership. The incurable folly of the Right got itself not only defeated, but the cause irretrievably besmirched. Still the Army Command would not give way : the review of the case forced upon it in 1898 still did not exonerate Dreyfus. But the momentum generated carried the Radicals to victory in the elections of 1898 and 1902. After the latter, the Socialist leader Jaurès became Vice-President of the Chamber and carried his party with him into collaboration with the Radicals in tackling the two outstanding problems : forcing the Army and then the Church to accept the implications of the Republic.

The political situation that followed was shortly after paralleled by that in England upon the immense Liberal victory of 1905. Indeed what is interesting is to observe the close similarity in the developments and events in England and

France : the same issues and problems present themselves at much the same time in the two most advanced areas of Western society. In England, too, the Liberals in power were supported hopefully by a growing Labour party. In both England and France the working-class movement experienced a sense of deception at the results of collaboration ; class-conflict and a fundamental difference in the attitude to property increasingly divided middle class and working class, Liberals and Labour people, Radicals and Socialists. The years of co-operation were succeeded by restiveness, a period of strikes and in-dustrial agitation, of syndicalist activism and the preaching of direct action, the cult of violence on the Left by Georges Sorel — whose ideas were the inspiration of both Mussolini and Laval.

But the alliance held together long enough to deal with the Church, and to carry through the separation of Church and State, for which the time had certainly come. This was mainly the work of the ministry of Combes (1902–5), a small-minded and bitter secularist, who nevertheless thus left a great mark — in some ways a wound — upon French life. But some dealing with the Church was indispensable : the *Ralliement* to the Republic brought about by the wise policy of Leo XIII was succeeded by the irreconcilable reactionism in every respect — doctrinal as well as political — of Pius X. The government expelled the militant religious orders which had taken so polemical a part in politics, dissolved the religious congregations engaged in teaching and determined to extend the control of the state over education in place of the Church. The state took over Church property, but was prepared to be generous in its financial provisions for the Church. 'Re-ligious associations' — trust bodies — were formed in which both sides were represented to administer the funds. These were rejected outright by Pius X, under the influence of his Secretary of State, the Irish-Spaniard, Merry del Val, who proceeded to order demonstrations of French Catholics against the government. Feelings were much embittered, and the issue became a rancorous one in French life. All the same, the policy of separation of Church and state was supported not only by militants like Combes, Jaurès, Clemenceau, but by a moderate like Poincaré. He once rejected an overture from the Right with the words, 'There is the whole extent of the religious question between us'. The French Church did not lose much by the divorce from the state : it may even have gained spiritually, as the Church of Wales is considered to have done with its Disestablishment a few years later.

With the solution of the Church question and the growth of the working-class movement, social questions came to the forefront in France as in other western countries. In social legislation France was very far behind England and Germany. A country of farmers and peasants, of small property-holders and numerous *rentiers*, put up a long resistance to social insurance, to the regulation of conditions of work for the benefit of the workers. French political institutions — particularly the Senate — were weighted in favour of country towns as against industrial areas. Not until the end of the war, in 1919, was the eight-hour day achieved ; not till the Popular Front government of Léon Blum in 1936 was substantial equality between working class and middle class in secondary education initiated, and the forty-hour week introduced. By then it was too late : there could not have been a more fatal moment for its introduction : Hitler's Germany was working all hours, arming for the conquest of Europe.

Undoubtedly the French propertied and rural classes held up any programme of social benefits and reforms, out of class-selfishness, until too late. This had the effect of exasperating the industrial workers into direct action in strikes, and increasing the irresponsibility of their political action. Again and again Jaurès pleaded and remonstrated with them : 'those who on the pretext of revolution and doctrinal purity hide miserably behind abstention from party politics are deserting socialist thought'. One recognises the necessity of the phrasing. In fact, Jaurès' policy of co-operation was

sabotaged by the extremists of the Left : such people as
Guesde who used his undoubted talents as orator and organiser
to preach pacifism up to 1914 — and then went over to a
detestable jingoism ; or Hervé, who, starting as a Boulangist,
became a pacifist, embarrassing Jaurès as leader all he could
— to pass over also to extreme chauvinism in 1914, and live
on, when the great leader was murdered as its victim, to
publish a pamphlet in 1935, *We Want Pétain*. One is re-
minded of Doriot, the Communist leader, who became a
Fascist thug and a collaborator with the Nazi S.S. in their
murderous work. Such people are the scum of politics.

But during the short period of co-operation between
Radicals and Socialists, Millerand, the most practical of the
Socialist leaders, joined the government and managed to pass
a law in 1899 limiting hours of work in factories and workshops to a ten-hour day for women and children, and he
initiated legislation regulating hours and conditions of work
in shops. This sensible good work was too much for the
militants, who insisted on forbidding Socialists from entering
bourgeois governments. The result was that Jaurès was kept
out of any responsibility for government all his life ; there
was a melancholy procession of the ablest and most practical
of socialist leaders away from the party into other and more
effective, if sometimes less desirable, associations : Millerand,
Viviani, Briand, even Laval and Déat.

The Trade Unions had formed a General Confederation
(*Confédération Générale du Travail*) in 1895. Millerand and
Jaurès strove hard to resist the tendency to violence and to
canalise Trade-Union activity into democratic parliamentary
action. But they had little success for all their efforts.
Throughout the Third Republic the industrial workers, by
their divisions, failed to correct its bias towards the countryside, the farmers and peasants ; the industrial workers received
scant justice from it — but they contributed to this state of
affairs by allowing themselves to be divided and by the
ineptitude of their leadership. In 1920 the irretrievable step

was committed — under the instructions of Lenin — of splitting the Trade-Union movement from top to bottom and
carrying large sections of it to form the C.G.T.U. (*Confédération Générale du Travail Unitaire*) under Communist
leadership. Hence further weakness and delay in the achievement of social services proper to a modern state — until the
Popular Front government of 1936, a generation late. That
government with its programme of benevolent — and indeed,
idealistic — social reforms was confronted by a series of stay-in
strikes. The ultimate position of the Socialist party under the
Fourth Republic is the best commentary on the bankruptcy
of its political line under the Third.

In any case feuds and squabbles, ineptitudes and *joie de
vivre* alike, the gaiety of society and the brilliance of French
culture, in literature, painting, music, the arts of life — all had
a shadow upon them, like the figure of Death that crosses
the stage at the end of *Love's Labour's Lost* : the shadow of
war, that Nietzsche foresaw would be the characteristic note
of the 20th century.

The fall of Bismarck in 1890 enabled France to breathe
more freely. So long as the victor of 1870–71 held power
France was held fast within her sphere by his system of
alliances, isolated and kept almost dependent, at one moment
— in the mid-seventies — terrorised by the threat of a pre-
ventive war. Bismarck's fall enabled France to cut free and
move for herself. In 1892 the Franco-Russian Alliance was
made. France gained perhaps less from it than Russia did ;
yet it was a turning-point : she was delivered from the
isolation that had kept her at the mercy of the Germans. The
Paris money-market, which organised the savings of millions
of thrifty Frenchmen, was thrown open to the insatiable
demands of Russia for credit. The Russian railway-system,
the Trans-Siberian, were the result. In the end millions of
small investors were to lose their savings by Russian default
and confiscation.

Delcassé s period as Foreign Minister, 1898–1905, was, as we have seen, even more important in its consequences. Bismarck's successors were convinced that Great Britain — isolated and rendered unpopular by the Boer War — would have to accept German terms for collaboration ; even before, Bismarck had initiated the policy of colonial blackmail in dealing with her — which had not been lost on the Foreign Office, or on Salisbury, Lansdowne or Grey. Later it became clear that Germany's rulers were determined on an expansion of naval power that was a challenge to Britain's very safety and existence, as German military power was a constant threat to both France and Russia. What more natural than that those threatened should draw together ?

Delcassé had the perspicacity to see the possibilities in the situation even at the moment of Britain's greatest unpopularity in France ; he had the tenacity and courage to follow it up with action. He wished to see the mess in Morocco cleared up and French power extended from Tunis and Algeria to the Atlantic. To secure British support over Morocco he was prepared to exchange French claims in Egypt. When Germany's rulers woke up to the consequences of the Franco-British Entente they deemed impossible, they reacted in the usual German manner, like bullies, and demanded the sacrifice of Delcassé. France was in no condition to face a war, and Delcassé was sacrificed at the behest of the Germans. But at the international conference that followed, though the Germans got a large slice of the French Cameroons in compensation, they found that the understanding between France and Britain was strengthened.

The great test for the Entente was the Russo-Japanese War, 1905–6 ; for Japan was an ally of Britain, while Russia was France's ally. But even this was surmounted, in view of the greater danger from Germany. Russia's defeat in the war with Japan turned out, paradoxically, to France's advantage ; for it forced Russia to look to the West again. Great Britain proceeded to clear up all her outstanding disagreements with

Russia to prepare the way for an understanding like that with France. The Dual Alliance was on the way to becoming a Triple, or even Quadruple, Alliance; for it was recognised that Italy would not in any case follow the Central Powers into war against Britain. Still Germany would not cease to threaten Britain's very existence as a sea-power, or France's existence with her enormous military and industrial predominance, her population more than half that of France again. When Germany resorted to a renewed attempt at colonial blackmail and to test the strength of the support of Britain and Russia for France — the Agadir crisis of 1911 — she found that even a Liberal Britain was prepared to submit to no more bullying and she was fairly warned by Lloyd George's Mansion House speech. With Italy's war against Turkey for Tripoli, and that of the Balkan powers for their independence and the liberation of their nationalities from Turkish rule (1912–13), the balance in Europe slipped still further against Germany. She found herself surrounded by enemies she had done her utmost to create and nothing to propitiate.

The danger bore immediately and most hardly upon France. Within the country there was a heightening of political tension and the question of military service became urgent. In his book, *L'Armée nouvelle*, Jaurès argued for a citizen army on democratic principles — idealistically as usual, the noble head of the great orator well in the air, his feet never quite on the ground. More practical persons with more sense — notably Poincaré — argued that with Germany's manpower far greater, the only hope was to increase the term of military service to three years. Thus it was fortunate for France that when war came an extra army-class existed.

Caillaux had hoped to achieve a deal with Germany over finance and economics, possibly to initiate an industrial collaboration between the Ruhr and Lorraine which could only have ended in France being carried into the orbit of German power. Jaurès hoped to ensure peace by mobilising the working class internationally: he was a century, if not for ever, before his time. He placed his hopes in the pacific assurances of the German socialists ; he assured his followers that there would be no invasion — when the plan of invasion was already prepared, to the last detail, and needed only the word from the German General Staff, the real holders of power in Germany, to be put into execution.

The approaching danger called out stronger men : in 1913 Poincaré was virtually imposed upon the politicians as President by public opinion. He was a Lorrainer, who had never forgotten his childhood memory of the German barbarians marching through his village in 1870 : a man of complete intellectual honesty, of great mental power, gifted with a marvellous lawyer's memory ; a grave, severe man, tenacious and proud, of an unquestioned rectitude. He was not a man of the Right, though pushed towards it by the unfailing silliness and irresponsibility of the Left. He was essentially a man of government, upright and responsible : as Napoleon said, 'probity is an interested disposition, but natural to men born for government'. Poincaré had himself introduced progressive death-duties (a progressive income-tax was not introduced till 1914), but he was as opposed to socialist collectivism as Clemenceau was ; like Clemenceau, he was a secularist, but no *mangeur de curés* ; he had come out on Dreyfus's side, but he was no enemy of the Army. He had felt a sense of disgust with party politics and stayed out of all governments for ten years, from 1895 to 1905, in protest against the 'distortions that the parliamentary system undergoes'. Now he was the man of the hour : he was on his way back from Russia, where he had been paying an official visit as President to cement the alliance, when Germany decided to give Austria a free hand and to let loose the war in which the old Europe foundered.

CHAPTER V

The War of 1914–18 and Recovery

It is impossible to do justice here to the grandiose, and degrading, theme of the German campaign for conquest which has dominated the first half of the 20th century, reduced Europe at times to the age of the barbarian invasions and ended her glorious ascendancy in the world — in terms of political and economic power, if still not in the arts and sciences. We are here concerned only with the effect of that bid for conquest upon France, for France was dominated — almost mesmerised — by it. Even so, we can only give the bare outlines of it, the framework rather than the content.

The period falls into four parts : (1) the war of 1914–18 ; (2) the twenty years between the wars, 1919–39, during the first half of which France tried hard to maintain the Versailles settlement and during the second was increasingly paralysed by German recovery and the renewed bid for conquest ; (3) the war of 1939–45, in which it culminated ; (4) the liberation of France and the Fourth Republic, essentially a continuation of the Third, with which our history merges into the affairs of today.

On the outbreak of war in 1914, the essential fact in the defence of France against the German invasion was that her frontier defences had not been continued behind the Belgian frontier. So that her fortifications could be turned by the long-prepared Schlieffen plan, which swept aside the international neutrality of Belgium that Germany had guaranteed along with others — though this brought Britain into the war — and directed the main thrust of the German armies through Belgium to the rear of the French forces. To this was added a second mistake : the French General Staff was a slave to the doctrine of the offensive à outrance, with even less reason than

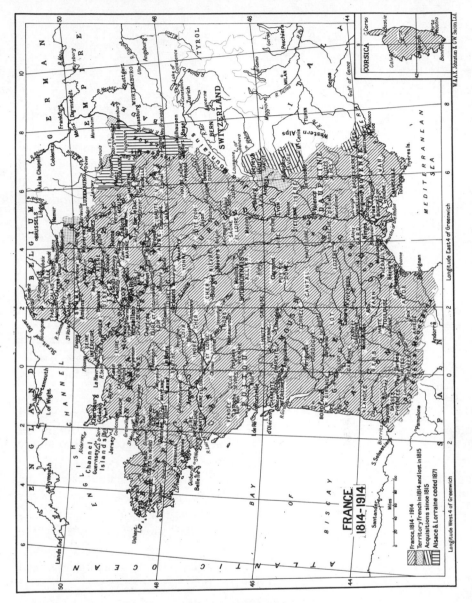

France 1814-1914

in 1870, and wasted precious time and energy in a forward move into Alsace. The result was that the French Army was turned by the immense wheeling movement of the Germans, and was only saved by a vast retreat on Paris from a great disaster of encirclement on a far larger scale than Sedan. Joffre, the Commander-in-Chief, kept a cool head and throughout the immense manœuvre rapidly transferred his strength from east to west, until at the moment when the French line was running from the eastern frontier to pivot on Paris in the west and the Germans were dangerously extended, he delivered his counter-blow — and turned their movement back on them. This was the victory of the Marne, that threw the Germans back from Paris. (In one small encounter in this vast movement of deliverance near Villeroy perished all that was mortal of Péguy.)

But the possibility of enveloping the Germans in turn was lost, and they were able to dig themselves in for a four-year-long occupation of eleven of the richest departments of north-eastern France, which contained also the largest concentration of French industry. For four years France — increasingly reinforced by Britain and, in the last phase, by America — held out along the Western Front in the dreadful trench-warfare that drained the life-blood of a whole generation of Frenchmen. It is this terrible blood-drain on a static population that gives the clue to so much of French history, both in attitude of mind and in action, in the decades that followed. It partly accounts for the natural preoccupation with security in the post-war years, for the progressive internal weakness of France — the absence of so many of the best men of their generation in all walks of life — and for the spreading defeat-ism that undermined French resistance to Hitler and paved the way to surrender in 1940. To quote Professor Brogan on these losses — a little historical imagination will reveal what they meant for France : 'By the end of 1915 France had lost in *dead* almost as many men as Great Britain was to lose in the whole course of the war and two-thirds of the total losses of the British Empire. In a period a little less than that during

which the United States was a belligerent, France lost seven
times as many men as the United States, out of a population a
little over a third as great ; *i.e.* over an approximately equal
period of belligerency, about twenty Frenchmen were killed
for one American.'

It was not until 1916 that, with conscription in Britain,
the British effort in man-power came to equal the French. It
was indeed high time, for throughout that year from February
to December, France was subjected to her greatest test of
endurance of the whole war : the martyrdom of Verdun
through which she came triumphantly, though terribly weakened. It was the aim of the Germans in this ghastly battle to
bleed her to death. By the same token Verdun became a
mystic symbol of life for the French people, and the watch-
word 'Ils ne passeront pas' an inspiration to resist to the last.
The attack began with a bombardment 'which far exceeded in
tempestuous violence anything yet seen in the world, and two
million shells were expended before the infantry began to
creep forward in the fading light'. The Germans had 1,400
guns — half of them heavy howitzers — for a front of attack
of barely eight miles. But the French artillery had achieved
great skill and even brilliance of technique ; the defensive
forts with which the region was studded held out against the
concentration of gun-fire far better than was expected ; and
in the course of the long *supplice* French morale gathered
strength. By the end of the year German losses were heavier
even than French, and at the end the terrible balance-sheet
showed fairly equal losses — over 300,000 on each side. It
was all the more surprising since the course of French military
history seems to show its most brilliant achievements in the
sphere of the offensive. 'The amazing toughness and self-
sacrifice of the French resistance before Verdun is perhaps the
most wonderful of "toutes les gloires de la France", just
because it ran so counter to the ordinary stream of national
temperament.'

Meanwhile, to the north, the new British armies were

making their great effort along with the French in the battle of the Somme. Here the fantastic bravery of the young British troops combined with the unimaginative obstinacy of the Command to make the losses stupendous : 'nearly 60,000, or 60 per cent of the officers and 40 per cent of the men engaged, probably the highest proportion in any great battle recorded in history'. In this battle total British casualties were twice those of the French, who were now fighting more skilfully and economically. The French had every reason to be proud of the exploits of their Army in 1916, but it was becoming terribly strained and war-weary — and no wonder. This became evident next year with the failure of Joffre's planned offensive. Joffre, who had rendered great services to the Allied cause, was removed from the Supreme Command at just the wrong moment ; the German retreat to their strongly fortified Hindenburg Line was a masterstroke : it ruined the Allied offensive. The French effort on the Chemin des Dames achieved a very small result for very large casualties. The strain and the disappointment were too much : all through the summer of 1917 the French armies were paralysed by a standstill on the part of the men — more like a strike than a mutiny : they would defend their trenches, but they would not make any more attacks that were both costly and useless.

It was in this situation that Pétain won his immense prestige with the French people. A cool man, he preserved an imperturbable calm in this dangerous juncture — fortunately the Germans did not realise how dangerous it was. He set himself to nurse the Army back to health and confidence in itself ; he worked tirelessly to achieve this end and succeeded. But something more was needed to win victory : to regain the offensive spirit. This was the work essentially of a civilian, but a very militant one, in fact an unconquerable spirit : Clemenceau. He became Prime Minister at the end of 1917. At once a new spirit manifested itself under this iron old man : traitors were rounded up, pro-Germans like Caillaux and Malvy put in prison, defeatists discountenanced. For the next year until victory was achieved, Clemenceau exerted a democratic dictatorship, a personal ascendancy, comparable to that of Lloyd George in Britain. Clemenceau's object was epically simple : 'Je fais la guerre'. His knowledge of English, his Anglo-Saxon sympathies — so disadvantageous to him in earlier years — were now a source of strength. France had borne the brunt of the German onslaught in 1914 and 1915 ; it was shared equally in 1916 ; in 1917 and 1918 it fell mainly upon Britain.

For the supreme phase of the struggle Clemenceau had his eye on Foch — the one general above all who had never lost the offensive spirit and who believed victory was possible. Clemenceau got the British to agree to making him Supreme Allied Commander and to a unified Command. It was only just in time, for in the spring of 1918 Ludendorff let loose the last and greatest of the German offensives, mainly upon the British. Pétain, who had ceased to believe victory was possible, expected to see them surrender. The Germans captured almost a quarter of a million prisoners, and once more reached the Marne to threaten Paris. But the Allies did not break, and it was now that the unquenchable courage of Clemenceau glowed brightest. 'I will fight before Paris, I will fight in Paris, I will fight behind Paris', he told the Chamber. These words must have been in Winston Churchill's mind in declaring his equal resolution to the British people in 1940.

'We shall be victorious if the public authorities are equal to their task', Clemenceau declared. Under him, in 1918, they were. And all the while that the Germans were advancing on Paris, Foch was preparing his great counter-stroke, to take place on the Marne as in 1914. He tried the endurance of the British to the uttermost ; he had absolute confidence that they would not break ; he made them hold on, he would not come to their rescue — he was saving every scrap of his reserves for the turning moment when the Germans had reached the limit of their momentum. The Americans were

beginning to arrive and to take their place in the line under
the gallant General Pershing.   At last in mid-July Foch's
hour came : he launched an offensive between Soissons and
Château-Thierry which was the beginning of the end.   On
August 8 — in Ludendorff's phrase, 'the black day of the
German Army' — the Hindenburg Line was breached.   From
then on, Foch gave the enemy no rest ; after all these years,
with victory in sight, the French fought like men possessed.
In September the final phase was reached : Foch's pincers,
200 miles apart, closed with two offensives, the British in
Flanders, the French on the Meuse.   The Hindenburg Line
was broken ; the German hordes rolled back to the frontier ;
Ludendorff's nerve broke and he insisted on capitulation.   On
9 November the Kaiser abdicated ; a new German government
took his place.   On 11 November the Allies, through Foch,
granted Germany an armistice.   This enabled Ludendorff and
the German General Staff to slip the responsibility for surrender on to the new German Republic : a move that was
parent of the disaster of much subsequent history in the next
two decades.

For France it was a great deliverance rather than a victory.
None of the exaltation of Péguy's

Heureux ceux qui sont morts dans les grandes batailles
Couchés dessus le sol à la face de Dieu . . .
Heureux ceux qui sont morts pour quatre coins de terre
Mais pourvu que ce soit dans une juste guerre . . .

There had been too many 'grandes batailles' — though there
could be no doubt that for France it had been a just war.

For the Germans — or rather for the occult forces that
ruled behind the scenes of German life — this was a temporary
truce rather than a permanent defeat.   After all, they had
so nearly brought off their grand bid for the domination of
Europe ; and as Germany recovered strength they did not
cease to plan for a second attempt — in more barbarous
manner, with few or none of the inhibitions of the civilised —

through the Nazis. It was not for nothing — indeed it has the greatest significance — that Ludendorff was the original promoter of Hitler and became the coadjutor of the little corporal in the first Nazi attempt on power, the Putsch of 1923.

Meanwhile, the Germans had achieved one of their great aims : the permanent reduction of France's relative position in Europe, along with the weakening of her strength. The true state of affairs was rather disguised by the fact of victory ; in spite of appearances, France's psychology was one of defeat : hence her preoccupation thenceforward with security. Though this was entirely legitimate and understandable, it was not shared by Britain, still less understood by America.

Against both Clemenceau and Foch, Poincaré wanted the defeat of Germany made complete and self-evident before concluding an armistice ; and perhaps he was right ; it would have prevented the Stab-in-the-back lie on which the Nazis rose to power. At the Peace Conference, which opened in January 1919, Poincaré wanted French security assured by the separation of the left bank of the Rhine from Germany. But Clemenceau willingly exchanged this for a military alliance with Great Britain and the United States. Poincaré was sceptical whether this would be implemented : as a lawyer he was only convinced by treaty guarantees. Foch protested in vain that effective help from America and Britain could not arrive in time to prevent France from being defeated and overrun. This turned out to be true when the time came in 1940. Poincaré warned the Allies that nothing would stop the Germans from remilitarising the Rhineland when it suited them. In vain. It was Hitler's first open defiance of Europe in 1936; its supine acceptance — by Britain rather than by France — rendered his subsequent course of aggression and conquest possible.

The Charter of the League of Nations, which was to give some semblance of order to a disrupted world, Poincaré criticised for having no operative force to make the organisation effective. He cannot be said to have been wrong. Five months after the opening of the Peace Conference, the United

States Senate refused to ratify either the Treaty or a pact with France. Great Britain followed suit, to the extent of refusing to give a sole guarantee to all the frontiers redrawn by the treaty, east as well as west. France was forced back on herself, to look to herself — though she could safely assume that Britain would make the ultimate defence of French territory her own. And, in fact, at Cannes in 1922 Lloyd George offered France a guarantee in the West, but could not go so far as to offer her a guarantee of the treaty frontiers in Eastern Europe.

For France this was not enough, now that she was thrown back on the system of alliances with her clients — especially Poland and Czecho-Slovakia — for security. What Britain and America failed to realise was that as the result of Russia's withdrawal to the limits of Eastern Europe and the fractionalising of Central and South-Eastern Europe, Germany's potential position was rendered far stronger, the moment she recovered sufficient strength to exploit it. Paradoxically, in spite of Germany's defeat in 1918, the balance of Europe had shifted in her favour.

No one — except possibly Hitler and the German General Staff — saw this at the time or appreciated its full significance. Nor did many perceive all that the war of 1914–18 portended in the decline of Europe, that a second such war would be its ruin — a ruin that Europe owes to the Germans, the people who by their situation and strength should have formed its keystone.

Actually the Treaty of Versailles was, on the political side, all too generous to a people who had wrecked Europe and were to do it again on a far worse scale. On the economic side the conflict was transferred to the subject of Reparations, which became the dominant issue of the next few years and had an unfortunate effect in dividing Britain from France. It was agreed that Germany should make reparation for the damage she had done ; but there was increasing disagreement as to how much she could pay. Germany took advantage of this, as her strength recovered, to pay less and less. As much American capital flowed into Germany as ever she paid in Reparations — capital investment much of which went on social amenities at first and later into gigantic expenditure on armaments. The Americans never saw their investments back : they went to rebuild the Germany that made the Second World War.

In the early stages of the controversy British policy, under the influence of the Bank of England and such economic experts as Keynes, was anxious to restore Germany's economy as soon as possible as part of the restoration of world trade and the pre-war world economic system. France, which had had eleven of her richest departments devastated, saw the matter in a different light. Poincaré, who became President of the Reparations Commission, defined the French point of view : Reparations were a matter of justice, not arising out of hatred or any desire for reprisals, but 'having the object of rendering to each his due and of not encouraging the renewal of the crime by impunity'. In fact, he had to watch the constant whittling down of French claims under English pressure, while he was convinced that Germany was playing fast and loose with her currency in order to default and cheat the Allies. Nor was he wrong.

By her own efforts, and with the aid of such Reparations as she got in the early years, France made a remarkable financial recovery from 1921 to 1924, and achieved a favourable balance of trade. The Reconstruction of the devastated areas cost 100 milliards — the greatest economic achievement of post-war Europe — and it was accomplished by the end of 1925. It must stand to the credit of the ministries of the National Bloc. France's recovery was the result of her own efforts.

The Genoa Conference of 1922 saw Lloyd George's bid for the settlement of Europe on the grand scale, bringing Russia back into the balance. To the Anglo-French discord over Reparations were by this time added serious disagree-

ments over the Near East, brought into the open by the war
between Greece and Turkey, in which Britain backed Greece
and France Turkey. All the same it is possible that Poincaré
made a mistake in holding France aloof at the Conference and
openly aiding its failure. The whole edifice crumbled with
the revelation of the Rapallo Treaty, the pact between Germany and Russia. Russian preferences stood revealed, as
they did again in the 1930's in spite of the sworn hatred of
Nazism and Communism : anything rather than the West,
with its hated values of freedom of thought, liberty of the
individual, the sanctity of human life, the inner core of its
political experience in the moral responsibility of self-govern-
ment — anything rather than that ! In a flash was revealed
the true character of Russian policy, the duplicity of German.
Germany had no intention of fulfilling the treaty ; her object
was deliberate evasion, playing East against West to recover
her military position.

At once Lloyd George fell, his policy in ruins. Poincaré,
in exasperation, turned down the new Reparations plan offered
by the new British government — which was a psychological
mistake : with no experience of foreign countries, Poincaré
was not happy in his dealings with Britain. He had been
proved right in his view of the Germans ; he was now left to
embark alone on the dangerous experiment of applying force.
In 1923 the French occupied the Ruhr. They were met with
passive resistance supported by the German government. It
was a test of endurance between France and Germany. After
some months German resistance gave way. Now was the
moment to clinch the issue, for France to get her own guarantees. The blunt and forceful Millerand, now President of the
Republic, pressed for direct negotiations with Germany,
France imposing her own security for the Rhine and uniting
the coal of the Ruhr to the iron of Lorraine. But at this pass
Poincaré's will — or his own legalistic moderation — failed
him. He let the moment for forcing things to a conclusion
escape him in favour of the well-worn legal track of Treaty,

Reparations, Commission. Great Britain took the opportunity
to get the argument back on to the financial plane, to leave it
to the judgment of the experts.

But indeed it had always been doubtful whether France
had the strength to impose her own solution. We know now
that France's strength had been much more seriously undermined than anyone realised, even Poincaré who said sadly,
'Frenchmen are too exhausted to follow me'. Therein lay
the truth. The fact was that only together could France and
Great Britain deal with Germany, and disunity or any failure
to co-ordinate policy between them enabled the malign forces
within Germany to get ahead with their campaign to capture
power and drive her along a more sinister and dangerous
course than ever ; for, as we have seen, the treaty had left a
vacuum around her, which she could exploit the moment she
was free to throw off her treaty shackles to re-arm.

After this failure of nerve, there remained nothing but
to try the policy of conciliation. This coincided with the
victory in 1924 of the Left, the Cartel des Gauches, of the
Radicals in alliance with the Socialists under Blum, who had
expected for the first time to emerge as the leading party at
the polls. Their first act was to force Millerand out of the
Presidency and to replace him by a colourless figure, Dou-
mergue. Their foreign policy was better : they agreed with the
first Labour government in Britain on the Geneva Protocol,
which would have initiated an international collective system,
giving guarantees of security, providing sanctions for its
breach and, on this basis, for agreed and controlled disarmament. It was a way of grappling with the essential problem
in the relations of the Powers and that which offered most
hope. But the Labour government fell and the Conservatives,
pressed by the Dominions, refused to ratify the Protocol. It
must be admitted that it was a long way ahead of opinion in
either country, which failed to appreciate the vital necessity
it would come to have.

The larger scheme for collective security having failed,

the direct approach to Germany was resumed which resulted in the Locarno Treaties (1925). The architect of the policy of conciliation was Briand, who had made his name as a conciliator at the time of the Separation of Church and state twenty years before. This remarkable Breton, in temperament very like Lloyd George with whom he got on too well, remained Foreign Minister from 1925 to 1932 : a period of office comparable to Delcassé's. At Locarno France's eastern frontier was guaranteed by Germany ; in return, Germany was to enter the League of Nations and the military occupation of Cologne to end. Soviet Russia did all she could to keep Germany from agreement with the Western powers ; and French confidence was hardly fortified by Germany's sudden renewal of the Rapallo Treaty with Russia or by the revelation of how cleverly Stresemann had finessed to avoid a specific renunciation of Alsace-Lorraine.

But Briand persevered with his conciliatory and pacific policy, trying to build up an effective system of collective security through the League of Nations and aiming ultimately at a federation of Europe. It was largely his work, his Celtic eloquence and his assiduous attendance that made Geneva something of a capital for all Europe during these years. France was much blamed for her militarism throughout this period — particularly in Anglo-Saxon countries, particularly by Liberal and Left opinion with its illusory hold on realities. Yet in fact Briand's liberal and pacific policy was always upheld by large majorities in the Chamber ; and France successively reduced the period of military service from three years to one year. Just before his death, Briand launched his last great effort on the world : his proposal for a European Federation. It was everywhere opposed, particularly by Britain ; it was not taken seriously even in France. Yet who can doubt now that the visionary was right?

In that year the economic storm broke that engulfed the world, sapped the foundations of its economic system, overturned all governments in power, swept away old landmarks and left nations and peoples face to face once more with the naked facts of the struggle for survival, for power and conquest, the forces of hatred and malign envy, the inculcation of evil for good, in a more terrible form than ever.

Internal politics in these years were dominated by financial questions, or, in a word, by the problem of the franc. Léon Say once said, somewhat unfairly, that 'Public intelligence, in economic questions, has made far less progress in France than anywhere else'. What is unmistakable is the rational objection of the French to being taxed — an objection endemic in French history, and one which, carried too far, has for long constituted the central weakness in the French state. For, rational enough from the point of view of the individual and his own interests, it ceases to be reasonable when carried to the point of paralysing society and holding up the social mechanism. The intelligent selfishness of the French, so evident in personal and individual matters, ceases to be so intelligent when it endangers the public well-being and threatens to bring the state to a stand-still. It may be said that an obvious and keen-eyed class-selfishness has, since before the great Revolution, been France's greatest weakness and the cause of many of her internal troubles. No-one, no class has been ready to compromise on its own self-interest in order to advance the well-being of the whole. It is sometimes a mistake to be too intelligent, or too clear-eyed, if a society is to make a going concern of itself.

In addition to the strain of the war there had been the economic drain of the German occupation of France's best industrial areas. The war was financed — to a much greater extent than in Britain, indeed mainly — not by taxation, but by borrowing, and afterwards devaluing the currency. That was a way; but it had the effect of weakening the middle classes, especially the best element among them, upon whom so many of the services of the modern state depend — the professional classes. No wonder they were further shaken, and alarmed, by the return of the Radicals in 1924 under the domination of the Socialists.   There soon set in a 'flight from the franc'; it was partly deliberate sabotage on the part of big finance and the larger capitalists, partly genuine fear on the part of smaller people for their savings.   There were no refinements of exchange-control in those happier days, and the franc took wings and fled to London and New York.

By 1926, after two years of Left government, the drain reached such alarming proportions that national bankruptcy was imminent.   Poincaré was called back to head a virtually national government on a simple programme of cutting expenditure and increasing taxation.   Confidence returned, the financial situation improved with each year 1927, 1928, 1929; economic recovery was achieved.   Poincaré accomplished it at the expense of his popularity; he knew that he would draw down all the rancours and injustices upon himself: 'What does it matter?' was his attitude.   He had never been a man to entertain illusions; he had long since ceased to expect any reward from public life other than the consciousness of performing his duty.   In the performance of duty, he was struck down by illness in 1929.   He was a man of absolute rectitude and conscientiousness.   Unlike Grévy, he had left the Presidency a poor man, who still needed to work for his living in illness and retirement.   He had above all a sense of responsibility for the well-being and security of the state —of which he had been a great servant.   La Bruyère's maxim was not only exemplified but satisfied in him: 'Le caractère des Français demande du sérieux dans le souverain'.

Poincaré's last ministry governed in a Chamber with a Left majority.   But the Radicals had come to the conclusion, as the result of their experience of 1924–26, that a financial policy under Socialist domination was not viable; and this had important consequences for the politics of the 1930's: it kept Radicals and Socialists at arm's length, even when forced to co-operate.   Meanwhile, Briand with his international outlook ruled foreign policy fairly independently of Poincaré.

The co-operation of these two men, each a great man in his way, saw the end of the good days for France.

With the late 1920's France recovered her position as the most civilised, the most highly cultivated, country in the world — everybody else's second country. It was still vastly agreeable, most livable in, with its climate, abundant food with the best cooking and wines, with the engaging variety of its landscape — Riviera, mountains and *plages*, and for the historically-minded, the châteaux round which so much of not merely French but European history had centred, in the Middle Ages, under the Valois, in the *Grand Siècle* ; or the churches of which Barrès had written in the *Grande Pitié des églises de France*, or Péguy of Chartres :

> Mais vous apparaissez, reine mystérieuse,
> Cette pointe là-bas dans le mouttonnement
> Des moissons et des bois et dans le flottement
> De l'extrême horizon ce n'est point une yeuse . . .

For this was the France of Valéry and Gide and the *Nouvelle Revue Française*, of the slow and sensational unfolding of Proust's *A la recherche du temps perdu* — the *Paradiso* as well as the *Inferno* of the modern world ; the France of Colette and the eternal Mistinguette, of Molyneux and Chanel ; of Claudel and Madame de Noailles ; of the *Vieux Colombier*, the Pitoëffs and the *Compagnie des Quinze* ; of Le Corbusier, of Ravel and *Les Six* ; of Borotra and the incomparable Suzanne Lenglen ; of the Curies and the early designs of Citroën and Renault.

CHAPTER VI

Defeat and Liberation

No lover of France, or of England, can regard the politics of the 1930's with anything but shame, humiliation, disgust. It is a disgusting, yet not a criminal, spectacle : the criminality was elsewhere. There was the mounting record of German bestiality under Nazi control, first at home, then abroad : the negation of freedom, the denial of human values, the inculcation of racial hatred, the calculated deformation of mind and spirit, the extermination of thousands of human beings. The modern world must never forget what 20th-century Germany showed itself capable of. Abroad, where Bismarck's technique was, in the words of his own ambassador in Paris, that of 'force, lying and trickery', Hitler's was the systematisation of perjury, of false assurances to intended victims, the ruthless treatment of the weaker with never a spark of generosity or mercy : a brilliant and malign genius for exploiting human baseness, always marching ahead of the degeneration of our age, contributing largely to it and pushing it forward to its catastrophe.

Everything that took place in this decade, in France, as in England, took place under this malignant spell, this growing shadow. In our decade the shadow has merely moved ; it is not less.

In all this the responsibility of the Western powers was a negative one — in not opposing with their combined force the onset of the evil thing, the extension of its power. In that Great Britain must bear a greater share of the blame than France. In the 1920's France had judged Germany and her true character far more accurately than either Britain or the United States, one so far removed from the scene and both victims of kindly illusions. And France had pursued a coherent policy into the 1930's. The whole position of the West was worsened and rendered insecure by the withdrawal of the United States. Even so, a unified and intelligent Anglo-French policy might have resisted Nazi Germany successfully and held the situation in control. That this was not done was mainly the fault of the unbelievable confusion and stupidity of British policy. Britain's vacillation between two courses in the early 1930's, her settling into the disastrous course of appeasement in the later, reduced French policy to incoherence. Gradually, as British policy settled under Chamberlain into the consistent appeasement of Hitler, the possibility of an independent course for France ceased : she could only follow, clearer-eyed and all the more paralysed in consequence.

It must be said that Britain's policy was not deliberately malign — as any intelligent person might suppose ; indeed its very disastrousness came from its good intentions. For it was profoundly mistaken in principle to entertain good intentions towards anything so evil as Nazism ; and it was equally mistaken in tactics to make any concessions to it whatever — that only increased its power and the danger from it. The only thing was to resist, to build up a stronger power against it, a grand alliance. In failing to do this Great Britain forsook the historic tradition of her European policy over centuries ; she paid a terrible price for it in the 1940's, from which she has not yet recovered. When one considers how often that policy had defeated France in previous centuries, it is ironical to think that in departing from it Britain now dragged France down with her to defeat.

The fundamental truth is that in the international politics of the 1930's, the old conflicts of national interest were cut across by those of class-interest within nations. And this, as might be expected, had a paralysing effect on the democracies, where there was freedom of opinion and action, as opposed to totalitarian powers — whether Nazi Germany or Soviet Russia — the purpose of whose totalitarianism was to suppress any such divergencies. Only the totalitarian powers could be sure of directing a unified policy as they willed ; the democracies were confused by contrary pulls ; in the end they were split wide open. In Britain the split was healed only by the terrible danger of the war it brought down upon it ; in France it was perpetuated by the defeat for which it was responsible. In unity only lay safety.

The whole period was dominated by the international conflict — of which the storm centre was the renewed attempt of Germany under Hitler at world-power. Everything that happened in internal French politics has to be seen in the light of this, or in the shadow of it. Events and developments in internal politics were often direct consequences of those in the international field, sometimes these came about in response to those or were manipulated by them. Never were the two so interwoven, particularly in France, paralysed by class-conflict at the moment of acute danger from Germany. The movement of forces, the course of events, the whole thing is so complex that it is impossible to write the history of it here ; one can only point to some of its leading themes.

France's last attempt at building a defensive alliance to withstand the German danger was brought to an end by the assassination of her Foreign Minister, Barthou, an old friend of Poincaré, and King Alexander of Jugo-Slavia, at Marseilles in 1934. In the event France paid grievously for the incompetence of her police and her security measures. But the police, the armed services and even the civil service were beginning to be riddled with disaffection ; as time went on the sympathies of whole sections went over to the enemy, Hitler and Mussolini. 'Better Hitler than Blum' became the view of many of the Right, and this prepared the ground for the defeatism that defeated France in 1940 before she had well begun to fight. The electoral system continued to produce Left majorities ; so the Right were preparing to use Fascist formations, like the *Croix de Feu*, some of them in collusion with the country's enemies. Earlier that year, on 6 February 1934, a premature attempt on their part succeeded in intimidating the government and forcing it out, but not in bringing Parliamentary institutions to an end. It was succeeded by a disingenuous compromise, of which the linchpin was Laval. The ambivalent personality and politics of this ex-Socialist are symbolic of the last years that remained to the Third Republic.

And yet for all his ambivalence and utter lack of candour or principle, there was a curious consistency in the career of Laval. His main object was to feather his own nest, and the grasping Auvergnat managed at length to buy the medieval castle overlooking the village where he had been born, the son of a butcher. For the rest, he was always a pacifist and a defeatist. In the critical year of the war, 1917, he was spreading defeatism ; he opposed the Treaty of Versailles. In 1920 he left the Left and got office ; but still he managed to keep in with both sides and proved a skilful negotiator, successful in ending strikes after the war. The only ideas that had any influence on him were those of Blanqui and Sorel — and what a comment on the value of their ideas ! Mussolini had been a follower of Sorel ; Laval and Mussolini understood each other.

The danger of having no principles in regard to world affairs was brought home on both sides of the Channel in 1935. Mussolini determined on the conquest of Abyssinia, and assumed that there would be no opposition from France and Britain, which needed Italy in the balance against Germany and to shore up the independent existence of Austria. But Italy's naked aggression aroused widespread opposition throughout the free world, and Britain took the lead in condemning it through the League of Nations. It became a test case for the very existence of the League and for the collective security that was the only hope of safety in a disintegrating world. But sanctions against Italy were not applied with any determination — though Italy's subsequent record in the war made it clear that she could easily have been brought to heel. Indeed, it is thought that Mussolini was fairly accurately informed by Laval just how seriously they were meant — so that the League's efforts were rendered null from the start. Laval was aiming at an understanding with Mussolini pleasing to the French Right. Meanwhile, the Baldwin government in Britain had won a large majority on a pledge of supporting the League and a full collective security policy. Immediately after, Laval inveigled Hoare, the British Foreign Secretary, into an agreement over Abyssinia clean contrary to the British government's pledges.

There was an immediate outcry in Britain; the Baldwin government was only saved by jettisoning its Foreign Secretary; in fact, the Prime Minister should have gone. The further consequences of the Abyssinian fiasco were unfathomable. In Britain, the Left would take nothing from a Conservative government again, after twice-repeated deceptions of this kind — even in regard to rearmament, now becoming urgent. Distrust was sown between Britain and France; no British statesman after this could co-operate with Laval. The collapse of the League system, through Mussolini's successful defiance, freed Hitler in turn from any fear of sanctions against the career of open external aggression he at once set in motion.

In March 1936 he set the Treaty of Versailles at defiance — and its guarantors, France and Britain — and remilitarised the Rhineland. This was the turning-point for Germany. It is now clear that if France and Britain had intervened against this deliberate defiance of the treaty settlement, Germany would have been saved from herself, Hitler thrown over and some régime at least compatible with civilisation would have taken his place. The French government was willing to intervene. It was discouraged by the British government, idiotically hypnotised by the quarrel with Mussolini and blind to where the real danger lay. From the moment that the Rhineland was effectively remilitarised it was impossible for France and Britain to intervene in Germany without incurring a war. Hitler's Germany had gained freedom of action to embark on her planned course of aggression aiming at the domination of Europe : step by step the campaign went forward : early in 1938 the invasion of Austria and the forced Anschluss ; in the autumn, Munich and the dismemberment of Czecho-Slovakia ; March 1939, the occupation of Prague and the extinction of Czecho-Slovak independence ; September, the attack on Poland and the outbreak of war.

In France, to torment the hopes of the faithful with a false dawn, the Popular Front of Radicals, Socialists, Communists gained a sweeping victory at the polls in 1936, largely by reaction against Laval and Fascist trends, and Léon Blum took power for the first time : too late. Blum, in his way, was as symptomatic a figure of these years, on the better side, as Laval was on the shady. A distinguished lawyer, of good Jewish family, he had been one of a brilliant group at the École Normale, who had made his mark young in intellectual circles with his study of Stendhal : contemporary of Péguy, friend of Proust. Then he was converted by Jaurès to Socialism, became his most faithful disciple and succeeded him as leader. Along with his intellectual distinction, his idealism and his personal probity, Blum took over some of Jaurès' worst illusions. If anything, Blum was even more of a pacifist, more bent on disarmament ; he placed an equal trust in German Social Democracy — with less reason, for there was the experience of the war and post-war Germany to learn from. He exemplified and encouraged by his leadership and his undoubted intellectual distinction all the illusions endemic in social democracy. There was no danger, he said, from the Fascists : he was badly beaten up in the streets of Paris to prove the worthlessness of his illusions. Hitler was miles away from power, he said, in 1930 : Hitler was in complete possession of power in 1933. Blum and the Socialists had opposed the raising of Army service from one to two years, an indispensable measure of defence : he and they lived to regret the gap in French defences in 1940. And yet Blum was a noble man, as Jaurès had been before him. It is questionable whether equal harm is not done in human affairs by idealists who cannot or will not face the truth about them, as by evil men who take advantage of their knowledge to advance evil causes. What is certain is that the one, all unintentionally, plays into the hands of the other. The profoundest truth about these matters has been uttered by an English philosopher, Bishop Butler, in a truism : 'Things are what they are and their consequences will be what they will be : why should we seek to deceive ourselves?'

Now, in 1936, the Socialists came into power for the first time, as the centre of a Left coalition. The great Paris exhibition that was to advertise the hopes of a new era could not be opened in time, because the workers were slacking ; the Prime Minister had to go down to ask them to work : what was exposed in the Paris exposition was, first, the indiscipline of the working class. It was true that decent treatment of the workers had been too long withheld by the bourgeois of the Third Republic. Now, by the usual irony of history, their demands were to be met at precisely the wrong moment. The forty-hour week and holidays with pay were introduced when the Germans were working night and day, arming for war. Collective bargaining and compulsory arbitration of labour disputes were enforced. Measures were brought in to nationalise the armaments industry ; meanwhile, France had no Air Force. The control of the Bank of France was rendered somewhat more democratic ; meanwhile, under the financial jugglery of Dr. Schacht, Germany was able to devote more than the total Reparations demanded of her by the Treaty of Versailles — and which Keynes had insisted she was incapable of paying — to armaments.

At the same time the life-blood of the Popular Front was exposed to a double drain : in the field of foreign affairs with the Spanish Civil War, and in finance. The incompetence of the Spanish Left in power, the inability of the Republic to hold on to power, the hopeless ineffectiveness of people who allowed themselves to be divided from top to bottom between Socialists and Anarchists, orthodox Communists and dissident Trotskyists — all served to provoke the military revolt such idiocy so richly deserved. It is probable that the revolt would have quickly succeeded, if the Republic had not received aid from abroad.   And no-one can doubt that that would have been better for all concerned, for Spain, both Right and Left, and paradoxically for democracy itself ; for there would have been no prolonged struggle draining the life-blood of the country — a million lives were lost in the course of it. Mussolini and Hitler intervened to send armed aid to Franco ; Soviet Russia sent more limited help to the Republic. The Spanish Civil War became an open battle-ground for Left and Right in Europe, and sympathies were aligned accordingly. It was to be expected that the Popular Front government in France would come to the rescue of the Spanish Republic, which was after all the legitimate elected government. But it dared not : France was already too divided, herself too near the edge of civil war ; if the government had intervened, it would have been faced with disaffection in the upper ranks of the Army and sabotage from the Right. And there was the growing danger from both Fascist Italy and Nazi Germany. When Blum considered allowing the Spanish Republic its right to buy armaments, he received the warning from London that if this led to conflict with the dictators, he could not count on England's support. That decided the fate of the Spanish Republic, and the foreign policy of the Popular Front bled to inanition on the battlefields of Spain.

But it was the financial *impasse* that brought the Popular Front, the *expérience Blum*, to an end — as it had done previous attempts to give more social content to the democracy of the Third Republic in the nineteen-twenties. Again it was the Senate, bulwark of conservatism, that imposed its veto and defeated the majority, now having lost confidence in itself and become disintegrated ; it was the old Radical, Caillaux, the pro-

German and friend of Laval, who forced Blum's resignation. The hopes of the Left were over.

Events now moved uncontrolled — or rather controlled by one who boasted of his somnambulist certainty — with the mesmerised fatality of a nightmare to the end which might have been foreseen, with a moderate degree of intelligence, from 1933 onwards. In 1938, when Hitler invaded Austria and annexed it to the Reich, France was without a government : no-one would take the responsibility. What a commentary on the decline of public spirit since Clemenceau and Poincaré! The Republic now failed to produce any leadership. As the climax approached, France abdicated : no positive course was possible, the division was too acute at the top : any possibility of leadership was destroyed by the divisions within. So France was reduced to leaning on British policy, which was set under an obstinate and ignorant old man upon a calamitous course. Britain and France paid the penalty of five years of confusion in policy at Munich, in September 1938, when the key to Central Europe — Czecho-Slovakia — was surrendered to Hitler. France was forced to assent, though Czecho-Slovakia was her ally ; but Frenchmen were not so stupid as to think that the surrender meant peace.

But the internal morale of the country was fast deteriorating, in contrast with Britain where it was hardening as the outbreak of war came nearer. It was in fact the British people who — after years of mistaken patience and muddled good intentions — came to the conclusion that it was impossible to avoid war with Hitler's Germany and imposed that conclusion on its government. After Hitler's open flouting of his pledge to Britain and France with the occupation of Prague (March 1939), a sudden reversal of policy was imposed upon the Chamberlain government : the British people had seen the danger signal. A guarantee was given Poland to come to her defence, in case of attack, without conditions and without prior agreement with Soviet Russia, which had indeed been left out of the charmed circle at Munich. It is likely, enough that no agreement could have been reached with Soviet Russia; certainly Russia showed far greater alacrity in reaching agreement with her 'enemy', Hitler's Germany — and that agreement, removing Hitler's fear of a war on two fronts, enabled him to attack Poland and start the Second World War.

These circumstances further weakened the morale of France in face of war: to the defeatism of the Right, the readiness of Fascist sympathisers to collaborate with the enemy, was now added the sabotage of the extreme Left, the Communists, for whom the war against Hitler was an 'imperialist' war — until the moment, in June 1941, when Hitler invaded the soil of Holy Russia. Then the war suddenly became one for 'democracy', a just war and a defensive war — which it had not been hitherto. It may be said, quite shortly, that both these elements, on the Right and on the Left, were traitors to France and to the French tradition. To some extent, as with the scum of German politics, they were interchangeable: Doriot, chief agent of the Gestapo under the later occupation, was a former Communist; Déat and Marquet, who became collaborators under Vichy, had been Socialists; Laval, we have seen, had a Socialist origin, a pacifist background. Already the name of Pétain was being whispered, as undertaker to, and successor of, the régime: he had the immense prestige of a Marshal of France, of his part in the first war, the defender of Verdun, the saviour of the Army in 1917: an octogenarian, he was still very much on the spot, *rusé*, immensely secretive, prepared. Of a peasant cunning, he kept his own counsel; but there could be no doubt that, with his underground contacts with Franco, he was an enemy of the régime and of democracy, and no friend to Britain.

In these circumstances, with the country's leadership worm-eaten from within, it was to France's credit that she remained loyal as she did to the British alliance. The nation responded well enough on the outbreak of war in September 1939 : at once five million men were mobilised under arms without difficulty and without opposition. Not since the days of Louis XIV had the Navy achieved a higher degree of efficiency and power : working together with the British Navy, it reached its highest point in modern times — largely the result of the professional work, alas, of Admiral Darlan. But two defects in her armed forces were fatal to France, as they nearly were to Britain : the Air Force was totally inadequate and armoured tanks hardly existed in any force. Germany was to revolutionise warfare in these very respects and by the tactical combination of the two, in the panzer divisions. Even worse was the spirit of passivity with which the military leadership, under Gamelin, awaited the German onslaught.

In each of these respects there was an officer of no great seniority in the Army who opposed a passionate and convincing negative : de Gaulle. But he did not convince the General Staff, under the domination of a lot of vain old men — the vainest of them, Pétain. At the École de Guerre, de Gaulle had exposed the defensive preconceptions which led to the Maginot Line and Maginot-mindedness. Again and again he had argued for mechanised divisions : his advice to create a tank-force would have prevented Hitler's break-through in 1940. He was convinced that passivity, standing on the defensive, meant defeat. That was what France and Britain proceeded to do, waiting to see what would turn up, from 3 September 1939 until May 1940 when the Barbarians once more engulfed Holland and Belgium — smashing Rotterdam from the air without a moment's warning — and bore down upon France.

It is impossible here to relate the swift and confused course of the war, or the slow and tortuous course of the occupation for France. In a matter of weeks, May-June 1940, France and the British Expeditionary Force (though not Britain) were beaten, overwhelmed and borne down. By a supreme effort, Britain managed to save the bulk of her forces, and almost as many French soldiers, from Dunkirk and Calais to carry on the fight. On June 14 Paris was yielded without a struggle — so different from Clemenceau's spirit in 1917. The government was in a state of collapse and demoralisation, flying from Tours to Bordeaux. In the whirlwind of the campaign de Gaulle had put up a remarkable performance in command of his tank regiment : he had shown what could be done with an aggressive spirit. The new Prime Minister of Britain, Winston Churchill, who incarnated the same spirit in his people, flew to Tours to make a last appeal to the government to remain true to the alliance and continue the war. There the idea of an indissoluble Union between France and Britain was conceived — it seems by de Gaulle — to hold them together in war and in peace. The offer, when made by Churchill, was described by Pétain as 'Fusion with a corpse'. Before leaving, Churchill saluted de Gaulle as the man of the future, *l'homme du destin*.

In the chaos of defeat the Third Republic, like the Second Empire before it, foundered. It had long been undermined from within and there were people waiting to take over its assets — notably Pétain. Of the civilian members of the government, some were in favour of carrying on the struggle from North Africa, others of a military capitulation without coming to terms with Hitler. Here the rôle of Weygand seems to have been decisive. He had been summoned from Syria to take over the supreme command at the moment of the German onslaught. He now — possibly with what had happened to Bazaine in mind — refused to take the responsibility for military surrender and insisted on the government's asking for an armistice. Neither Norway nor Denmark, nor Holland nor Belgium, nor Poland — though all alike defeated and overrun — had done this. By a malign providence Reynaud's government in the confusion had never received Churchill's request that the French fleet should sail for British ports. Even Weygand recognises that that would have

created a secret union between France and England more
effective than the proposed external union could have been ;
it would have shortened the war ; it was a tragic accident that
it should never have been received.

The last government of the Third Republic broke up,
like so many of its predecessors, in confusion : Weygand as
Commander-in-Chief was able to use the instability of its
governments as a reproach against the Republic in his argument for surrender. Reynaud resigned and advised President
Lebrun to call on Pétain. Pétain and Weygand at once sued
Hitler for an armistice (16 June). Two days later de Gaulle,
who had been flown from Bordeaux to Britain, broadcast his
appeal to the French nation, assuming the leadership of all
Frenchmen who were willing to continue the struggle. On
21 June the French representatives signed an armistice in
humiliating terms in the same railway coach brought to the
same spot in the forest of Compiègne, where the Germans
had signed the Armistice in 1918 : a nice example of the
essential meanness of the German mentality and a poor
augury as to what France might expect from collaboration
with Germany. Indeed, Hitler warned Laval later that year
at Montoire that if Britain offered a compromise peace he
would not hesitate to sacrifice France. But Britain never did
offer him a compromise peace.

Britain's reply to the armistice was at once to recognise
de Gaulle as leader of all the Free French. But the National
Assembly voted the ratification of the Armistice and 569
members voted full powers to Pétain. This provided the
legal basis on which the Vichy régime rested and by which it
secured the adhesion of the colonial administrations throughout
the French Empire. The fact was that not only France, but
practically the whole world, assumed that Britain would soon
be forced to surrender and that this was the end of the war.
No-one can blame France for this mistaken calculation — it
was made by everyone else, except Britain, President Roosevelt
and the free fighting forces of the smaller nations who had so

often made common cause with Britain before in history. No-
one can blame France for surrender — she had been beaten ;
nor did Churchill reproach her with one word in that speech
of magnanimous release, which moved to tears all those who
heard it with any imaginative sense of all the history between
France and England that lay behind it : 'Good night, then :
sleep to gather strength for the morning. For the morning
will come. Brightly will it shine on the brave and true, kindly
upon all who suffer for the cause, glorious upon the tombs of
heroes. Thus will shine the dawn. *Vive la France!*'

What was unforgivable was not defeat, but the Armistice,
the coming to terms with Hitler. It was this that did such
damage to France's good name — one had almost said irreparable, except that history shows that nothing is quite irreparable,
and France in especial has always shown marvellous powers of
recovery. Although the Vichy régime rested upon an historic
error, for Britain had no intention of giving in, the régime
had certain assets to begin with and a coherent, if not very
respectable, policy. But the assets were wasting and as the
war continued the policy lost all coherence. Of Vichy's chief
assets the Fleet, we have seen, it owed to an accident. Britain,
in mortal danger, could not afford the terrible risk of the
French Fleet's passing under the control of Germany : hence
the 'cruel necessity' of the fleet-action at Oran. On Britain's
survival now depended the survival of France. Vichy's
second asset was the obedience to its authority of the French
Empire overseas. With the progress of the war, with the
winning of West African territories and Syria by Free French
forces based on Britain, with the Allied invasion of North
Africa and the scuttling of the remainder of the Fleet in
Toulon harbour, Vichy's assets successively vanished ; until,
in the end, with the approaching liberation of France, the
deplorable régime lost *raison d'être*, coherence and all respect.

It may be argued — as it is by Weygand — that Vichy had
served its turn. It kept a good deal of France intact while
the brunt of the struggle with Germany was borne by others

— Britain, Russia, the United States. It may be said that France had no desire to repeat the experience of 1914–18 ; that France, alone of occupied territories in Hitler's Europe, escaped being a Gestapo-run country, until the very end with the approach of D-Day. And that is about all that can profitably be said for it. It was not a noble policy, but a self-preservative one ; it was based upon calculations of intelligent self-interest ; it was wrecked upon the courage and endurance, the loyalty and faith of the common man. The record of those years shows — such is the irony of history — that calculations of self-interest are not necessarily the most intelligent ones, that faith in the future may sometimes be more so.

That germ of faith was carried by a very small body of men to begin with around de Gaulle in London. But it was to be seen more and more in the little groups of men escaping from occupied France and crossing the Channel to come into the battered ports of Britain, bastion of Europe's ultimate freedom ; in the simple people of the French countryside who saved Allied airmen at the risk of their own lives ; in the increasing number of men within the country, who against every refinement of German savagery, maintained the Resistance, and prepared the way internally for the day of liberation. For that day, that morning spoken of in Mr. Churchill's 'Good night' speech, came with the stormy, glorious morning of D-Day, 6 June 1944. On 23 August the Allies were in Paris and France was shortly freed.

We have brought this history to the point at which the separate histories of France and England — those old and famous neighbours, enemies and friends, to whom Western civilisation chiefly owes what it is — have ceased to have their former importance. For indeed the defence of the West must in contemporary circumstances be a common effort, and no one country is the sole exponent of what Western civilisation is. But no-one can doubt — looking back over the history of France, the infinitely rich and diverse character of her creative effort, *mère des arts, des armes et des lois* — that hers has been the leading part in constituting what that idea of civilisation is. And we remember when we are apt to be overborne in the 20th century by considerations of mere size and mass and power, the word of the great mathematician, Henri Poincaré, that it is 'par les sciences et les arts que les civilisations valent'.

INDEX

Abd-el-Kader, 389
Abélard, 103
Aboukir, battle of, 351, 360
Abyssinia, 466-7
Academies, 246 ; Academy, the French, 231, 380
Adalbéron, Archbishop of Rheims, 73-74
Aedui, the, 21-3, 25-8, 83
Africa, French West, 298, 414, 433, 445, 476
Agadir, 446
Agincourt, 156-7
Agriculture, 374, 407
Aigues-Mortes, 126, 171
Aix-en-Provence, 23
Aix-la-Chapelle, 60, 65 ; — Treaty of, 285-6
Alais, Peace of, 227, 263
Alaric, 40
Albigenses, the, 111-12
Albret, Jeanne d', 212, 218
Alemanni, the, 55
Alexander I, Emperor of Russia, 360, 362, 363, 365
Alexander VI, Pope, 187
Algeria, 389, 413-14, 433 ; Algiers, 382
Allobroges, the, 22
Alphonse of Poitiers, 125
Alsace, 8, 12, 25, 41, 176, 229, 240, 258, 323, 326, 328 ; Alsace-Lorraine, 410, 418, 422, 431, 459
Ambiorix, 26
Amboise, 202, 213 ; — Edict of, 213
America, 195, 297, 304-6, 405, 414-15, 449, 450, 452-3, 454-5, 456 ; and v. United States
Amiens, Peace of (1802), 354-5
Ampère, A. M., 375
Anagni, 117, 119
Anjou, county of, 82 ; — 'King' René of, 177, 184, 189
Antioch, 101
Antwerp, 183
Aquitaine, 48, 55, 58, 83 ; — Eleanor of, 83, 107, 193 ; Aquitania, 14, 18, 30

Aragon, 126, 194
Argenson, Marquis d', 282-3, 284-5
Ariovistus, 25
Arles, 35, 65, 105
Armagnac party, 156-7, 166, 169
Artois, 110, 194, 197 ; — Comte d', v. Charles X
Arverni, the, 8, 21-3
Attila, 40
Augsburg, League of, 265, 266
Aumale, Duc d', 389
Austerlitz, battle of, 360-61, 401
Austria, 200, 223, 228-9, 250, 266, 267-8, 277-82, 296-7, 343, 354, 360-61, 367, 372, 415-16, 471 ; — Anne of, 225, 227, 236-8, 241, 242 ; Austrian Succession, War of, 280-82
Autun, 54, 55
Auvergne, 105, 111, 114, 196
Avignon, 119, 136, 184, 325, 326, 328

Babœuf, G., 346
Baldwin Government, 467
Barbarians (German), 29, 39-45
Barras, P. de, 338, 340, 346, 352
Barry, Comtesse du, 301
Basel, Treaty of (1795), 343
Basques, the, 14, 61
Bastille, the, 222, 320
Bayle, Pierre, 291
Baylen, Capitulation of, 363
Bazaine, Marshal, 414, 419, 421, 474
Beaujeu, Anne de, 178-9, 196
Beaumont, Christophe de, 294
Bedford, Duke of, 163, 168, 169
Belfort, 421
Belgae, 26 ; Belgians, 325 ; Belgium, 30, 342, 388, 416, 418, 448
Belle-Isle, Marshal, 280-81
Beresina, battle of, 366
Berlin, 265, 361
Berry, Duc de, 379 ; — Duchesse de, 385
Béziers, 112
Bibracte, 19, 25
Biron, Marshal, 221

Bismarck, Prince, 411, 415-18, 420, 421-422, 444, 445, 463
Black Death, the, 146
Black Prince, the, 147
Blanche of Castile, 108, 111, 126
Blenheim, battle of, 267
Blois, 216 ; — county of, 82
Blücher, Marshal, 368, 370
Blum, Léon, 442, 458, 465, 468-71
Bologna, Concordat of, 191
Bonaparte, Jerome, 362 ; — Joseph, 361, 363 ; — Louis, 361, 398 ; — Lucien, 352 ; — Napoleon, v. Napoleon I
'Bonhommes', order of, 89
Boniface VIII, Pope, 117-19
Bordeaux, 55, 474, 475
Borodino, battle of, 365-6
Bossuet, J. B., 261
Boulanger, General, 436-8
Bourbon, family, 152 ; — Antoine de, 212, 213, 214; — Cardinal de, 216, 218 ; — Constable de, 196 ; — Duc de, 275, 276, 277
Bourges, 19, 27, 58, 163 ; — Pragmatic Sanction of, 171
Bouvines, battle of, 110
Brandenburg, 61, 265
Brest, 360
Brétigny, Treaty of, 150-51
Briand, Aristide, 459, 461-2
Brienne, Loménie de, 308-9
Brissot, J. P., 327, 328
Britain, 26, 43 ; — Great, 445-6, 449-51, 452-3, 454-9, 463-5, 466-8, 471, 473-7 ; v. also England
Brittany, 10, 26, 43, 75, 82, 109, 147, 270, 300, 344 ; — Anne, Duchess of, 179
Broglie, Louis, Duc de, 386 ; — Albert, —, 427, 429
Bruges, 136
Brünhilde, Frankish queen, 50
Budé, Guillaume, 203
Bugeaud, Marshal, 389, 391, 434
Burgundy, 40-41, 47, 48, 54, 82-3, 89, 163, 176, 184-5, 188, 198, 218 ; — Dukes of, 97, 172, 197 ; Burgundian party, 156-7, 169 ; Burgundians, the, 40-41, 44, 45
Byzantine Empire, the, 54, 55, 58, 62, 63, 99, 100

Caen, 105
Caesar, Julius, 18, 19, 21, 23-8

Caillaux, J., 446, 451, 470-71
Calais, 145, 200, 474
Calonne, C. A., 307-8
Calvin, Jean, 204, 208-9, 210
Cambon, J., 341
Campo Formio, Peace of, 350
Canada, 195, 223, 253, 268, 285, 297
Capet, Hugh, King, 72, 73-5
Carnot, Lazare, 343, 346, 348
Carthage, 16, 17, 434
Carthusians, order of, 89
Cartier, Jacques, 195
Castle, the medieval, 92-3
Cateau-Cambrésis, Treaty of, 201, 211
Catherine de Medici, 202, 211-16, 263, 287
Cauchon, Pierre, 168-9
Cavaignac, General, 397, 398, 401
Cavour, C. B., 411, 412
Celts, the, 15, 17-20
Cévennes, the, 265
Chamberlain, Neville, 464
Chambord, Comte de, 401, 427
Champagne, 136, 163 ; — county of, 82, 111
Champaigne, Philippe de, 230
Chardin, J. B. S., 290
Charlemagne, 59-66, 67, 68, 70, 80, 86, 102, 120
Charles V, 148-9, 151-4, 157 ; Charles VI, 142, 154-7; Charles VII, 142, 163, 165-71, 173, 175, 177, 287 ; Charles VIII, 176, 178-9, 189, 191 ; Charles IX, 211, 214-15 ; Charles X, 307, 378, 379-82 ; Charles of Anjou, 124, 125, 126, 128 ; Charles-Martel, 55-6 ; Charles of Navarre, 146-7, 148, 149, 150, 153 ; Charles the Fat, Emperor, 69, 72-3 ; Charles V, Emperor, 187, 194, 196, 197-200 ; Charles VI, Emperor, 278, 280
Chartres, 462
Chateaubriand, F. R. de, 355, 359, 376, 379, 380
Château-Gaillard, 109, 113
Cherbourg, 374
China, 136
Chivalry, 142-3
Choiseul, Duc de, 295, 297, 298, 301
Churchill, Winston, 452, 474-5, 476-7
Cinq-Mars, 228-9
Cîteaux, abbey of, 90 ; — order of, 90, 104

Clairvaux, abbey of, 90
Clemenceau, G., 436, 437, 439, 440, 447, 451-2, 454
Clement V, Pope, 119, 122
Clément, Jacques, 217
Clothair I, Clothair II, 47
Clotilde, 44, 45
Clovis, 41, 43-5
Cluny, abbey of, 83, 86, 87-9, 90, 97, 99, 104, 105
Code, the Civil, 341-2, 355-6, 408, 432
Cœur, Jacques, 170, 172, 184, 185
Colbert, J. B., 249-55, 256, 257, 258, 269, 372, 374
Coligny, Admiral, 212, 214-15
Colombe, Michel, 202
Columbus, Christopher, 187
Combes, E., 441, 442
Comte, Auguste, 376
Concini, C., 224, 225
Concordat (1801), 355
Condé, Louis I, Prince of, 212-14 ; — Louis II, 'le Grand', 238-41
Congo, French, 433
Constance, Council of, 164, 206
Constantine, Emperor, 34
Constantinople, 98, 100, 186
Constitution, of the Year I (1793), 340-341 ; — of the Year III (1795), 341 ; — of the Year VIII (1799), 352-3 ; — of the Year X (1802), 357
Corday, Charlotte, 334
Corneille, Pierre, 230, 231
Corsica, 200, 298, 343
Coster, Laurent, 183
Courtrai, battle of, 111, 118
Cousin, Victor, 376
Crécy, battle of, 145
Crusades, the, 99-101, 136, 181
Cuvier, G., 375
Czecho-Slovakia, 455, 468, 471

Dagobert, 47, 49-50
Dante, 138
Danton, G. J., 324, 327, 330, 332, 335, 336, 342
Darlan, Admiral, 473
Dauphiné, 144
Delcassé, T., 434-5, 445
Delorme, Philibert, 201-2
Denmark, 415
Descartes, René, 230

Desmoulins, Camille, 336
Dominican Order, 129-30
Domrémy, 164, 165
Dreyfus Affair, the, 439-40
Druids, the, 20
Dubois, Cardinal, 277
Dubois, Pierre, 117
Duguesclin, Bertrand de, 152-3
Dumouriez, General, 332, 333, 342
Dunkirk, 268, 306, 474
Dupleix, Marquis de, 285, 293
Duruy, Victor, 404

École Normale, the, 343, 468
Edward III, King of England, 143, 144-145 ; Edward IV, —, 176
Egypt, 126, 130, 134, 350-51, 354, 445
Elba, 368-9, 370
Elizabeth I, Queen of England, 212
England, 97-9, 143-4, 193, 197, 277, 278, 279-80, 287, 292, 296, 304-6, 342, 350-351, 354, 360, 362, 372, 388, 409, 410, 411-12, 440-41, 445-6
Erasmus, 203
Eugene, Prince, of Savoy, 267, 268
Eugénie, Empress, 403, 408, 417, 419
Eyck, Hubert and Jan van, 183

Falloux, Comte de, 399-400
Favre, Jules, 420, 421, 422
Fénelon, Archbishop, 246
Ferdinand II, Emperor, 228-9
Ferry, Jules, 420, 429, 432, 436-8
Flanders, 81, 134, 135, 144, 183, 214 ; — Count of, 110, 111
Flemings, the, 133
Fleury, Cardinal, 275-82
Florence, 181
Flote, Pierre, 117, 118
Foch, Marshal, 452-3, 454
Fontenoy, battle of, 282, 285
Fontévrault, abbey of, 89
Fornovo, battle of, 189
Fouché, J., 338, 363, 371, 378
Foucquet, Jean, 185
Fouquet, N., 248-9
Fouquier-Tinville, A. Q., 335, 337, 339
Franche-Comté, 257, 258
Francis I, 186, 190, 191, 194-9, 202, 208-209, 215, 222, 434 ; Francis II, 211, 213
Francis II, Emperor, 328, 360, 364

Franciscan Order, 129-30
Franco, General, 470, 472
Franco-Russian Alliance, 444, 445-6
Frankfort, Treaty of (1871), 422, 426
Franklin, Benjamin, 305
Frederick II, Emperor, 119, 128
Frederick II, King of Prussia, 280-81, 285-6, 296-8
Freycinet, C. S. de, 420, 430, 431
Friedland, battle of, 361
Froissart, Jean, 159
Fronde, the, 237-9

Gallican Church, 261-2
Gambetta, L., 404, 420, 421, 423, 429, 436
Garibaldi, G., 413
Garonne, R., 43
Gascony, 144
Gaulle, General de, 473, 474, 475, 477
Gauls, the, 8, 13, 15, 17-31, 41-2
Geneva, 209; — Protocol, the, 458
Genoa Conference, the, 456-7
Gergovia, 19, 27
German Empire, the, 410; — General Staff, the, 453, 455; Germans, the, 28; Germany, 61, 183, 210, 240, 361, 367, 372, 413, 442, 445-7; — Nazi, 453-4, 463-5
Gibraltar, 267
Girondins, the, 327-8, 332, 333, 335
Godfrey of Bouillon, 100-101
Goujon, Jean, 202
Grasse, Admiral de, 305-6
Greece, 98, 457; Greeks, the, 15, 19, 32, 33
Gregory of Tours, 50
Grenoble, 36
Guesde, Jules, 443
Guise, François, Duc de, 200, 212, 213; — Henri, —, 214-15, 216
Guizot, F., 378, 386-7, 390-91
Gustavus Adolphus, 229
Guyenne, 110, 163, 169

Habsburgs, the, 200, 228-9, 240, 361
Hanse, the, 135, 177, 183
Hastings, battle of, 98
Haussmann, Baron, 406
Hébert, J. R., 335, 336
Helvetians, the, 25
Helvétius, C. A., 289

Henry II, 199-201, 218; Henry III, 215-217; Henry IV, 214, 216-25, 228, 243, 263, 313
Henry II, King of England, 107, 109; Henry III, —, 110; Henry V, —, 156-7; Henry VI, —, 163; Henry VIII, —, 198, 199, 210
Hindenburg Line, the, 451, 453
Hitler, Adolf, 442, 454, 455, 463, 464, 465, 466-7, 468, 470, 471-2, 473, 474, 475-7
Hoche, General, 343, 344, 346
Holland, 257-8, 267
Hugo, Victor, 389, 401, 402, 403, 423

Iberians, the, 14, 18
Ile-de-France, 8, 131
India, French in, 293, 297-8
Indies, French West, 253, 279, 298, 306, 354; — Company of the, 274-5
Indo-China, French, 414, 432
Industrialism, 374-5, 407
Innocent III, Pope, 112, 118
Inquisition, the Holy, 112, 122, 130
Isabel (of Bavaria), Queen, 155-6
Italians, the, 182-3; Italy, 7, 127, 182, 188-92, 197, 200, 202-3, 277, 349-50, 354, 412-13, 446, 466-7
Ivry, battle of, 217

Jacobins, the, 322, 324, 327, 329, 338-9, 346
Jacquerie, the, 149-50
Jansenists, the, 262, 273, 276-7, 294-5
Japan, 445
Jarnac, battle of, 214
Jaurès, Jean, 436, 439, 440, 442-3, 446-7, 468, 469
Jena, battle of, 361
Jerusalem, 101
Jesuits, the, 210-11, 262, 294-5
Jews, the, 120-21, 146
Joan of Arc, 141, 164-9, 185
Joffre, Marshal, 449, 451
John II (the Good), 151, 154, 270
John, King of England, 109, 110, 111, 116
John the Fearless, Duke of Burgundy, 156-7
Joinville, the Sire de, 124, 138
Joseph, Father, 229
Joseph II, Emperor, 304, 325
Josephine, Empress, 364
Jouarre, 36

Keynes, Lord, 456, 469
Knighthood, order of, 93-4
Kovno, 365, 366
Kutusov, General, 365, 366

La Bourdonnais, B. F. M. de, 285
La Bruyère, J. de, 264, 461
Lafayette, Marquis de, 305, 320, 321, 322, 324, 329, 331, 379, 384
La Hogue, battle of, 266
Languedoc, 111, 112, 120, 147
La Rochelle, 110, 171, 227
La Salle, Cavelier de, 253
Laval, Pierre, 443, 466-7, 472, 475
Lavalette, Father, 295
La Vendée, 333, 336, 340, 343-4
Lavigerie, Cardinal, 434
Lavoisier, A. L. de, 337
Law, John, 273-5, 289
League, the (1576), 216-18; — of Nations, 454-5, 459, 466-7; — of the Public Good (1465), 175
Le Brun, C., 247
Ledru-Rollin, A. A., 397, 398, 399, 400
Lefèvre d'Étaples, G., 208
Legion of Honour, the, 356
Le Havre, 195
Leipzig, battle of, 367
Leoben, Peace of, 350
Leonardo da Vinci, 201, 202
Leopold I, Emperor, 266, 267; Leopold II, Emperor, 326, 328
Lesseps, F. de, 407, 439
Ligurians, the, 14, 18
Lille, 81, 111, 268
Limoges, 83, 163, 202
Lloyd George, D., 452, 455, 456-7, 459
Locarno Treaties, 459
Locke, John, 292
Loire, R., 21, 27; — Valley, 163, 202
Lombards, the, 55, 57, 60; 'Lombards' (Italian bankers), 120, 121
Lorient, 275
Lorraine, 8, 12, 69, 176, 278-9, 298, 331, 374; —, Charles de Guise, Cardinal of, 212
Louis VI (the Fat), 107; Louis VII, 107; Louis VIII, 108, 110, 112; Louis IX (St. Louis), 108, 109, 110, 114, 115, 116, 117-22, 123-8, 130, 132, 133, 134, 138, 139, 141; Louis XI, 173-8, 184, 185, 188, 195; Louis XII, 179, 189-90; Louis XIII, 220, 224-30, 242, 244,

254; Louis XIV, 220, 235-6, 241-71, 273, 280, 285, 300, 310; Louis XV, 272-302, 311; Louis XVI, 300, 302, 303, 307-16, 318-30, 332-3, 382; Louis XVII, 340; Louis XVIII, 326, 327, 340, 356, 369-70, 371, 377-9; Louis Napoleon, v. Napoleon III; Louis-Philippe, 381, 382, 383-91, 399, 411
Louisbourg, 285
Louisiana, 253-97
Louvois, Marquis, 255-6, 260, 264, 266
Ludendorff, General, 452, 453, 454
Lunéville, Treaty of (1801), 354
Luther, Martin, 208, 209
Luxemburg, 258, 416; — Marshal, 266
Luynes, Duc de, 225
Lyautey, Marshal, 434-5
Lyons, 30, 33, 43, 111, 171, 177, 184-5, 195, 251, 336, 385

Machault d'Arnouville, J. B., 284, 294
Machiavelli, Niccolo, 203, 206
MacMahon, Marshal, 412, 418, 419-20, 425, 427, 429-30
Madagascar, 432, 434
Madras, 285
Madrid, 362, 363, 367; — Treaty of, 198
Maintenon, Madame de, 261, 273
Malesherbes, C. G. de L. de, 302, 303, 332
Malplaquet, battle of, 268
Malta, 350, 354, 360
Marat, J. P., 324, 331, 333, 334
Marcel, Étienne, 148-9
Marchand, Colonel, 433
Marco Polo, 136, 138
Marengo, battle of, 354
Margaret of Angoulême, 208; — of Valois, 214; Marguerite of Provence, 125
Maria Theresa, Empress, 280-82, 296
Marie-Antoinette, 302, 303, 304, 307, 308-9, 326, 329, 335
Marie-Louise, Empress, 364
Marie de Medici, 224-8, 231
Marignano, battle of, 190
Marigny, Enguerrand de, 117
Marlborough, Duke of, 267
Marne, battle of, 449
Marot, Clément, 203
Marseilles, 15-17, 22, 130, 172, 295, 465

Marx, Karl, 408
Maupeou, Chancellor, 301, 304
Maurepas, J. F. P. de, 302, 306, 307
Maurras, Charles, 440
Maximilian I, Emperor, 177, 189
Maximum, Law of the, 335
Mayenne, Duc de, 216, 217, 218
Mazarin, Cardinal, 236-41, 248, 249, 251, 262, 263
Medici family, the, 181
Mediterranean, the, 14, 15, 16, 135, 136, 180, 186, 187, 306, 372
Mercury, cult of, 20
Metternich, Prince, 367
Metz, 198, 200, 240, 323, 419, 421, 422
Milan, 189-90, 198, 349-50 ; — Edict of, 34 ; — Decree, 362
Millerand, Alexandre, 443, 457, 458
Mirabeau, Marquis de, 319
Mississippi, R., 253, 297
Molière, J. B. P., 246
Moltke, Field-Marshal, 416, 418
Moncontour, battle of, 214
Montaigne, Michel de, 204
Montcalm, Marquis de, 297
Montereau, battle of, 157
Montesquieu, C. de S., 291, 292, 293
Montmorency, Constable de, 200, 202, 212, 214
Montpellier, 136, 140, 172
Montpensier, Mademoiselle de, 238-9
Moreau, General, 349, 354
Morny, Duc de, 401, 402, 403, 404
Moscow, 365-6
Munich (1938), 471-2
Mussolini, B., 465, 466-7

Nancy, 176, 290
Nantes, Edict of, 218-19 ; — Revocation of —, 263-6
Naples, 189, 191, 197, 278, 354, 361
Napoleon I, Emperor, 340, 346, 347-75, 410, 447 ; Napoleon III, 398-420
Narbonne, 23, 36, 65
Navy, the French, 199, 252-3, 258, 304, 306, 473, 474-5, 476
Necker, J., 289, 306-7, 310, 319, 320
Nelson, Lord, 351, 360
Nerra, Fulk, 82
Netherlands, the, 7, 258, 267, 268
Ney, Marshal, 363, 370, 377
Nibelungenlied, the, 138
Nice, 8, 16, 22, 342, 412

Nijmegen, Peace of, 258, 266
Nîmes, 65
Nogaret, Guillaume de, 117, 118-19, 120, 122
Normandy, 71, 75, 81-2, 98-9, 107, 109, 110, 134, 145, 156-7, 163, 167, 169

Odo, Count of Paris, 72, 73
Ollivier, Émile, 404, 405, 417
Orange, William of, 258, 266, 267
Orléans, 19, 40, 47, 140, 166-7, 213 ; — Gaston, Duke of, 227-8 ; — Louis I, —, 155-6 ; — Louis, — (v. also Louis XII), 179 ; — Philip, —, Regent, 272-5 ; Orleanist party, 384, 399, 403, 427, 437
Orsini, F., 403, 412
Oudenarde, battle of, 268

Palatinate, the, 266
Palissy, Bernard, 202
Panama Canal, 439
Paré, Ambroise, 204
Paris, 30, 31, 43, 45, 47, 72, 75, 113, 135, 137, 138, 148-9, 154, 163, 167, 169, 214-15, 216, 217, 237-9, 251, 294, 303, 318, 320-21, 329-30, 331-2, 336, 366, 368, 373, 375, 381, 386, 395, 396-7, 400, 403, 406, 407, 452, 469 ; — Commune, 424-5 ; — Parliament of, 170, 208, 237, 246, 272, 273, 294, 295, 301, 308-9 ; — Siege of, 420-21, 423 ; — Treaty of (1763), 297-8 ; — (1814), 369 ; — Treaty of (1856), 412 ; — University of, 139-40, 209
Parliaments, provincial, 115, 170, 294, 295, 300-301, 307, 308-9
Pascal, Blaise, 230, 262
Paul IV, Pope, 200
'Paulette', the, 222
Pavia, 58, 60 ; — battle of, 198
Péguy, Charles, 438, 440, 449, 453, 462
Pepin, of Héristal, 53, 55
Pepin the Short, 56-9
Périer, Casimir, 384-5
Périgord, 10, 12
Péronne, Treaty of, 6
Pershing, General, 453
Philip Augustus, 108-14, 117, 137 ;
Philip the Fair, 108, 109, 113, 114, 115, 116, 117, 118-22, 127, 142, 143 ;
Philip III, 126-7 ; Philip VI, 142, 143-146

Philip II, King of Spain, 200, 201, 212, 218, 267, 268, 277
Philip the Bold, Duke of Burgundy, 154-155 ; Philip the Good, —, 172-3, 175
Picardy, 218
Picquigny, Treaty of, 176
Pillnitz, Declaration of, 326
Pitt, William, 342
Pius VII, Pope, 355, 359 ; Pius X, 441
Poincaré, Raymond, 438, 442, 446, 447, 454, 456-8, 461-2 ; — Henri, 478
Poissy, Colloquy of, 213
Poitiers, 35, 36, 55, 105, 163, 166 ; — battle of, 147
Poitou, 107, 109, 110
Poland, 276, 278-9, 298, 325, 343, 455, 471 ; Polish Succession, War of, 278-279
Pompadour, Marquise de, 283-4, 293, 294, 296, 301
Port-Royal, 262
Portugal, 97, 186, 187, 362
Poussin, Nicolas, 230
Prague, 281, 468
Prémontré, abbey of, 89
Pressburg, Treaty of (1805), 361
Proudhon, P. J., 386, 389, 408
Proust, Marcel, 462, 468
Provence, 47, 56, 88, 177, 184, 188, 198, 199, 285 ; — Comte de, v. Louis XVIII
Prussia, 240, 281, 287, 296-8, 361-2, 363, 366-7, 370-71, 372, 413, 415-18
Pyrenees, 14, 54, 61, 97 ; — Peace of, 241

Quebec, 223, 297
Quiberon, 340

Rabelais, François, 203-4
Racine, Jean, 246
Railways, 387, 406-7, 431
Rapallo Treaty, 457, 459
Rastadt, Treaty of, 268
Ratisbon, Diet of, 229 ; — Truce of, 258
Ravaillac, François, 223
Reparations, German, 455-8
Reynaud, Paul, 474, 475
Rheims, 19, 44, 47, 166, 167
Rhine, 16, 26, 343, 350 ; — Confederation of the, 361, 364 ; Rhineland, 454, 467

Rhône, 8, 14, 22-3, 43, 107
Richard Cœur de Lion, King of England, 109
Richelieu, Cardinal, 226-30, 231, 236, 241, 250, 252, 254, 263
Robert the Pious, 86
Robespierre, Maximilian, 327, 329, 332, 334-8
Rocroi, battle of, 239
Roland, Duke, 60 ; Chanson de Roland, 61, 102
Rollo, 71, 81
Romanesque art, 103-5, 131, 132
Romanticism, 376, 389, 396
Rome, 22, 29, 63, 413
Ronceval, pass of, 54, 60
Rouen, 81-2, 137, 157, 168, 202, 213
Rouher, E., 404
Rousseau, J. J., 293, 318
Roussillon, 84, 189, 229
Ruhr, occupation of the, 457
Russia, 296, 351, 354, 360-62, 365-6, 372, 410, 411-12, 444, 445-6, 447, 455, 457, 459, 471-2
Ryswick, Peace of, 266

Sadowa, 415, 416
St. Bartholomew, Massacre of, 214-15
St. Bernard, 89-90, 103, 104, 107, 120
St. Boniface, 56, 57
St.-Cyr, military school of, 342
St.-Denis, abbey of, 50, 57, 58, 75, 153, 218 ; — fair of, 51, 136
St. Dominic, 129, 130
St. Éloi, 50, 51
St. Francis, 129, 130
St. Geneviève, 40, 45
St.-Germain, Comte de, 302, 303-4
St.-Germain-des-Prés, 65, 72, 75
St. Gregory (Pope Gregory III), 56
St. Helena, island of, 371, 387
St. Hilary, bishop of Poitiers, 35
St. Irenaeus, bishop of Lyons, 32-3, 35
St.-Just, L. de, 332, 334, 337, 338
St. Lawrence, River, 195, 223, 268, 297
St. Louis, v. Louis IX
St. Martin, bishop of Tours, 37-8, 55
St.-Médard, convulsives of, 277
St. Pothinus, bishop of Lyons, 32
St.-Quentin, 184 ; — battle of, 200
St. Radigund, 51
St. Remi, bishop of Rheims, 44

St.-Simon, Comte de, 386; St.-Simon-
ism, 406, 407; — Duc de, 245, 269,
270, 277
St. Symphorian, 32
St. Thomas Aquinas, 130
St. Vincent de Paul, 230
Saintes, battle of, 110
Saône, R., 21, 43, 82
Savoy, 8, 197, 198, 201, 223, 268, 412
Schleswig-Holstein, 415-16
Sebastopol, 412
Sedan, 317, 419-20
Seine, R., 27, 43
Senegal, 298, 306
Serres, Olivier de, 222
Servetus, Michael, 204, 209
Sévigné, Madame de, 245, 246, 249
Sicily, 97-8, 125, 126; 'Sicilian Vespers',
126
Sieyès, E. J., 351, 352, 377
Silesia, 281, 286, 296, 298
Simon de Montfort, 58, 112
Sluys, battle of, 144
Socialism, 396-7, 442-4, 461-2, 468-71
Soissons, 43, 44, 57, 73
Somme, battle of the, 451
Sorbon, Robert de, 139-40
Sorbonne, the, 140, 208, 231
Sorel, Agnes, 170
Sorel, George, 441, 466
Soult, Marshal, 363
Spain, 47, 199-201, 223, 228, 229, 240-41,
257-8, 267, 268, 297, 362-3, 366, 367,
417, 469-70; Spanish Succession, war
of the, 267-8
Stanislas Leczinski, King of Poland, 276,
278, 298
State, French, character of, 6-7, 188,
254-5
States General, the, 147-8, 179, 216, 218,
308, 309-10, 318-19
Stephen II, Pope, 57
Strasbourg, 240; — Oath of, 69
Sudan, 432, 433
Suessiones, the, 21
Suez Canal, the, 407, 414
Suger, abbot of St.-Denis, 107-30
Sully, Duc de, 220-23, 228, 243
Syria, 16, 126, 412, 474

Tahiti, 388, 389
Taillebourg, battle of, 110

Talleyrand, Prince, 322, 351, 363, 368,
378
Tarascon, 14
Templars, the, 121-2
Tennis-Court, Oath of the, 319
Thiers, Adolphe, 381, 386-7, 390, 391,
401, 403, 422, 423, 424-6
Tilsit, Treaty of, 362
Toulon, 336, 343, 348, 360, 476
Toulouse, 23, 40, 112, 140, 368; —
county of, 83-4, 112
Touraine, 109, 114
Tournai, 43
Tours, 35, 37, 50, 65, 75, 420, 474
Trade Unions, 431, 442, 443-4
Trafalgar, battle of, 360
Trent, Council of, 210
Trochu, General, 420
Troyes, 40; — Treaty of, 157
Tunisia, 413-14, 433
Turenne, Marshal, 239-40, 256, 257, 258
Turgot, Baron de, 302-3, 306, 308
Turkey, 279, 411-12, 446, 457; the
Turks, 100-101, 186, 197, 199, 279

Ulm, Capitulation of, 360
'Unigenitus', Papal Bull, 262, 276, 294
United States, 305, 414-15, 449-50, 454-
455, 463-4; v. also America
Urban II, Pope, 100
Utrecht, Treaty of, 268, 277

Valmy, battle of, 332
Varennes, Flight to, 323
Vasco da Gama, 186
Vassy, 213
Vauban, Marshal, 244, 256-7, 264, 270
Vendôme, Duke of, 267
Venetii, the, 26
Venice, 136, 181, 190, 251, 413
Vercingetorix, 27-8
Verdun, 198, 240, 450; — Treaty of,
68-9
Vergennes, Comte de, 302, 304-5
Versailles, 246-7, 421-2, 423-5; —
Treaty of (1783), 306; — Treaty of
(1919), 438, 454-6, 467, 469
Vervins, Treaty of, 218
Vichy Régime, the, 475-7
Vienna, 199, 360, 364; — Treaty of
(1809), 364; — Congress of (1815),
372
Villars, Marshal, 265, 267, 268, 278

Villehardouin, Geoffrey, 138
Villèle, Comte de, 378, 379, 380
Villon, François, 185
Voltaire, F. M. A., 203, 204, 266, 291, 292, 298, 317, 318

Wagram, battle of, 364
Waldeck-Rousseau, R., 431
Walpole, Sir Robert, 278
Warsaw, Grand Duchy of, 364, 365, 367
Washington, George, 305-6
Waterloo, battle of, 370-71

Watteau, Antoine, 289, 290
Wellington, Duke of, 367, 368, 370-71
Westphalia, kingdom of, 362, 364; — peace of, 237, 239-40
Weygand, Marshal, 474-5, 476
William the Conqueror, 98-9; William I, German Emperor, 415, 417, 422
Wolfe, General, 297

Yorktown, 306

Zola, Émile, 440

THE END